NILES
NUTRIENTS
PATENT PENDING

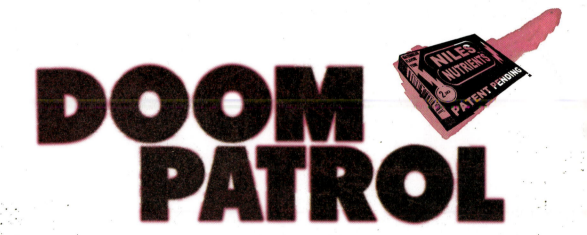

DOOM PATROL

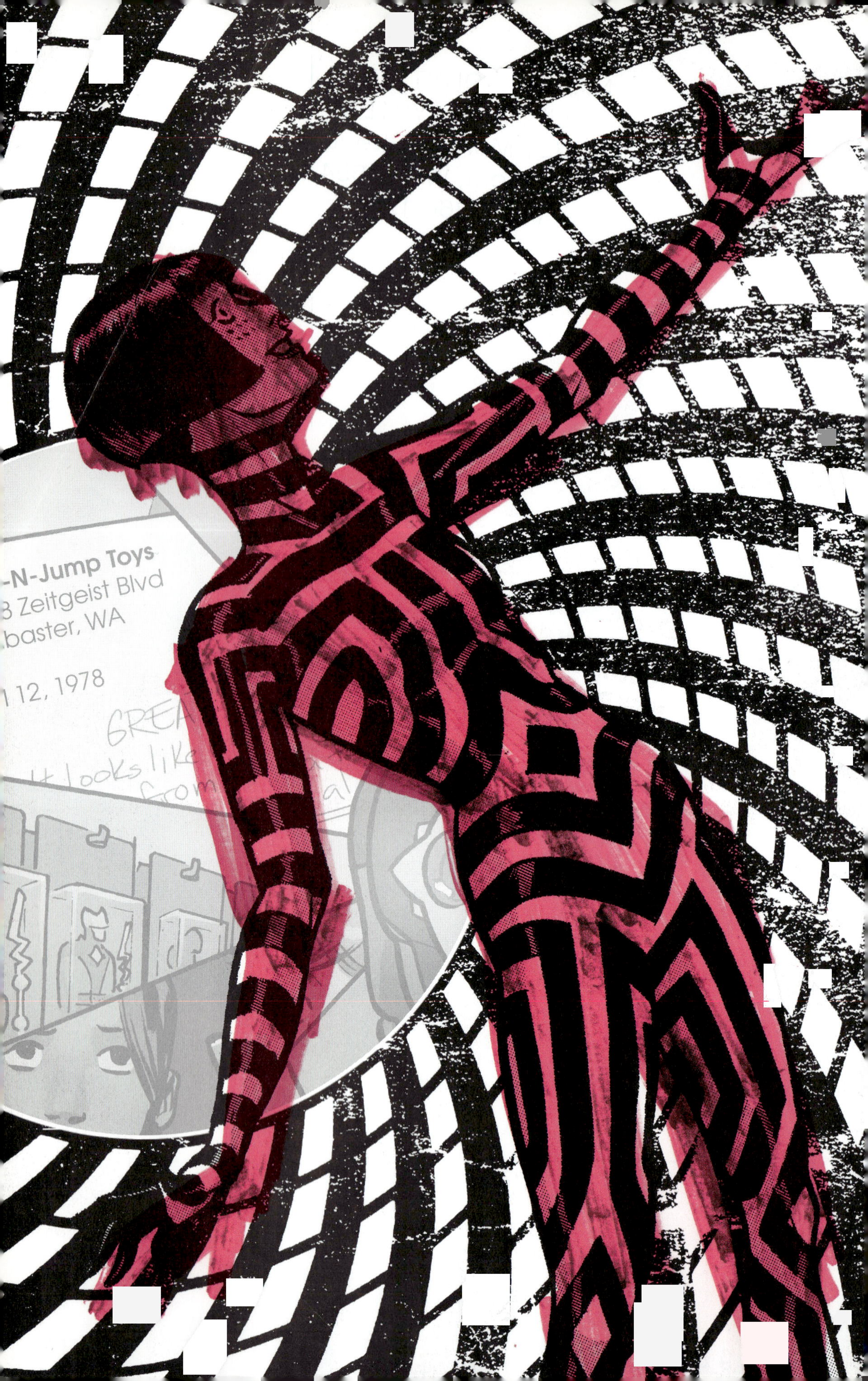
-N-Jump Toys
3 Zeitgeist Blvd
baster, WA
12, 1978

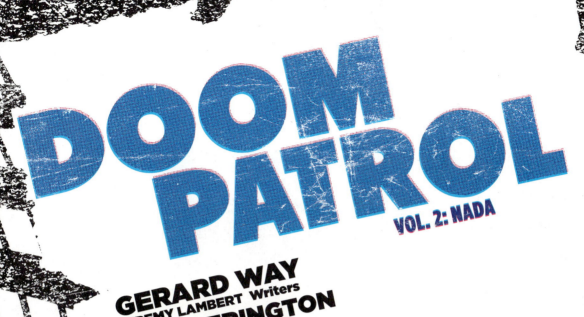

DOOM PATROL

VOL. 2: NADA

GERARD WAY
JEREMY LAMBERT Writers

NICK DERINGTON
TOM FOWLER
MICHAEL ALLRED
DAN McDAID Artists

TAMRA BONVILLAIN LAURA ALLRED Colorists

TODD KLEIN Letterer

NICK DERINGTON Collection Cover Art

NICK DERINGTON
MICHAEL and LAURA ALLRED Original Series Covers

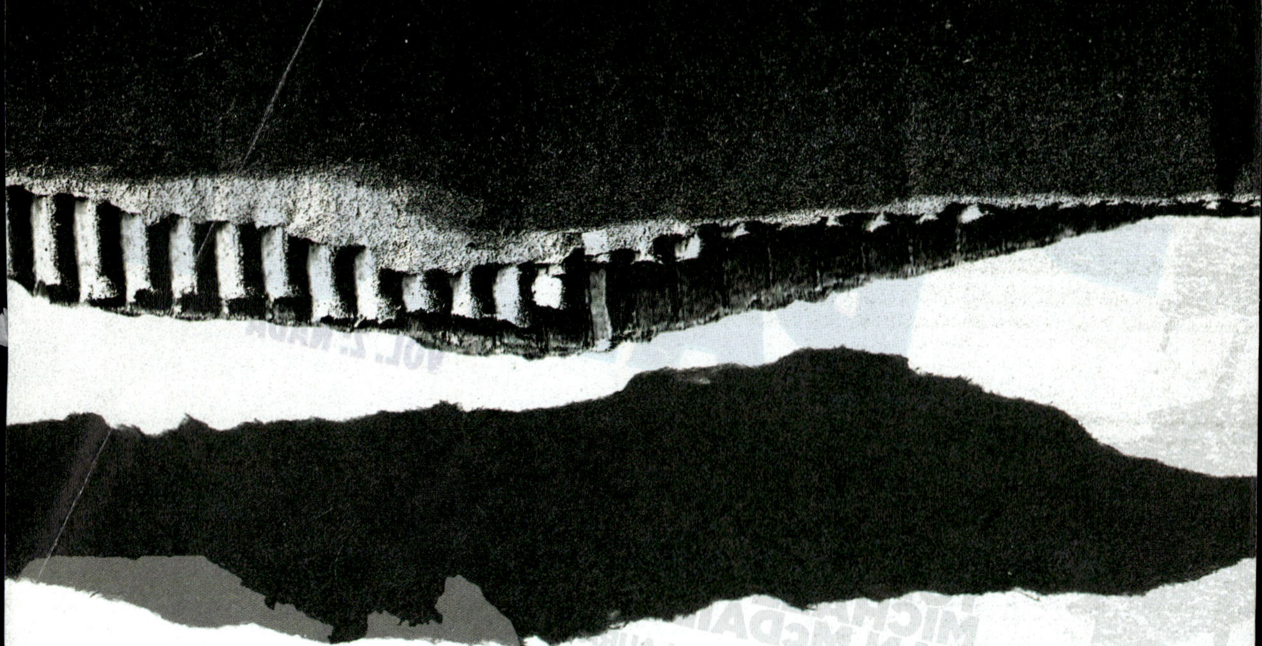

Jamie S. Rich Molly Mahan Editors – Original Series
Maggie Howell Assistant Editor – Original Series
Jeb Woodard Group Editor – Collected Editions
Scott Nybakken Editor – Collected Edition
Steve Cook Design Director – Books
Louis Prandi Publication Design

Bob Harras Senior VP – Editor-in-Chief, DC Comics
Mark Doyle Executive Editor, Vertigo & Black Label

Dan DiDio Publisher
Jim Lee Publisher & Chief Creative Officer
Amit Desai Executive VP – Business & Marketing Strategy, Direct to Consumer & Global Franchise Management
Bobbie Chase VP & Executive Editor, Young Reader & Talent Development
Mark Chiarello Senior VP – Art, Design & Collected Editions
John Cunningham Senior VP – Sales & Trade Marketing
Briar Darden VP – Business Affairs
Anne DePies Senior VP – Business Strategy, Finance & Administration
Don Falletti VP – Manufacturing Operations
Lawrence Ganem VP – Editorial Administration & Talent Relations
Alison Gill Senior VP – Manufacturing & Operations
Jason Greenberg VP – Business Strategy & Finance
Hank Kanalz Senior VP – Editorial Strategy & Administration
Jay Kogan Senior VP – Legal Affairs
Nick J. Napolitano VP – Manufacturing Administration
Lisette Osterloh VP – Digital Marketing & Events
Eddie Scannell VP – Consumer Marketing
Courtney Simmons Senior VP – Publicity & Communications
Jim (Ski) Sokolowski VP – Comic Book Specialty Sales & Trade Marketing
Nancy Spears VP – Mass, Book, Digital Sales & Trade Marketing
Michele R. Wells VP – Content Strategy

DOOM PATROL VOL. 2: NADA

DC Comics
2900 West Alameda Avenue
Burbank, CA 91505
Printed by LSC Communications, Owensville, MO, USA. 11/16/18. First printing.
ISBN: 978-1-4012-7500-6

Library of Congress Cataloging-in-Publication Data is available.

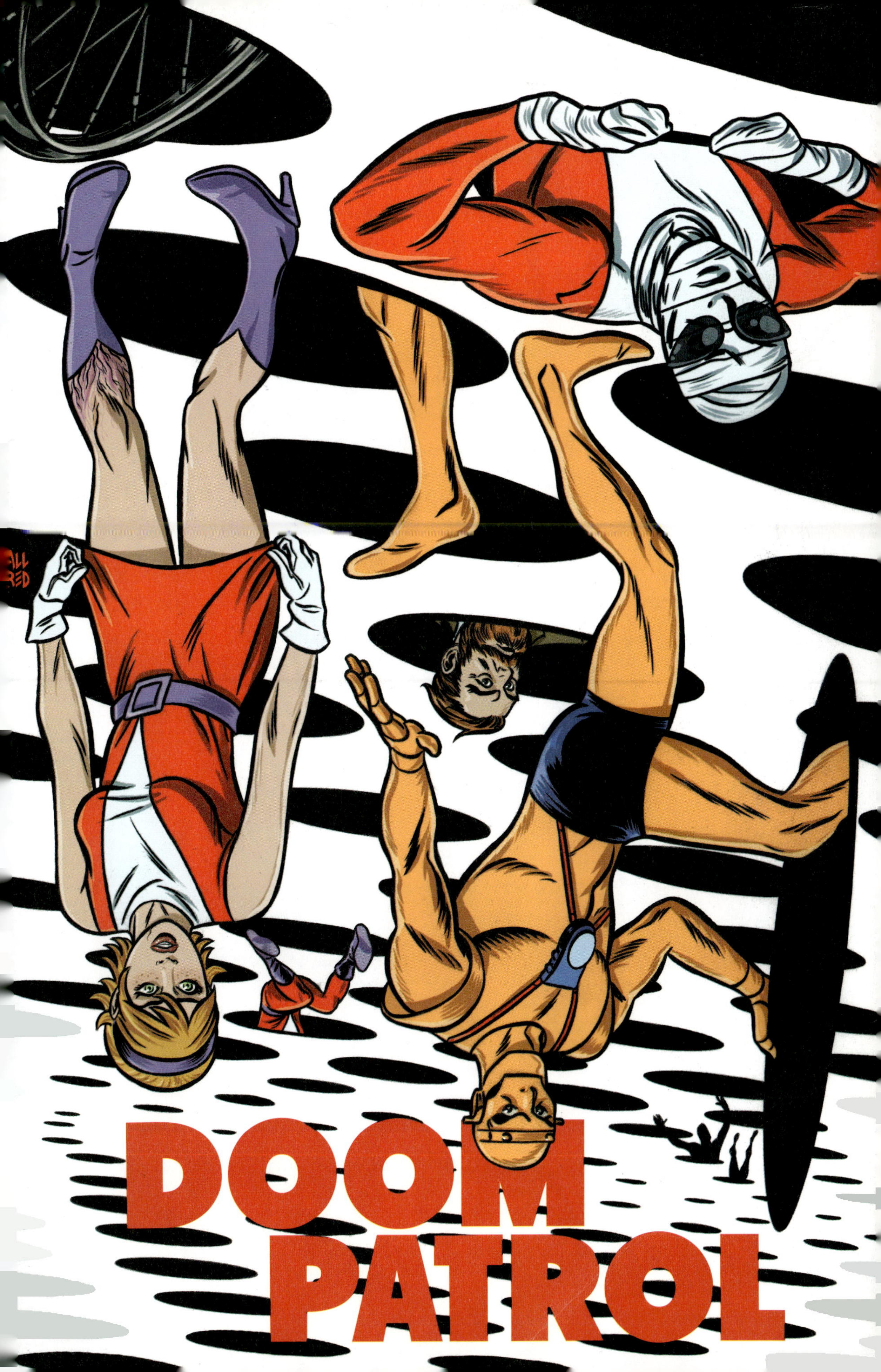
DOOM
PATROL

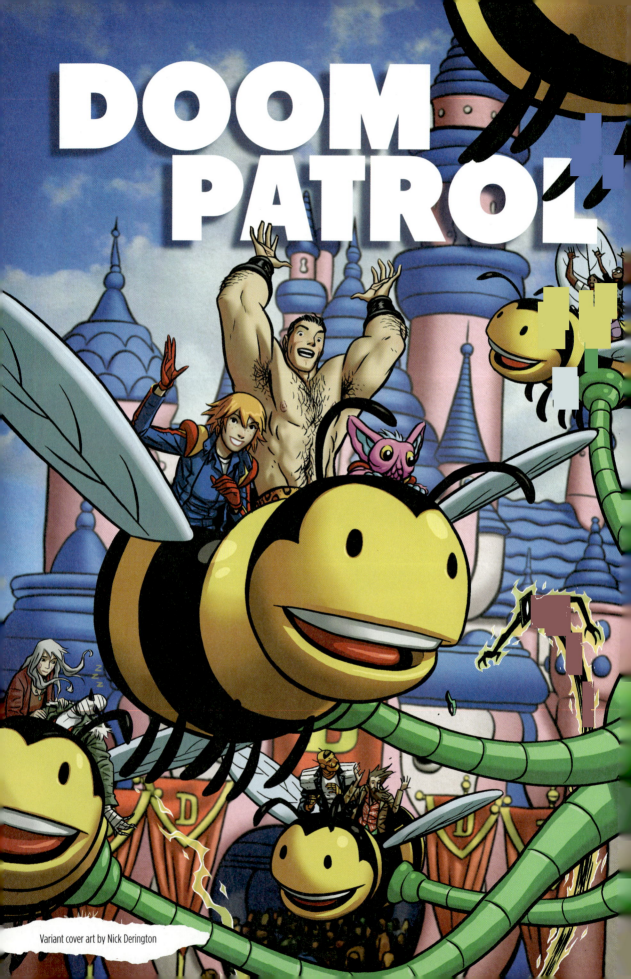

Variant cover art by Nick Derington

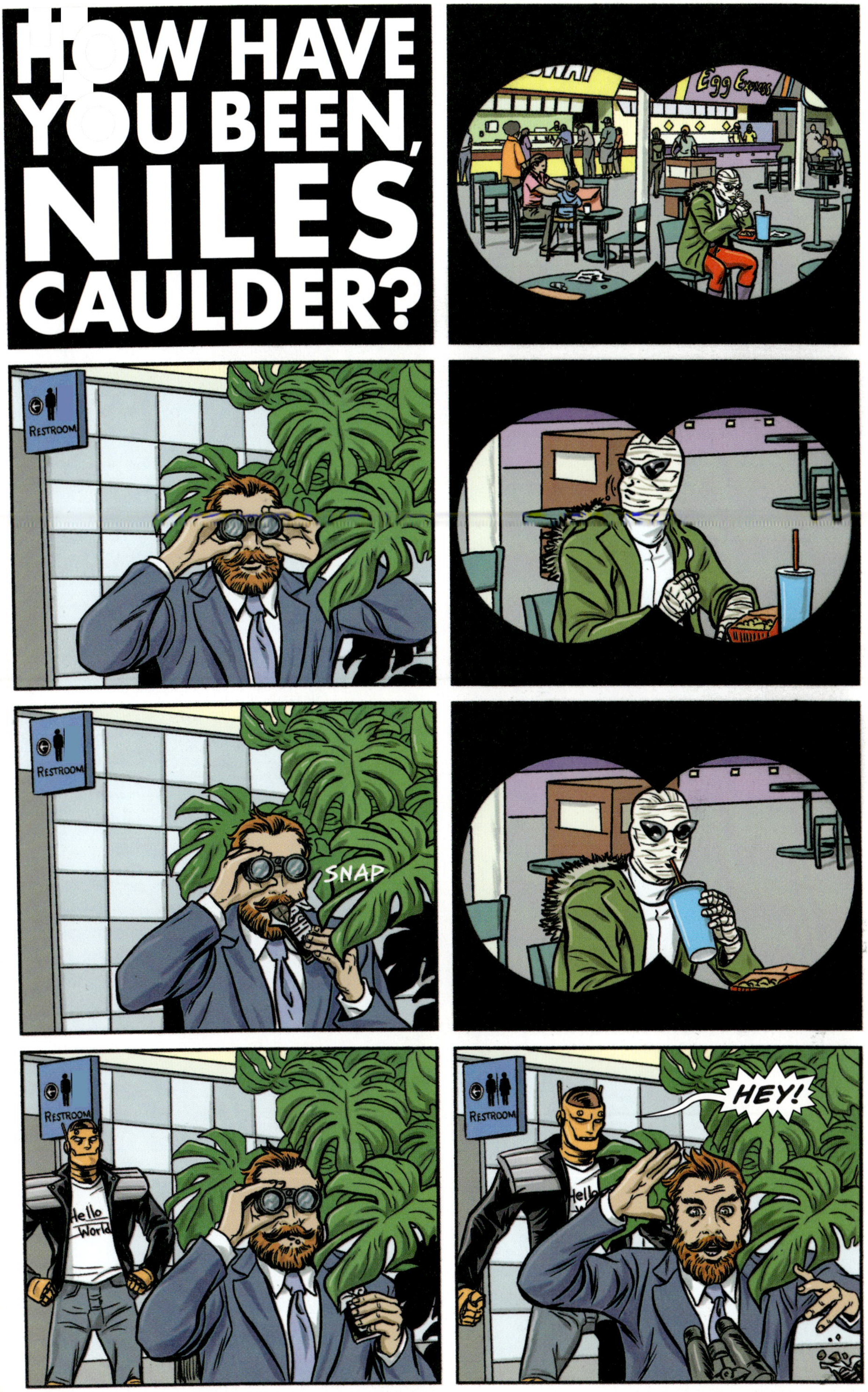
HOW HAVE YOU BEEN, NILES CAULDER?
Egg Express
RESTROOM
SNAP
Hello World
HEY!

INTO THE SCANTOVERSE
or EMOTIONAL ROBOTS AND PSYCHIC WEREWOLVES: A Doom Patrol Adventure

GERARD WAY writer
MICHAEL ALLRED artist
LAURA ALLRED colorist
TODD KLEIN letterer
MICHAEL & LAURA ALLRED cover
NICK DERINGTON pencils pages 23-24
MOLLY MAHAN assoc. ed. JAMIE S. RICH editor

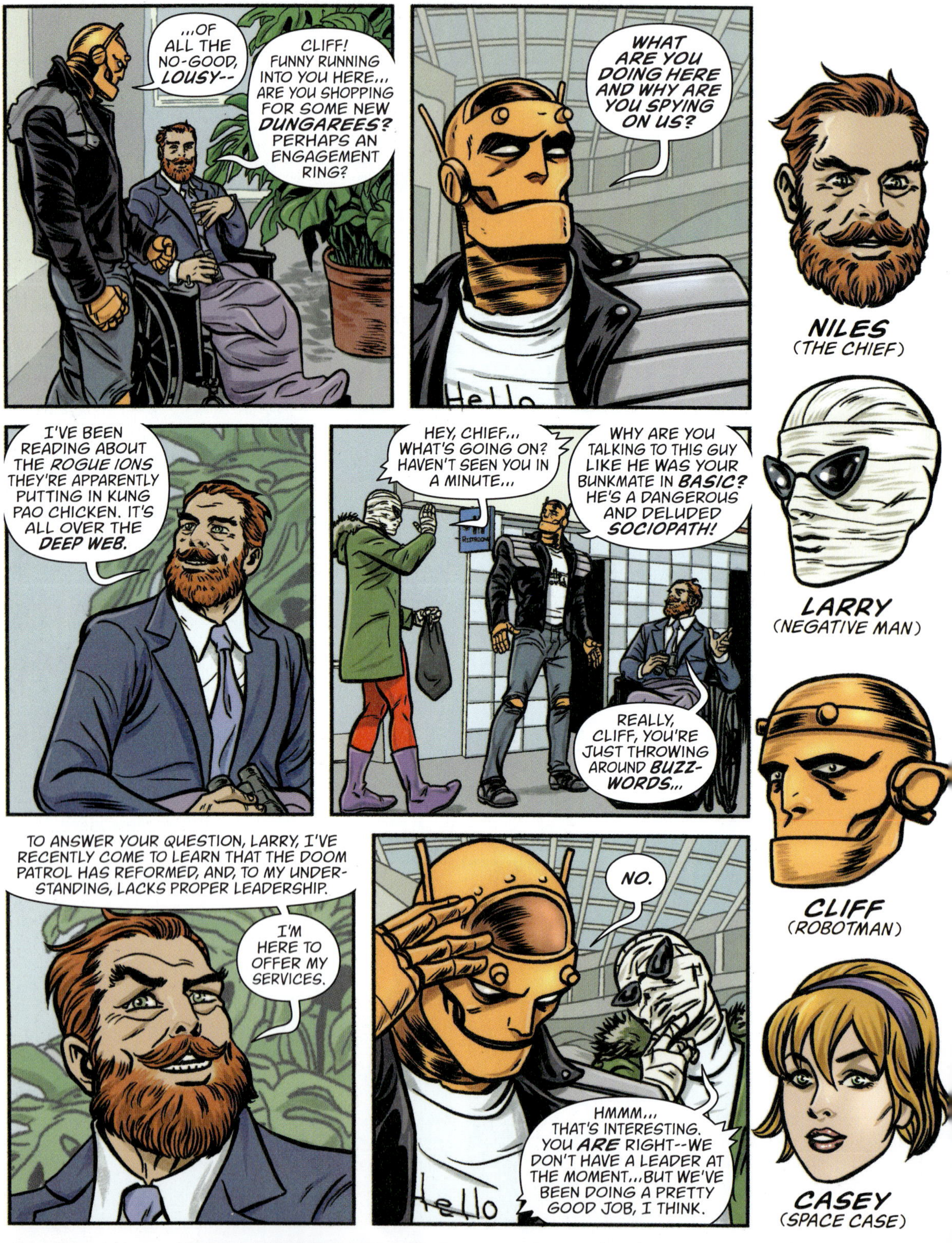

...OF ALL THE NO-GOOD, LOUSY--
CLIFF! FUNNY RUNNING INTO YOU HERE... ARE YOU SHOPPING FOR SOME NEW DUNGAREES? PERHAPS AN ENGAGEMENT RING?
WHAT ARE YOU DOING HERE AND WHY ARE YOU SPYING ON US?
Hello
I'VE BEEN READING ABOUT THE ROGUE IONS THEY'RE APPARENTLY PUTTING IN KUNG PAO CHICKEN. IT'S ALL OVER THE DEEP WEB.
HEY, CHIEF... WHAT'S GOING ON? HAVEN'T SEEN YOU IN A MINUTE...
WHY ARE YOU TALKING TO THIS GUY LIKE HE WAS YOUR BUNKMATE IN BASIC? HE'S A DANGEROUS AND DELUDED SOCIOPATH!
REALLY, CLIFF, YOU'RE JUST THROWING AROUND BUZZ-WORDS...
TO ANSWER YOUR QUESTION, LARRY, I'VE RECENTLY COME TO LEARN THAT THE DOOM PATROL HAS REFORMED, AND, TO MY UNDER-STANDING, LACKS PROPER LEADERSHIP.
I'M HERE TO OFFER MY SERVICES.
NO.
HMMM... THAT'S INTERESTING. YOU ARE RIGHT--WE DON'T HAVE A LEADER AT THE MOMENT... BUT WE'VE BEEN DOING A PRETTY GOOD JOB, I THINK.
Hello
NILES (THE CHIEF)
LARRY (NEGATIVE MAN)
CLIFF (ROBOTMAN)
CASEY (SPACE CASE)

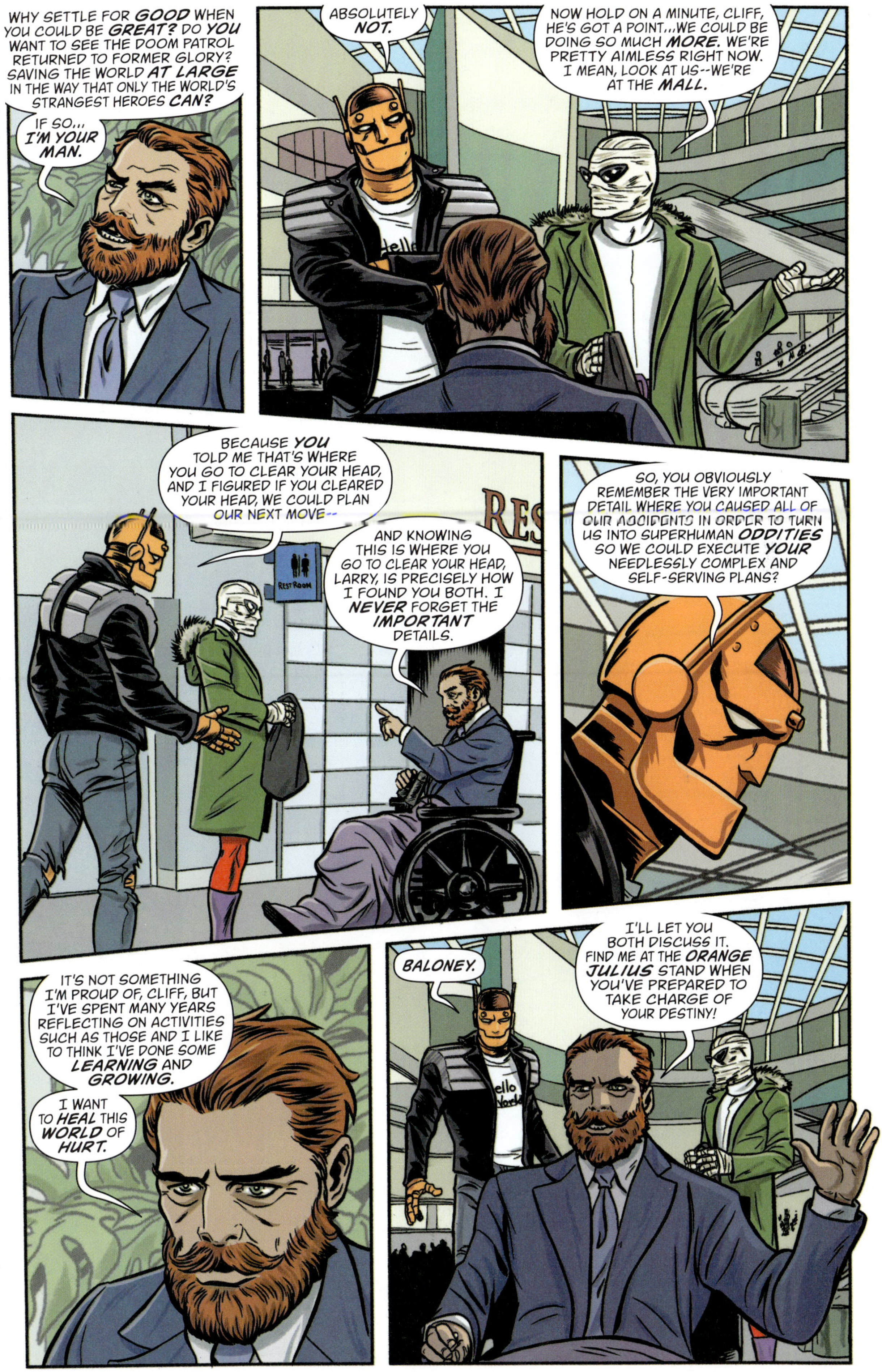
WHY SETTLE FOR GOOD WHEN YOU COULD BE GREAT? DO YOU WANT TO SEE THE DOOM PATROL RETURNED TO FORMER GLORY? SAVING THE WORLD AT LARGE IN THE WAY THAT ONLY THE WORLD'S STRANGEST HEROES CAN?
IF SO... I'M YOUR MAN.
ABSOLUTELY NOT.
NOW HOLD ON A MINUTE, CLIFF, HE'S GOT A POINT...WE COULD BE DOING SO MUCH MORE. WE'RE PRETTY AIMLESS RIGHT NOW. I MEAN, LOOK AT US--WE'RE AT THE MALL.
BECAUSE YOU TOLD ME THAT'S WHERE YOU GO TO CLEAR YOUR HEAD, AND I FIGURED IF YOU CLEARED YOUR HEAD, WE COULD PLAN OUR NEXT MOVE--
RESTROOM
AND KNOWING THIS IS WHERE YOU GO TO CLEAR YOUR HEAD, LARRY, IS PRECISELY HOW I FOUND YOU BOTH. I NEVER FORGET THE IMPORTANT DETAILS.
SO, YOU OBVIOUSLY REMEMBER THE VERY IMPORTANT DETAIL WHERE YOU CAUSED ALL OF OUR ACCIDENTS IN ORDER TO TURN US INTO SUPERHUMAN ODDITIES SO WE COULD EXECUTE YOUR NEEDLESSLY COMPLEX AND SELF-SERVING PLANS?
IT'S NOT SOMETHING I'M PROUD OF, CLIFF, BUT I'VE SPENT MANY YEARS REFLECTING ON ACTIVITIES SUCH AS THOSE AND I LIKE TO THINK I'VE DONE SOME LEARNING AND GROWING.
I WANT TO HEAL THIS WORLD OF HURT.
BALONEY.
I'LL LET YOU BOTH DISCUSS IT. FIND ME AT THE ORANGE JULIUS STAND WHEN YOU'VE PREPARED TO TAKE CHARGE OF YOUR DESTINY!

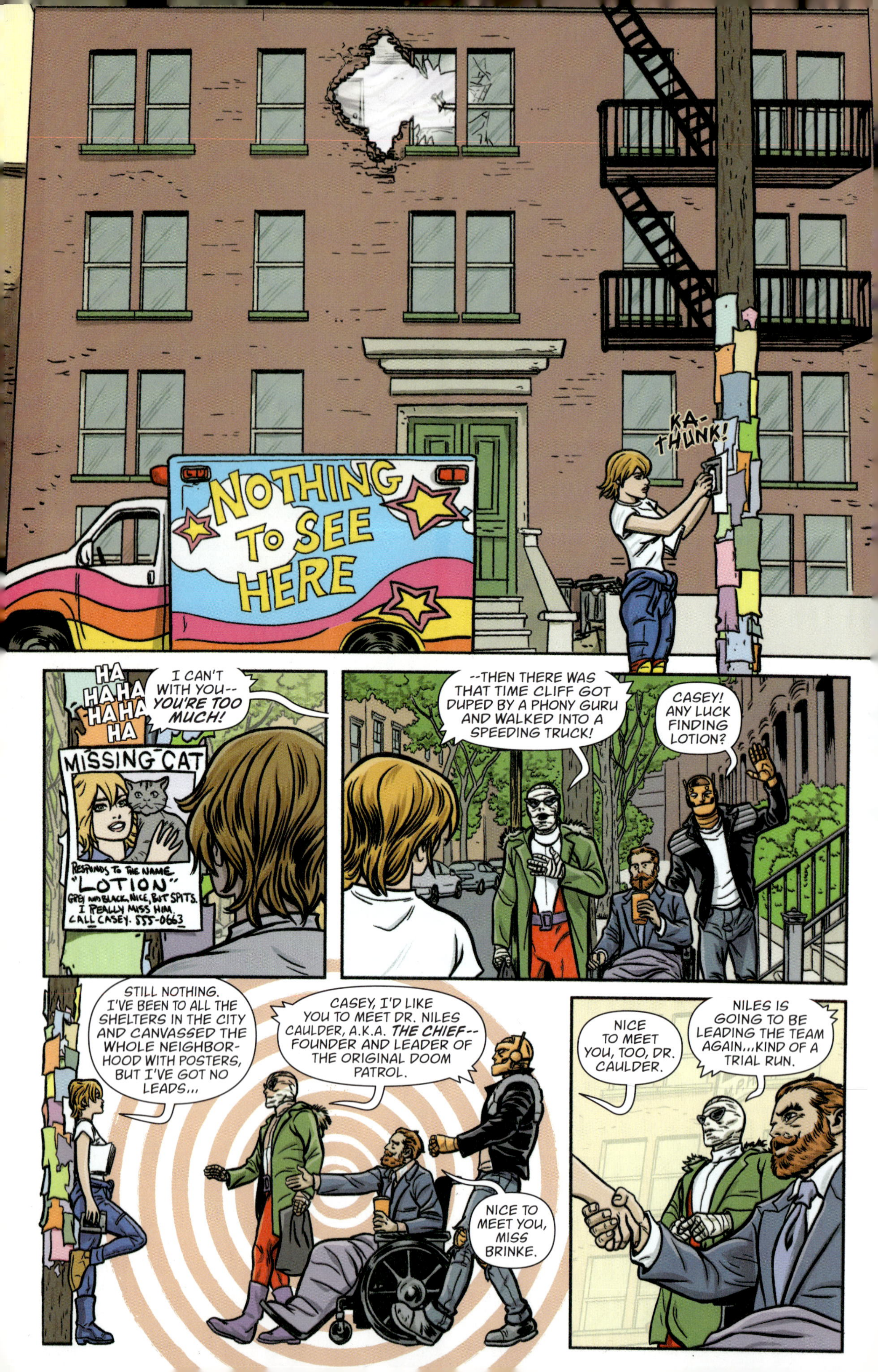
NOTHING TO SEE HERE
KA-THUNK!
HA HA HA HA HA HA
I CAN'T WITH YOU-- YOU'RE TOO MUCH!
MISSING CAT
RESPONDS TO THE NAME "LOTION"
GREY AND BLACK. NICE, BUT SPITS.
I REALLY MISS HIM.
CALL CASEY. 555-0663
--THEN THERE WAS THAT TIME CLIFF GOT DUPED BY A PHONY GURU AND WALKED INTO A SPEEDING TRUCK!
CASEY! ANY LUCK FINDING LOTION?
STILL NOTHING. I'VE BEEN TO ALL THE SHELTERS IN THE CITY AND CANVASSED THE WHOLE NEIGHBORHOOD WITH POSTERS, BUT I'VE GOT NO LEADS...
CASEY, I'D LIKE YOU TO MEET DR. NILES CAULDER, A.K.A. THE CHIEF-- FOUNDER AND LEADER OF THE ORIGINAL DOOM PATROL.
NICE TO MEET YOU, MISS BRINKE.
NICE TO MEET YOU, TOO, DR. CAULDER.
NILES IS GOING TO BE LEADING THE TEAM AGAIN...KIND OF A TRIAL RUN.

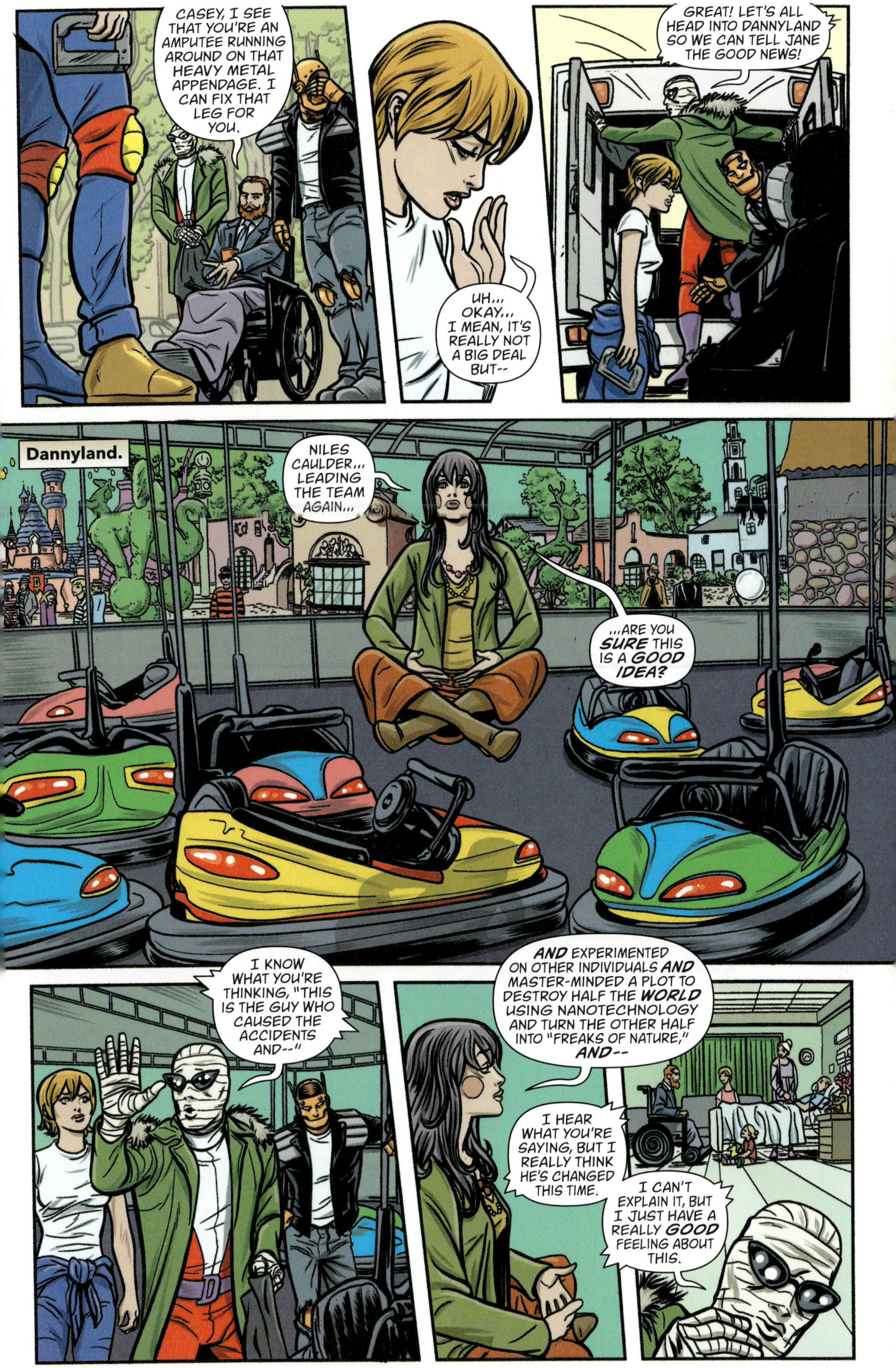
CASEY, I SEE THAT YOU'RE AN AMPUTEE RUNNING AROUND ON THAT HEAVY METAL APPENDAGE. I CAN FIX THAT LEG FOR YOU.
UH... OKAY... I MEAN, IT'S REALLY NOT A BIG DEAL BUT--
GREAT! LET'S ALL HEAD INTO DANNYLAND SO WE CAN TELL JANE THE GOOD NEWS!
Dannyland.
NILES CAULDER... LEADING THE TEAM AGAIN...
...ARE YOU SURE THIS IS A GOOD IDEA?
I KNOW WHAT YOU'RE THINKING, "THIS IS THE GUY WHO CAUSED THE ACCIDENTS AND--"
AND EXPERIMENTED ON OTHER INDIVIDUALS AND MASTER-MINDED A PLOT TO DESTROY HALF THE WORLD USING NANOTECHNOLOGY AND TURN THE OTHER HALF INTO "FREAKS OF NATURE," AND--
I HEAR WHAT YOU'RE SAYING, BUT I REALLY THINK HE'S CHANGED THIS TIME.
I CAN'T EXPLAIN IT, BUT I JUST HAVE A REALLY GOOD FEELING ABOUT THIS.

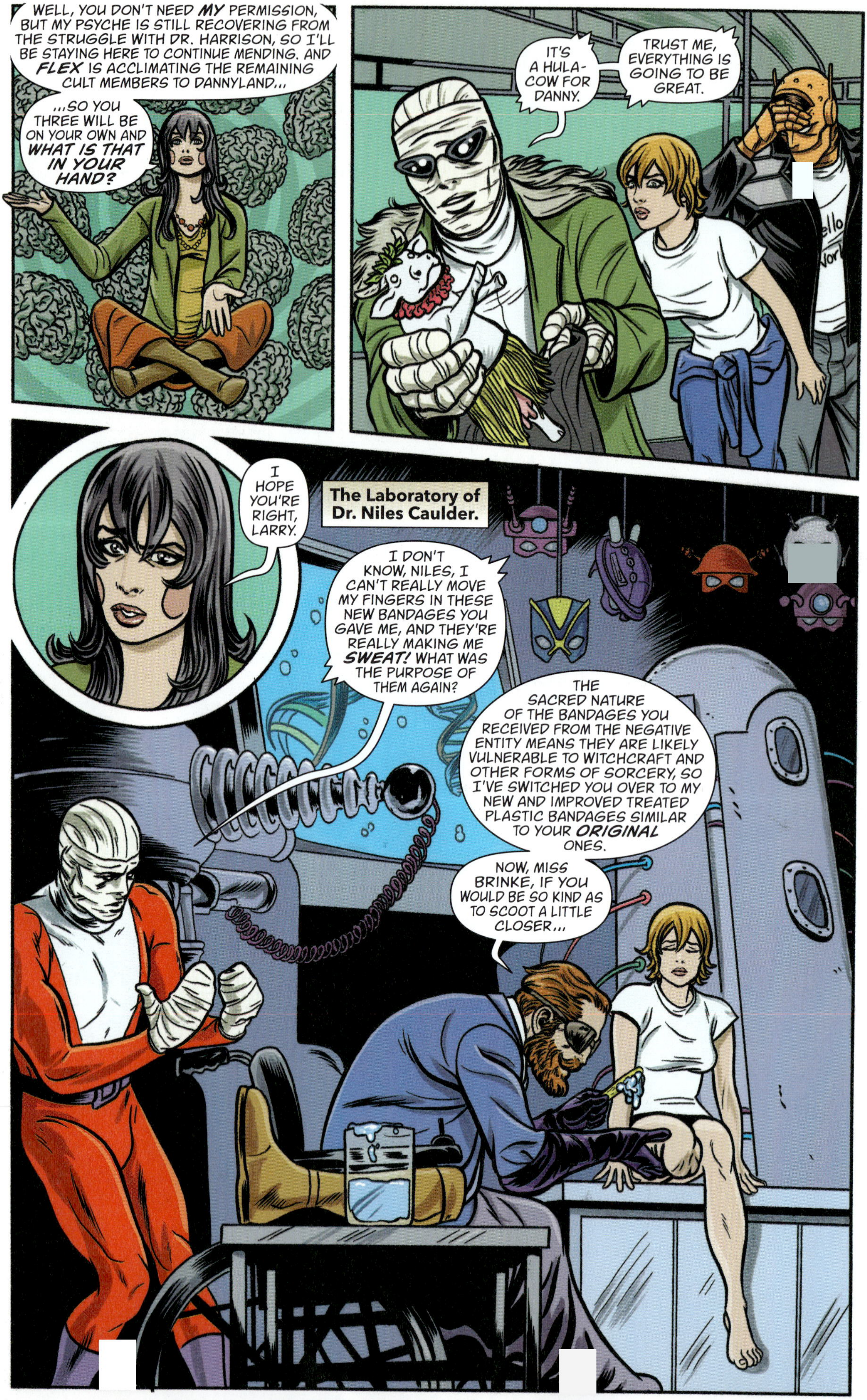
WELL, YOU DON'T NEED MY PERMISSION, BUT MY PSYCHE IS STILL RECOVERING FROM THE STRUGGLE WITH DR. HARRISON, SO I'LL BE STAYING HERE TO CONTINUE MENDING. AND FLEX IS ACCLIMATING THE REMAINING CULT MEMBERS TO DANNYLAND...
...SO YOU THREE WILL BE ON YOUR OWN AND WHAT IS THAT IN YOUR HAND?
IT'S A HULA-COW FOR DANNY.
TRUST ME, EVERYTHING IS GOING TO BE GREAT.
I HOPE YOU'RE RIGHT, LARRY.
The Laboratory of Dr. Niles Caulder.
I DON'T KNOW, NILES, I CAN'T REALLY MOVE MY FINGERS IN THESE NEW BANDAGES YOU GAVE ME, AND THEY'RE REALLY MAKING ME SWEAT! WHAT WAS THE PURPOSE OF THEM AGAIN?
THE SACRED NATURE OF THE BANDAGES YOU RECEIVED FROM THE NEGATIVE ENTITY MEANS THEY ARE LIKELY VULNERABLE TO WITCHCRAFT AND OTHER FORMS OF SORCERY, SO I'VE SWITCHED YOU OVER TO MY NEW AND IMPROVED TREATED PLASTIC BANDAGES SIMILAR TO YOUR ORIGINAL ONES.
NOW, MISS BRINKE, IF YOU WOULD BE SO KIND AS TO SCOOT A LITTLE CLOSER...

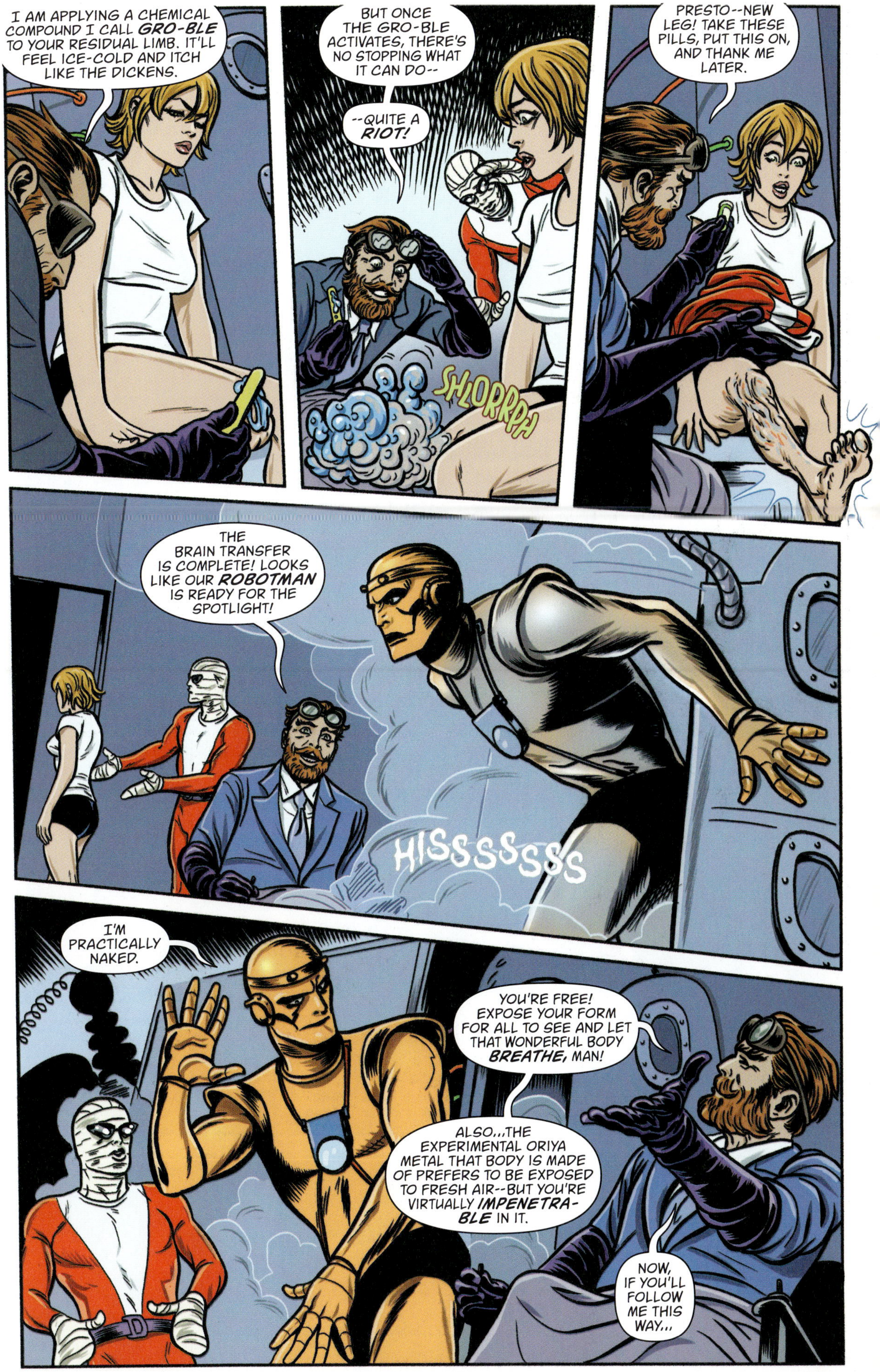

I AM APPLYING A CHEMICAL COMPOUND I CALL **GRO-BLE** TO YOUR RESIDUAL LIMB. IT'LL FEEL ICE-COLD AND ITCH LIKE THE DICKENS.
BUT ONCE THE GRO-BLE ACTIVATES, THERE'S NO STOPPING WHAT IT CAN DO--
--QUITE A **RIOT!**
SHLORRPH
PRESTO--NEW LEG! TAKE THESE PILLS, PUT THIS ON, AND THANK ME LATER.
THE BRAIN TRANSFER IS COMPLETE! LOOKS LIKE OUR **ROBOTMAN** IS READY FOR THE SPOTLIGHT!
HISSSSSSS
I'M PRACTICALLY NAKED.
YOU'RE FREE! EXPOSE YOUR FORM FOR ALL TO SEE AND LET THAT WONDERFUL BODY ***BREATHE,*** MAN!
ALSO...THE EXPERIMENTAL ORIYA METAL THAT BODY IS MADE OF PREFERS TO BE EXPOSED TO FRESH AIR--BUT YOU'RE VIRTUALLY ***IMPENETRA-BLE*** IN IT.
NOW, IF YOU'LL FOLLOW ME THIS WAY...

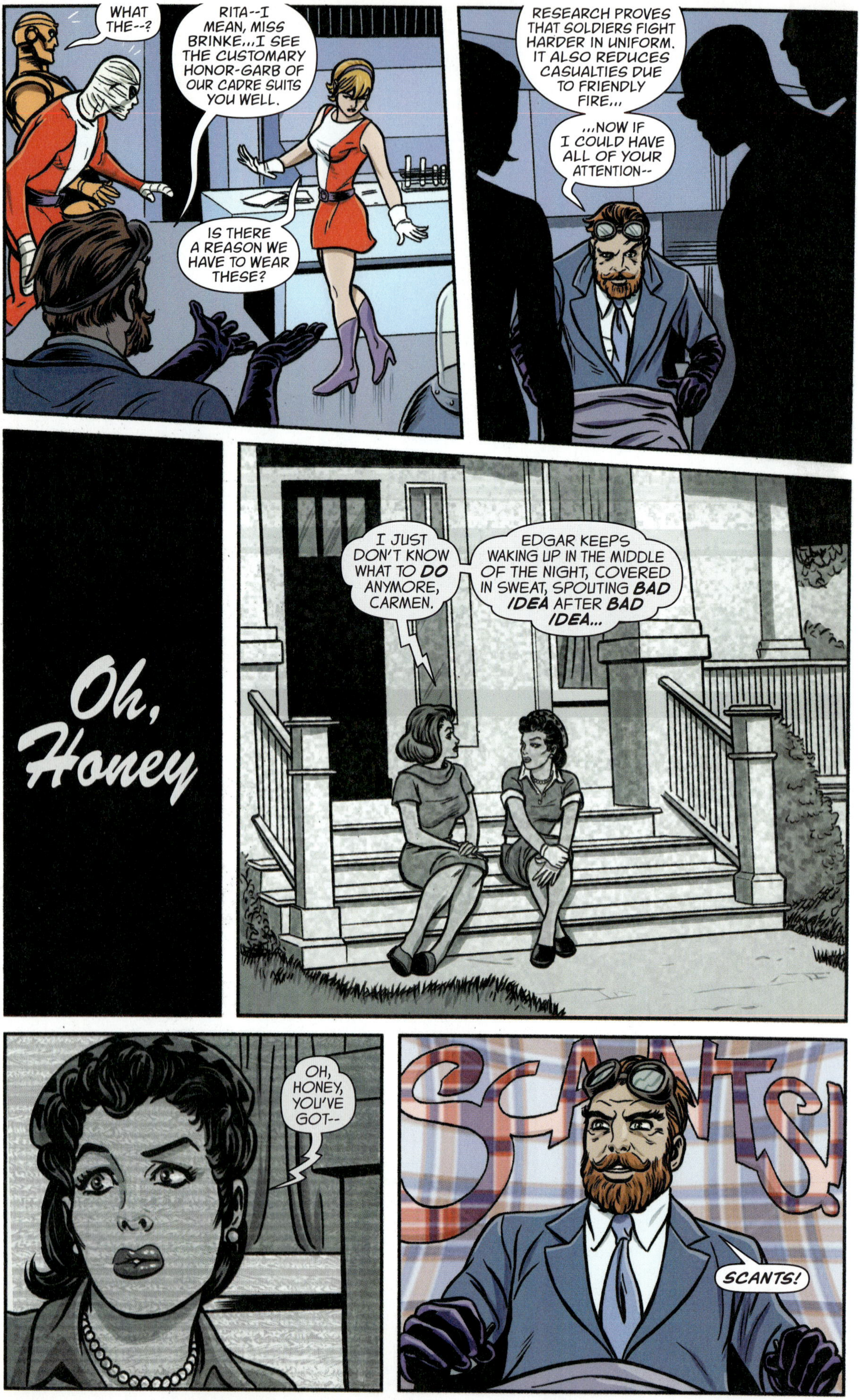
WHAT THE--?
RITA--I MEAN, MISS BRINKE...I SEE THE CUSTOMARY HONOR-GARB OF OUR CADRE SUITS YOU WELL.
IS THERE A REASON WE HAVE TO WEAR THESE?
RESEARCH PROVES THAT SOLDIERS FIGHT HARDER IN UNIFORM. IT ALSO REDUCES CASUALTIES DUE TO FRIENDLY FIRE...
...NOW IF I COULD HAVE ALL OF YOUR ATTENTION--
Oh, Honey
I JUST DON'T KNOW WHAT TO DO ANYMORE, CARMEN.
EDGAR KEEPS WAKING UP IN THE MIDDLE OF THE NIGHT, COVERED IN SWEAT, SPOUTING BAD IDEA AFTER BAD IDEA...
OH, HONEY, YOU'VE GOT--
SCANTS!
SCANTS!

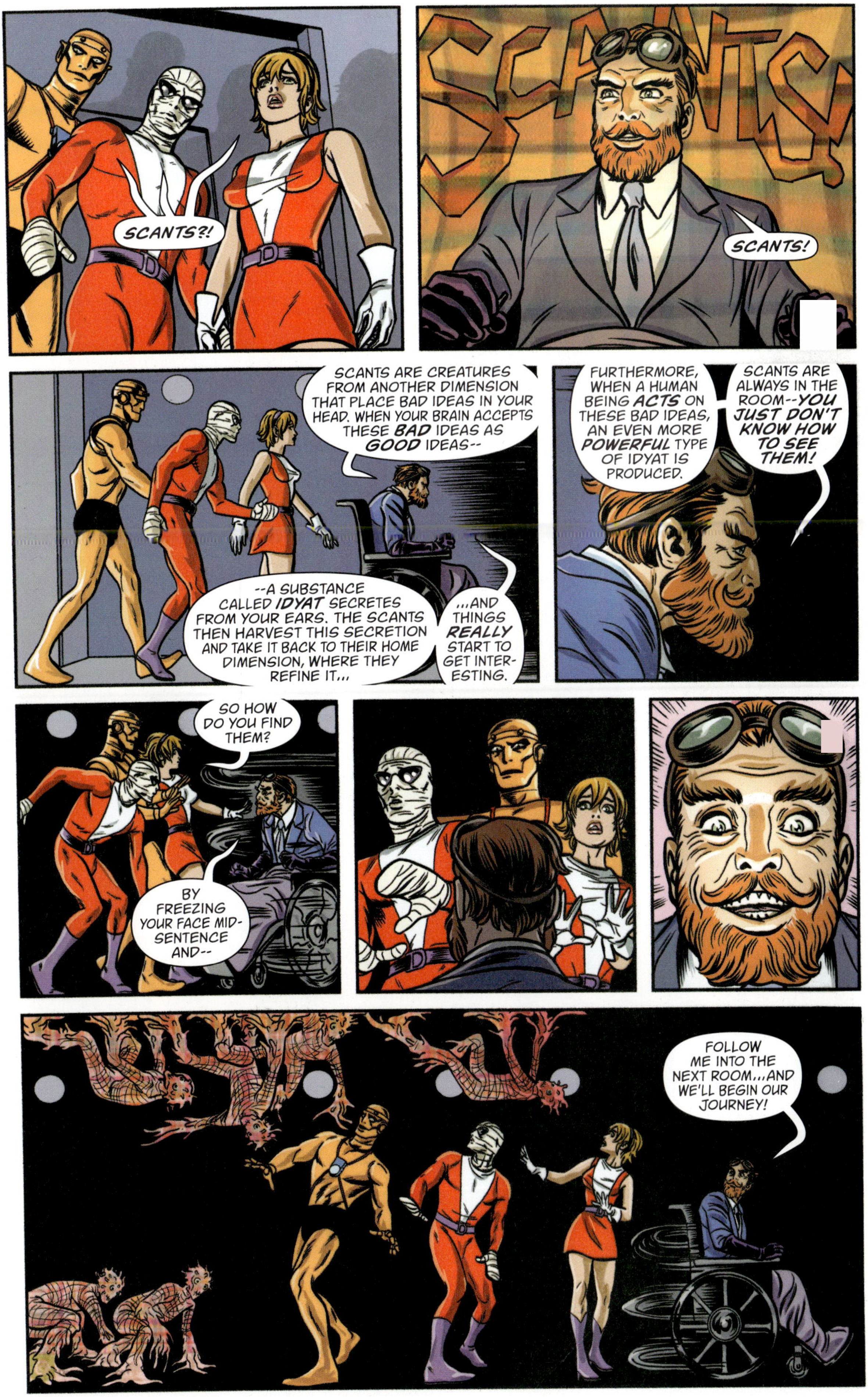
SCANTS?!
SCANTS!
SCANTS ARE CREATURES FROM ANOTHER DIMENSION THAT PLACE BAD IDEAS IN YOUR HEAD. WHEN YOUR BRAIN ACCEPTS THESE BAD IDEAS AS GOOD IDEAS--
--A SUBSTANCE CALLED IDYAT SECRETES FROM YOUR EARS. THE SCANTS THEN HARVEST THIS SECRETION AND TAKE IT BACK TO THEIR HOME DIMENSION, WHERE THEY REFINE IT...
...AND THINGS REALLY START TO GET INTERESTING.
FURTHERMORE, WHEN A HUMAN BEING ACTS ON THESE BAD IDEAS, AN EVEN MORE POWERFUL TYPE OF IDYAT IS PRODUCED.
SCANTS ARE ALWAYS IN THE ROOM--YOU JUST DON'T KNOW HOW TO SEE THEM!
SO HOW DO YOU FIND THEM?
BY FREEZING YOUR FACE MID-SENTENCE AND--
FOLLOW ME INTO THE NEXT ROOM...AND WE'LL BEGIN OUR JOURNEY!

WELCOME HOME, VALERIÉ REYNOLDS

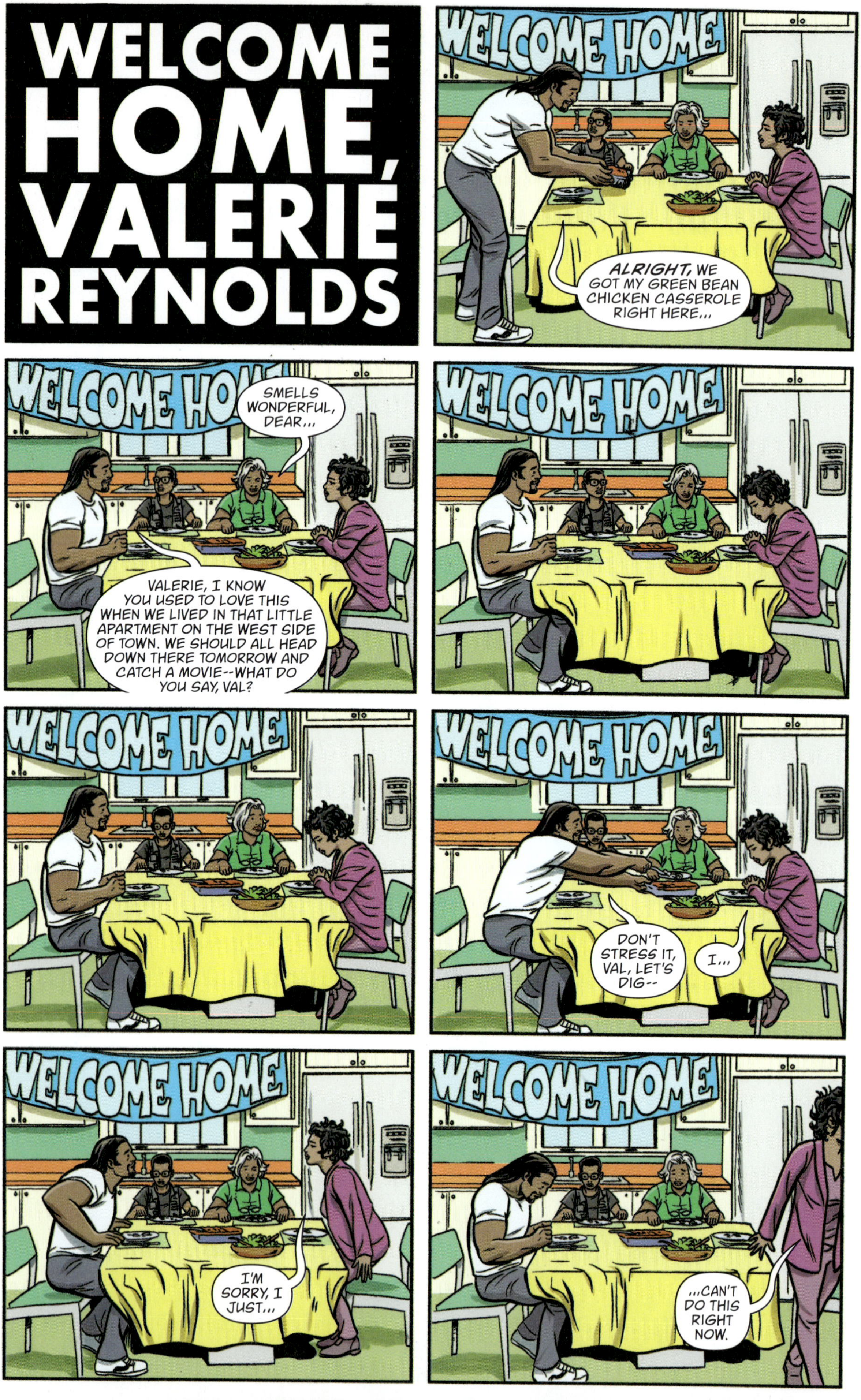
WELCOME HOME
ALRIGHT, WE GOT MY GREEN BEAN CHICKEN CASSEROLE RIGHT HERE...
SMELLS WONDERFUL, DEAR...
VALERIE, I KNOW YOU USED TO LOVE THIS WHEN WE LIVED IN THAT LITTLE APARTMENT ON THE WEST SIDE OF TOWN. WE SHOULD ALL HEAD DOWN THERE TOMORROW AND CATCH A MOVIE--WHAT DO YOU SAY, VAL?
DON'T STRESS IT, VAL, LET'S DIG--
I...
I'M SORRY, I JUST...
...CAN'T DO THIS RIGHT NOW.

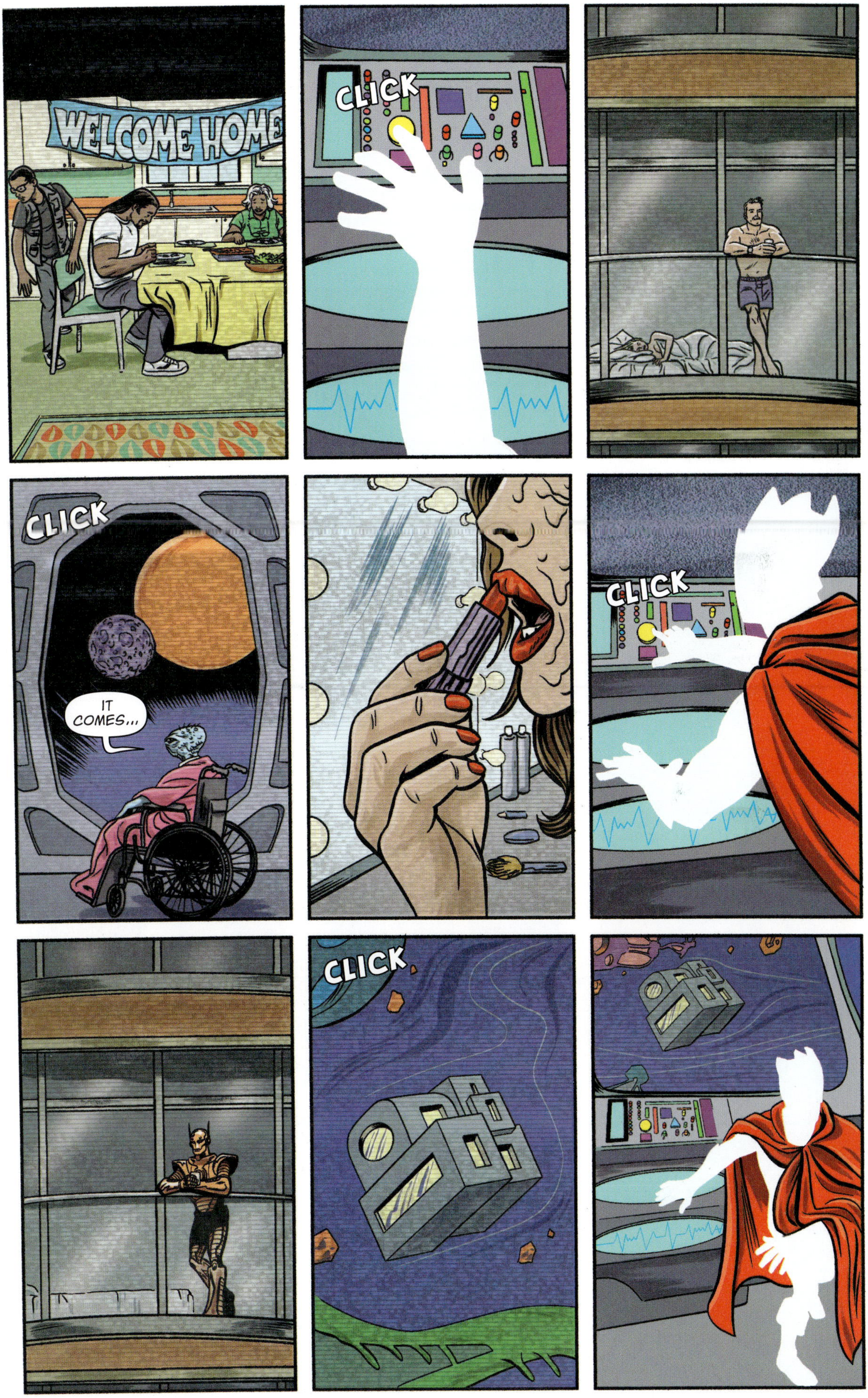

WELCOME HOME
CLICK
CLICK
IT COMES...
CLICK
CLICK

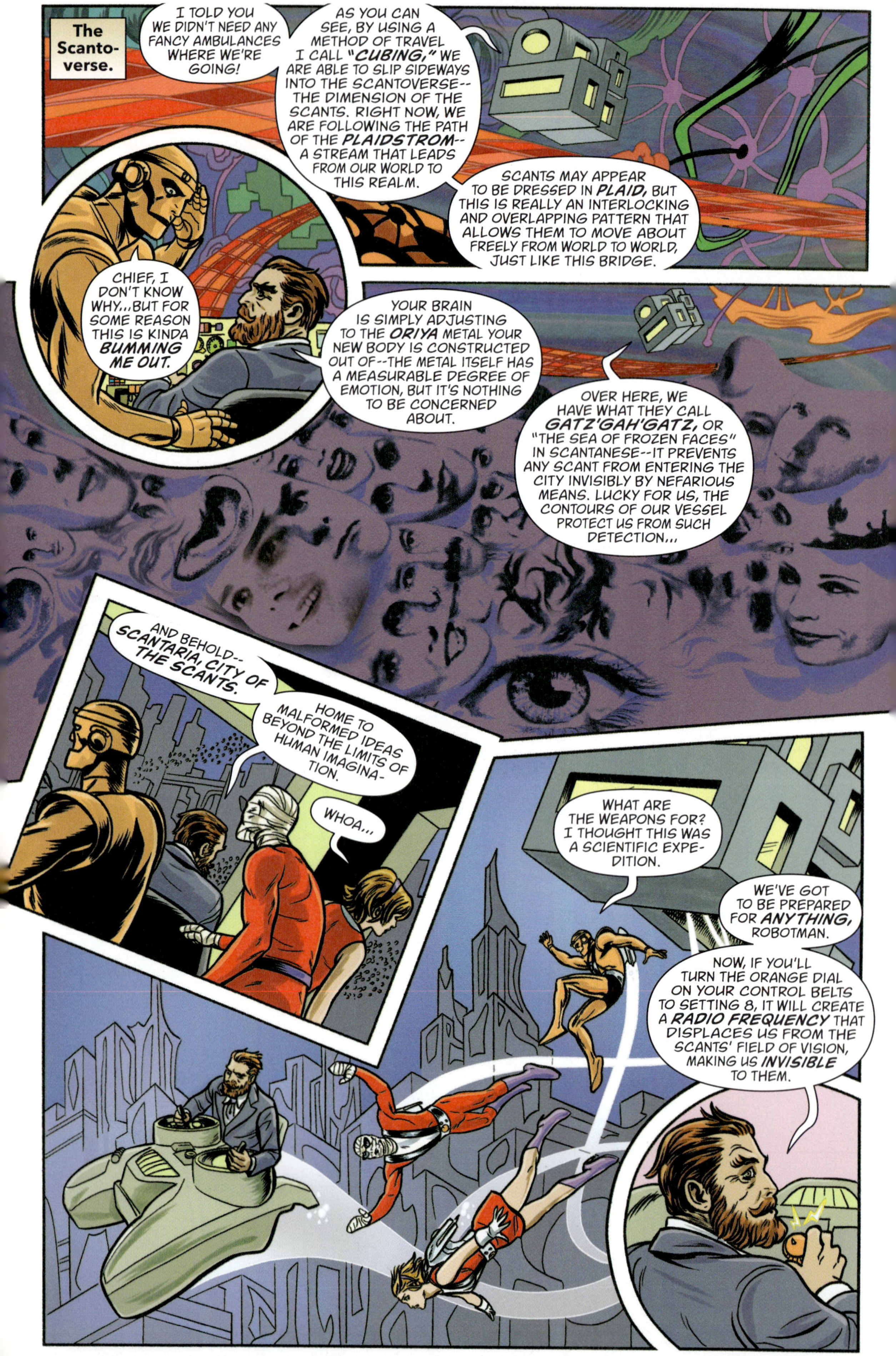
The Scantoverse.
I TOLD YOU WE DIDN'T NEED ANY FANCY AMBULANCES WHERE WE'RE GOING!
AS YOU CAN SEE, BY USING A METHOD OF TRAVEL I CALL "CUBING," WE ARE ABLE TO SLIP SIDEWAYS INTO THE SCANTOVERSE--THE DIMENSION OF THE SCANTS. RIGHT NOW, WE ARE FOLLOWING THE PATH OF THE PLAIDSTROM--A STREAM THAT LEADS FROM OUR WORLD TO THIS REALM.
SCANTS MAY APPEAR TO BE DRESSED IN PLAID, BUT THIS IS REALLY AN INTERLOCKING AND OVERLAPPING PATTERN THAT ALLOWS THEM TO MOVE ABOUT FREELY FROM WORLD TO WORLD, JUST LIKE THIS BRIDGE.
CHIEF, I DON'T KNOW WHY...BUT FOR SOME REASON THIS IS KINDA BUMMING ME OUT.
YOUR BRAIN IS SIMPLY ADJUSTING TO THE ORIYA METAL YOUR NEW BODY IS CONSTRUCTED OUT OF--THE METAL ITSELF HAS A MEASURABLE DEGREE OF EMOTION, BUT IT'S NOTHING TO BE CONCERNED ABOUT.
OVER HERE, WE HAVE WHAT THEY CALL GATZ'GAH'GATZ, OR "THE SEA OF FROZEN FACES" IN SCANTANESE--IT PREVENTS ANY SCANT FROM ENTERING THE CITY INVISIBLY BY NEFARIOUS MEANS. LUCKY FOR US, THE CONTOURS OF OUR VESSEL PROTECT US FROM SUCH DETECTION...
AND BEHOLD--SCANTARIA, CITY OF THE SCANTS.
HOME TO MALFORMED IDEAS BEYOND THE LIMITS OF HUMAN IMAGINATION.
WHOA...
WHAT ARE THE WEAPONS FOR? I THOUGHT THIS WAS A SCIENTIFIC EXPEDITION.
WE'VE GOT TO BE PREPARED FOR ANYTHING, ROBOTMAN.
NOW, IF YOU'LL TURN THE ORANGE DIAL ON YOUR CONTROL BELTS TO SETTING 8, IT WILL CREATE A RADIO FREQUENCY THAT DISPLACES US FROM THE SCANTS' FIELD OF VISION, MAKING US INVISIBLE TO THEM.

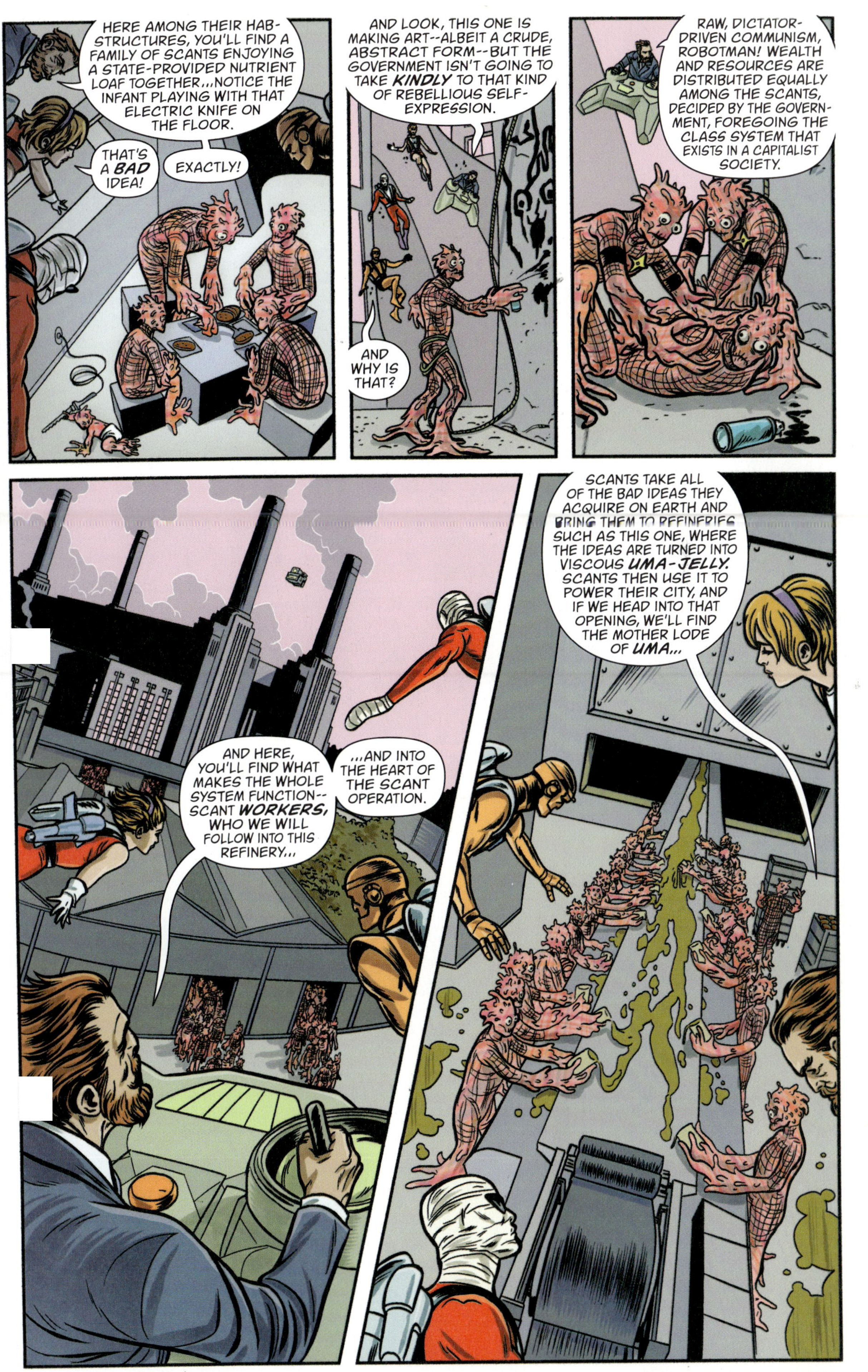
HERE AMONG THEIR HAB-STRUCTURES, YOU'LL FIND A FAMILY OF SCANTS ENJOYING A STATE-PROVIDED NUTRIENT LOAF TOGETHER... NOTICE THE INFANT PLAYING WITH THAT ELECTRIC KNIFE ON THE FLOOR.
THAT'S A BAD IDEA!
EXACTLY!
AND LOOK, THIS ONE IS MAKING ART--ALBEIT A CRUDE, ABSTRACT FORM--BUT THE GOVERNMENT ISN'T GOING TO TAKE KINDLY TO THAT KIND OF REBELLIOUS SELF-EXPRESSION.
AND WHY IS THAT?
RAW, DICTATOR-DRIVEN COMMUNISM, ROBOTMAN! WEALTH AND RESOURCES ARE DISTRIBUTED EQUALLY AMONG THE SCANTS, DECIDED BY THE GOVERNMENT, FOREGOING THE CLASS SYSTEM THAT EXISTS IN A CAPITALIST SOCIETY.
AND HERE, YOU'LL FIND WHAT MAKES THE WHOLE SYSTEM FUNCTION-- SCANT WORKERS, WHO WE WILL FOLLOW INTO THIS REFINERY...
...AND INTO THE HEART OF THE SCANT OPERATION.
SCANTS TAKE ALL OF THE BAD IDEAS THEY ACQUIRE ON EARTH AND BRING THEM TO REFINERIES SUCH AS THIS ONE, WHERE THE IDEAS ARE TURNED INTO VISCOUS UMA-JELLY. SCANTS THEN USE IT TO POWER THEIR CITY, AND IF WE HEAD INTO THAT OPENING, WE'LL FIND THE MOTHER LODE OF UMA...

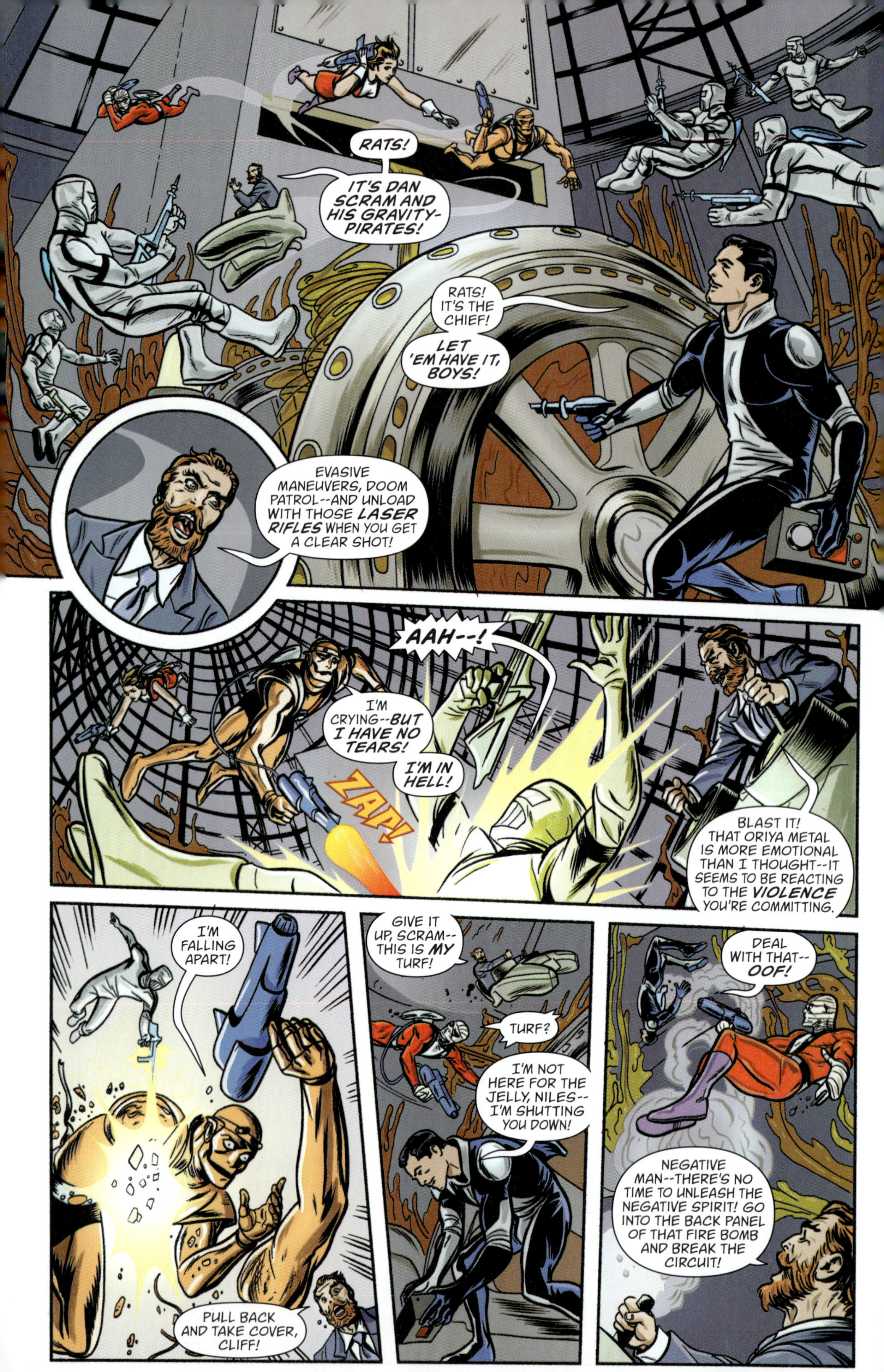
RATS!
IT'S DAN SCRAM AND HIS GRAVITY-PIRATES!
RATS! IT'S THE CHIEF!
LET 'EM HAVE IT, BOYS!
EVASIVE MANEUVERS, DOOM PATROL--AND UNLOAD WITH THOSE LASER RIFLES WHEN YOU GET A CLEAR SHOT!
AAH--!
I'M CRYING--BUT I HAVE NO TEARS!
I'M IN HELL!
ZAP!
BLAST IT! THAT ORIYA METAL IS MORE EMOTIONAL THAN I THOUGHT--IT SEEMS TO BE REACTING TO THE VIOLENCE YOU'RE COMMITTING.
I'M FALLING APART!
PULL BACK AND TAKE COVER, CLIFF!
GIVE IT UP, SCRAM--THIS IS MY TURF!
TURF?
I'M NOT HERE FOR THE JELLY, NILES--I'M SHUTTING YOU DOWN!
DEAL WITH THAT--OOF!
NEGATIVE MAN--THERE'S NO TIME TO UNLEASH THE NEGATIVE SPIRIT! GO INTO THE BACK PANEL OF THAT FIRE BOMB AND BREAK THE CIRCUIT!

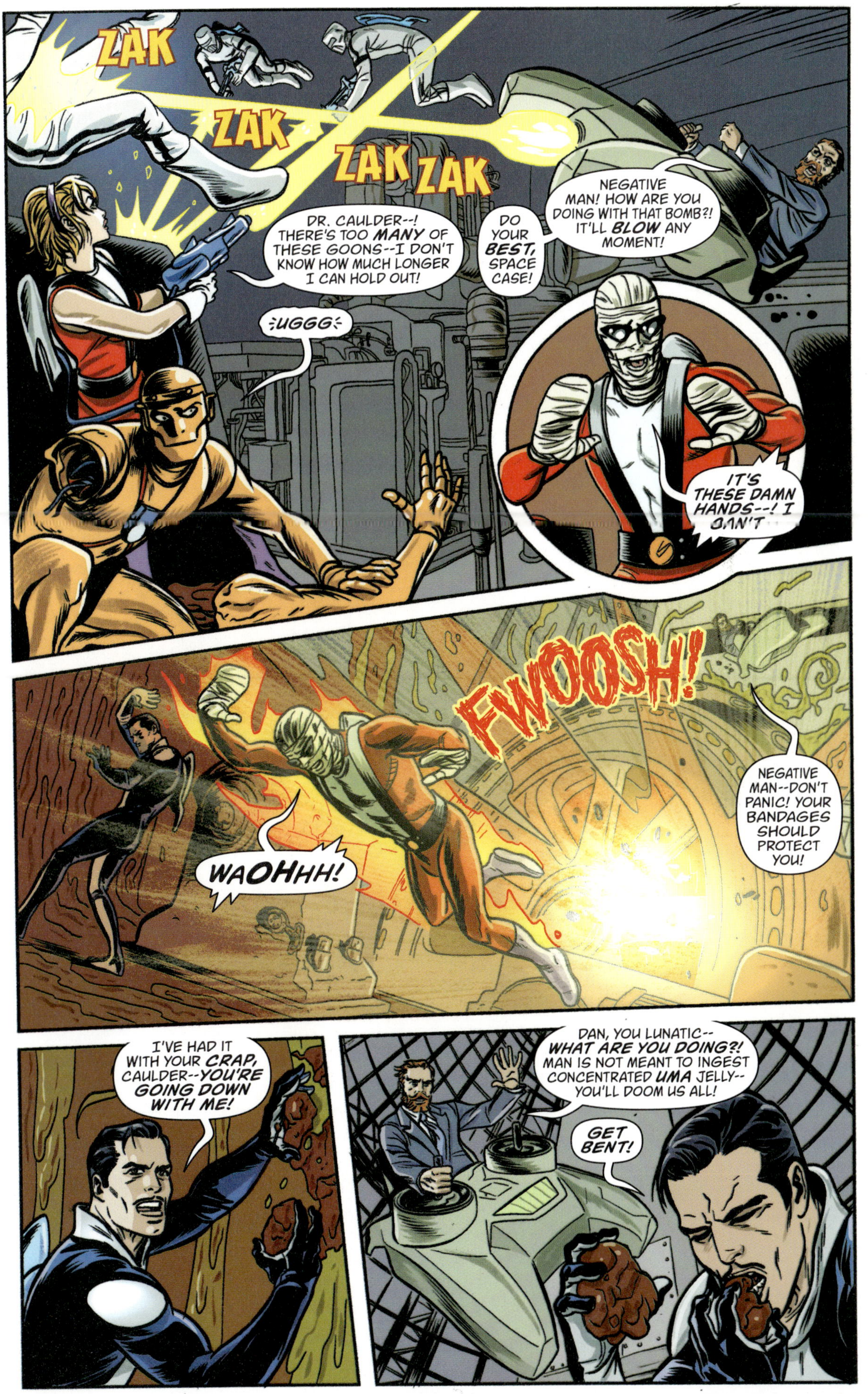

ZAK
ZAK
ZAK ZAK
DR. CAULDER--! THERE'S TOO MANY OF THESE GOONS--I DON'T KNOW HOW MUCH LONGER I CAN HOLD OUT!
DO YOUR BEST, SPACE CASE!
NEGATIVE MAN! HOW ARE YOU DOING WITH THAT BOMB?! IT'LL BLOW ANY MOMENT!
UGGG
IT'S THESE DAMN HANDS--! I CAN'T
FWOOSH!
WAOHHH!
NEGATIVE MAN--DON'T PANIC! YOUR BANDAGES SHOULD PROTECT YOU!
I'VE HAD IT WITH YOUR CRAP, CAULDER--YOU'RE GOING DOWN WITH ME!
DAN, YOU LUNATIC-- WHAT ARE YOU DOING?! MAN IS NOT MEANT TO INGEST CONCENTRATED UMA JELLY-- YOU'LL DOOM US ALL!
GET BENT!

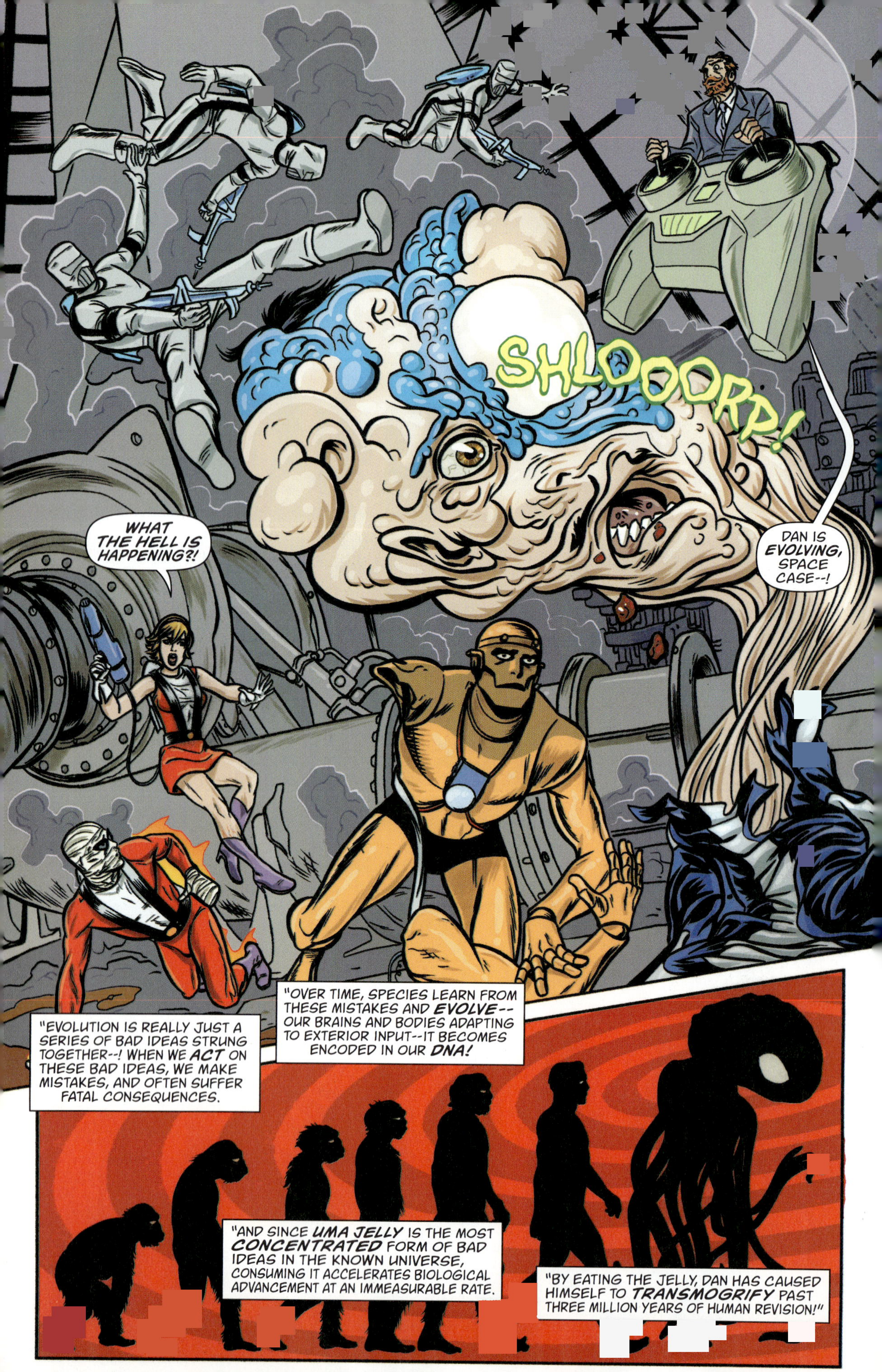
SHLOOORP!
WHAT THE HELL IS HAPPENING?!
DAN IS EVOLVING, SPACE CASE--!
"EVOLUTION IS REALLY JUST A SERIES OF BAD IDEAS STRUNG TOGETHER--! WHEN WE ACT ON THESE BAD IDEAS, WE MAKE MISTAKES, AND OFTEN SUFFER FATAL CONSEQUENCES.
"OVER TIME, SPECIES LEARN FROM THESE MISTAKES AND EVOLVE--OUR BRAINS AND BODIES ADAPTING TO EXTERIOR INPUT--IT BECOMES ENCODED IN OUR DNA!
"AND SINCE UMA JELLY IS THE MOST CONCENTRATED FORM OF BAD IDEAS IN THE KNOWN UNIVERSE, CONSUMING IT ACCELERATES BIOLOGICAL ADVANCEMENT AT AN IMMEASURABLE RATE.
"BY EATING THE JELLY, DAN HAS CAUSED HIMSELF TO TRANSMOGRIFY PAST THREE MILLION YEARS OF HUMAN REVISION!"

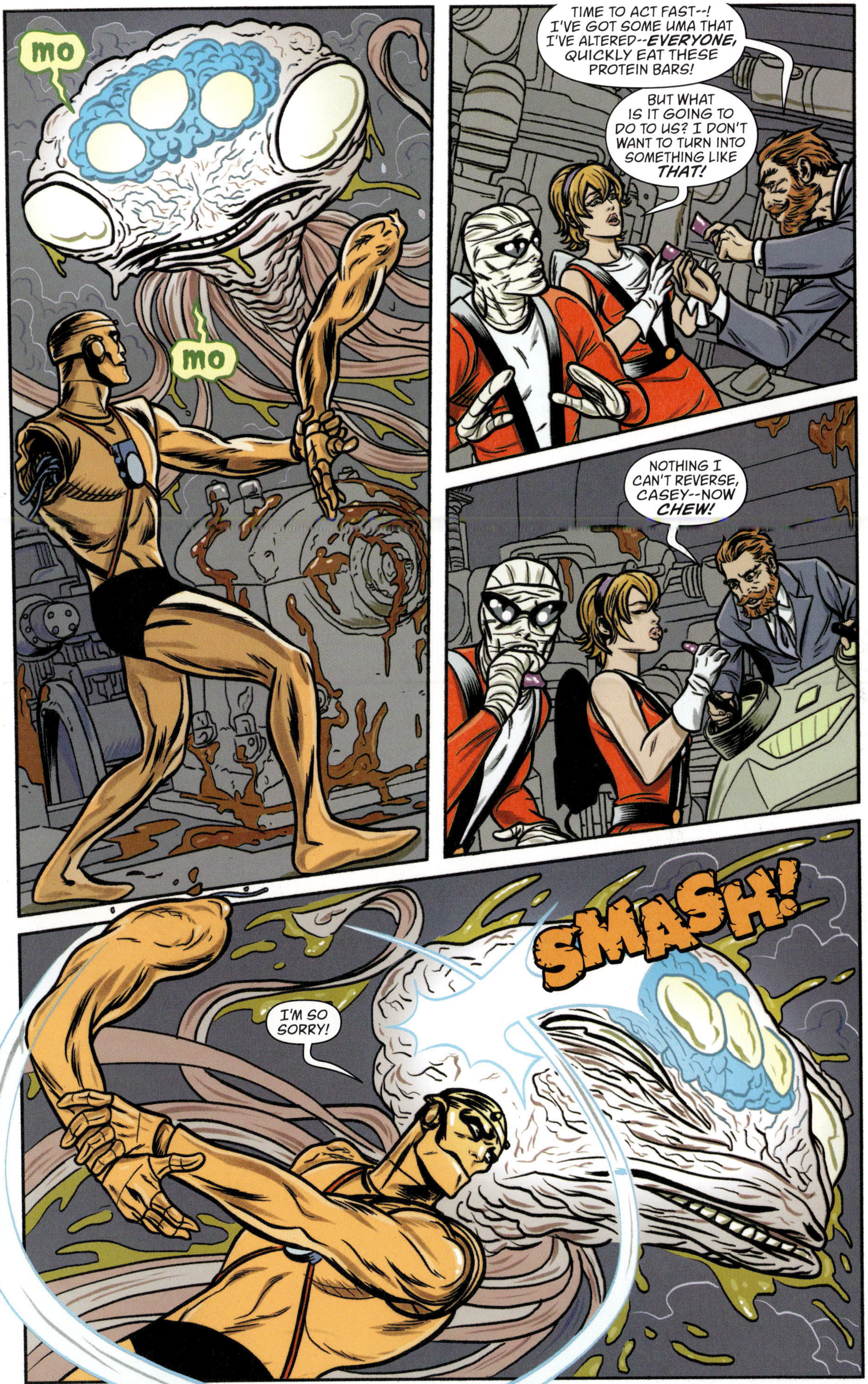
mo
mo
TIME TO ACT FAST--! I'VE GOT SOME UMA THAT I'VE ALTERED--*EVERYONE,* QUICKLY EAT THESE PROTEIN BARS!
BUT WHAT IS IT GOING TO DO TO US? I DON'T WANT TO TURN INTO SOMETHING LIKE *THAT!*
NOTHING I CAN'T REVERSE, CASEY--NOW *CHEW!*
SMASH!
I'M SO SORRY!

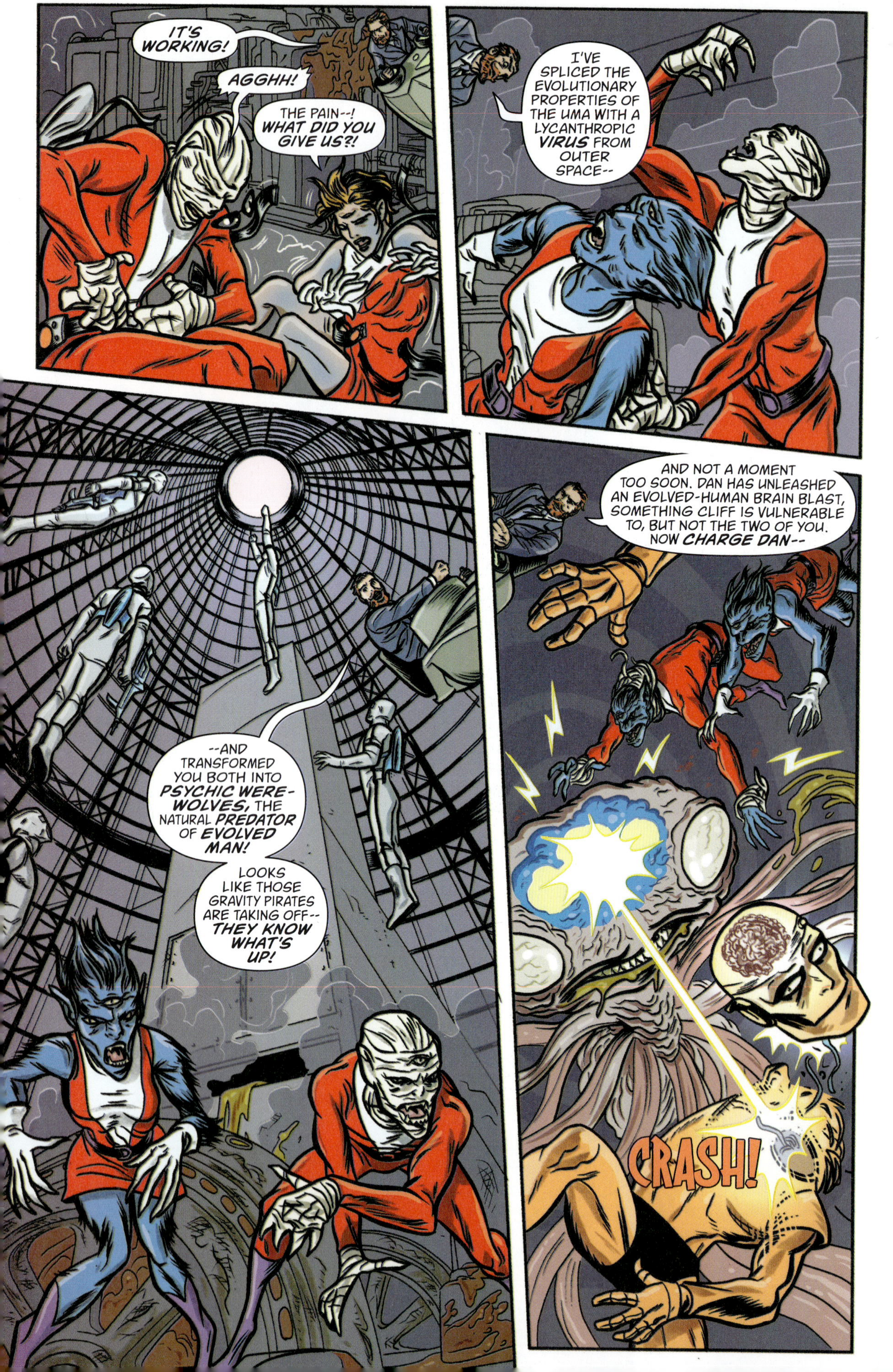
IT'S WORKING!
AGGHH!
THE PAIN--! WHAT DID YOU GIVE US?!
I'VE SPLICED THE EVOLUTIONARY PROPERTIES OF THE UMA WITH A LYCANTHROPIC VIRUS FROM OUTER SPACE--
--AND TRANSFORMED YOU BOTH INTO PSYCHIC WERE-WOLVES, THE NATURAL PREDATOR OF EVOLVED MAN!
LOOKS LIKE THOSE GRAVITY PIRATES ARE TAKING OFF-- THEY KNOW WHAT'S UP!
AND NOT A MOMENT TOO SOON. DAN HAS UNLEASHED AN EVOLVED-HUMAN BRAIN BLAST, SOMETHING CLIFF IS VULNERABLE TO, BUT NOT THE TWO OF YOU. NOW CHARGE DAN--
CRASH!

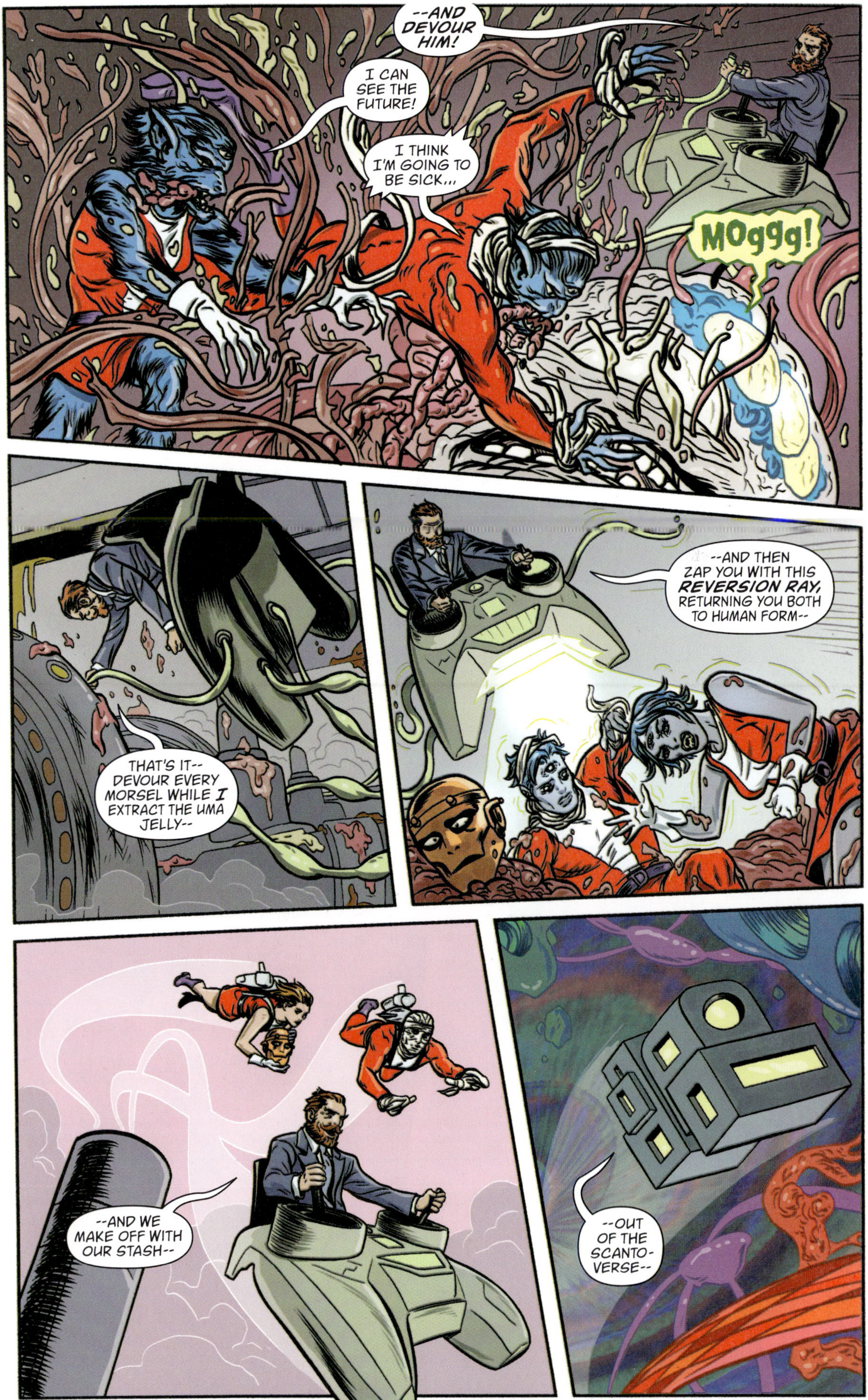
--AND DEVOUR HIM!
I CAN SEE THE FUTURE!
I THINK I'M GOING TO BE SICK...
MOggg!
THAT'S IT-- DEVOUR EVERY MORSEL WHILE I EXTRACT THE UMA JELLY--
--AND THEN ZAP YOU WITH THIS REVERSION RAY, RETURNING YOU BOTH TO HUMAN FORM--
--AND WE MAKE OFF WITH OUR STASH--
--OUT OF THE SCANTO-VERSE--

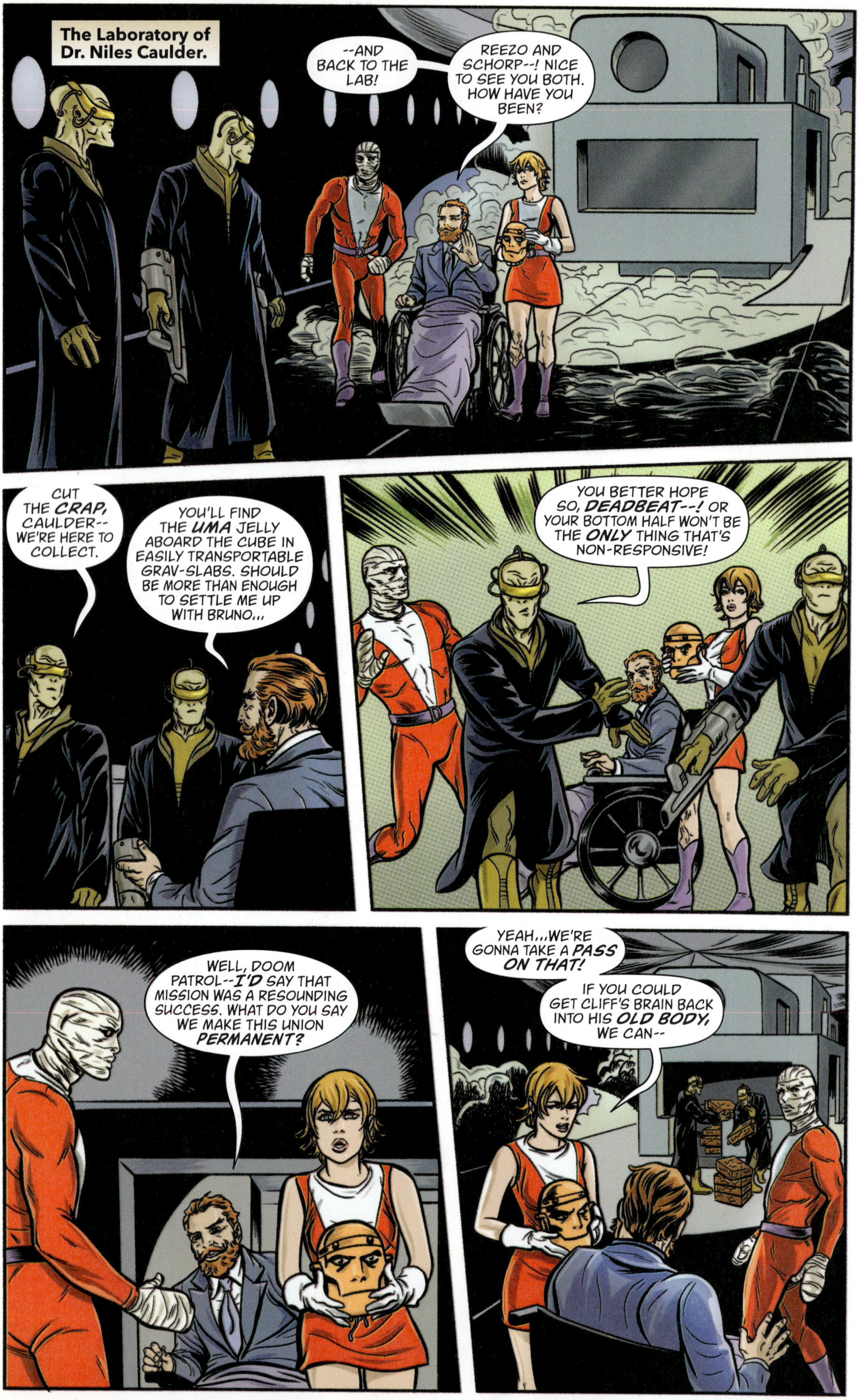

The Laboratory of Dr. Niles Caulder.
--AND BACK TO THE LAB!
REEZO AND SCHORP--! NICE TO SEE YOU BOTH. HOW HAVE YOU BEEN?
CUT THE CRAP, CAULDER-- WE'RE HERE TO COLLECT.
YOU'LL FIND THE UMA JELLY ABOARD THE CUBE IN EASILY TRANSPORTABLE GRAV-SLABS. SHOULD BE MORE THAN ENOUGH TO SETTLE ME UP WITH BRUNO...
YOU BETTER HOPE SO, DEADBEAT--! OR YOUR BOTTOM HALF WON'T BE THE ONLY THING THAT'S NON-RESPONSIVE!
WELL, DOOM PATROL--I'D SAY THAT MISSION WAS A RESOUNDING SUCCESS. WHAT DO YOU SAY WE MAKE THIS UNION PERMANENT?
YEAH...WE'RE GONNA TAKE A PASS ON THAT!
IF YOU COULD GET CLIFF'S BRAIN BACK INTO HIS OLD BODY, WE CAN--

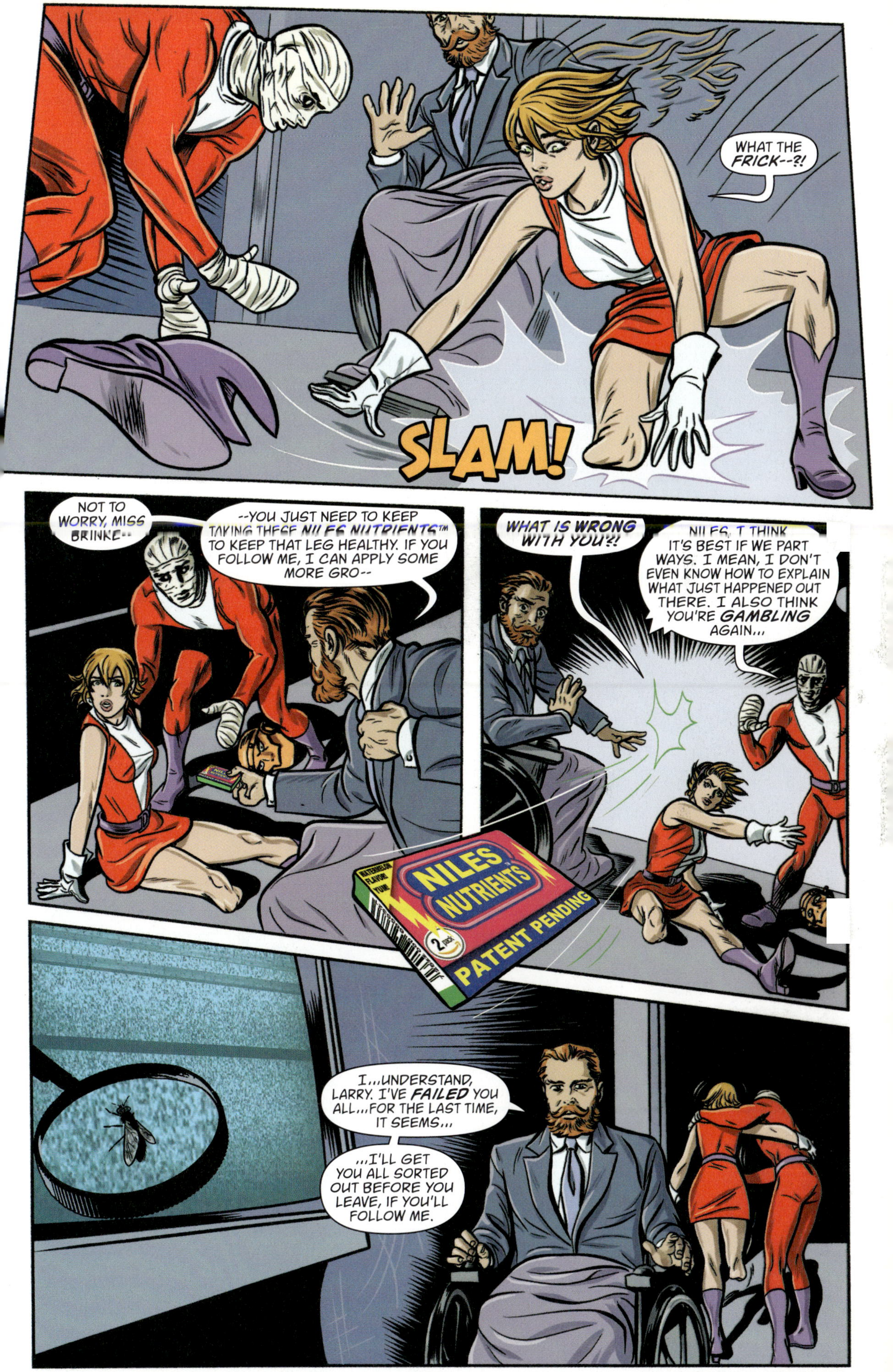
WHAT THE FRICK--?!
SLAM!
NOT TO WORRY, MISS BRINKE--
--YOU JUST NEED TO KEEP TAKING THESE NILES NUTRIENTS™ TO KEEP THAT LEG HEALTHY. IF YOU FOLLOW ME, I CAN APPLY SOME MORE GRO--
WHAT IS WRONG WITH YOU?!
NILES, I THINK IT'S BEST IF WE PART WAYS. I MEAN, I DON'T EVEN KNOW HOW TO EXPLAIN WHAT JUST HAPPENED OUT THERE. I ALSO THINK YOU'RE GAMBLING AGAIN...
NILES NUTRIENTS
PATENT PENDING
I...UNDERSTAND, LARRY. I'VE FAILED YOU ALL...FOR THE LAST TIME, IT SEEMS...
...I'LL GET YOU ALL SORTED OUT BEFORE YOU LEAVE, IF YOU'LL FOLLOW ME.

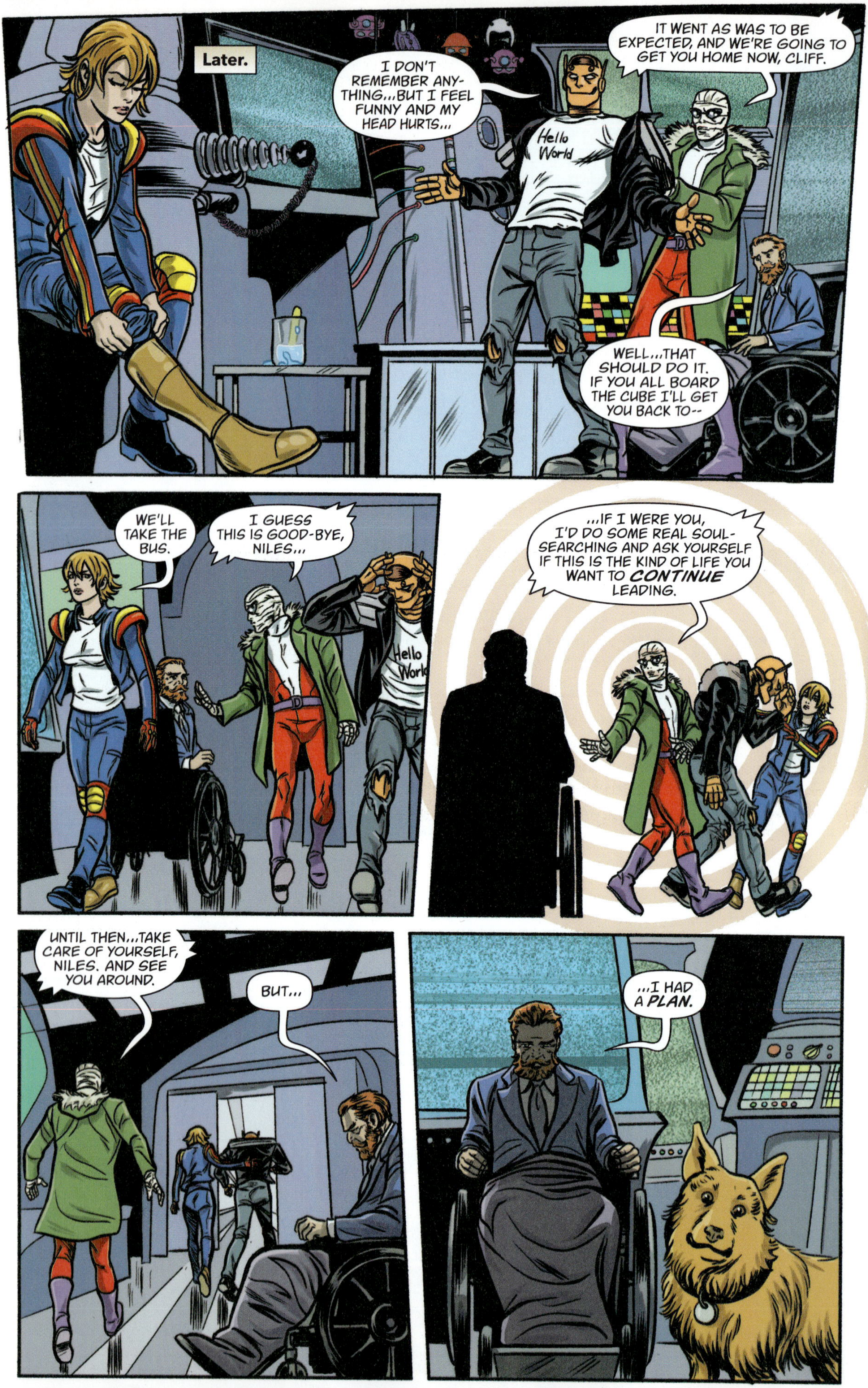
Later.
I DON'T REMEMBER ANYTHING...BUT I FEEL FUNNY AND MY HEAD HURTS...
IT WENT AS WAS TO BE EXPECTED, AND WE'RE GOING TO GET YOU HOME NOW, CLIFF.
Hello World
WELL...THAT SHOULD DO IT. IF YOU ALL BOARD THE CUBE I'LL GET YOU BACK TO--
WE'LL TAKE THE BUS.
I GUESS THIS IS GOOD-BYE, NILES...
...IF I WERE YOU, I'D DO SOME REAL SOUL-SEARCHING AND ASK YOURSELF IF THIS IS THE KIND OF LIFE YOU WANT TO CONTINUE LEADING.
UNTIL THEN...TAKE CARE OF YOURSELF, NILES. AND SEE YOU AROUND.
BUT...
...I HAD A PLAN.

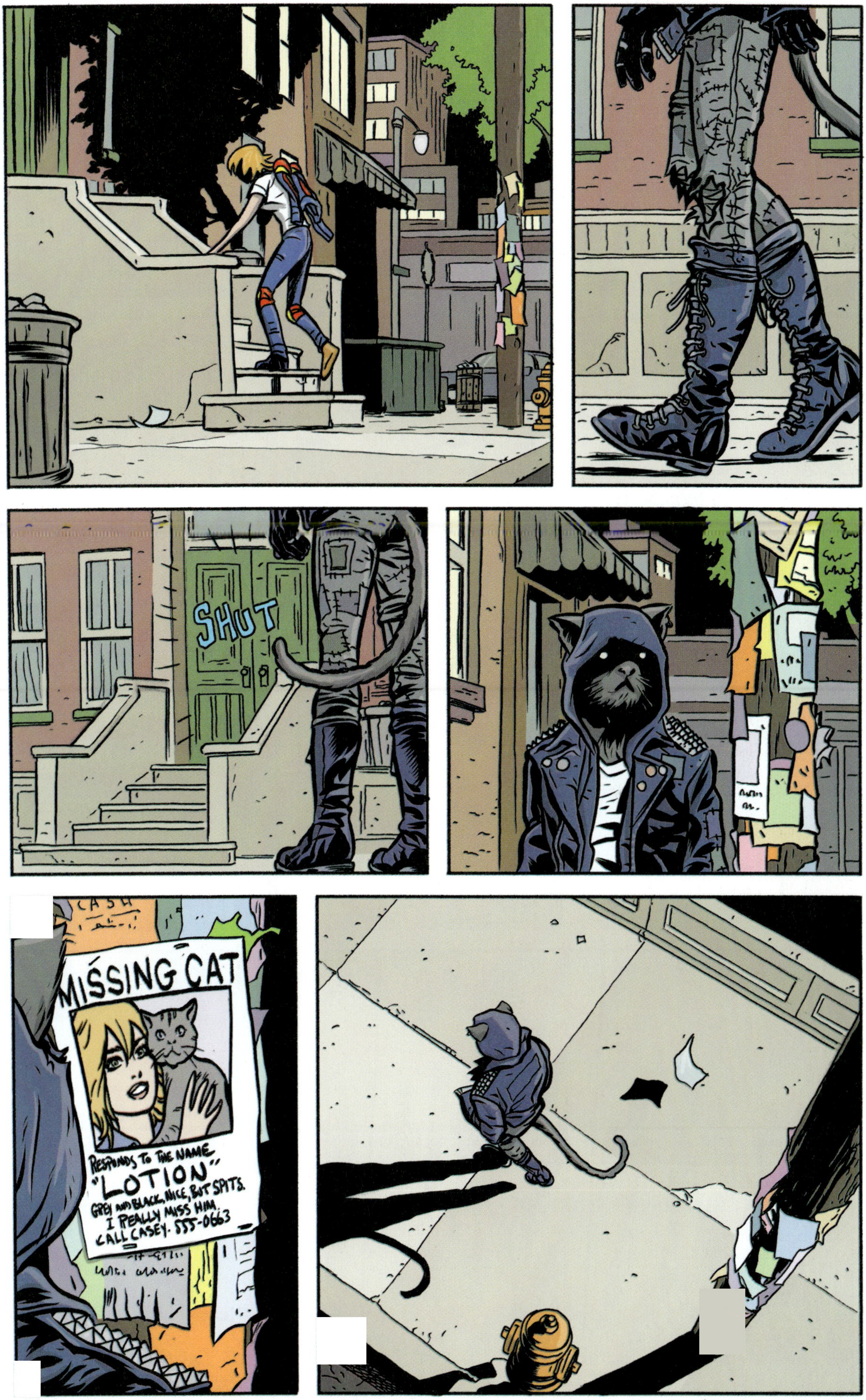
SHUT
CASH
MISSING CAT
RESPONDS TO THE NAME
"LOTION"
GREY AND BLACK, NICE, BUT SPITS.
I REALLY MISS HIM.
CALL CASEY. 555-0663

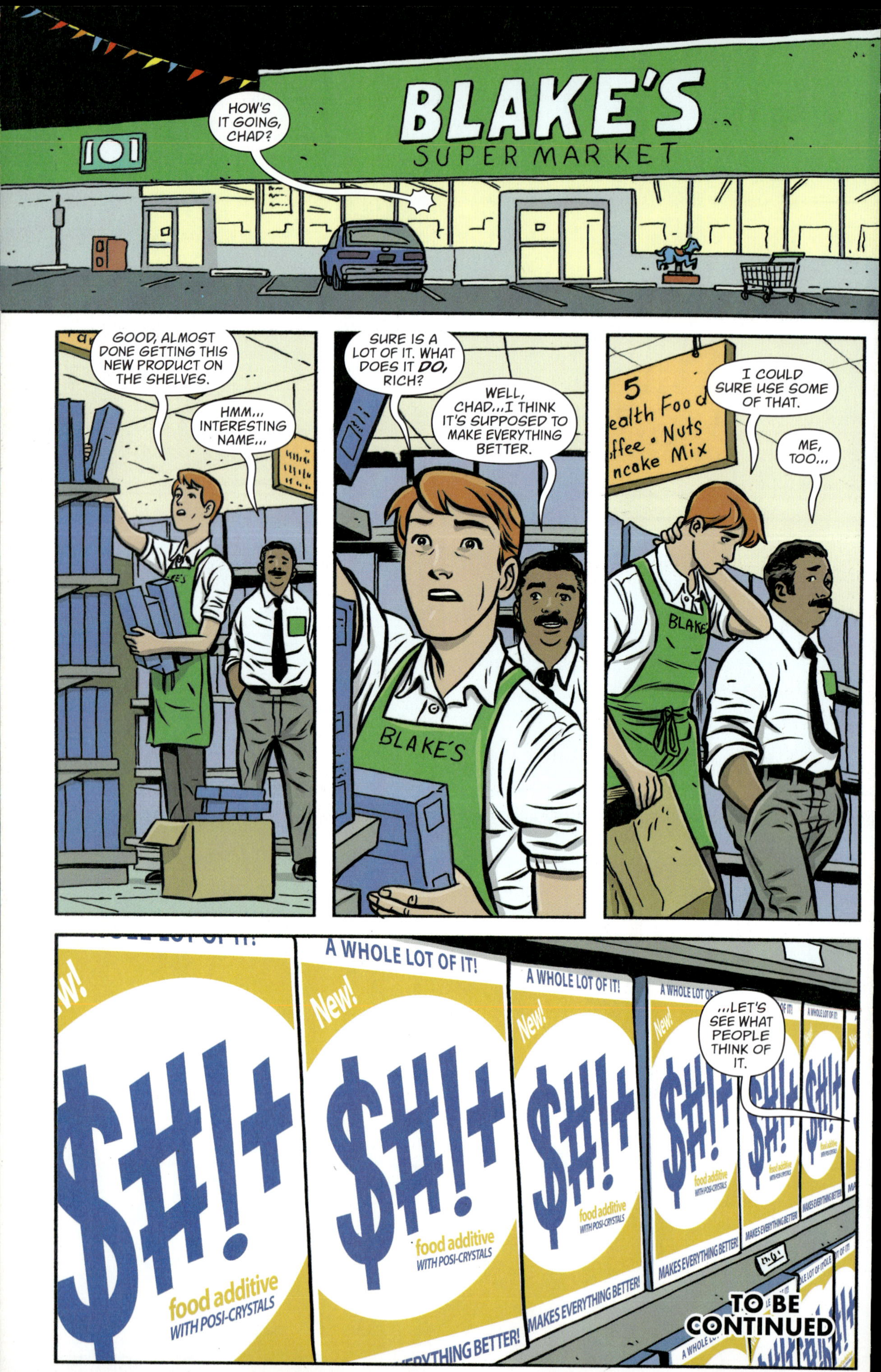
BLAKE'S
SUPER MARKET
HOW'S IT GOING, CHAD?
GOOD, ALMOST DONE GETTING THIS NEW PRODUCT ON THE SHELVES.
HMM... INTERESTING NAME...
SURE IS A LOT OF IT. WHAT DOES IT *DO,* RICH?
WELL, CHAD...I THINK IT'S SUPPOSED TO MAKE EVERYTHING BETTER.
BLAKE'S
5
ealth Food
ffee • Nuts
ncake Mix
I COULD SURE USE SOME OF THAT.
ME, TOO...
A WHOLE LOT OF IT!
New!
$#!+
food additive
WITH POSI-CRYSTALS
MAKES EVERYTHING BETTER!
...LET'S SEE WHAT PEOPLE THINK OF IT.
TO BE CONTINUED

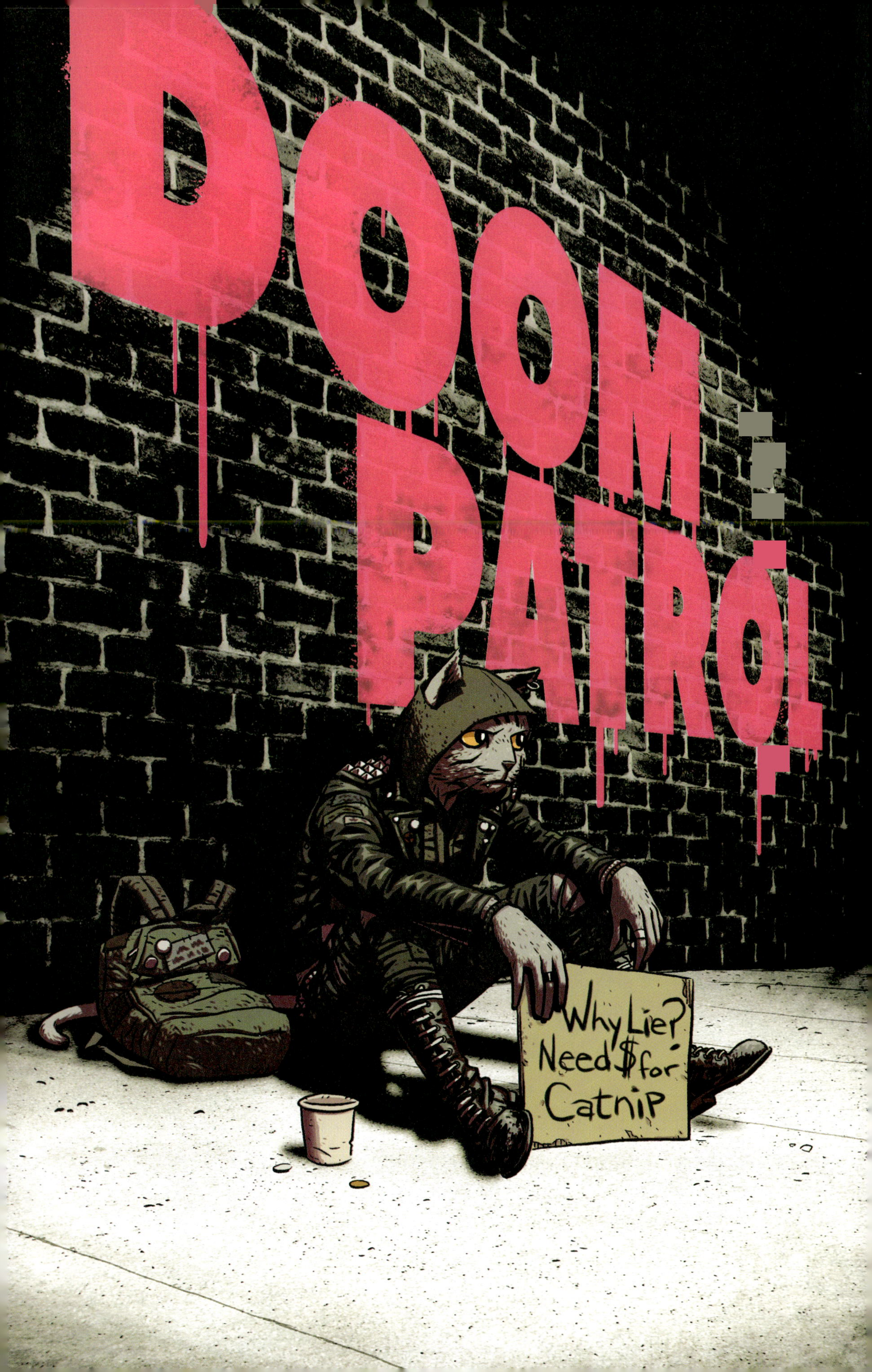
DOOM PATROL
Why Lie?
Need $ for
Catnip

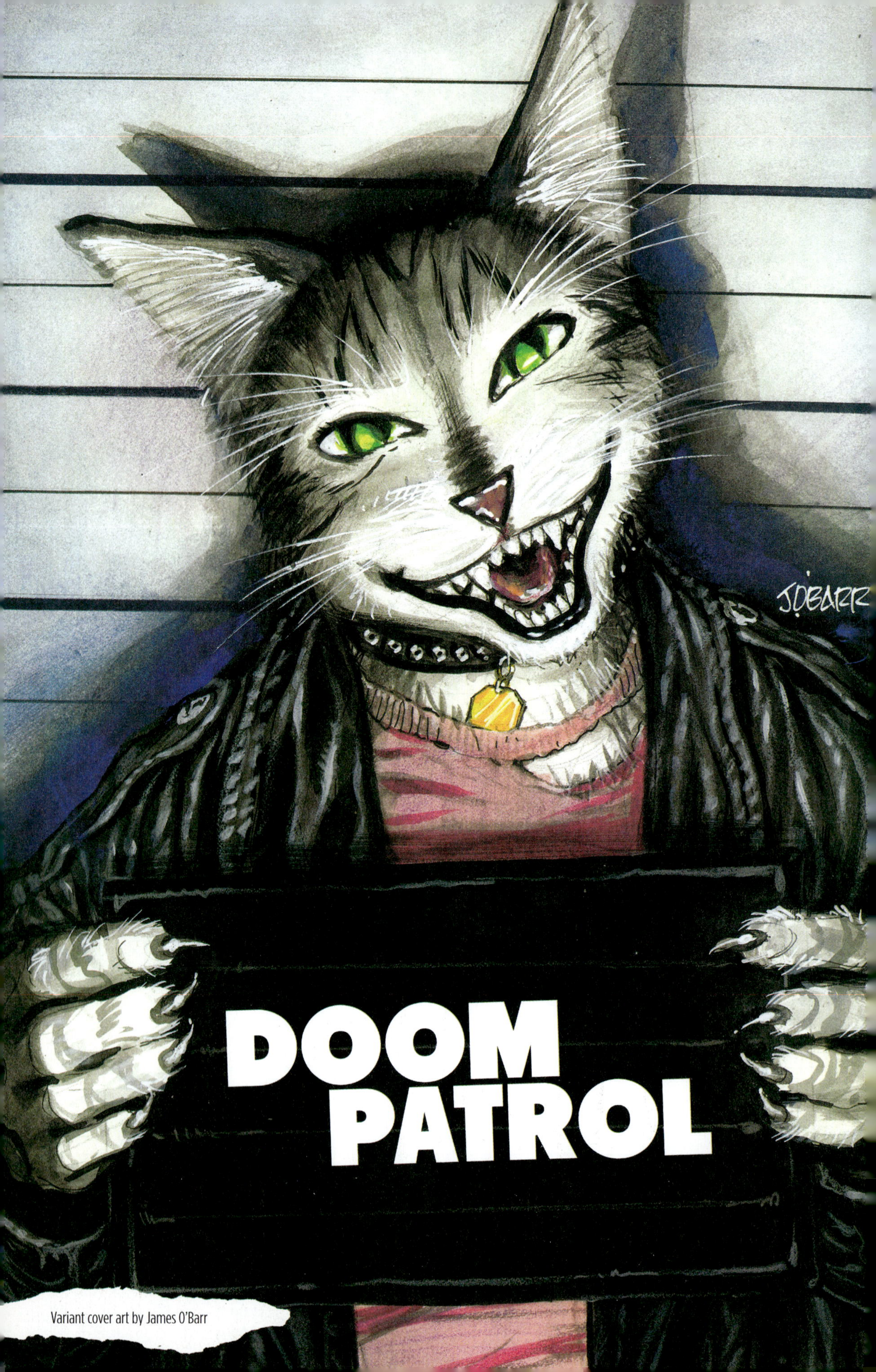
J. O'BARR
DOOM
PATROL

Variant cover art by James O'Barr

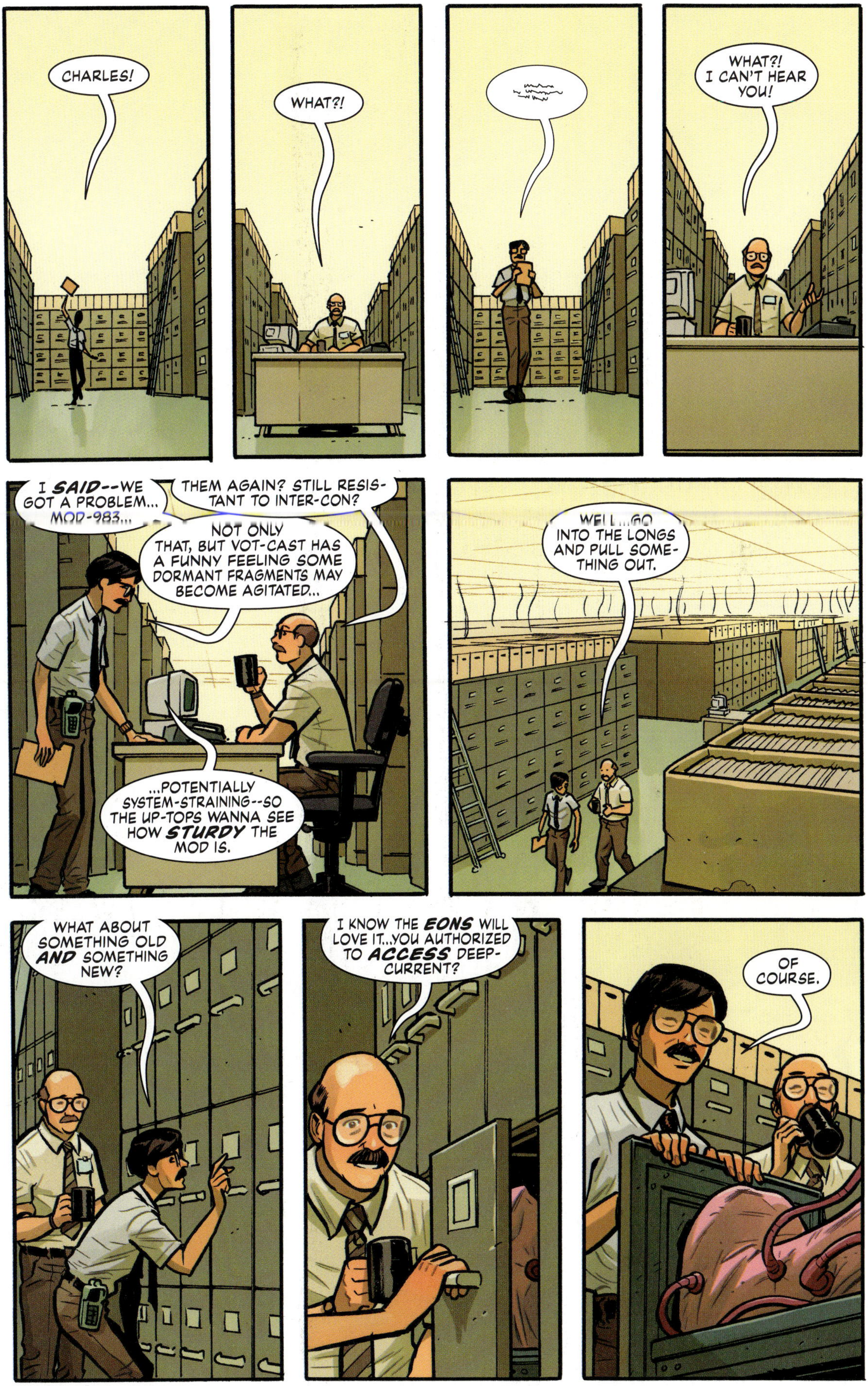
CHARLES!
WHAT?!
WHAT?! I CAN'T HEAR YOU!
I SAID--WE GOT A PROBLEM... MOD-983...
THEM AGAIN? STILL RESIS-TANT TO INTER-CON?
NOT ONLY THAT, BUT VOT-CAST HAS A FUNNY FEELING SOME DORMANT FRAGMENTS MAY BECOME AGITATED...
...POTENTIALLY SYSTEM-STRAINING--SO THE UP-TOPS WANNA SEE HOW STURDY THE MOD IS.
WELL...GO INTO THE LONGS AND PULL SOME-THING OUT.
WHAT ABOUT SOMETHING OLD AND SOMETHING NEW?
I KNOW THE EONS WILL LOVE IT...YOU AUTHORIZED TO ACCESS DEEP-CURRENT?
OF COURSE.

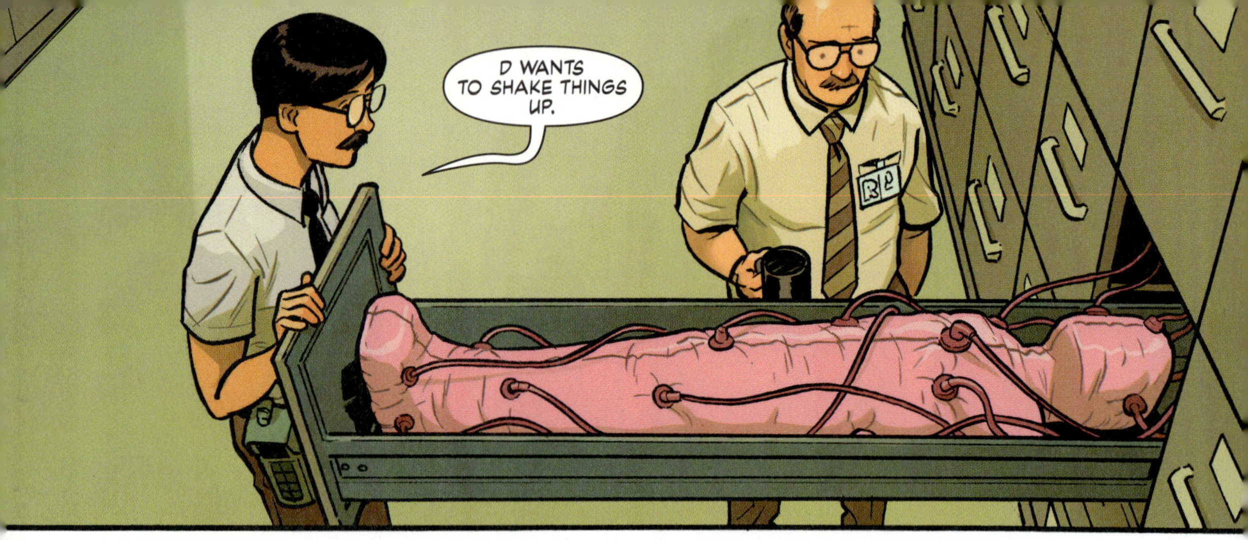
D WANTS TO SHAKE THINGS UP.

NOTHING MATTERS Part 1 of NADA

GERARD WAY writer
NICK DERINGTON penciller & cover
TOM FOWLER inker
TAMRA BONVILLAIN colorist
TODD KLEIN letterer
MAGGIE HOWELL assistant editor
JAMIE S. RICH editor

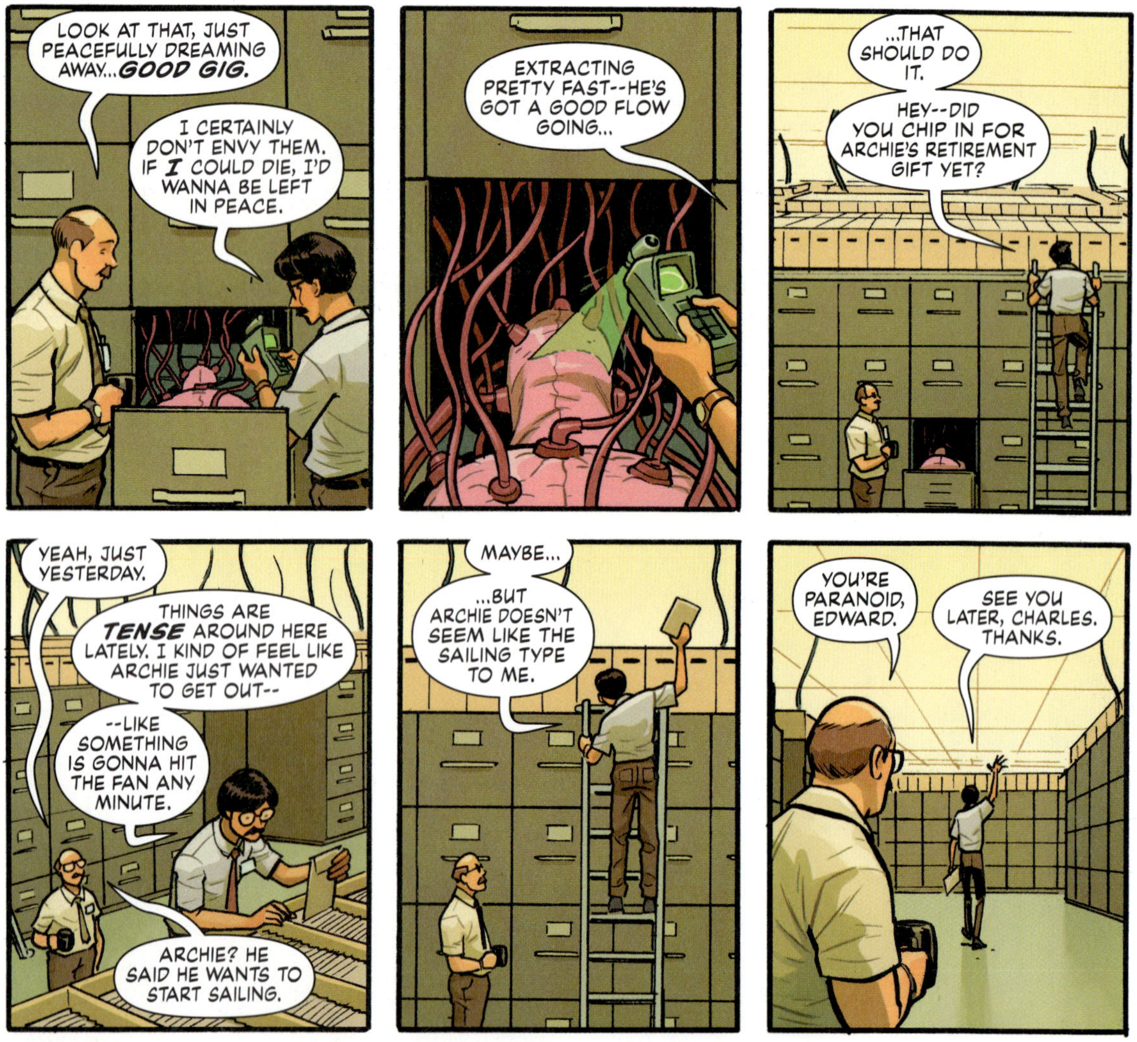
LOOK AT THAT, JUST PEACEFULLY DREAMING AWAY...GOOD GIG.
I CERTAINLY DON'T ENVY THEM. IF I COULD DIE, I'D WANNA BE LEFT IN PEACE.
EXTRACTING PRETTY FAST--HE'S GOT A GOOD FLOW GOING...
...THAT SHOULD DO IT.
HEY--DID YOU CHIP IN FOR ARCHIE'S RETIREMENT GIFT YET?
YEAH, JUST YESTERDAY.
THINGS ARE TENSE AROUND HERE LATELY. I KIND OF FEEL LIKE ARCHIE JUST WANTED TO GET OUT--
--LIKE SOMETHING IS GONNA HIT THE FAN ANY MINUTE.
ARCHIE? HE SAID HE WANTS TO START SAILING.
MAYBE...
...BUT ARCHIE DOESN'T SEEM LIKE THE SAILING TYPE TO ME.
YOU'RE PARANOID, EDWARD.
SEE YOU LATER, CHARLES. THANKS.

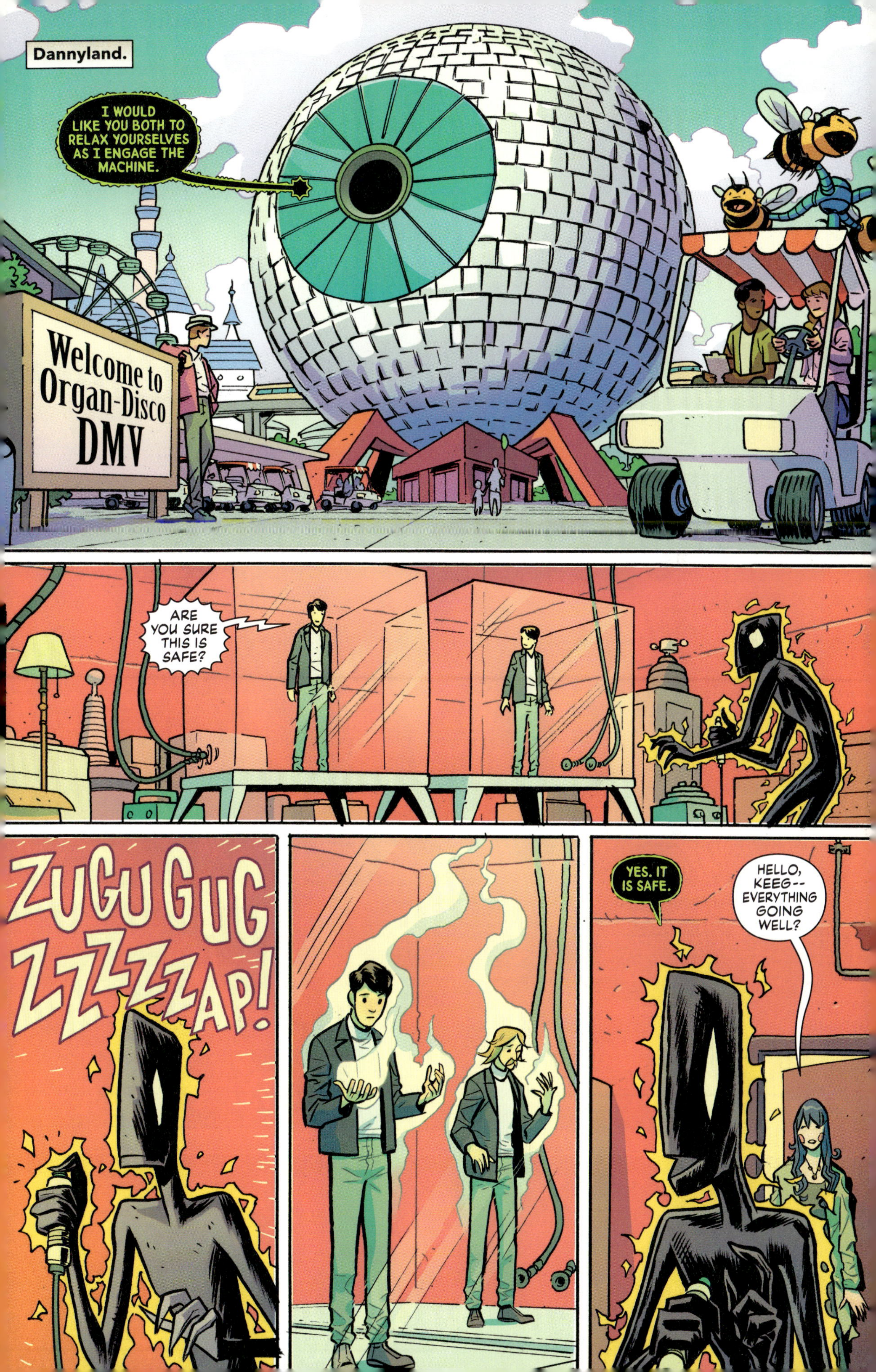

Dannyland.
I WOULD LIKE YOU BOTH TO RELAX YOURSELVES AS I ENGAGE THE MACHINE.
Welcome to Organ-Disco DMV
ARE YOU SURE THIS IS SAFE?
ZUGU GUG ZZZZZAP!
YES. IT IS SAFE.
HELLO, KEEG-- EVERYTHING GOING WELL?

JANE. MAKING PROGRESS. I HAVE BEGUN TO ALTER THE BIOLOGICAL MAKEUP OF THE *DUPLICATE* DANNYLAND INHABITANTS. PICKED UP FROM OUR TIME-TRAVEL RESCUE MISSION ABOARD THE VECTRA'S MOBILE SLAUGHTER UNIT.

HUMAN THINGS-- IF YOU SO DESIRE, YOU MAY NOW TOUCH EACH OTHER WITHOUT ERASING YOURSELVES FROM EXISTENCE.

BUT THERE'S STILL TWO OF US!

WE ONLY HAVE ONE WIFE AND SON LEFT ALIVE.

DIVIDE RESPONSIBILITIES. YOU WILL BE KNOWN AS "BEN" AND "BENTOO."

JANE, PLEASE STEP OVER TO MY TERMINAL. I CAN SHOW YOU THE RESULTS OF OUR TESTS--

WHERE'S LARRY?

CAPTAIN TRAINOR IS DISCOVERING THE MEANING OF EXISTENCE. AS ONE DOES WHILE CONSTANTLY REPEATING A LIFETIME UNCONSCIOUSLY. OR PARASAILING IN BELIZE. HE ALLOWS ME TO CONTINUE MY WORK WHILE HE "EXPLORES."

AS FOR THE TESTS I RAN ON YOU, I CAN DETECT NO REMNANTS OF DR. HARRISON IN YOUR PSYCHE--AT LEAST, NOTHING THAT WASN'T SHARED BETWEEN YOU.

SHARED?

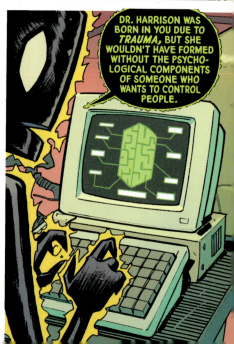

DR. HARRISON WAS BORN IN YOU DUE TO *TRAUMA*, BUT SHE WOULDN'T HAVE FORMED WITHOUT THE PSYCHO-LOGICAL COMPONENTS OF SOMEONE WHO WANTS TO CONTROL PEOPLE.

"CONTROL" PEOPLE?

OFTEN IN THE GUISE OF FIXING PEOPLE, HELD AS A CONSCIOUS OR SUBCONSCIOUS DESIRE.

DO NOT JUDGE YOURSELF HARSHLY. FROM WHAT I HAVE LEARNED, IT IS HUMAN NATURE TO DESIRE CONTROL OR DISMANTLEMENT. POSSIBLY COMPOUNDED BY BAD MODELING FROM A PARENTAL FIGURE.

"BAD MODELING" IS AN UNDERSTATEMENT. MY FATHER WAS A BASTARD.

FRAGILE

I MUST GO BACK INSIDE OF CAPTAIN TRAINOR BEFORE THE TEAM ASSEMBLY--WE WILL BE ALONG IN A MOMENT.

MIGHT I SUGGEST TALK THERAPY? IT SEEMS TO WORK FOR SOME HUMANS.

NO THANKS--I JUST DROPPED A PSYCHIC BOMB ON MYSELF TO GET RID OF THE LAST DOCTOR IN MY LIFE. SEE YOU IN THE OCULUS, KEEG.

ZZZ

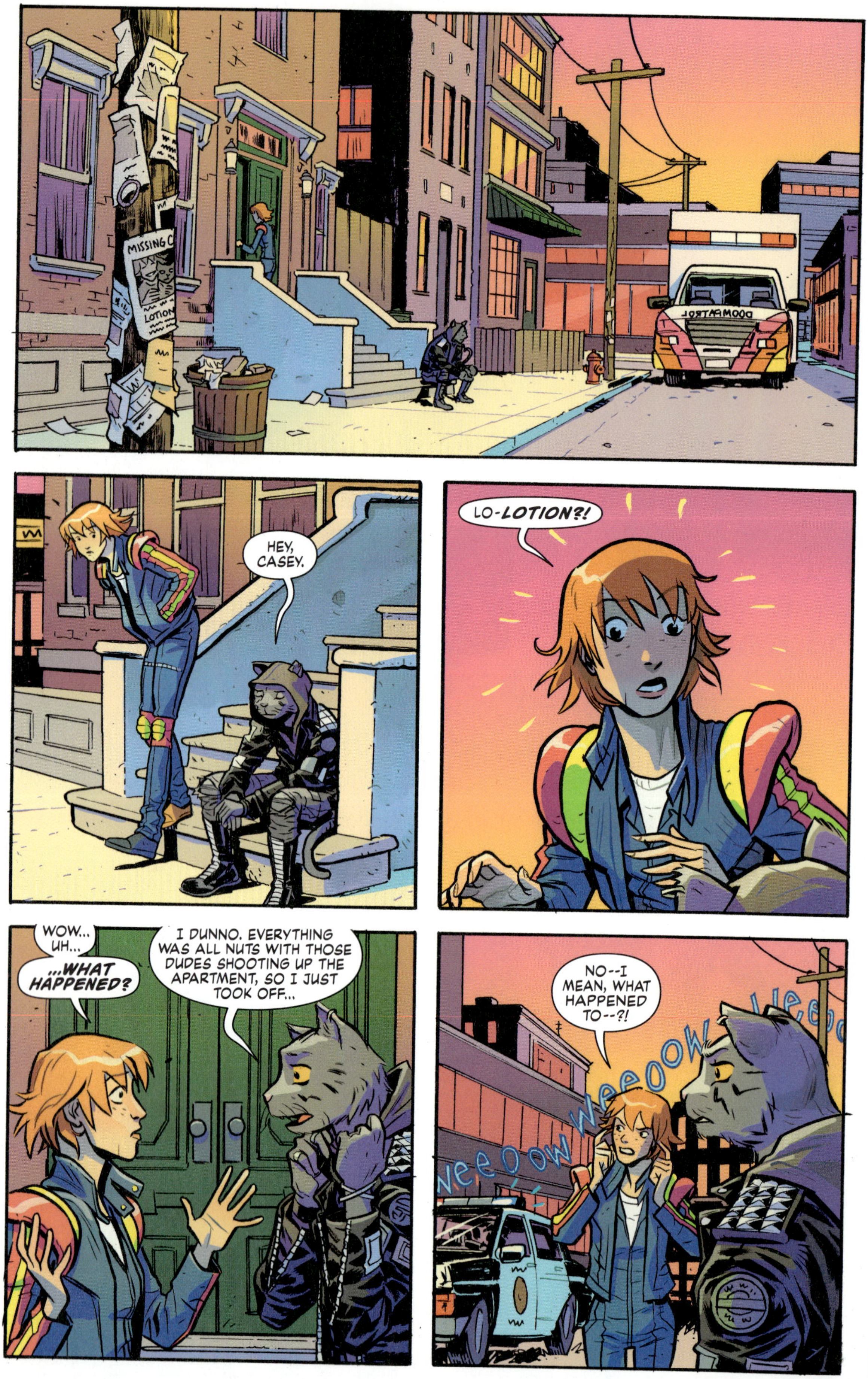
MISSING C
LOTION
HEY, CASEY.
LO-LOTION?!
WOW... UH...
...WHAT HAPPENED?
I DUNNO. EVERYTHING WAS ALL NUTS WITH THOSE DUDES SHOOTING UP THE APARTMENT, SO I JUST TOOK OFF...
NO--I MEAN, WHAT HAPPENED TO--?!
weeoow weeoow

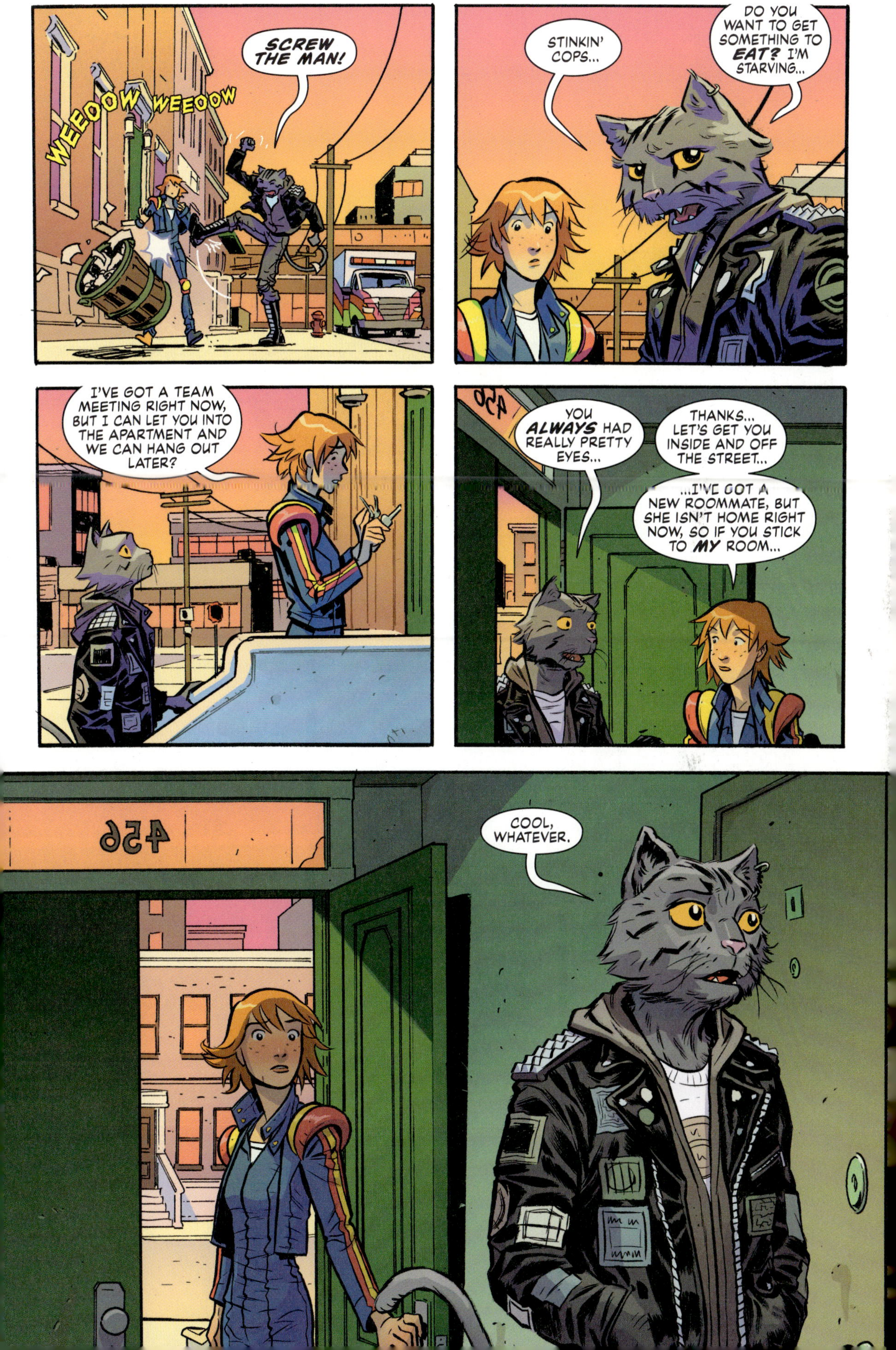

WEEOOW WEEOOW
SCREW THE MAN!
STINKIN' COPS...
DO YOU WANT TO GET SOMETHING TO EAT? I'M STARVING...
I'VE GOT A TEAM MEETING RIGHT NOW, BUT I CAN LET YOU INTO THE APARTMENT AND WE CAN HANG OUT LATER?
456
YOU ALWAYS HAD REALLY PRETTY EYES...
THANKS... LET'S GET YOU INSIDE AND OFF THE STREET...
...I'VE GOT A NEW ROOMMATE, BUT SHE ISN'T HOME RIGHT NOW, SO IF YOU STICK TO MY ROOM...
456
COOL, WHATEVER.

Dannyland.

I THINK WE MAY BE MISSING A PERSON, BUT WE BETTER GET STARTED. YOU CAN BEGIN, KEEG...

THANK YOU, JANE. RICARDO, IF YOU WOULD SHIFT TO THE FIRST SLIDE...

CLIK-IK

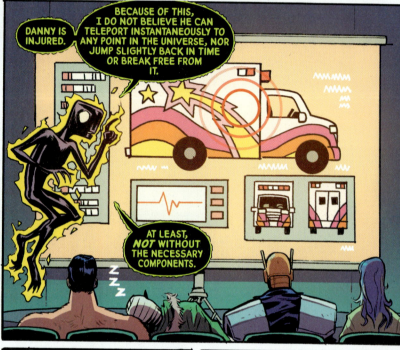

DANNY IS INJURED.

BECAUSE OF THIS, I DO NOT BELIEVE HE CAN TELEPORT INSTANTANEOUSLY TO ANY POINT IN THE UNIVERSE, NOR JUMP SLIGHTLY BACK IN TIME OR BREAK FREE FROM IT.

AT LEAST, *NOT* WITHOUT THE NECESSARY COMPONENTS.

ZZZ

CLIK-IK

COMPONENT B IS JOY. HAPPINESS. WHAT DANNY LIKES TO CALL "POSITIVE VIBRATIONS." IT IS WHY HE CREATED THE DANNYLAND INHABITANTS. THEY WOULD KEEP HIM HAPPY, STRONG, AND CAPABLE OF TRAVEL.

FOR A TIME, COMPONENT B WAS ALL DANNY NEEDED TO TELEPORT. NOW COMPONENT B IS NOT ENOUGH. DANNY MUST INTERFACE WITH...

$$A + B = 0$$
$$A + C = 98\%$$

...COMPONENT C.

SORRY I'M LATE--MY CAT CAME BACK!

OKAY, SO DANNY NEEDS *CASEY* TO GET AROUND. PROVIDED SHE'S ON TIME, WE SHOULD BE GOOD.

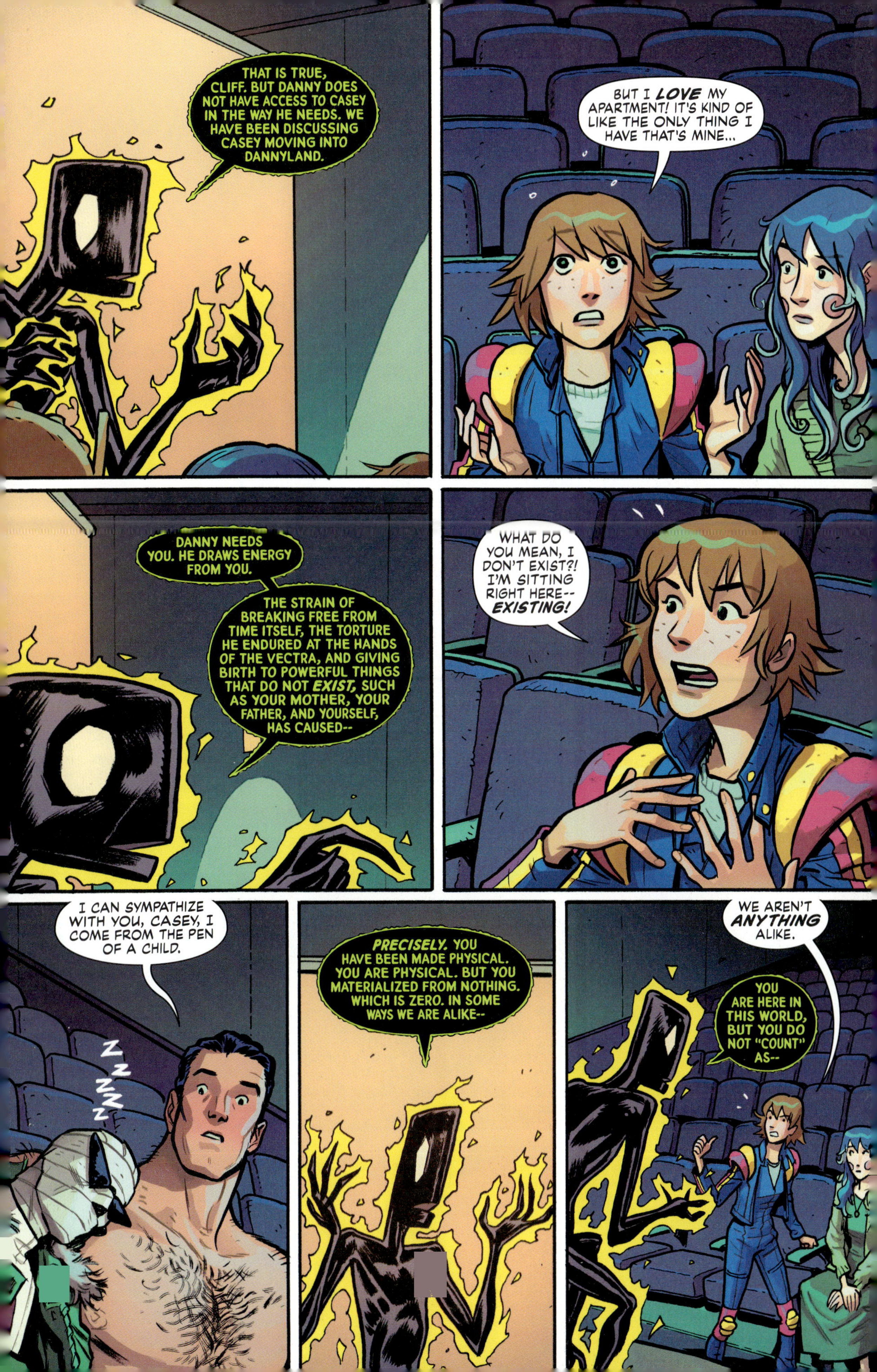
THAT IS TRUE, CLIFF. BUT DANNY DOES NOT HAVE ACCESS TO CASEY IN THE WAY HE NEEDS. WE HAVE BEEN DISCUSSING CASEY MOVING INTO DANNYLAND.
BUT I LOVE MY APARTMENT! IT'S KIND OF LIKE THE ONLY THING I HAVE THAT'S MINE...
DANNY NEEDS YOU. HE DRAWS ENERGY FROM YOU.
THE STRAIN OF BREAKING FREE FROM TIME ITSELF, THE TORTURE HE ENDURED AT THE HANDS OF THE VECTRA, AND GIVING BIRTH TO POWERFUL THINGS THAT DO NOT EXIST, SUCH AS YOUR MOTHER, YOUR FATHER, AND YOURSELF, HAS CAUSED--
WHAT DO YOU MEAN, I DON'T EXIST?! I'M SITTING RIGHT HERE-- EXISTING!
I CAN SYMPATHIZE WITH YOU, CASEY, I COME FROM THE PEN OF A CHILD.
Z Z Z Z
PRECISELY. YOU HAVE BEEN MADE PHYSICAL. YOU ARE PHYSICAL. BUT YOU MATERIALIZED FROM NOTHING. WHICH IS ZERO. IN SOME WAYS WE ARE ALIKE--
WE AREN'T ANYTHING ALIKE.
YOU ARE HERE IN THIS WORLD, BUT YOU DO NOT "COUNT" AS--

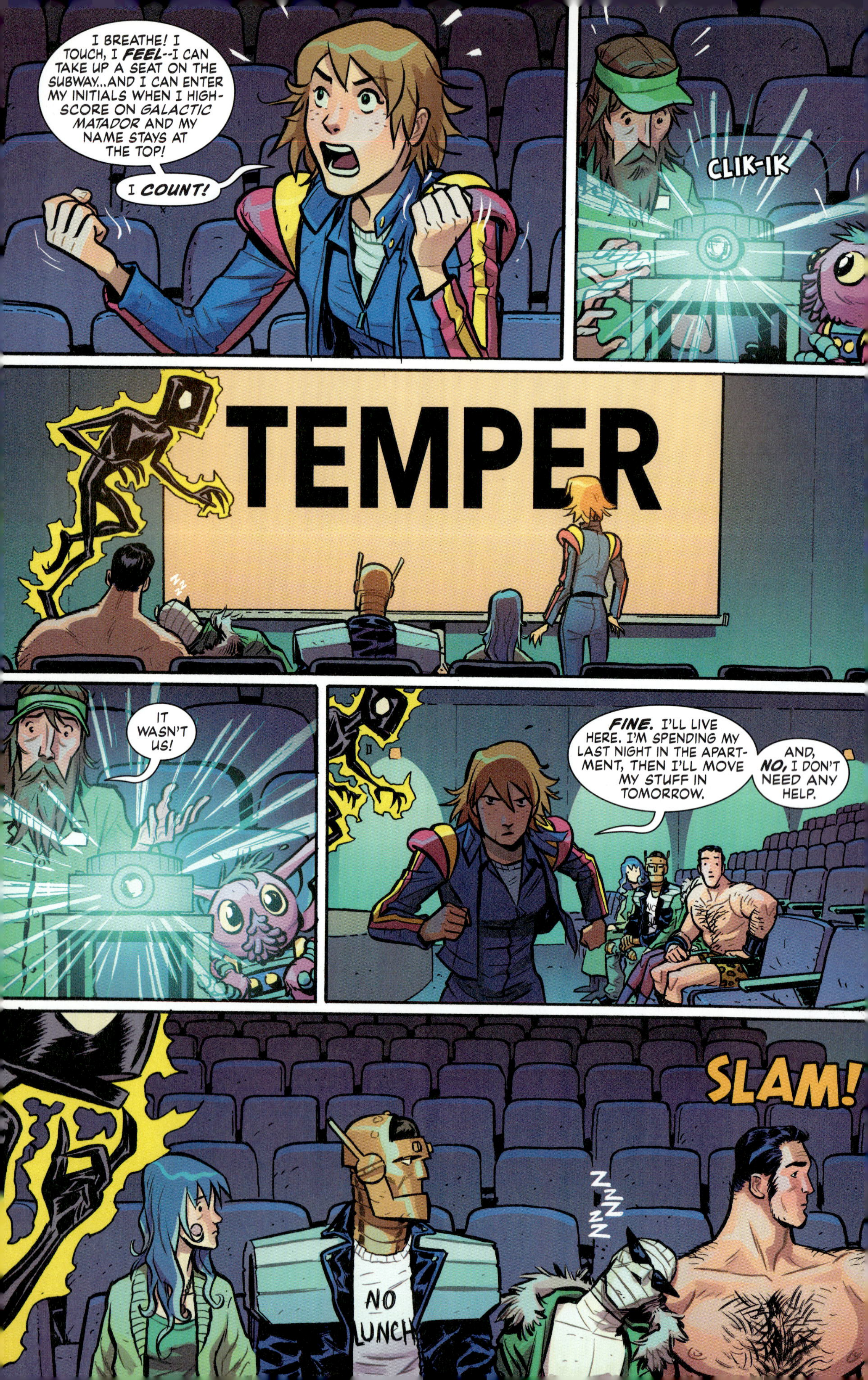

I BREATHE! I TOUCH, I FEEL--I CAN TAKE UP A SEAT ON THE SUBWAY...AND I CAN ENTER MY INITIALS WHEN I HIGH-SCORE ON GALACTIC MATADOR AND MY NAME STAYS AT THE TOP!
I COUNT!
CLIK-IK
TEMPER
IT WASN'T US!
FINE. I'LL LIVE HERE. I'M SPENDING MY LAST NIGHT IN THE APARTMENT, THEN I'LL MOVE MY STUFF IN TOMORROW.
AND, NO, I DON'T NEED ANY HELP.
SLAM!
NO LUNCH

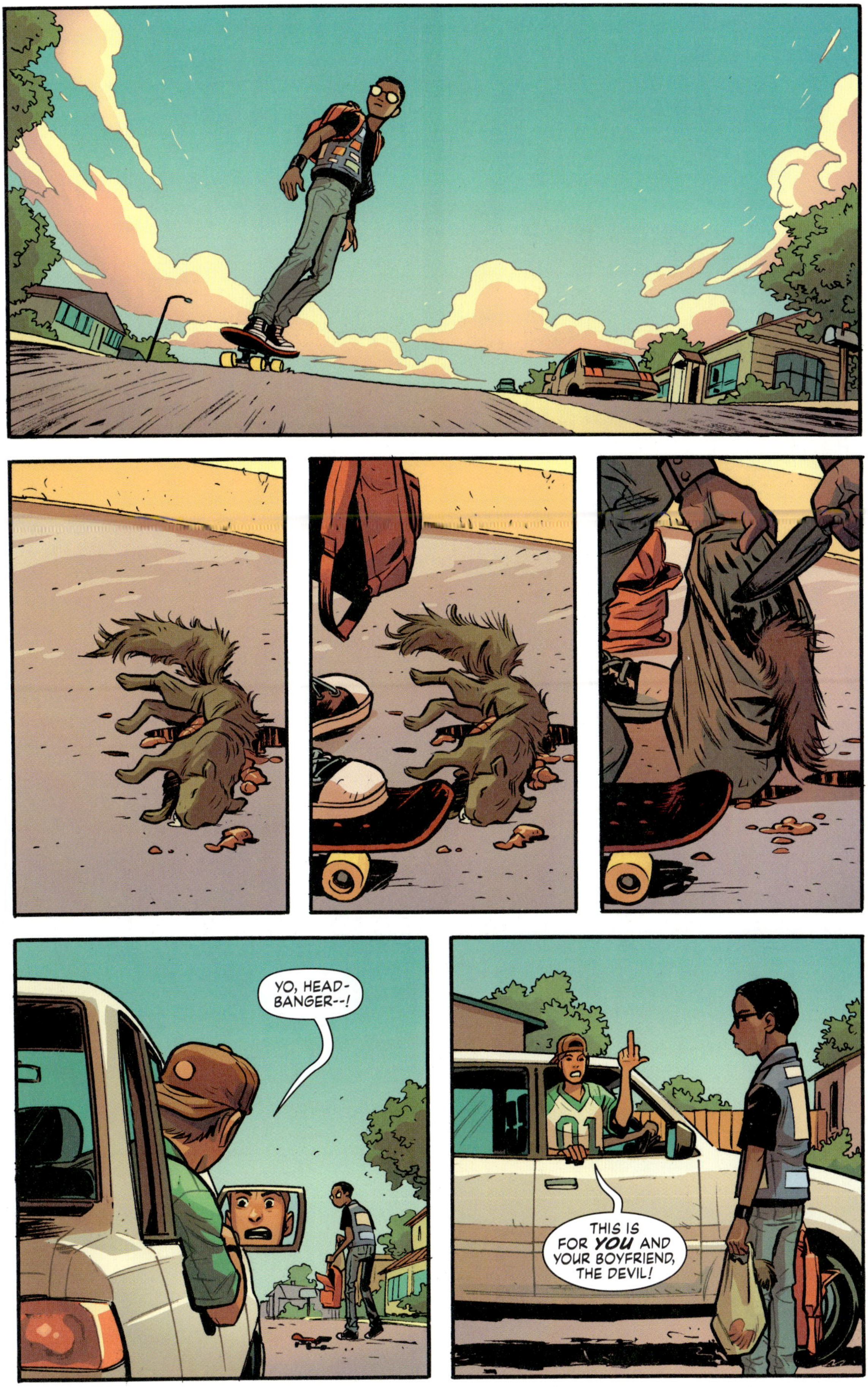
YO, HEAD-BANGER--!
THIS IS FOR YOU AND YOUR BOYFRIEND, THE DEVIL!

WATCH YOUR-SELF!

SCREECH

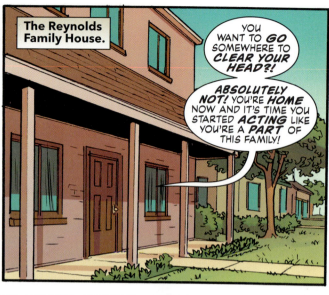

The Reynolds Family House.

YOU WANT TO *GO* SOMEWHERE TO *CLEAR YOUR HEAD?!*

ABSOLUTELY NOT! YOU'RE *HOME* NOW AND IT'S TIME YOU STARTED *ACTING* LIKE YOU'RE A *PART* OF THIS FAMILY!

I DON'T WANT TO BE ACTING, SAM--I WANT IT TO BE *REAL.* WE CAN'T JUST FORCE THIS, I'VE BEEN THROUGH A LOT...

WE'VE *ALL* BEEN THROUGH A LOT.

YES. AND *YES,* JANE USED HER POWERS TO INFLUENCE ALL OF US IN THE CULT, BUT SOMETHING IN MY LIFE CAUSED ME TO SEEK HER *OUT...* SOMETHING LINGERS...

...AND I CAN'T TELL IF IT WAS *PUT* THERE OR IF IT WAS *ALWAYS* THERE.

I'M JUST ASKING FOR A LITTLE TIME TO FIGURE THIS OUT, SAM.

WE NEED TO BE *MAKING UP TIME,* VAL, NOT SPENDING *MORE OF IT APART!*

FOUR YEARS!

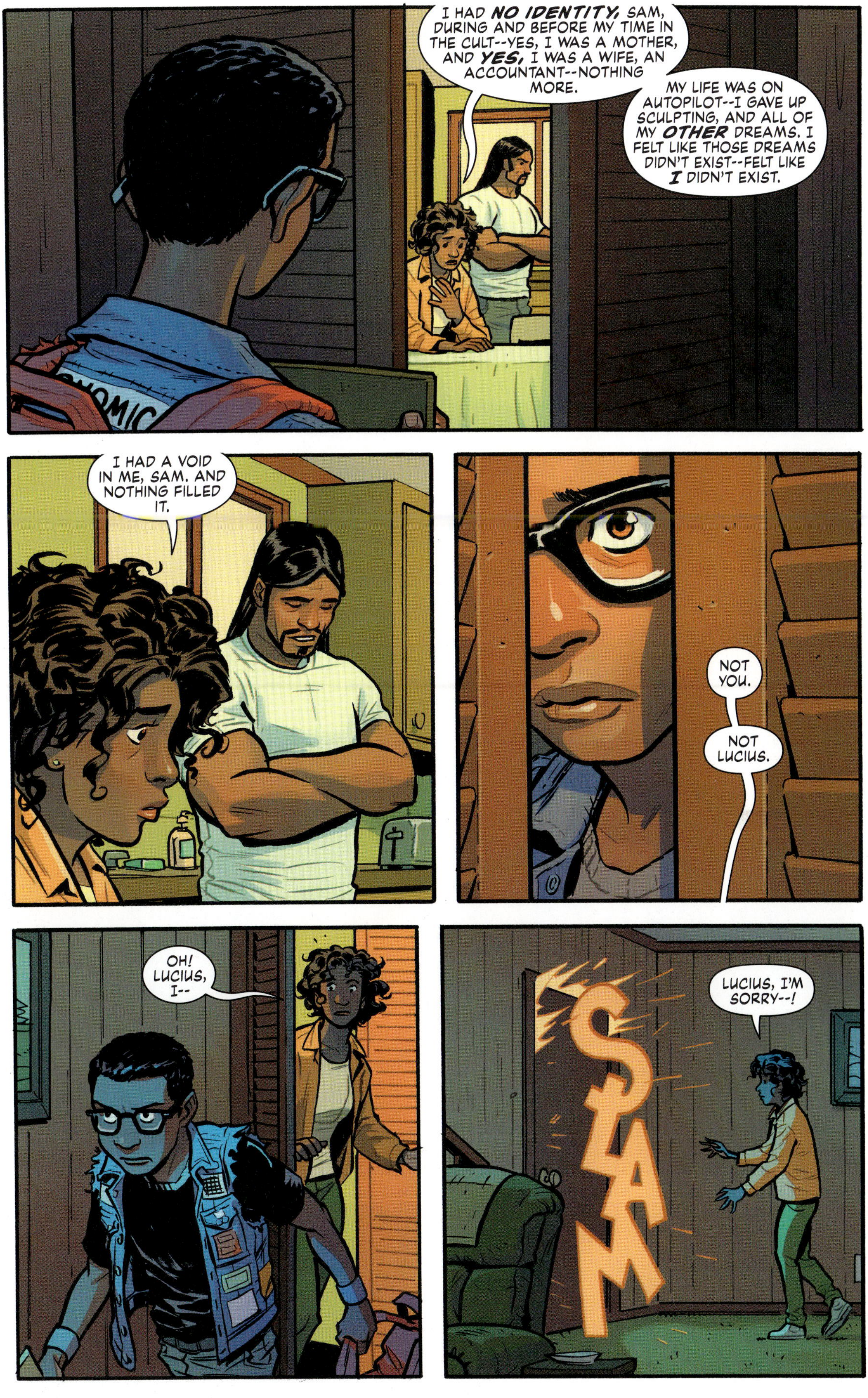
I HAD NO IDENTITY, SAM, DURING AND BEFORE MY TIME IN THE CULT--YES, I WAS A MOTHER, AND YES, I WAS A WIFE, AN ACCOUNTANT--NOTHING MORE.
MY LIFE WAS ON AUTOPILOT--I GAVE UP SCULPTING, AND ALL OF MY OTHER DREAMS. I FELT LIKE THOSE DREAMS DIDN'T EXIST--FELT LIKE I DIDN'T EXIST.
I HAD A VOID IN ME, SAM. AND NOTHING FILLED IT.
NOT YOU.
NOT LUCIUS.
OH! LUCIUS, I--
SLAM
LUCIUS, I'M SORRY--!

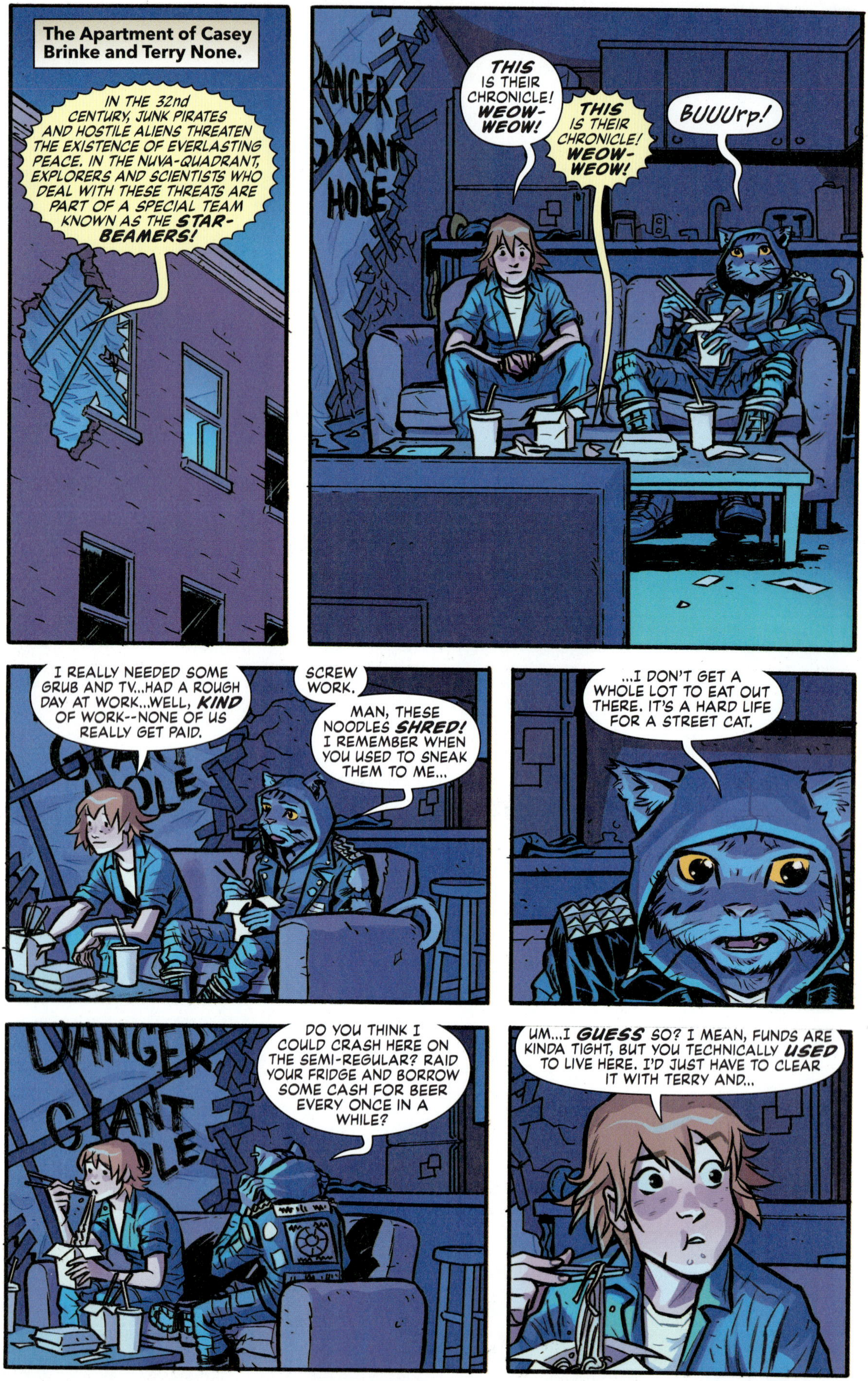

The Apartment of Casey Brinke and Terry None.
IN THE 32nd CENTURY, JUNK PIRATES AND HOSTILE ALIENS THREATEN THE EXISTENCE OF EVERLASTING PEACE. IN THE NUVA-QUADRANT, EXPLORERS AND SCIENTISTS WHO DEAL WITH THESE THREATS ARE PART OF A SPECIAL TEAM KNOWN AS THE STAR-BEAMERS!
DANGER GIANT HOLE
THIS IS THEIR CHRONICLE! WEOW-WEOW!
THIS IS THEIR CHRONICLE! WEOW-WEOW!
BUUUrp!
I REALLY NEEDED SOME GRUB AND TV...HAD A ROUGH DAY AT WORK...WELL, KIND OF WORK--NONE OF US REALLY GET PAID.
SCREW WORK.
MAN, THESE NOODLES SHRED! I REMEMBER WHEN YOU USED TO SNEAK THEM TO ME...
...I DON'T GET A WHOLE LOT TO EAT OUT THERE. IT'S A HARD LIFE FOR A STREET CAT.
DO YOU THINK I COULD CRASH HERE ON THE SEMI-REGULAR? RAID YOUR FRIDGE AND BORROW SOME CASH FOR BEER EVERY ONCE IN A WHILE?
UM...I GUESS SO? I MEAN, FUNDS ARE KINDA TIGHT, BUT YOU TECHNICALLY USED TO LIVE HERE. I'D JUST HAVE TO CLEAR IT WITH TERRY AND...

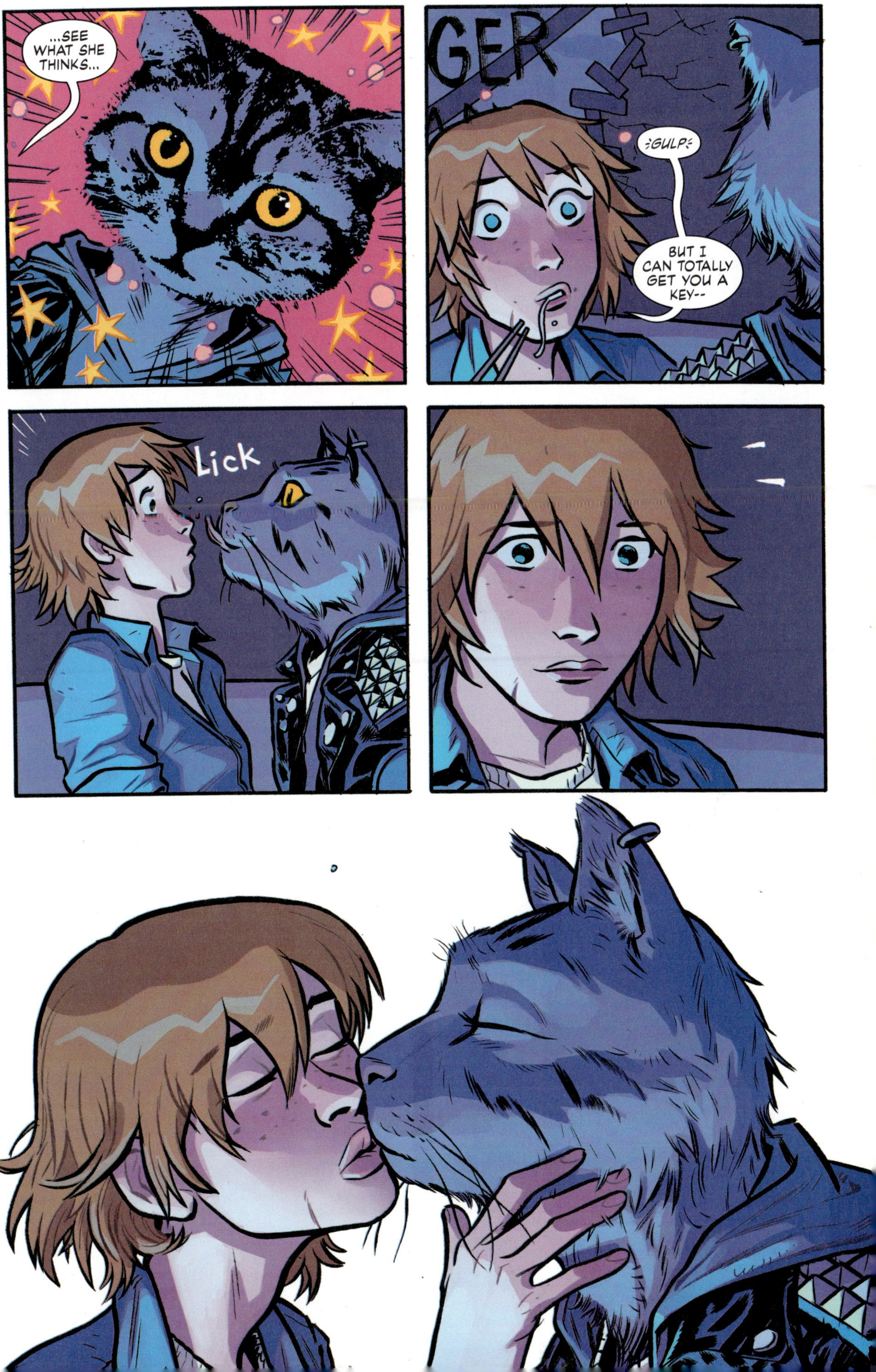
...SEE WHAT SHE THINKS...
GER
GULP
BUT I CAN TOTALLY GET YOU A KEY--
Lick

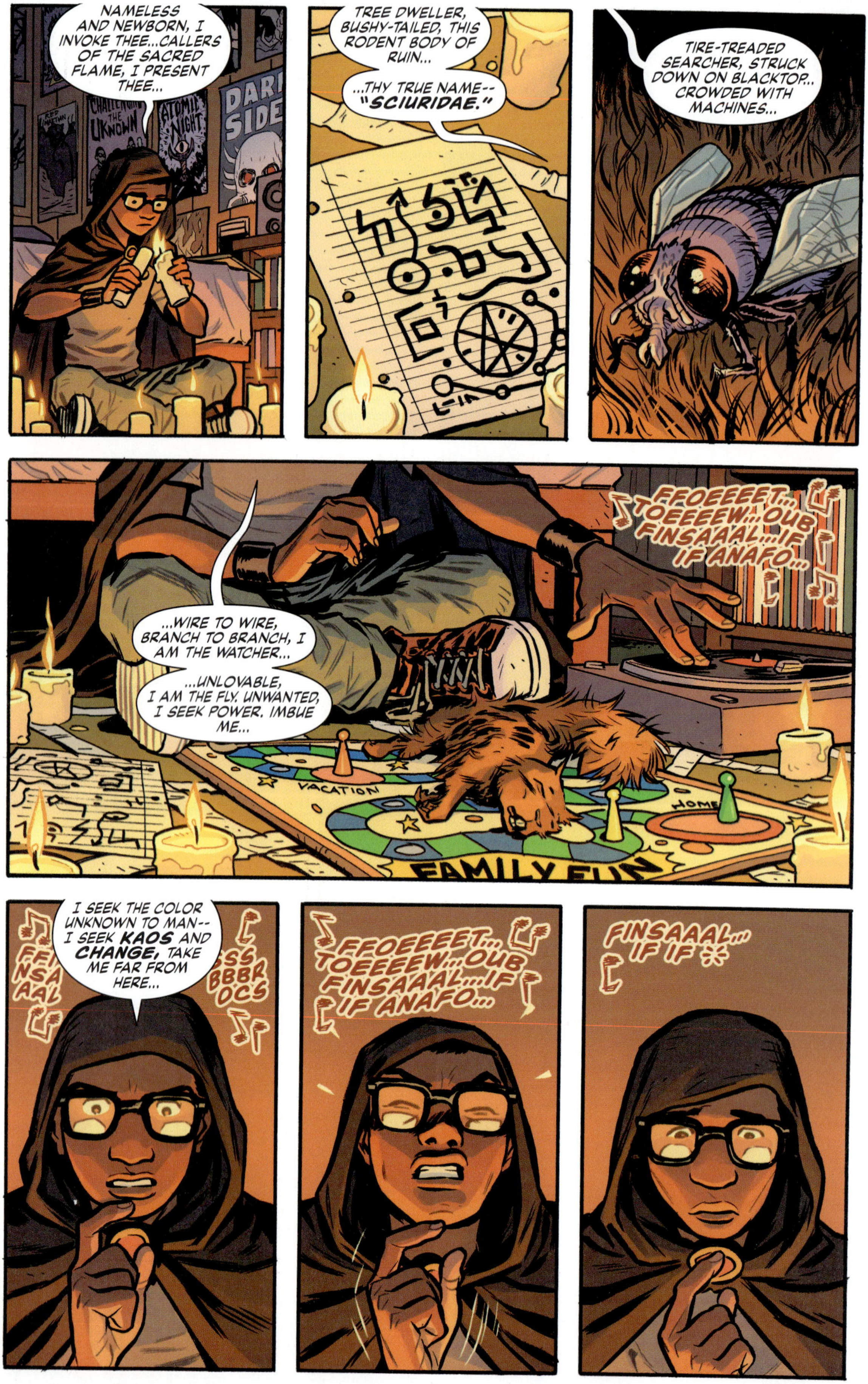
NAMELESS AND NEWBORN, I INVOKE THEE...CALLERS OF THE SACRED FLAME, I PRESENT THEE...
TREE DWELLER, BUSHY-TAILED, THIS RODENT BODY OF RUIN...
...THY TRUE NAME-- "SCIURIDAE."
TIRE-TREADED SEARCHER, STRUCK DOWN ON BLACKTOP... CROWDED WITH MACHINES...
FFOEEEET... TOEEEEW...OUB FINSAAAL...IF IF ANAFO...
...WIRE TO WIRE, BRANCH TO BRANCH, I AM THE WATCHER...
...UNLOVABLE, I AM THE FLY. UNWANTED, I SEEK POWER. IMBUE ME...
VACATION
HOME
FAMILY FUN
I SEEK THE COLOR UNKNOWN TO MAN-- I SEEK KAOS AND CHANGE, TAKE ME FAR FROM HERE...
FFOEEEET... TOEEEEW...OUB FINSAAAL...IF IF ANAFO...
FINSAAAL... IF IF

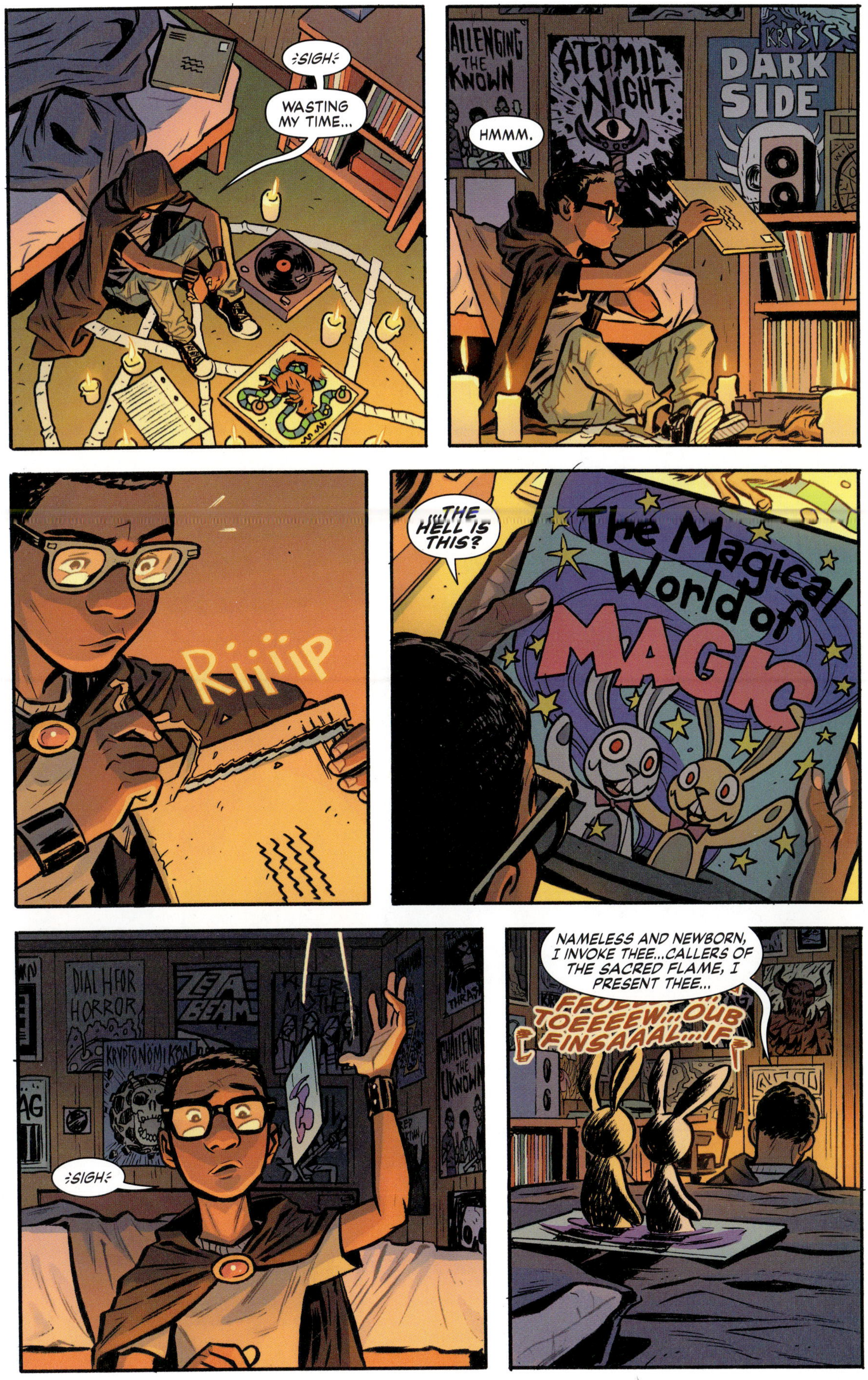
SIGH
WASTING MY TIME...
ATOMIC NIGHT
KRISIS
DARK SIDE
HMMM.
Riiiip
...THE HELL IS THIS?
The Magical World of MAGIC
DIAL H FOR HORROR
ZETA BEAM
SIGH
NAMELESS AND NEWBORN, I INVOKE THEE...CALLERS OF THE SACRED FLAME, I PRESENT THEE...

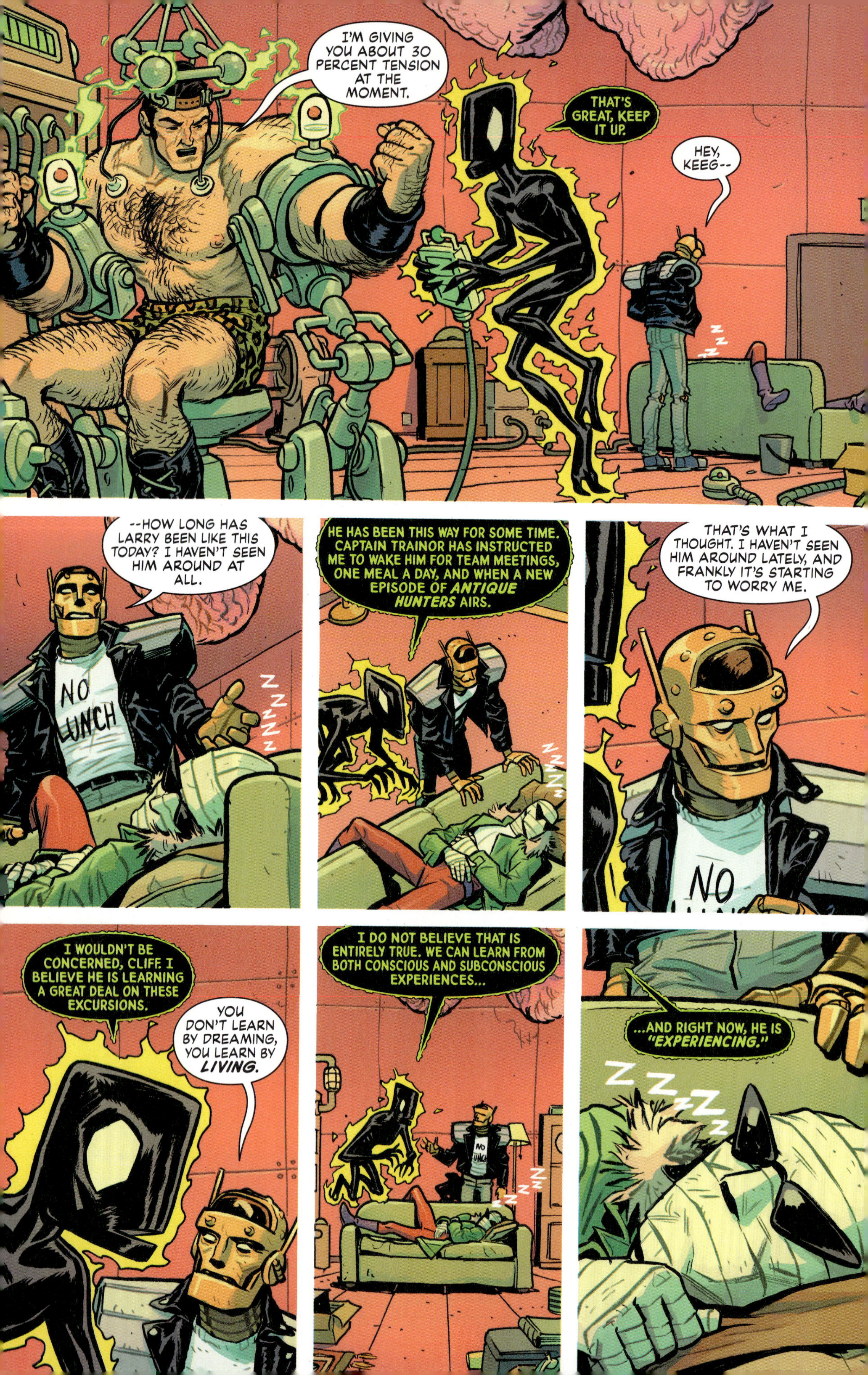
I'M GIVING YOU ABOUT 30 PERCENT TENSION AT THE MOMENT.
THAT'S GREAT, KEEP IT UP.
HEY, KEEG--
--HOW LONG HAS LARRY BEEN LIKE THIS TODAY? I HAVEN'T SEEN HIM AROUND AT ALL.
NO LUNCH
HE HAS BEEN THIS WAY FOR SOME TIME. CAPTAIN TRAINOR HAS INSTRUCTED ME TO WAKE HIM FOR TEAM MEETINGS, ONE MEAL A DAY, AND WHEN A NEW EPISODE OF *ANTIQUE HUNTERS* AIRS.
THAT'S WHAT I THOUGHT. I HAVEN'T SEEN HIM AROUND LATELY, AND FRANKLY IT'S STARTING TO WORRY ME.
I WOULDN'T BE CONCERNED, CLIFF. I BELIEVE HE IS LEARNING A GREAT DEAL ON THESE EXCURSIONS.
YOU DON'T LEARN BY DREAMING, YOU LEARN BY ***LIVING.***
I DO NOT BELIEVE THAT IS ENTIRELY TRUE. WE CAN LEARN FROM BOTH CONSCIOUS AND SUBCONSCIOUS EXPERIENCES...
...AND RIGHT NOW, HE IS ***"EXPERIENCING."***

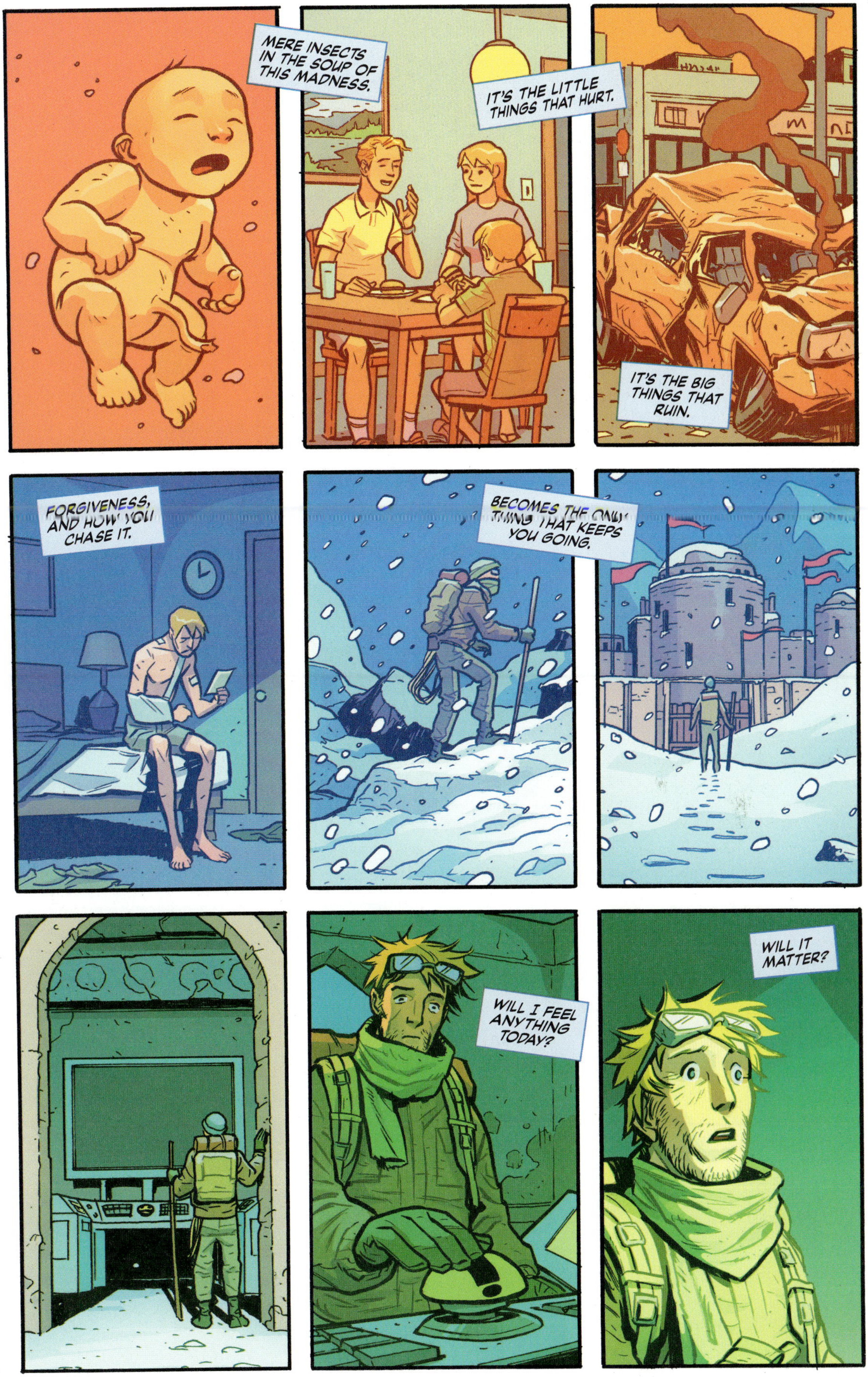
MERE INSECTS IN THE SOUP OF THIS MADNESS.
IT'S THE LITTLE THINGS THAT HURT.
IT'S THE BIG THINGS THAT RUIN.
FORGIVENESS, AND HOW YOU CHASE IT.
BECOMES THE ONLY THING THAT KEEPS YOU GOING.
WILL I FEEL ANYTHING TODAY?
WILL IT MATTER?

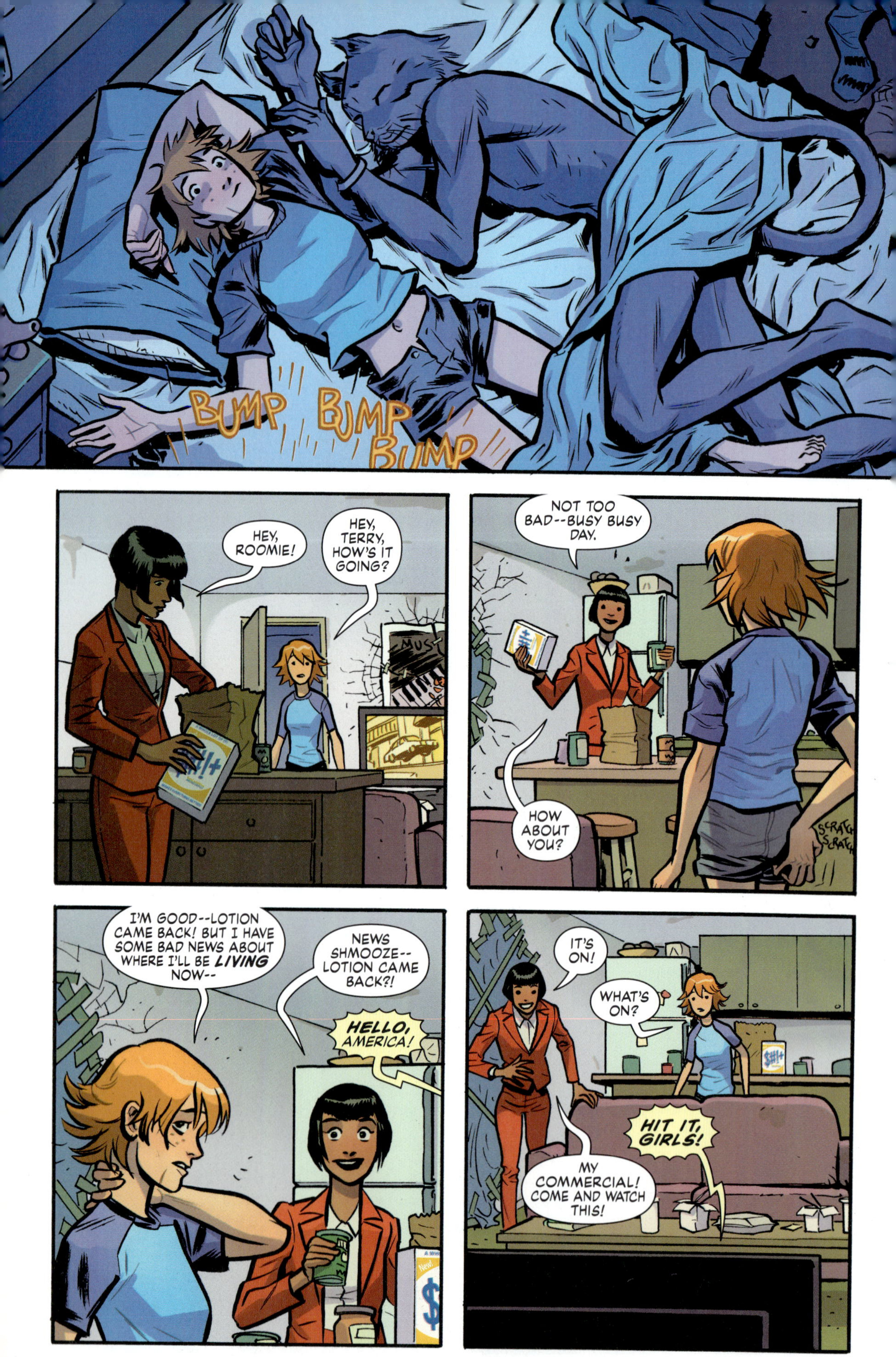
BUMP BUMP BUMP
HEY, ROOMIE!
HEY, TERRY, HOW'S IT GOING?
NOT TOO BAD--BUSY BUSY DAY.
HOW ABOUT YOU?
SCRATCH SCRATCH
I'M GOOD--LOTION CAME BACK! BUT I HAVE SOME BAD NEWS ABOUT WHERE I'LL BE *LIVING* NOW--
NEWS SHMOOZE--LOTION CAME BACK?!
HELLO, AMERICA!
IT'S ON!
WHAT'S ON?
HIT IT, GIRLS!
MY COMMERCIAL! COME AND WATCH THIS!

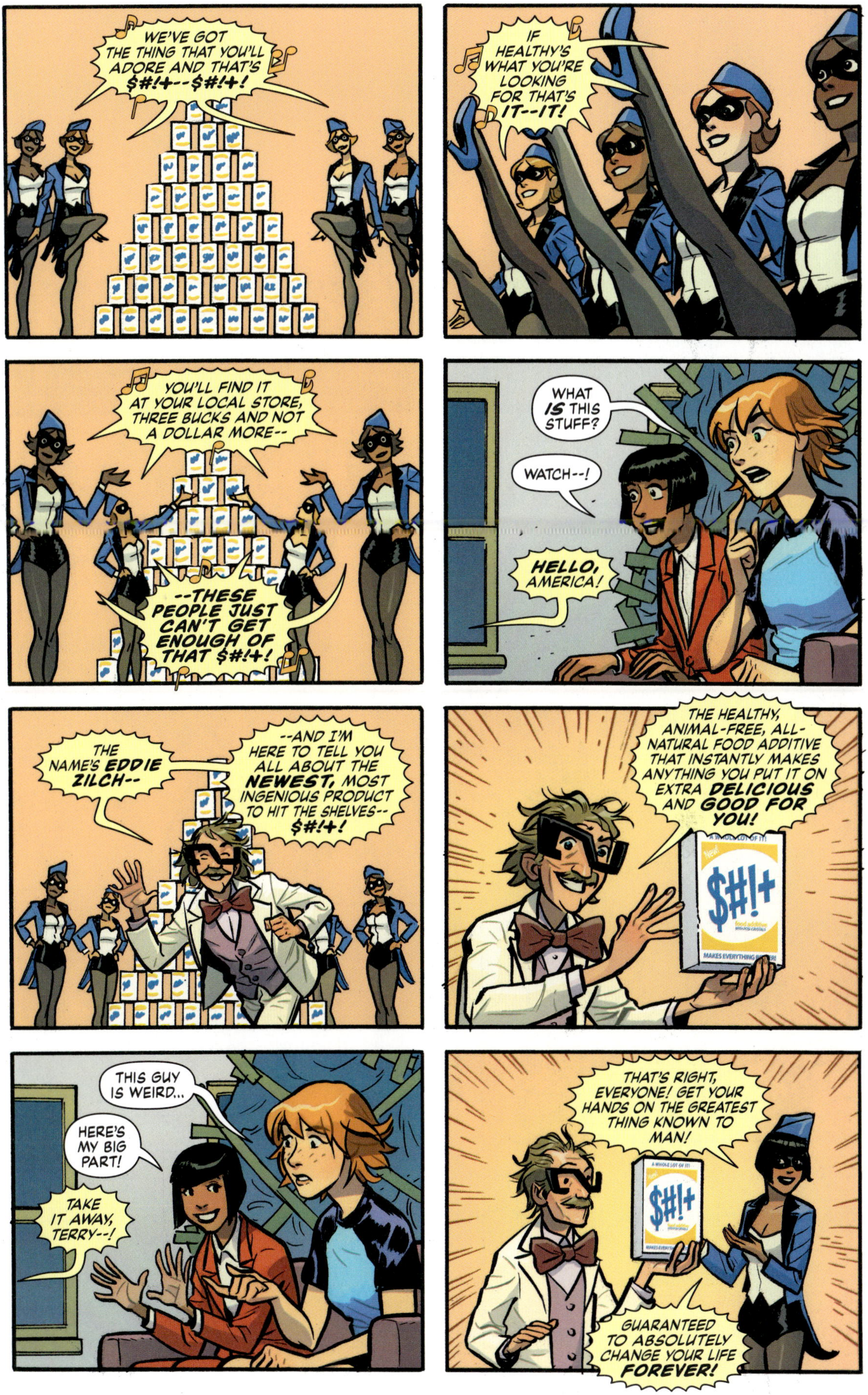

WE'VE GOT THE THING THAT YOU'LL ADORE AND THAT'S $#!+--$#!+!
IF HEALTHY'S WHAT YOU'RE LOOKING FOR THAT'S IT--IT!
YOU'LL FIND IT AT YOUR LOCAL STORE, THREE BUCKS AND NOT A DOLLAR MORE--
--THESE PEOPLE JUST CAN'T GET ENOUGH OF THAT $#!+!
WHAT IS THIS STUFF?
WATCH--!
HELLO, AMERICA!
THE NAME'S EDDIE ZILCH--
--AND I'M HERE TO TELL YOU ALL ABOUT THE NEWEST, MOST INGENIOUS PRODUCT TO HIT THE SHELVES-- $#!+!
THE HEALTHY, ANIMAL-FREE, ALL-NATURAL FOOD ADDITIVE THAT INSTANTLY MAKES ANYTHING YOU PUT IT ON EXTRA DELICIOUS AND GOOD FOR YOU!
$#!+
THIS GUY IS WEIRD...
HERE'S MY BIG PART!
TAKE IT AWAY, TERRY--!
THAT'S RIGHT, EVERYONE! GET YOUR HANDS ON THE GREATEST THING KNOWN TO MAN!
$#!+
GUARANTEED TO ABSOLUTELY CHANGE YOUR LIFE FOREVER!

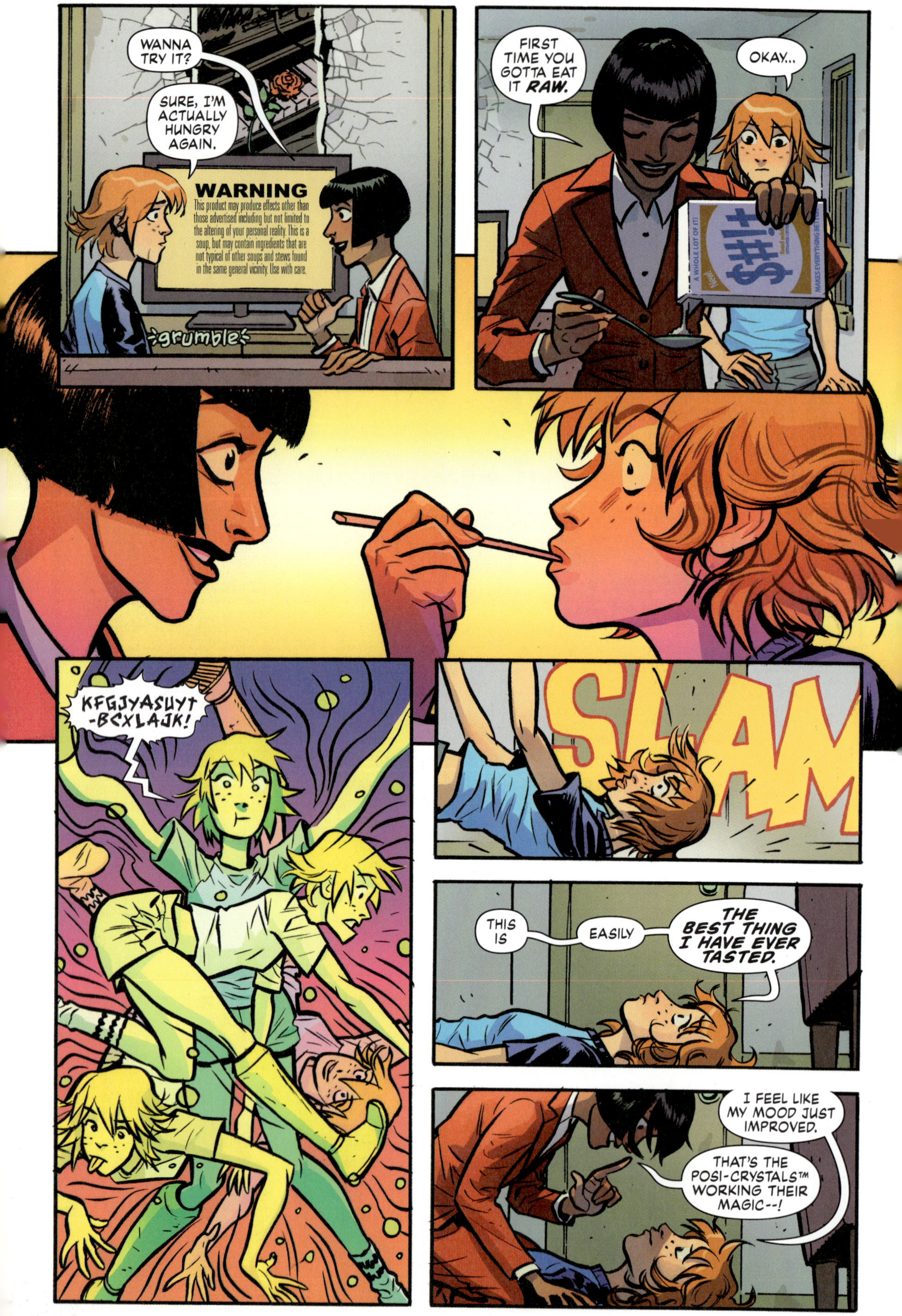
WANNA TRY IT?
SURE, I'M ACTUALLY HUNGRY AGAIN.
WARNING
This product may produce effects other than those advertised including but not limited to the altering of your personal reality. This is a soup, but may contain ingredients that are not typical of other soups and stews found in the same general vicinity. Use with care.
grumble
FIRST TIME YOU GOTTA EAT IT RAW.
OKAY...
A WHOLE LOT OF IT!
KFGJYASUYT-BCXLAJK!
SLAM
THIS IS EASILY THE BEST THING I HAVE EVER TASTED.
I FEEL LIKE MY MOOD JUST IMPROVED.
THAT'S THE POSI-CRYSTALS™ WORKING THEIR MAGIC--!

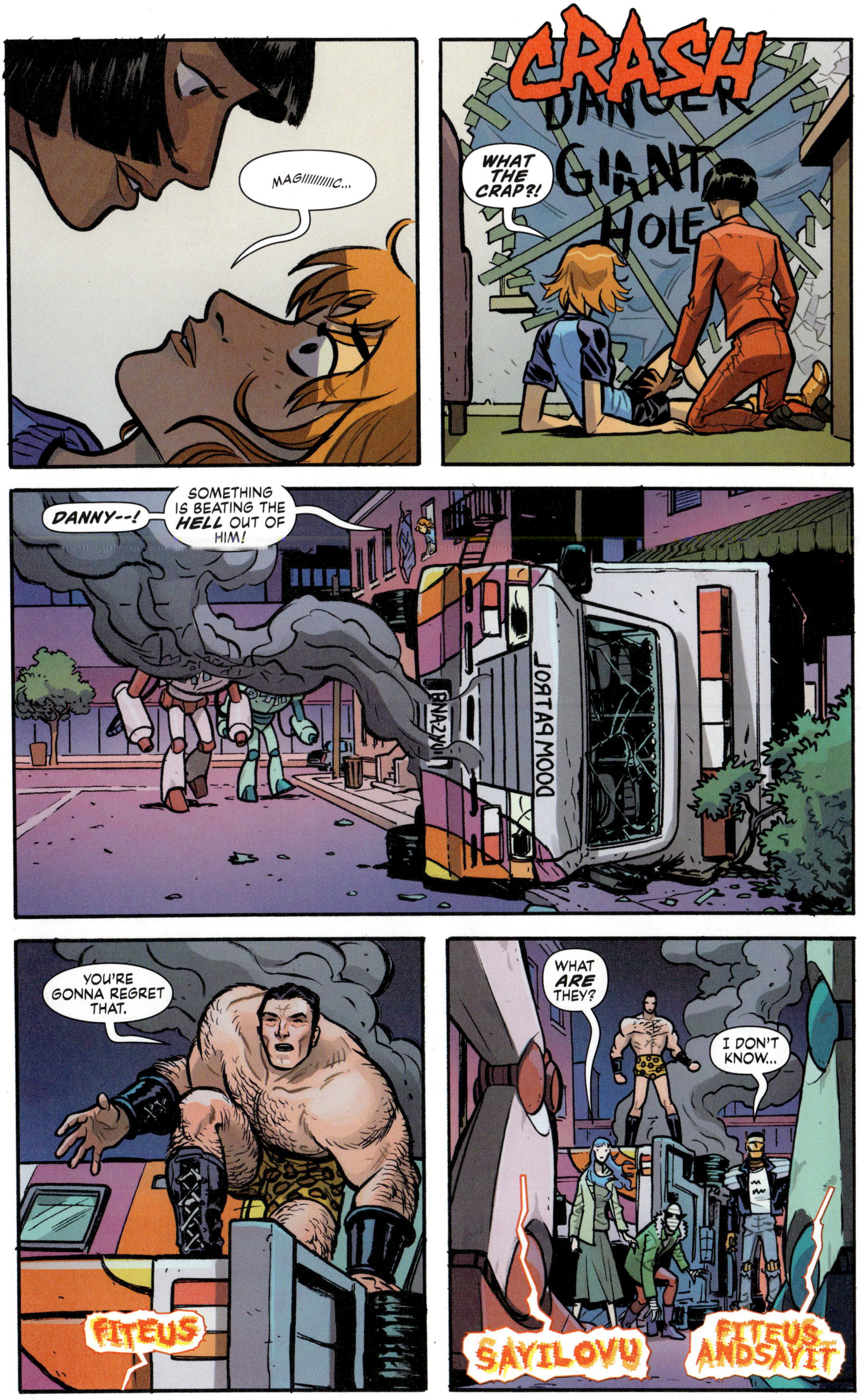
MAGIIIIIIIIC...
CRASH
DANGER
GIANT HOLE
WHAT THE CRAP?!
DANNY--!
SOMETHING IS BEATING THE HELL OUT OF HIM!
YOU'RE GONNA REGRET THAT.
FITEUS
WHAT ARE THEY?
I DON'T KNOW...
SAYILOVU
FITEUS ANDSAYIT

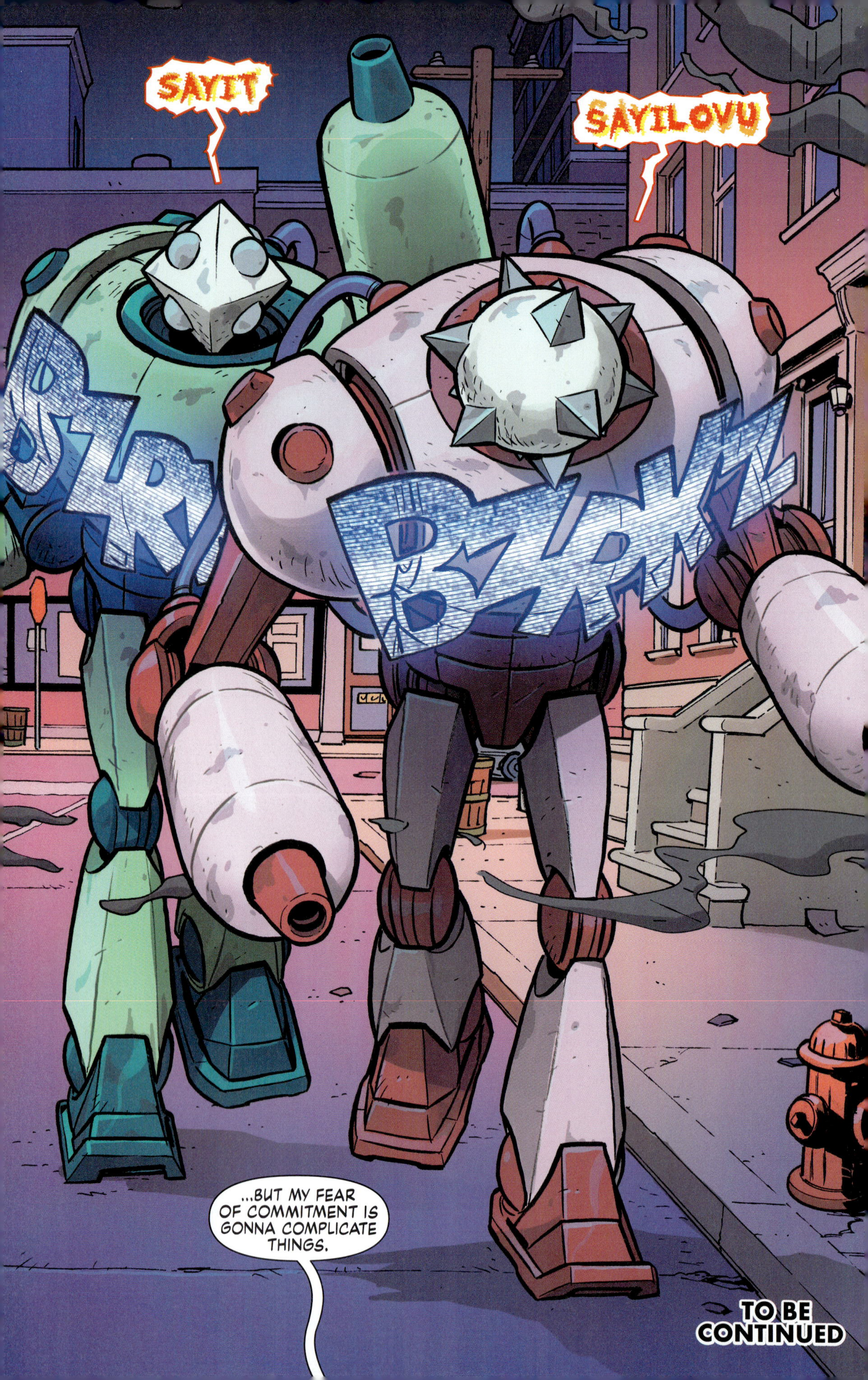
SAYIT
SAYILOVU
BZRK
BZRKZZ
...BUT MY FEAR OF COMMITMENT IS GONNA COMPLICATE THINGS.
TO BE CONTINUED

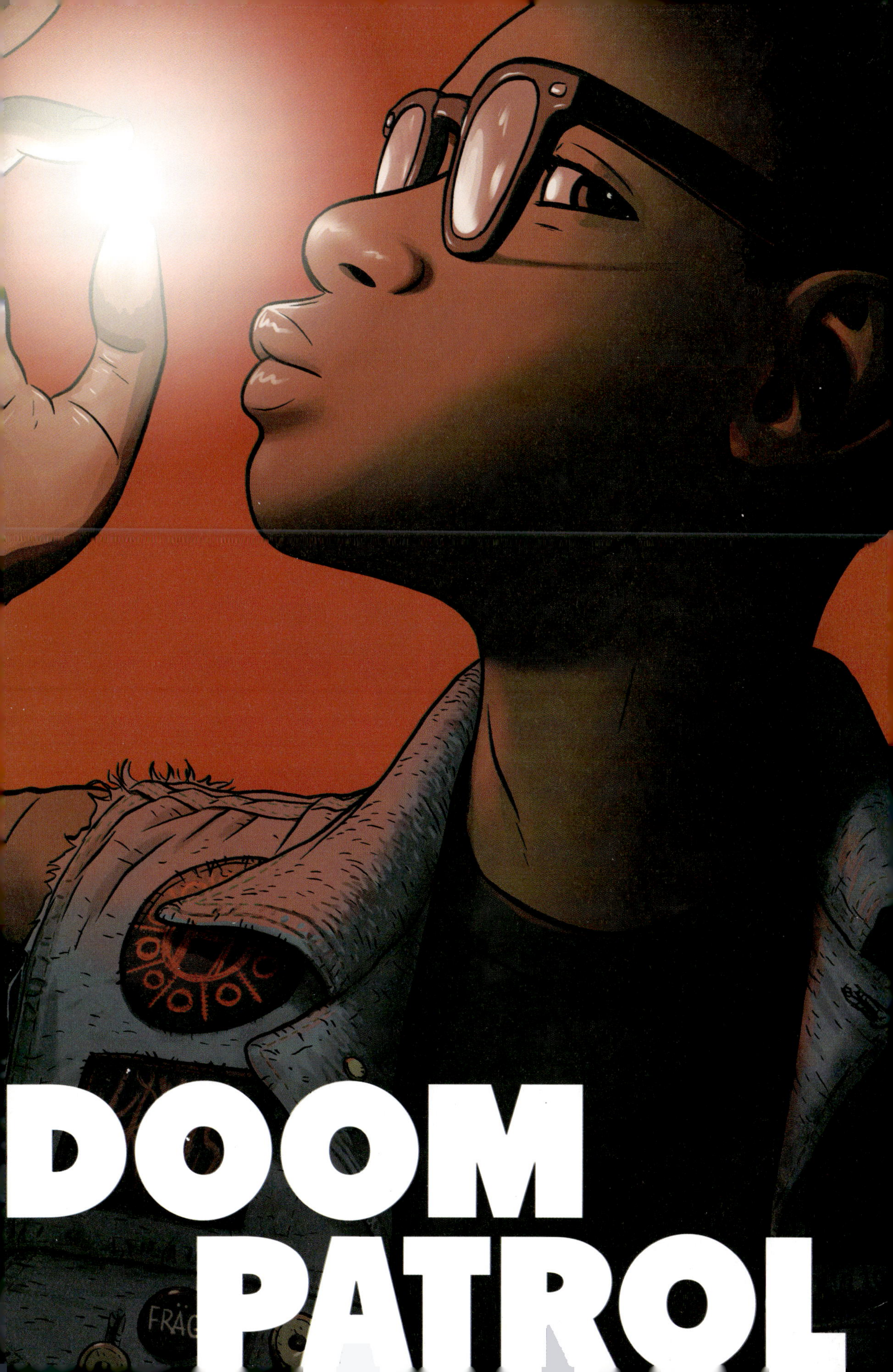
DOOM
PATROL
FRÄG

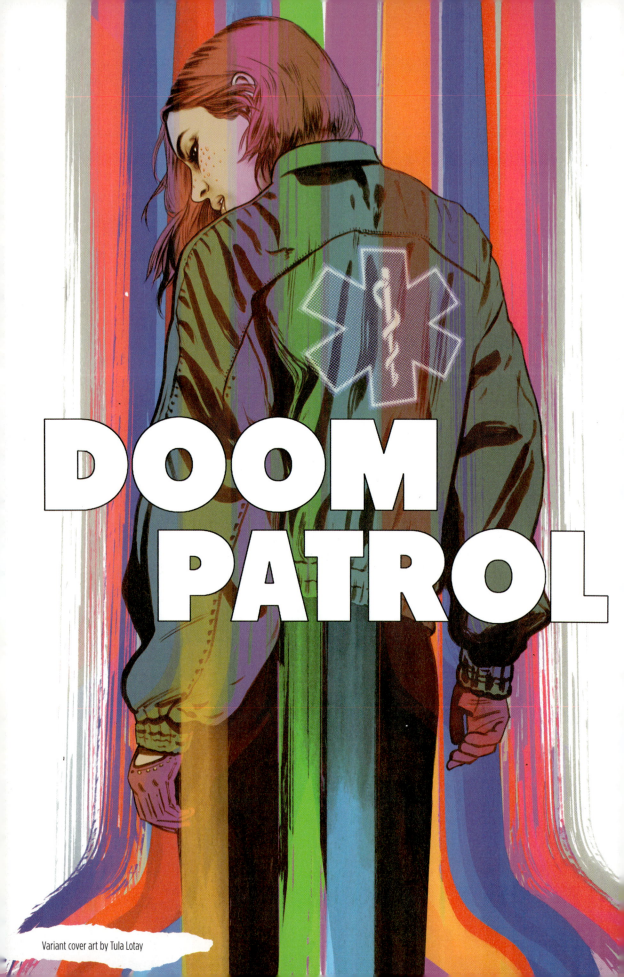

DOOM PATROL

Variant cover art by Tula Lotay

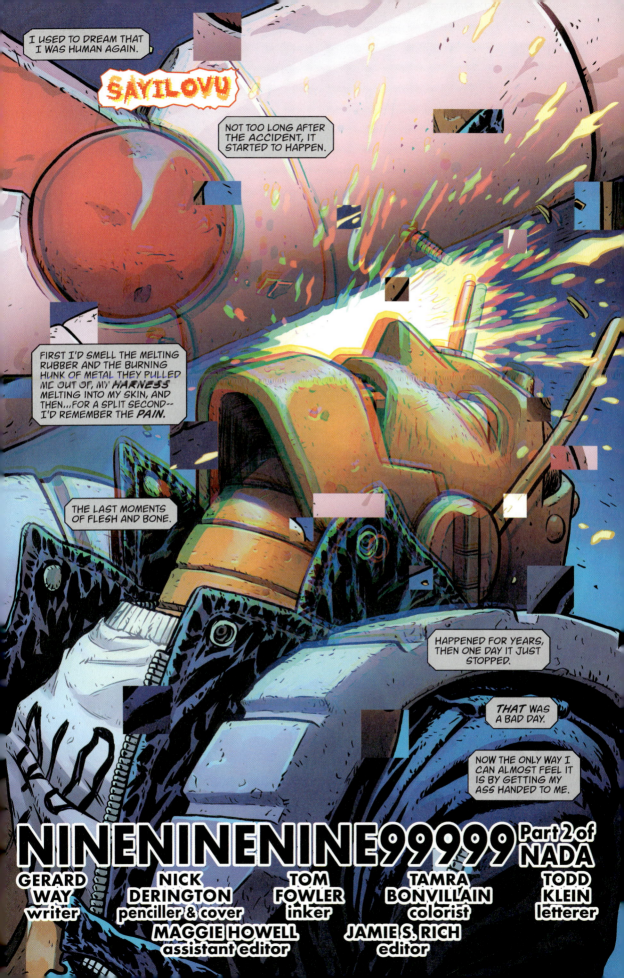

I USED TO DREAM THAT I WAS HUMAN AGAIN.

SAYILOVU

NOT TOO LONG AFTER THE ACCIDENT, IT STARTED TO HAPPEN.

FIRST I'D SMELL THE MELTING RUBBER AND THE BURNING HUNK OF METAL THEY PULLED ME OUT OF, MY *HARNESS* MELTING INTO MY SKIN, AND THEN...FOR A SPLIT SECOND-- I'D REMEMBER THE *PAIN.*

THE LAST MOMENTS OF FLESH AND BONE.

HAPPENED FOR YEARS, THEN ONE DAY IT JUST STOPPED.

THAT WAS A BAD DAY.

NOW THE ONLY WAY I CAN ALMOST FEEL IT IS BY GETTING MY ASS HANDED TO ME.

NINENINENINE99999 Part 2 of NADA

GERARD WAY writer **NICK DERINGTON** penciller & cover **TOM FOWLER** inker **TAMRA BONVILLAIN** colorist **TODD KLEIN** letterer

MAGGIE HOWELL assistant editor **JAMIE S. RICH** editor

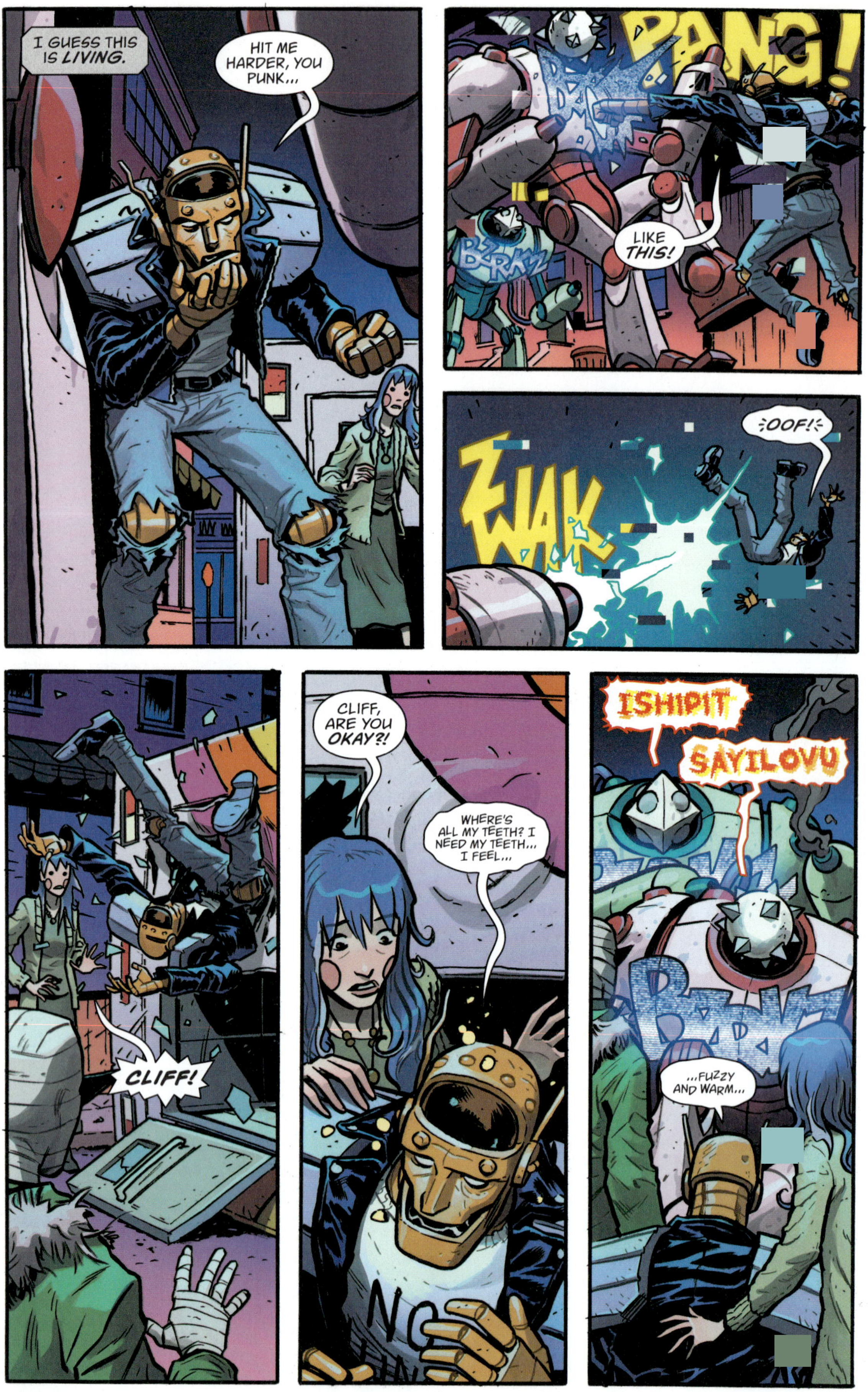
I GUESS THIS IS *LIVING.*
HIT ME HARDER, YOU PUNK...
PANG!
LIKE *THIS!*
OOF!
CLIFF!
CLIFF, ARE YOU *OKAY?!*
WHERE'S ALL MY TEETH? I NEED MY TEETH... I FEEL...
ISHIPIT
SAYILOVU
...FUZZY AND WARM...

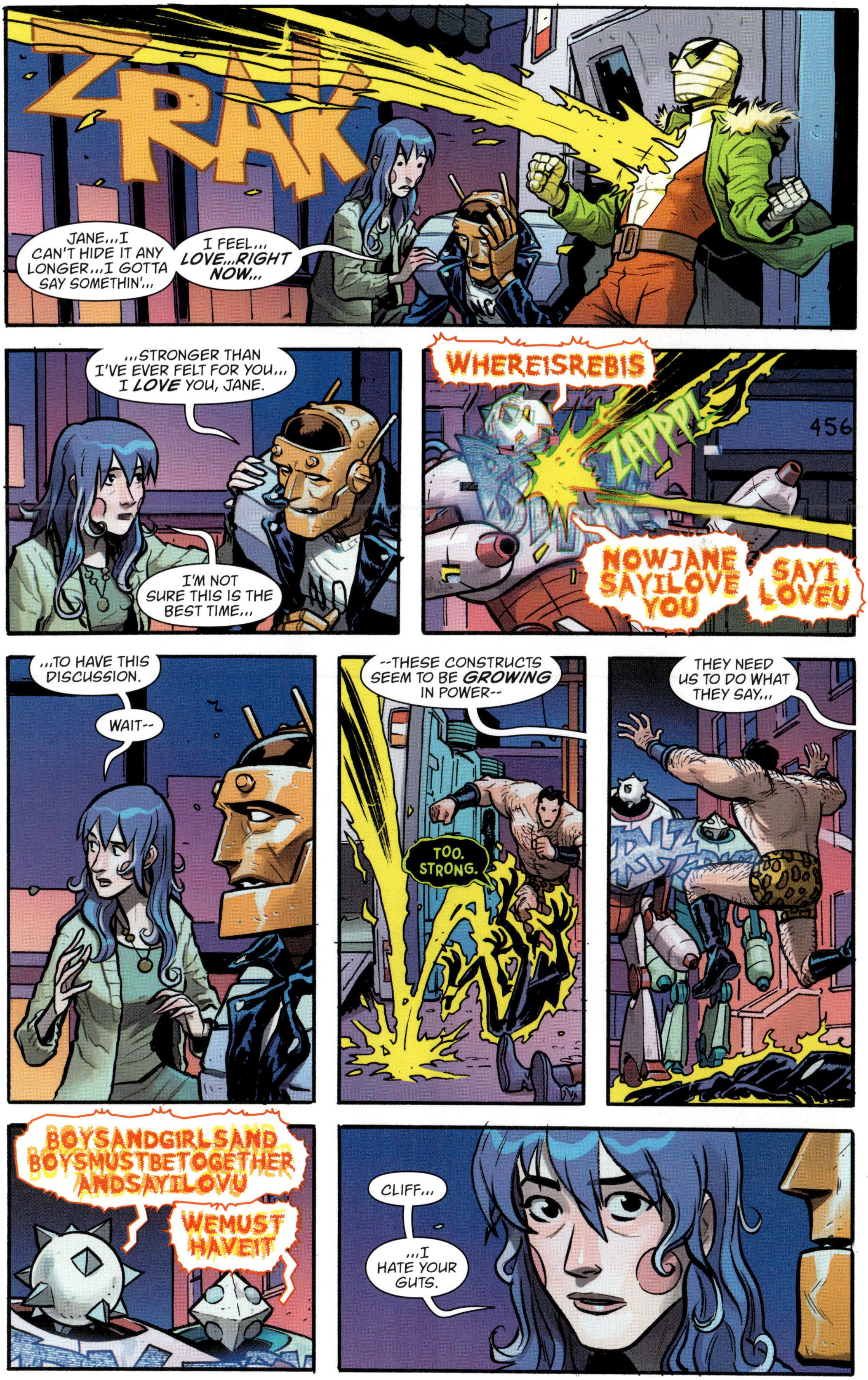
ZRAK
JANE...I CAN'T HIDE IT ANY LONGER...I GOTTA SAY SOMETHIN'...
I FEEL... LOVE...RIGHT NOW...
...STRONGER THAN I'VE EVER FELT FOR YOU... I LOVE YOU, JANE.
I'M NOT SURE THIS IS THE BEST TIME...
WHEREISREBIS
ZAPPP!
456
NOWJANE SAYILOVE YOU
SAYI LOVEU
...TO HAVE THIS DISCUSSION.
WAIT--
--THESE CONSTRUCTS SEEM TO BE GROWING IN POWER--
TOO. STRONG.
THEY NEED US TO DO WHAT THEY SAY...
BOYSANDGIRLSAND BOYSMUSTBETOGETHER ANDSAYILOVU
WEMUST HAVEIT
CLIFF...
...I HATE YOUR GUTS.

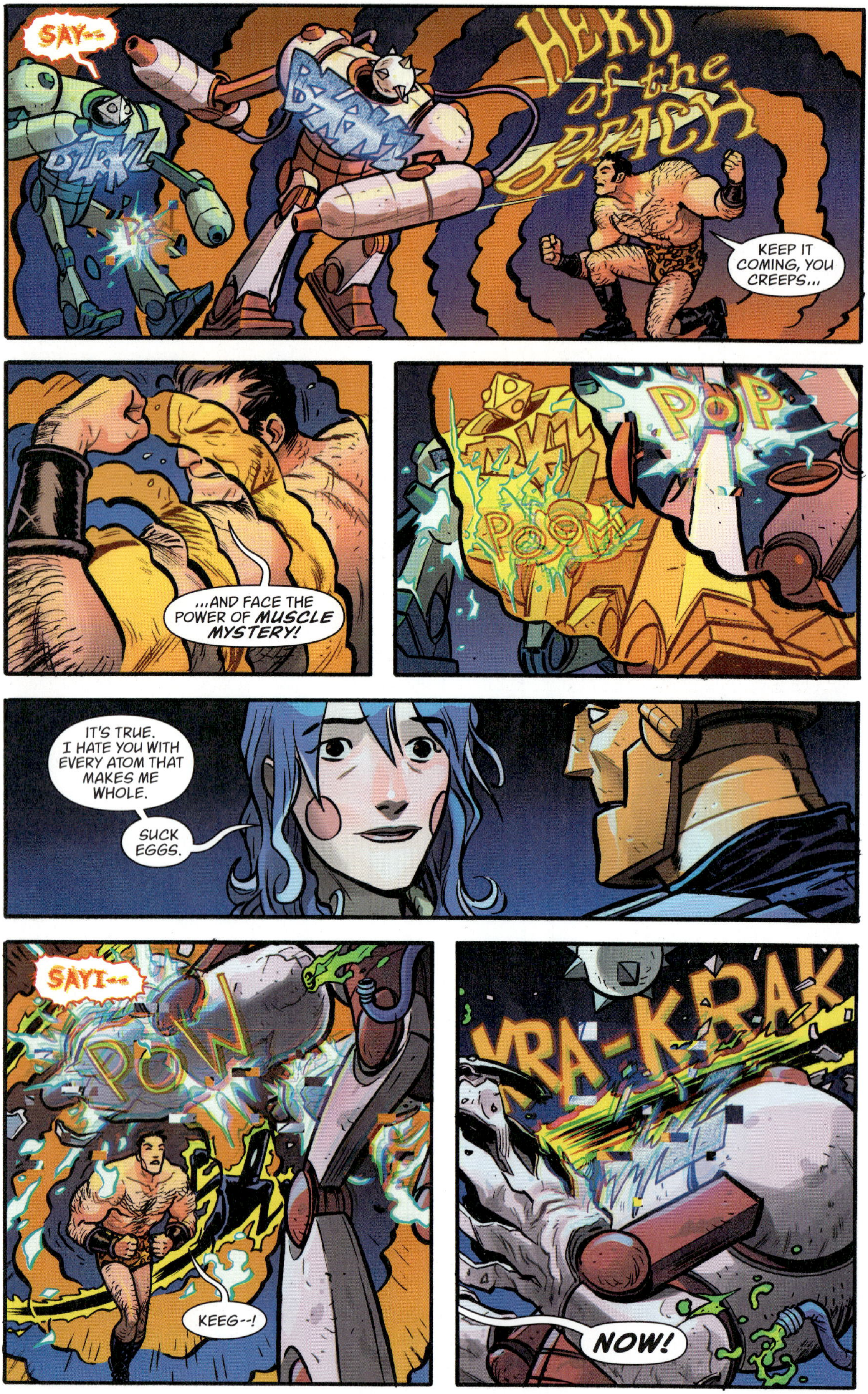
SAY--
BZRKL
BZAKKZ
POW
HERO of the BEACH
KEEP IT COMING, YOU CREEPS...
...AND FACE THE POWER OF MUSCLE MYSTERY!
POP
POOM
IT'S TRUE. I HATE YOU WITH EVERY ATOM THAT MAKES ME WHOLE.
SUCK EGGS.
SAYI--
POW
KEEG--!
KRA-KRAK
NOW!

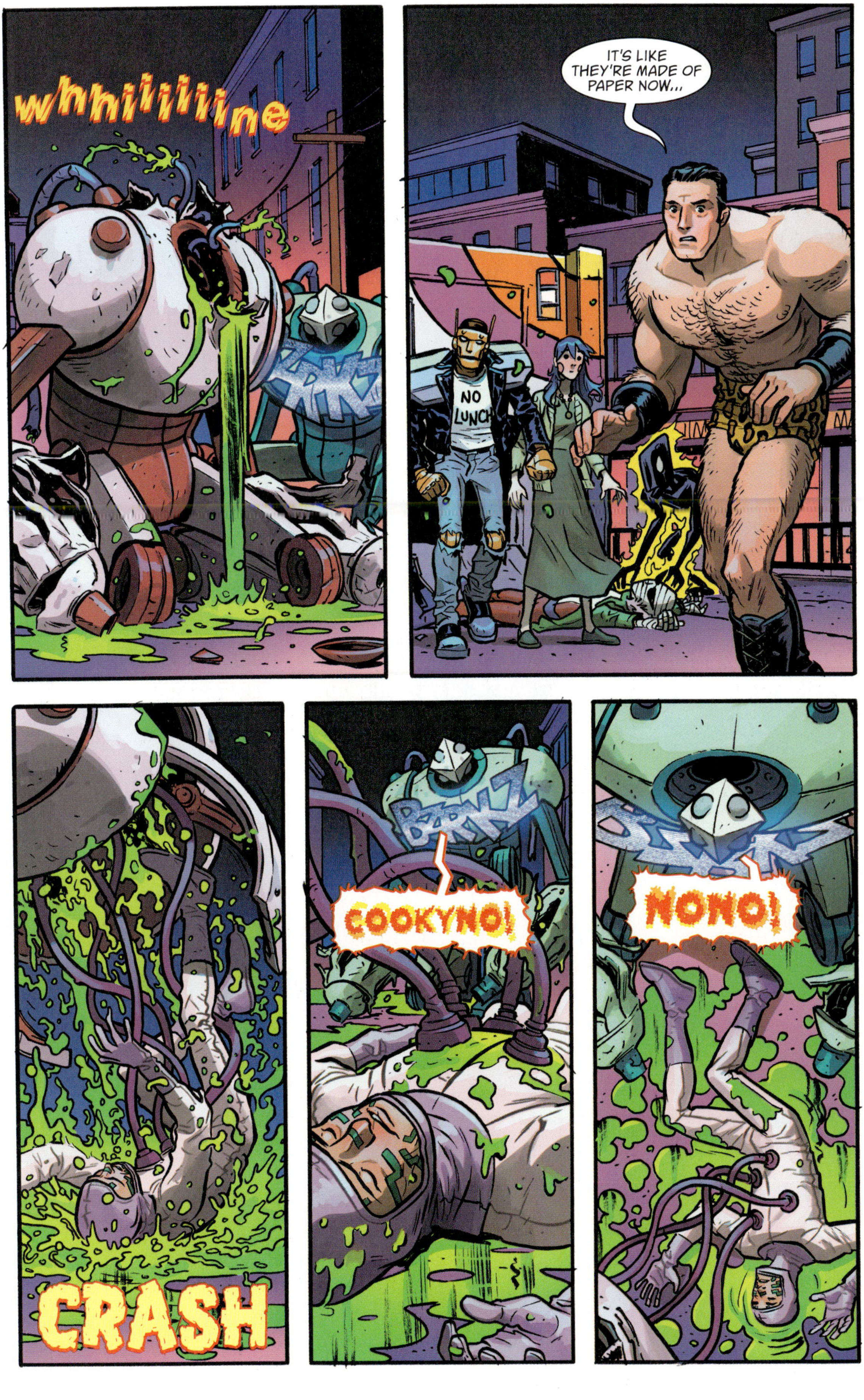

whhiiiiiine
IT'S LIKE THEY'RE MADE OF PAPER NOW...
NO LUNCH
CRASH
COOKYNO!
NONO!

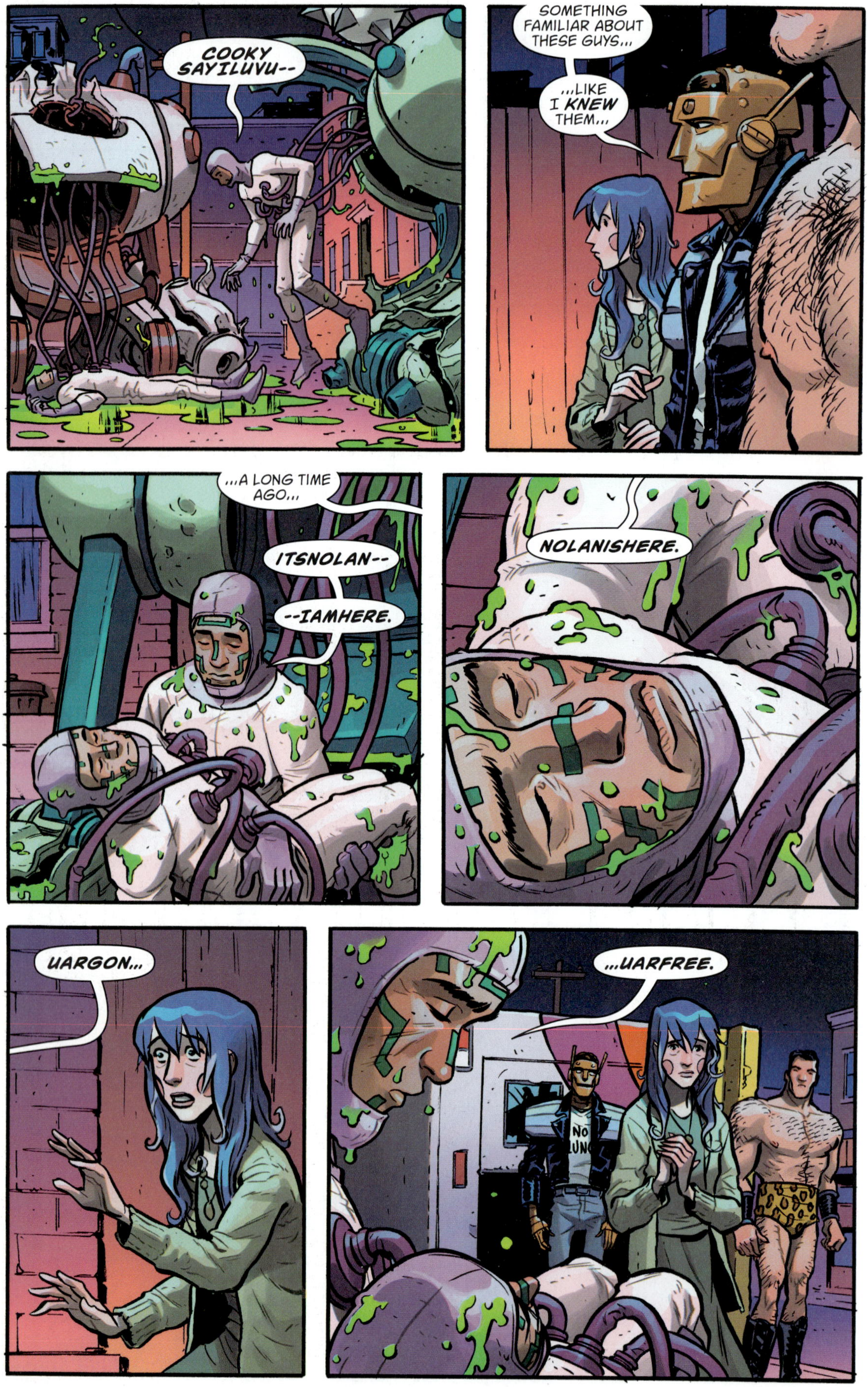
COOKY SAYILUVU--
SOMETHING FAMILIAR ABOUT THESE GUYS...
...LIKE I KNEW THEM...
...A LONG TIME AGO...
ITSNOLAN--
--IAMHERE.
NOLANISHERE.
UARGON...
...UARFREE.
NO
LUNC

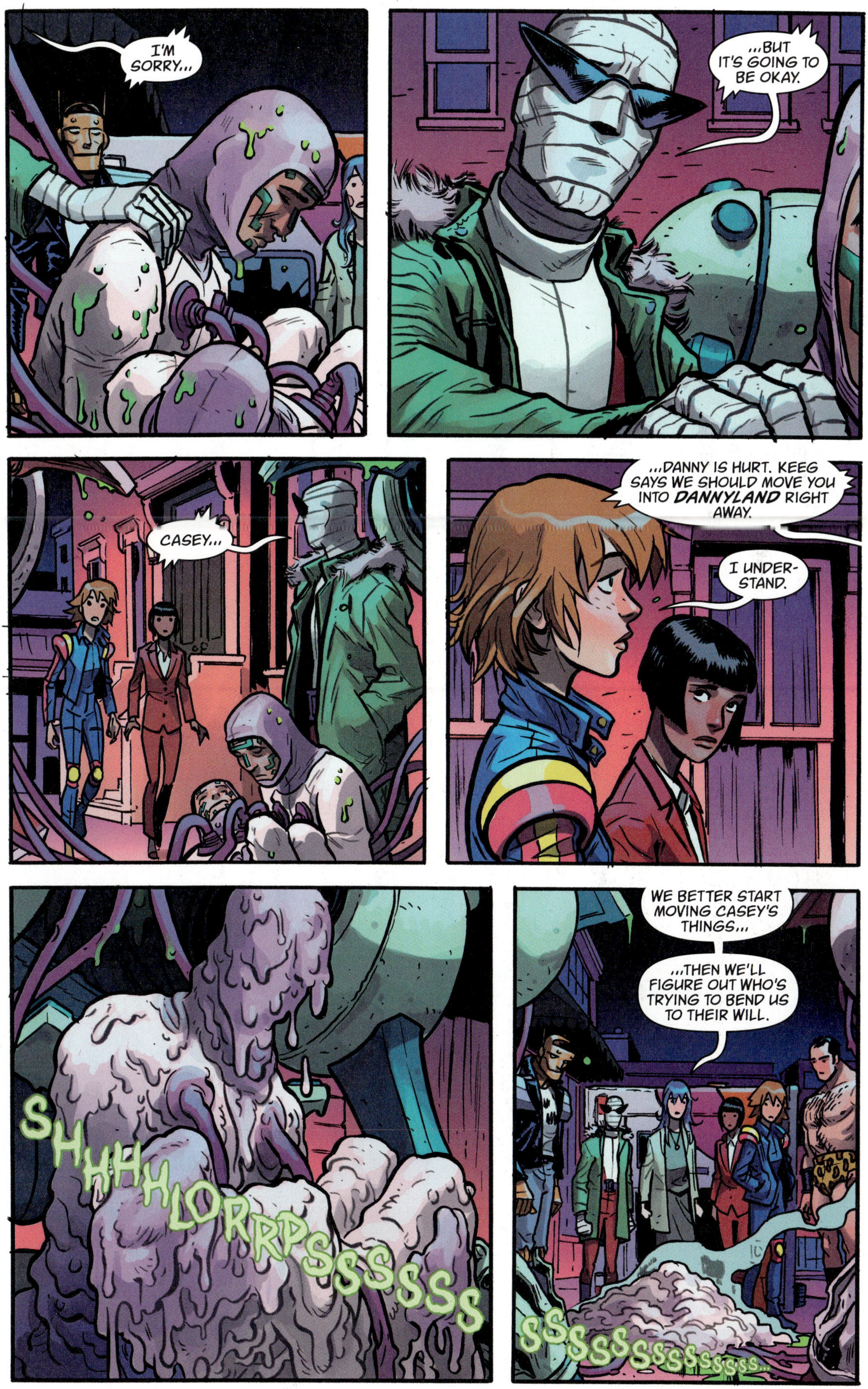

I'M SORRY...
...BUT IT'S GOING TO BE OKAY.
CASEY...
...DANNY IS HURT. KEEG SAYS WE SHOULD MOVE YOU INTO DANNYLAND RIGHT AWAY.
I UNDERSTAND.
SHHHHLORRRPSSSSSSS
WE BETTER START MOVING CASEY'S THINGS...
...THEN WE'LL FIGURE OUT WHO'S TRYING TO BEND US TO THEIR WILL.
SSSSSSSSSSSSSS...

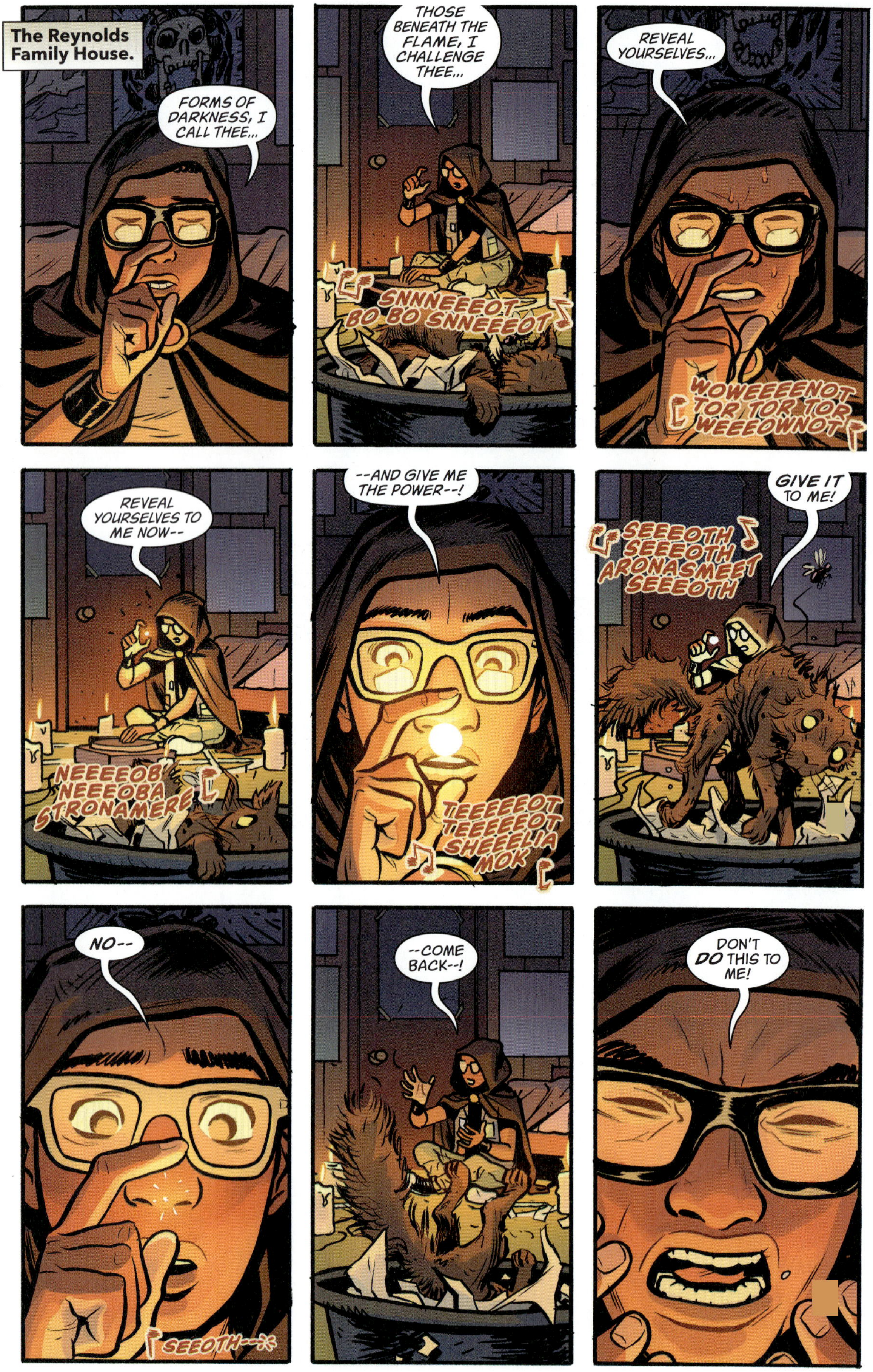
The Reynolds Family House.
FORMS OF DARKNESS, I CALL THEE...
THOSE BENEATH THE FLAME, I CHALLENGE THEE...
SNNNEEEOT BO BO SNNEEEOT
REVEAL YOURSELVES...
WOWEEEEENOT TOR TOR TOR WEEEOWNOT
REVEAL YOURSELVES TO ME NOW--
NEEEEOB NEEEOBA STRONAMERE
--AND GIVE ME THE POWER--!
TEEEEEOT TEEEEEOT SHEEELIA MOK
GIVE IT TO ME!
SEEEOTH SEEEOTH ARONASMEET SEEEOTH
NO--
SEEOTH--
--COME BACK--!
DON'T DO THIS TO ME!

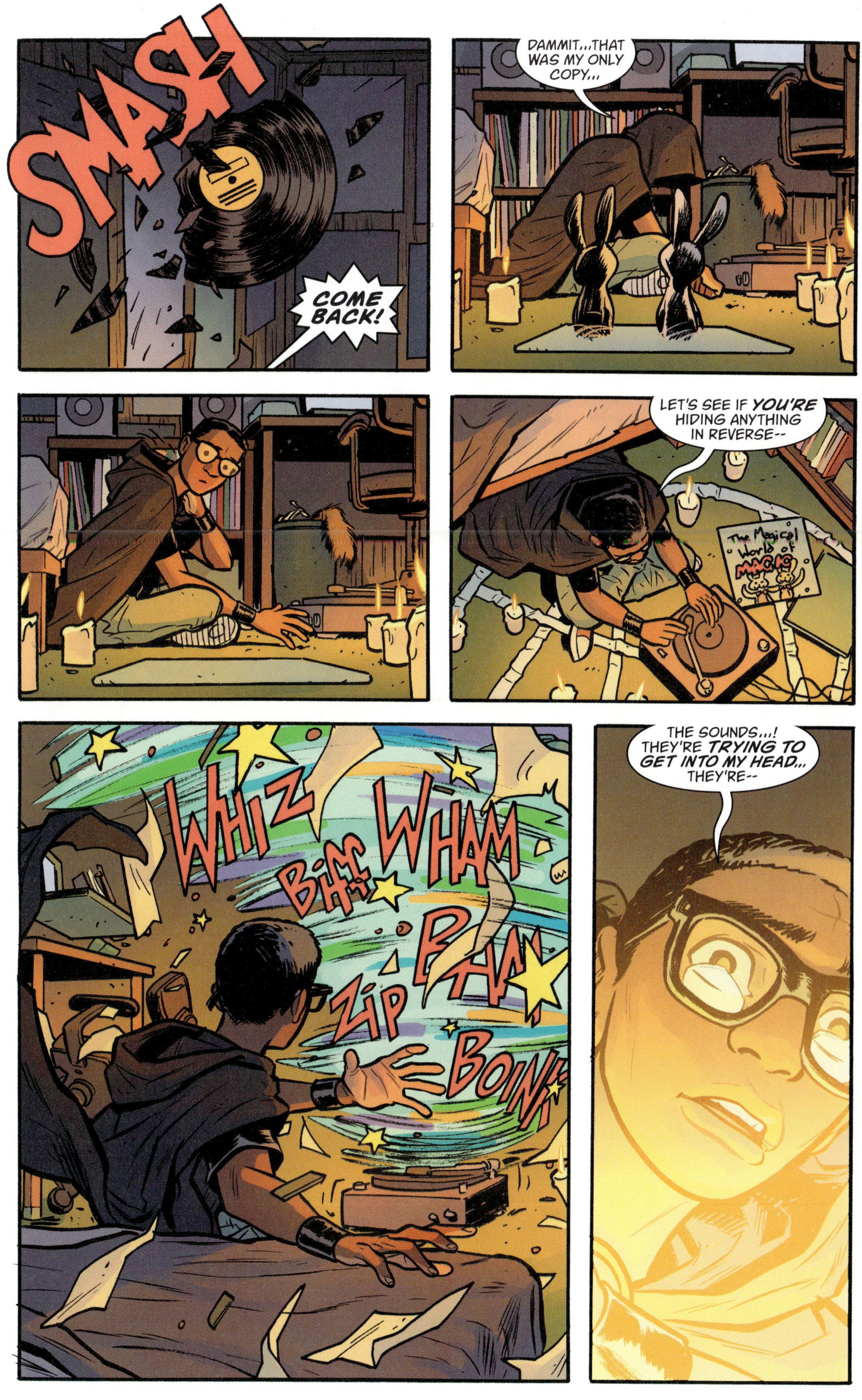
SMASH
COME BACK!
DAMMIT...THAT WAS MY ONLY COPY...
LET'S SEE IF *YOU'RE* HIDING ANYTHING IN REVERSE--
The Magical World of MAGIC
WHIZ
Biff
WHAM
ZIP
BOINK
THE SOUNDS...! THEY'RE *TRYING TO GET INTO MY HEAD...* THEY'RE--

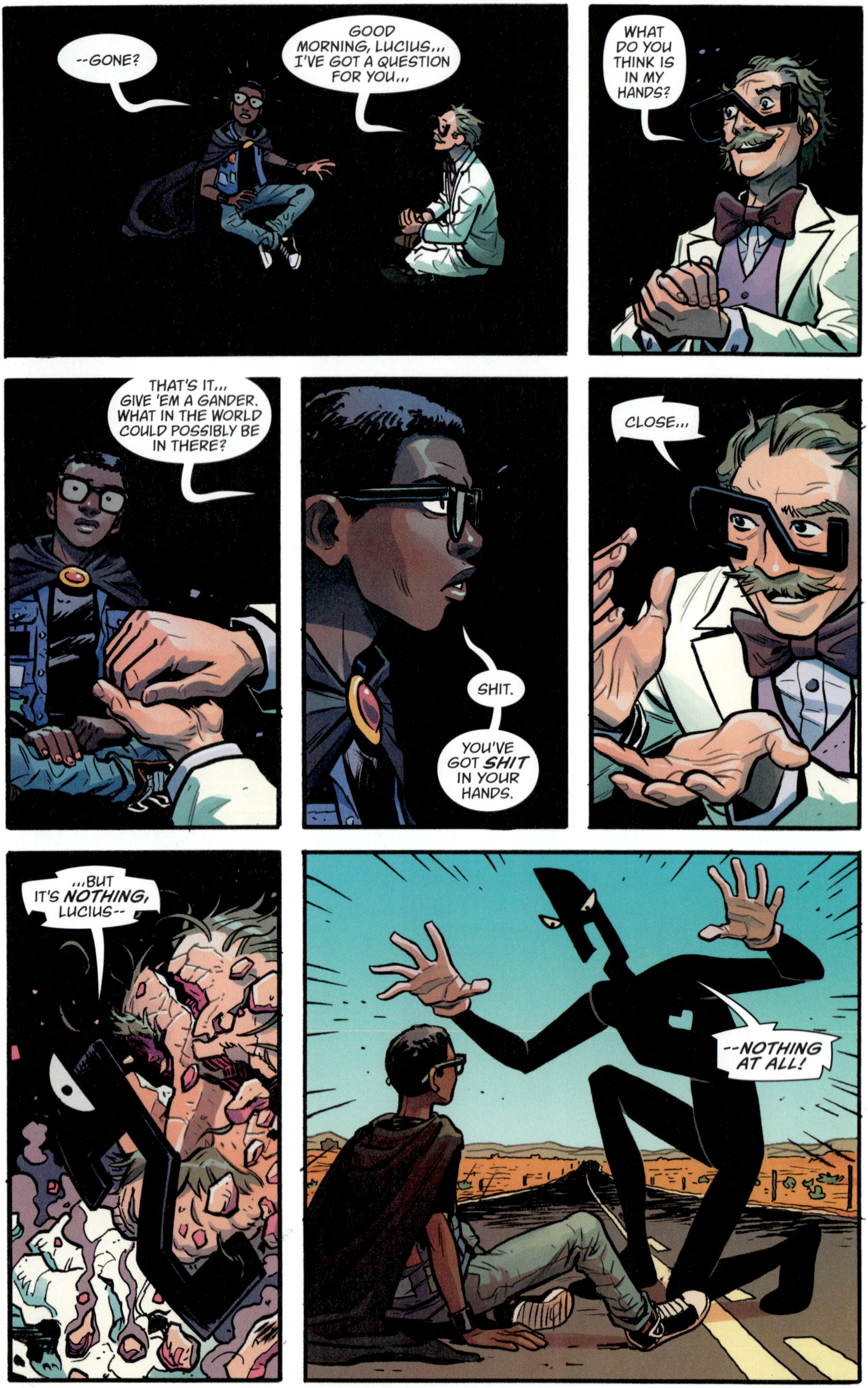
--GONE?
GOOD MORNING, LUCIUS... I'VE GOT A QUESTION FOR YOU...
WHAT DO YOU THINK IS IN MY HANDS?
THAT'S IT... GIVE 'EM A GANDER. WHAT IN THE WORLD COULD POSSIBLY BE IN THERE?
SHIT.
YOU'VE GOT SHIT IN YOUR HANDS.
CLOSE...
...BUT IT'S NOTHING, LUCIUS--
--NOTHING AT ALL!

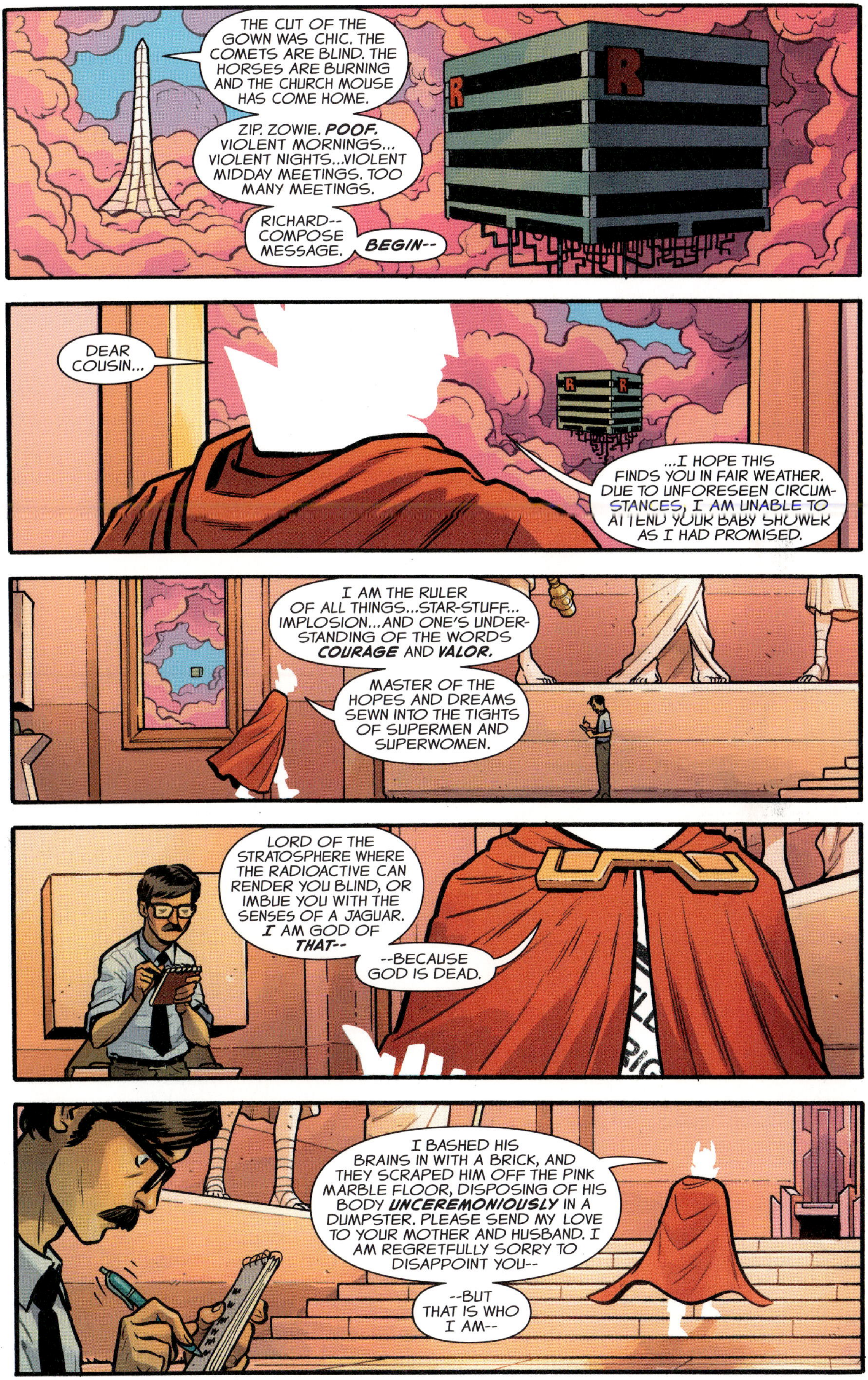
THE CUT OF THE GOWN WAS CHIC. THE COMETS ARE BLIND. THE HORSES ARE BURNING AND THE CHURCH MOUSE HAS COME HOME.
ZIP. ZOWIE. **POOF.** VIOLENT MORNINGS... VIOLENT NIGHTS...VIOLENT MIDDAY MEETINGS. TOO MANY MEETINGS.
RICHARD-- COMPOSE MESSAGE.
BEGIN--
DEAR COUSIN...
...I HOPE THIS FINDS YOU IN FAIR WEATHER. DUE TO UNFORESEEN CIRCUMSTANCES, I AM UNABLE TO ATTEND YOUR BABY SHOWER AS I HAD PROMISED.
I AM THE RULER OF ALL THINGS...STAR-STUFF... IMPLOSION...AND ONE'S UNDERSTANDING OF THE WORDS ***COURAGE*** AND ***VALOR.***
MASTER OF THE HOPES AND DREAMS SEWN INTO THE TIGHTS OF SUPERMEN AND SUPERWOMEN.
LORD OF THE STRATOSPHERE WHERE THE RADIOACTIVE CAN RENDER YOU BLIND, OR IMBUE YOU WITH THE SENSES OF A JAGUAR. ***I*** AM GOD OF ***THAT--***
--BECAUSE GOD IS DEAD.
I BASHED HIS BRAINS IN WITH A BRICK, AND THEY SCRAPED HIM OFF THE PINK MARBLE FLOOR, DISPOSING OF HIS BODY ***UNCEREMONIOUSLY*** IN A DUMPSTER. PLEASE SEND MY LOVE TO YOUR MOTHER AND HUSBAND. I AM REGRETFULLY SORRY TO DISAPPOINT YOU--
--BUT THAT IS WHO I AM--

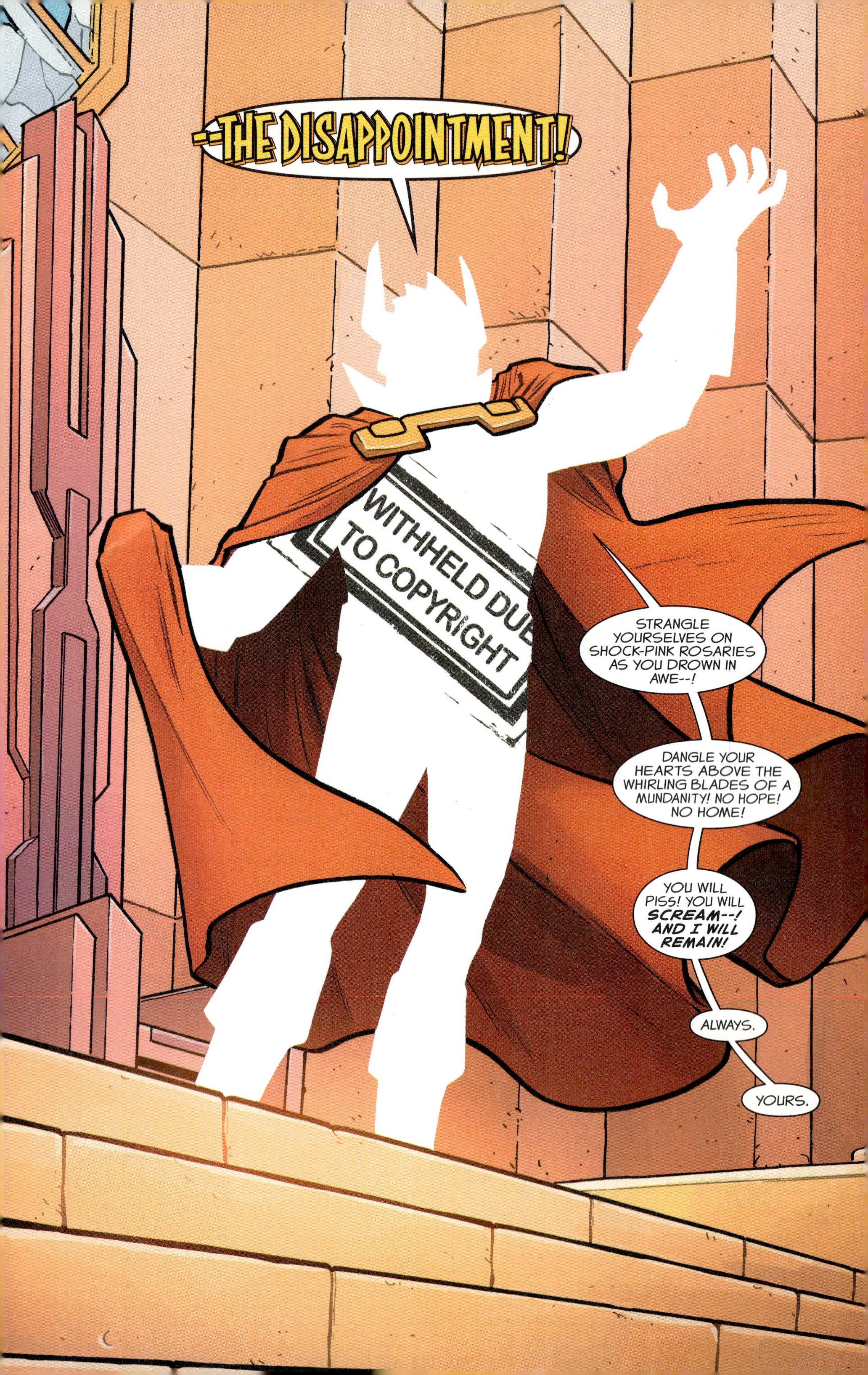
--THE DISAPPOINTMENT!
WITHHELD DUE TO COPYRIGHT
STRANGLE YOURSELVES ON SHOCK-PINK ROSARIES AS YOU DROWN IN AWE--!
DANGLE YOUR HEARTS ABOVE THE WHIRLING BLADES OF A MUNDANITY! NO HOPE! NO HOME!
YOU WILL PISS! YOU WILL SCREAM--! AND I WILL REMAIN!
ALWAYS.
YOURS.

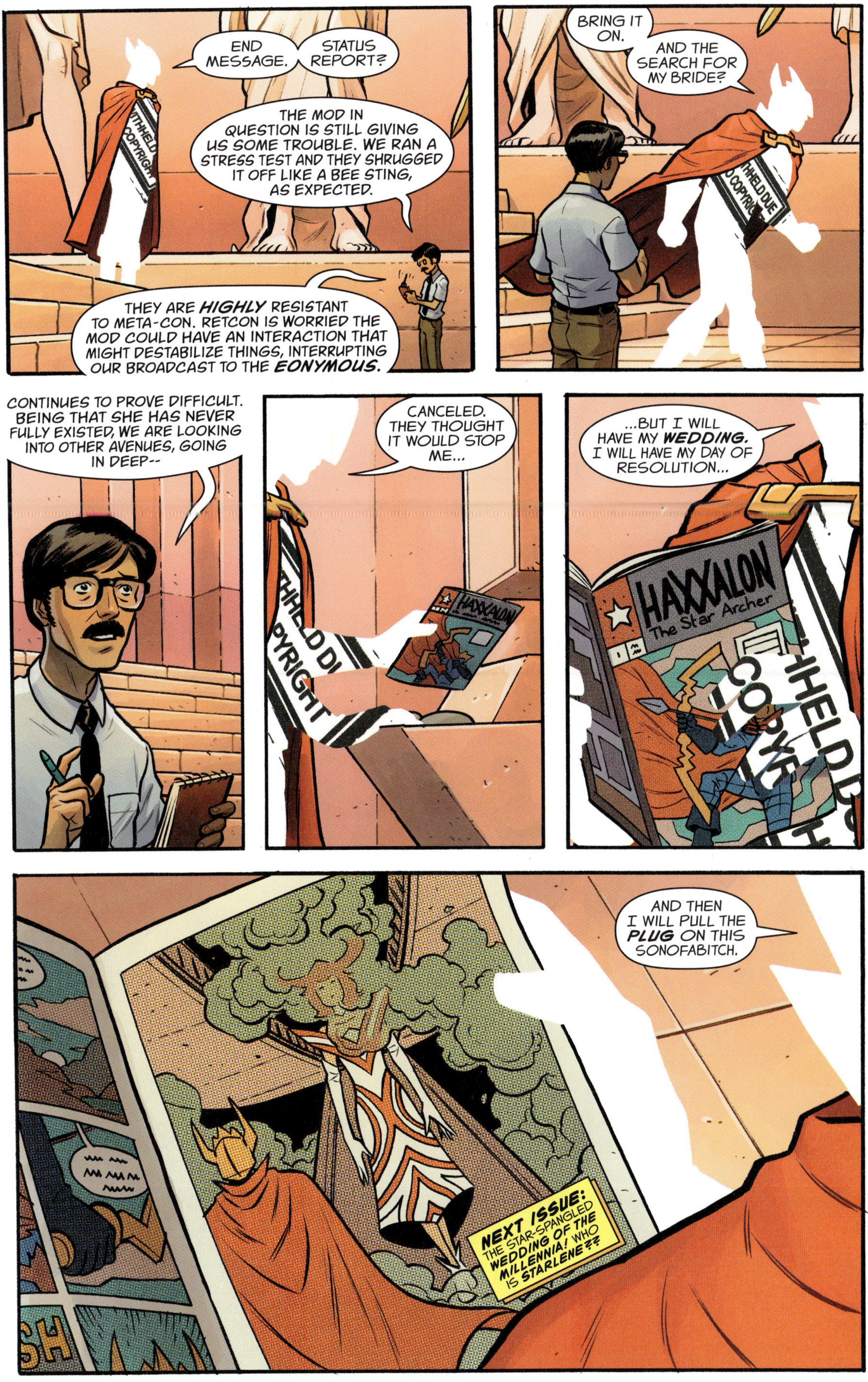
END MESSAGE.
STATUS REPORT?
THE MOD IN QUESTION IS STILL GIVING US SOME TROUBLE. WE RAN A STRESS TEST AND THEY SHRUGGED IT OFF LIKE A BEE STING, AS EXPECTED.
THEY ARE **HIGHLY** RESISTANT TO META-CON. RETCON IS WORRIED THE MOD COULD HAVE AN INTERACTION THAT MIGHT DESTABILIZE THINGS, INTERRUPTING OUR BROADCAST TO THE **EONYMOUS**.
BRING IT ON.
AND THE SEARCH FOR MY BRIDE?
CONTINUES TO PROVE DIFFICULT. BEING THAT SHE HAS NEVER FULLY EXISTED, WE ARE LOOKING INTO OTHER AVENUES, GOING IN DEEP--
CANCELED. THEY THOUGHT IT WOULD STOP ME...
...BUT I WILL HAVE MY **WEDDING**. I WILL HAVE MY DAY OF RESOLUTION...
HAXXALON
The Star Archer
AND THEN I WILL PULL THE **PLUG** ON THIS SONOFABITCH.
NEXT ISSUE: THE STAR-SPANGLED **WEDDING OF THE MILLENNIA!** WHO IS **STARLENE??**

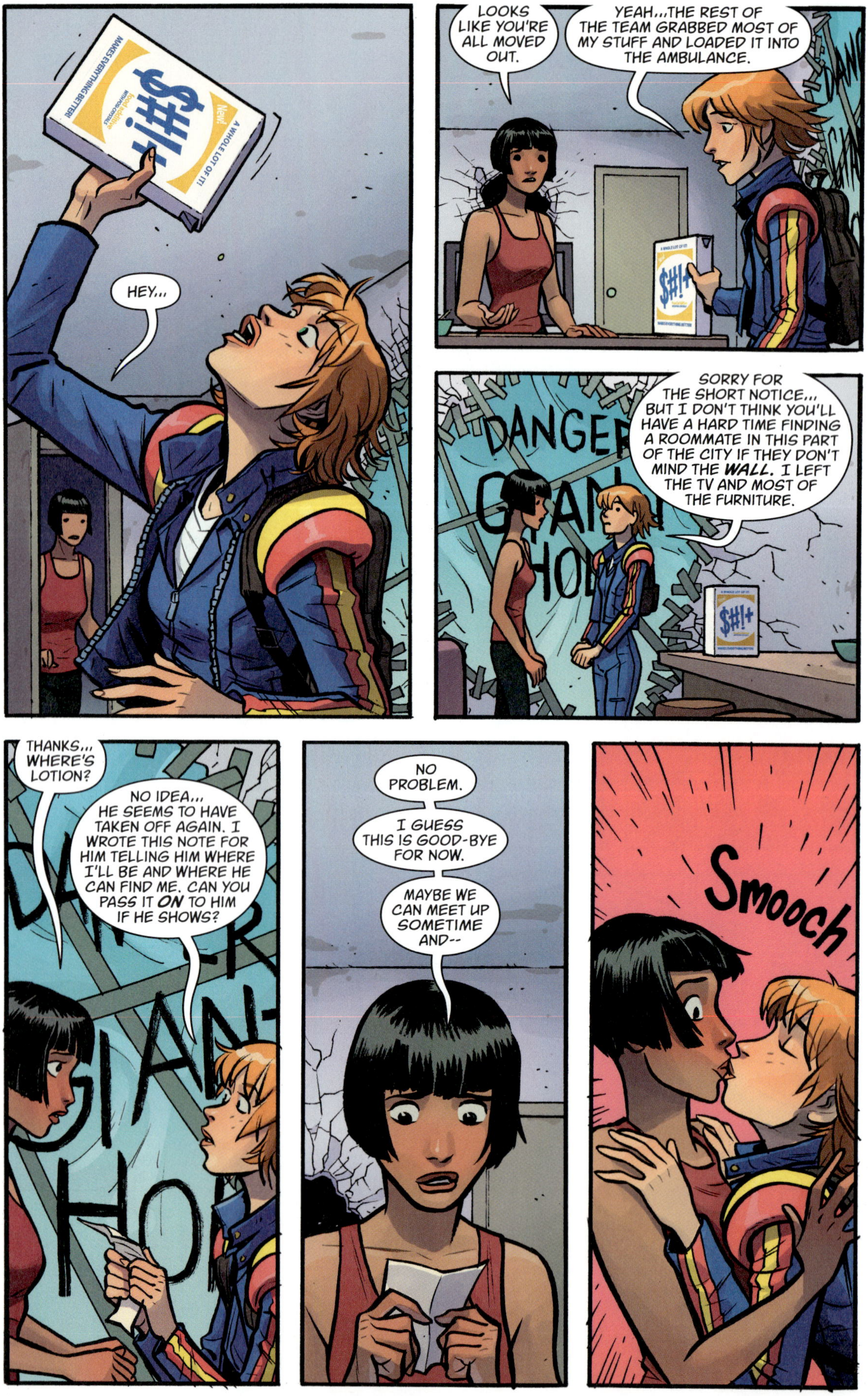
$#!+
New!
A WHOLE LOT OF IT!
MAKES EVERYTHING BETTER
HEY...
LOOKS LIKE YOU'RE ALL MOVED OUT.
YEAH...THE REST OF THE TEAM GRABBED MOST OF MY STUFF AND LOADED IT INTO THE AMBULANCE.
DANGER
SORRY FOR THE SHORT NOTICE... BUT I DON'T THINK YOU'LL HAVE A HARD TIME FINDING A ROOMMATE IN THIS PART OF THE CITY IF THEY DON'T MIND THE *WALL*. I LEFT THE TV AND MOST OF THE FURNITURE.
THANKS... WHERE'S LOTION?
NO IDEA... HE SEEMS TO HAVE TAKEN OFF AGAIN. I WROTE THIS NOTE FOR HIM TELLING HIM WHERE I'LL BE AND WHERE HE CAN FIND ME. CAN YOU PASS IT *ON* TO HIM IF HE SHOWS?
NO PROBLEM.
I GUESS THIS IS GOOD-BYE FOR NOW.
MAYBE WE CAN MEET UP SOMETIME AND--
Smooch

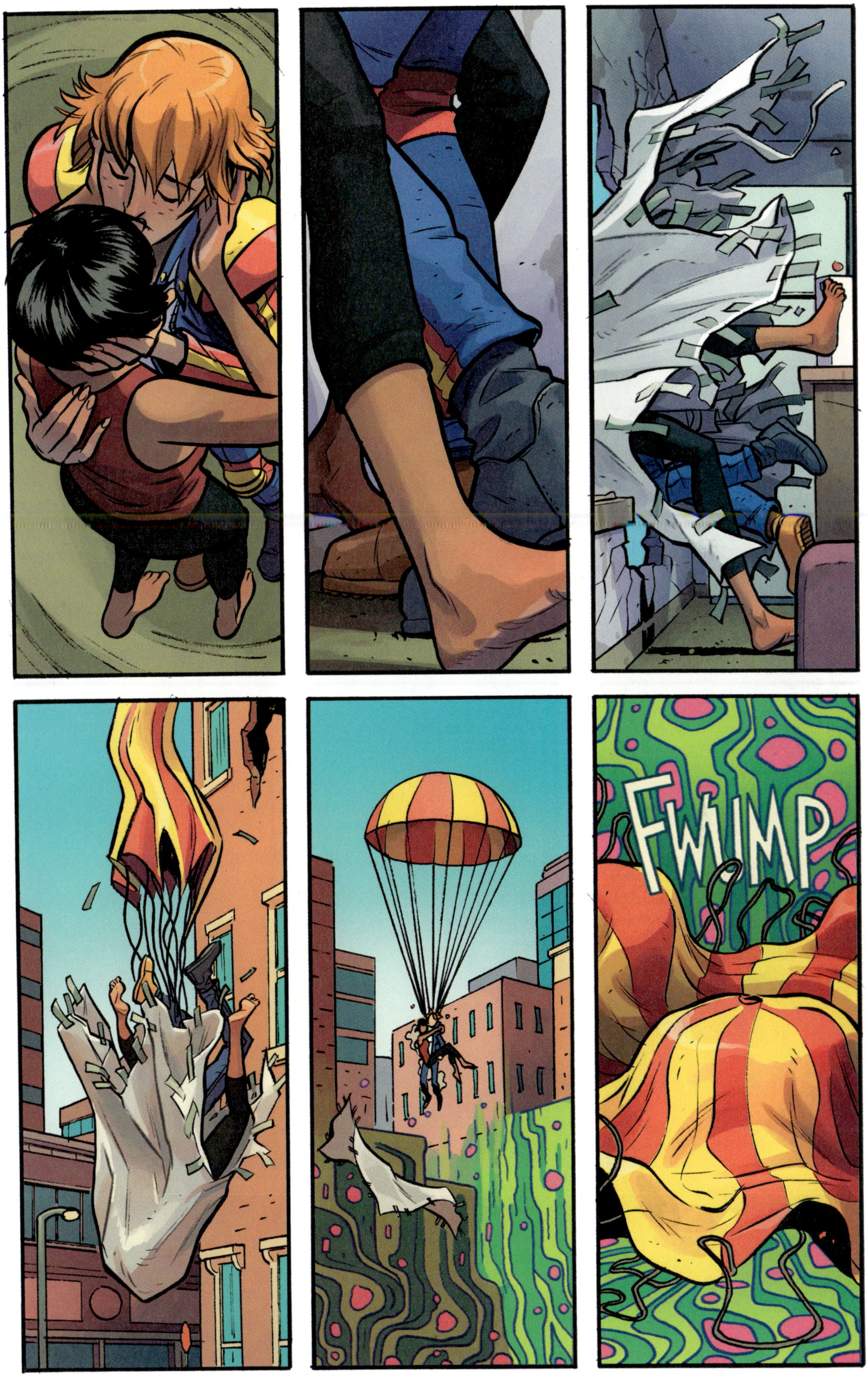
FWIMP

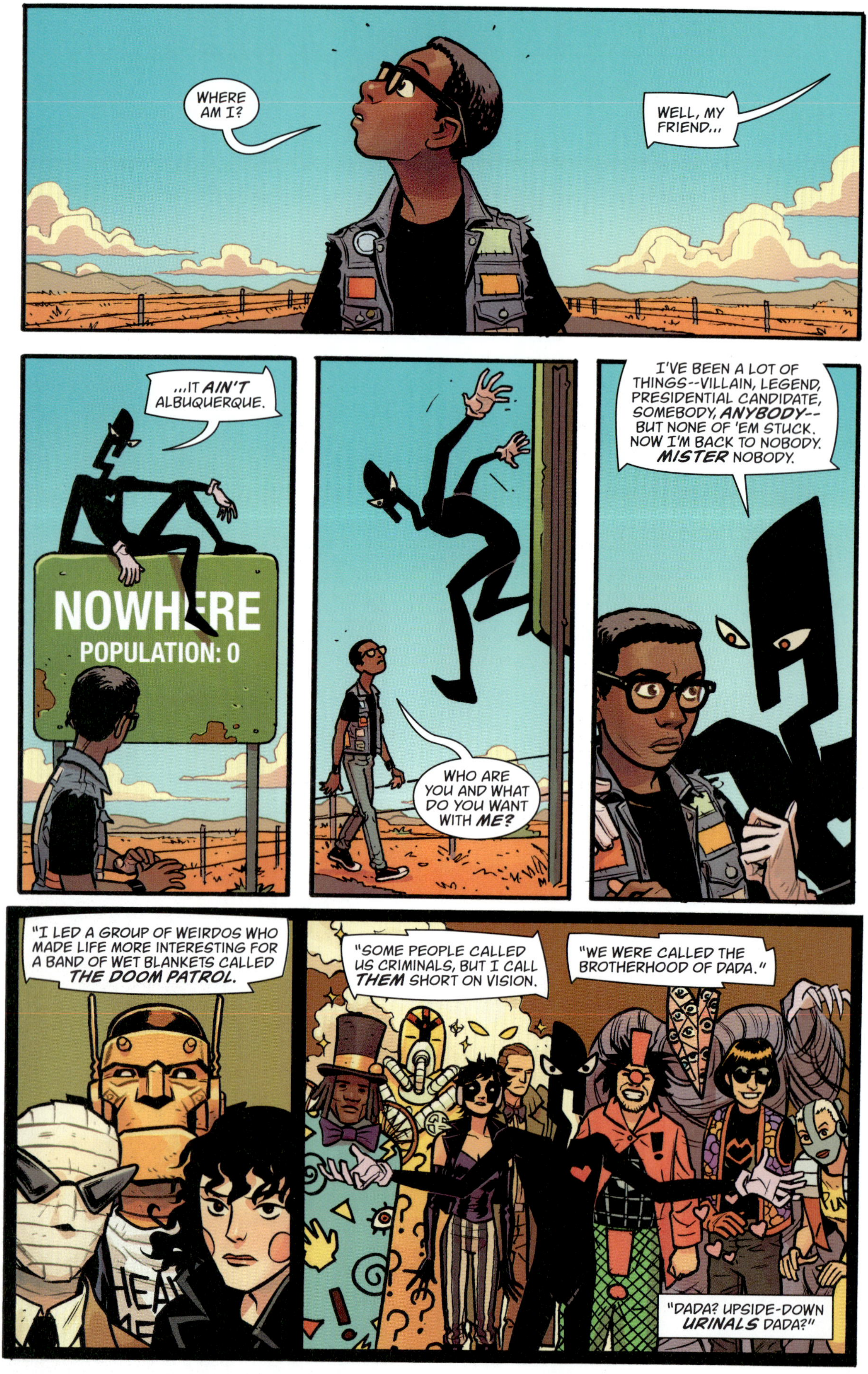

WHERE AM I?
WELL, MY FRIEND...
...IT AIN'T ALBUQUERQUE.
NOWHERE
POPULATION: 0
WHO ARE YOU AND WHAT DO YOU WANT WITH ME?
I'VE BEEN A LOT OF THINGS--VILLAIN, LEGEND, PRESIDENTIAL CANDIDATE, SOMEBODY, ANYBODY-- BUT NONE OF 'EM STUCK. NOW I'M BACK TO NOBODY. MISTER NOBODY.
"I LED A GROUP OF WEIRDOS WHO MADE LIFE MORE INTERESTING FOR A BAND OF WET BLANKETS CALLED THE DOOM PATROL.
"SOME PEOPLE CALLED US CRIMINALS, BUT I CALL THEM SHORT ON VISION.
"WE WERE CALLED THE BROTHERHOOD OF DADA."
"DADA? UPSIDE-DOWN URINALS DADA?"

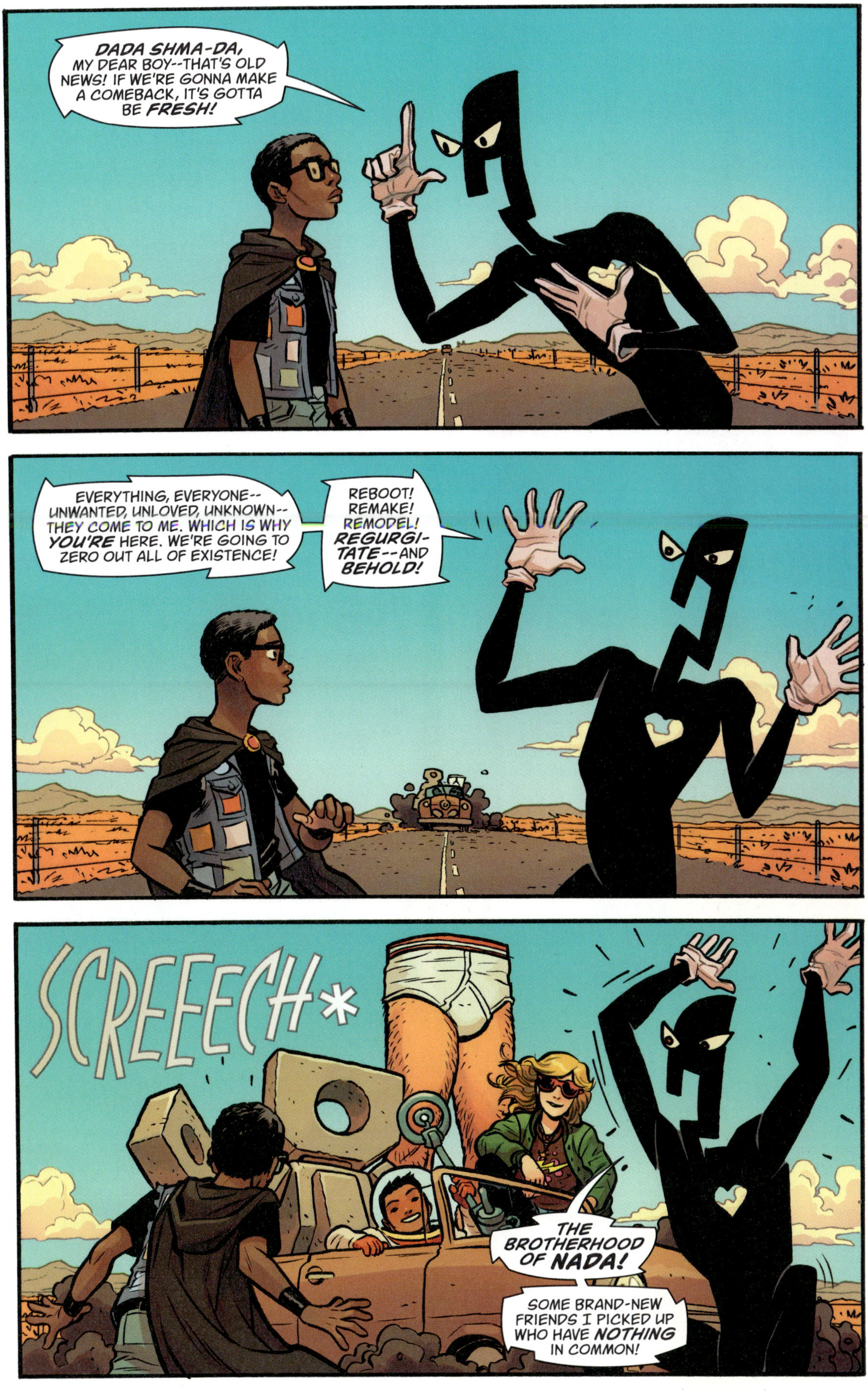
DADA SHMA-DA, MY DEAR BOY--THAT'S OLD NEWS! IF WE'RE GONNA MAKE A COMEBACK, IT'S GOTTA BE FRESH!
EVERYTHING, EVERYONE--UNWANTED, UNLOVED, UNKNOWN--THEY COME TO ME. WHICH IS WHY YOU'RE HERE. WE'RE GOING TO ZERO OUT ALL OF EXISTENCE!
REBOOT! REMAKE! REMODEL! REGURGI-TATE--AND BEHOLD!
SCREEECH*
THE BROTHERHOOD OF NADA!
SOME BRAND-NEW FRIENDS I PICKED UP WHO HAVE NOTHING IN COMMON!

"DAISY LANGDON: A PROMISING YOUNG SCIENTIST WHO HAD THE MISFORTUNE OF BOTCHING AN EXPERIMENT WITH RADIOACTIVE CEMENT.

"THE ACCIDENT RENDERED HER COLD AND INHUMAN. THE ONLY THING THAT KEEPS HER ALIVE IS FEEDING ON THE PAIN AND MISFORTUNE OF OTHERS, WHICH SHE'LL GLADLY BRING ABOUT WITH HER MONSTROUS STRENGTH--

"SHE'S KNOWN AS... *THE BRUTALIST!*

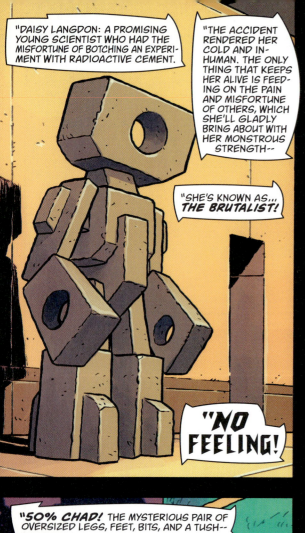

"*NO FEELING!*

"HECTOR ALVAREZ WAS JUST A MILD-MANNERED BOY WHO LOVED BUILDING SAND CASTLES AT THE BEACH, WHEN ONE DAY HE FOUND A METAL DETECTOR OF ALIEN ORIGIN. NOW HE UNCOVERS ADVENTURE, LOOSE CHANGE, AND ANYTHING ELSE! WHEREVER HE GOES, HE'S *HECTOR THE BOY DETECTOR!*

"*NO HIDING!*

"*50% CHAD!* THE MYSTERIOUS PAIR OF OVERSIZED LEGS, FEET, BITS, AND A TUSH--

"NOBODY KNOWS WHERE THEY COME FROM! DID THEY BELONG TO SOMEONE ELSE?! SOMEONE *LARGE?!* IS THERE MORE CHAD?!

"THE WHIFF OF FAILURE, THE CLAMMY SKIN-- THE MERE SIGHT OF THESE HAM HOCKS AND A BREATH OF HIS *CLOUD OF DESPERATION* WILL MAKE *ANYONE* QUIT!

"*NO PANTS!*

"*ALICE DEBRIES, 'THE BREEZE'!* EVEN FROM A YOUNG AGE, ALICE WAS AN ACE AT EVERYTHING! WHIZ KID, TRACK STAR, DARTS CHAMP--ALICE WAS SO GOOD AT EVERYTHING THAT PEOPLE JUST GOT BORED OF HER! SHE'S NEVER HAD IT HARD, AND THERE'S NOTHING THAT DON'T COME EASY!

"*NO PROBLEM!*"

AND YOU!

UN-*LOVED*. UN-*WANTED*. UN-*COOPERATIVE*--!

THE GREAT LUDINI, THE TEENAGE NOTHING!

THE MOST POWERFUL *WIELDER* OF *GONZO-SORCERY* THIS SIDE OF *CRAMALOT!*

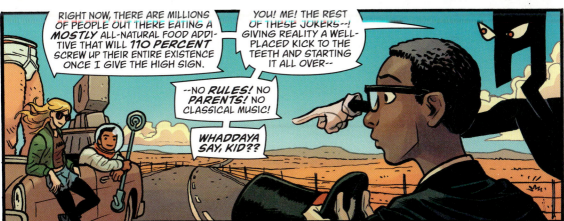

RIGHT NOW, THERE ARE MILLIONS OF PEOPLE OUT THERE EATING A *MOSTLY* ALL-NATURAL FOOD ADDITIVE THAT WILL *110 PERCENT* SCREW UP THEIR ENTIRE EXISTENCE ONCE I GIVE THE HIGH SIGN.

--NO *RULES!* NO *PARENTS!* NO CLASSICAL MUSIC!

WHADDAYA SAY, KID??

YOU! ME! THE REST OF THESE *JOKERS*--! GIVING REALITY A WELL-PLACED KICK TO THE TEETH AND STARTING IT ALL OVER--

SURE... WHY NOT? I DON'T HAVE ANY BETTER OFFERS.

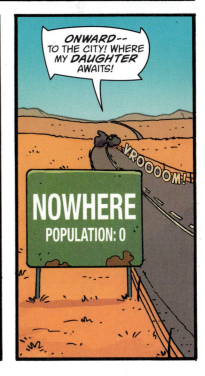

ONWARD-- TO THE CITY! WHERE MY *DAUGHTER* AWAITS!

VROOOOM!

NOWHERE
POPULATION: 0

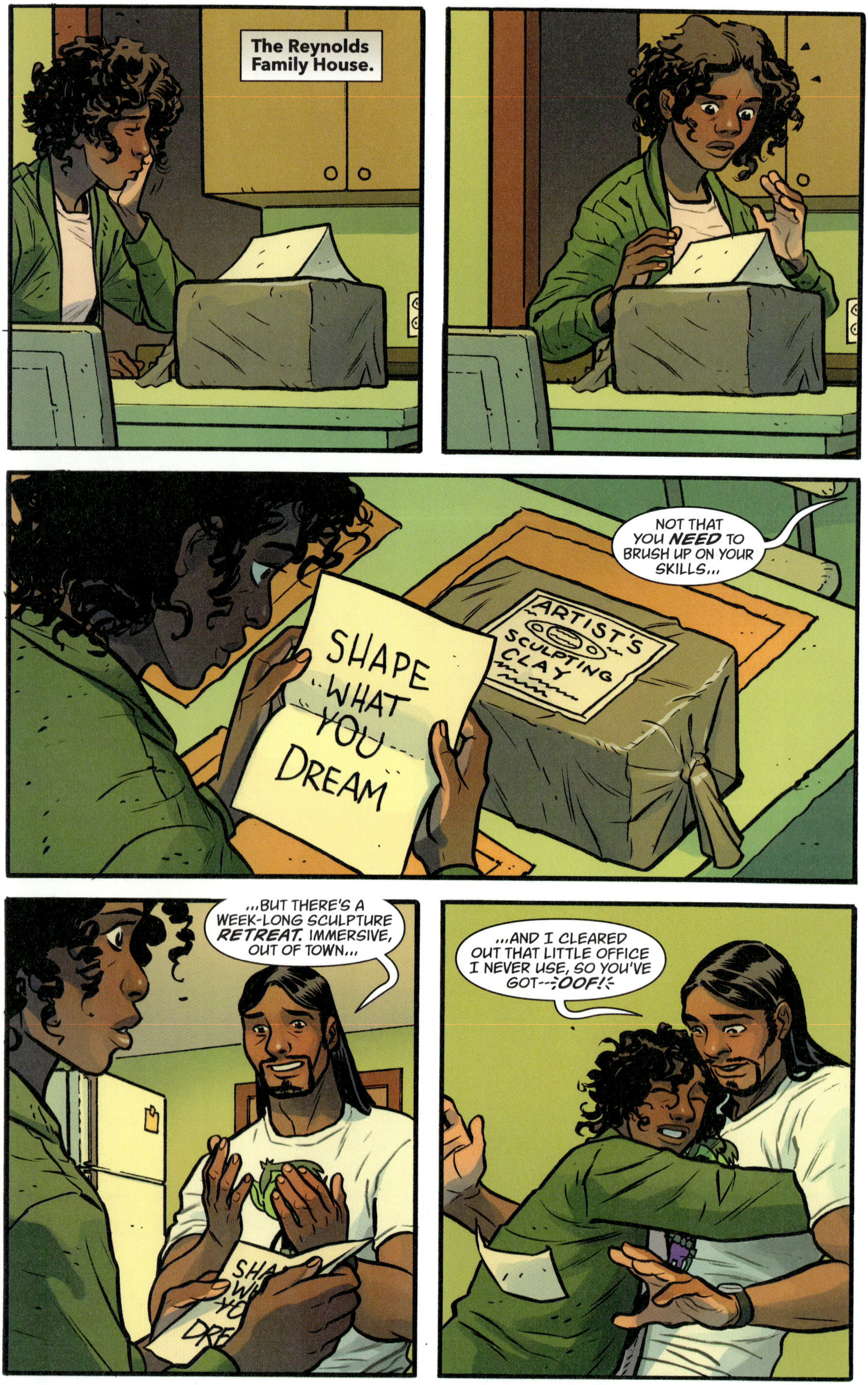
The Reynolds Family House.
NOT THAT YOU NEED TO BRUSH UP ON YOUR SKILLS...
SHAPE WHAT YOU DREAM
ARTIST'S SCULPTING CLAY
...BUT THERE'S A WEEK-LONG SCULPTURE RETREAT. IMMERSIVE, OUT OF TOWN...
...AND I CLEARED OUT THAT LITTLE OFFICE I NEVER USE, SO YOU'VE GOT-- OOF!

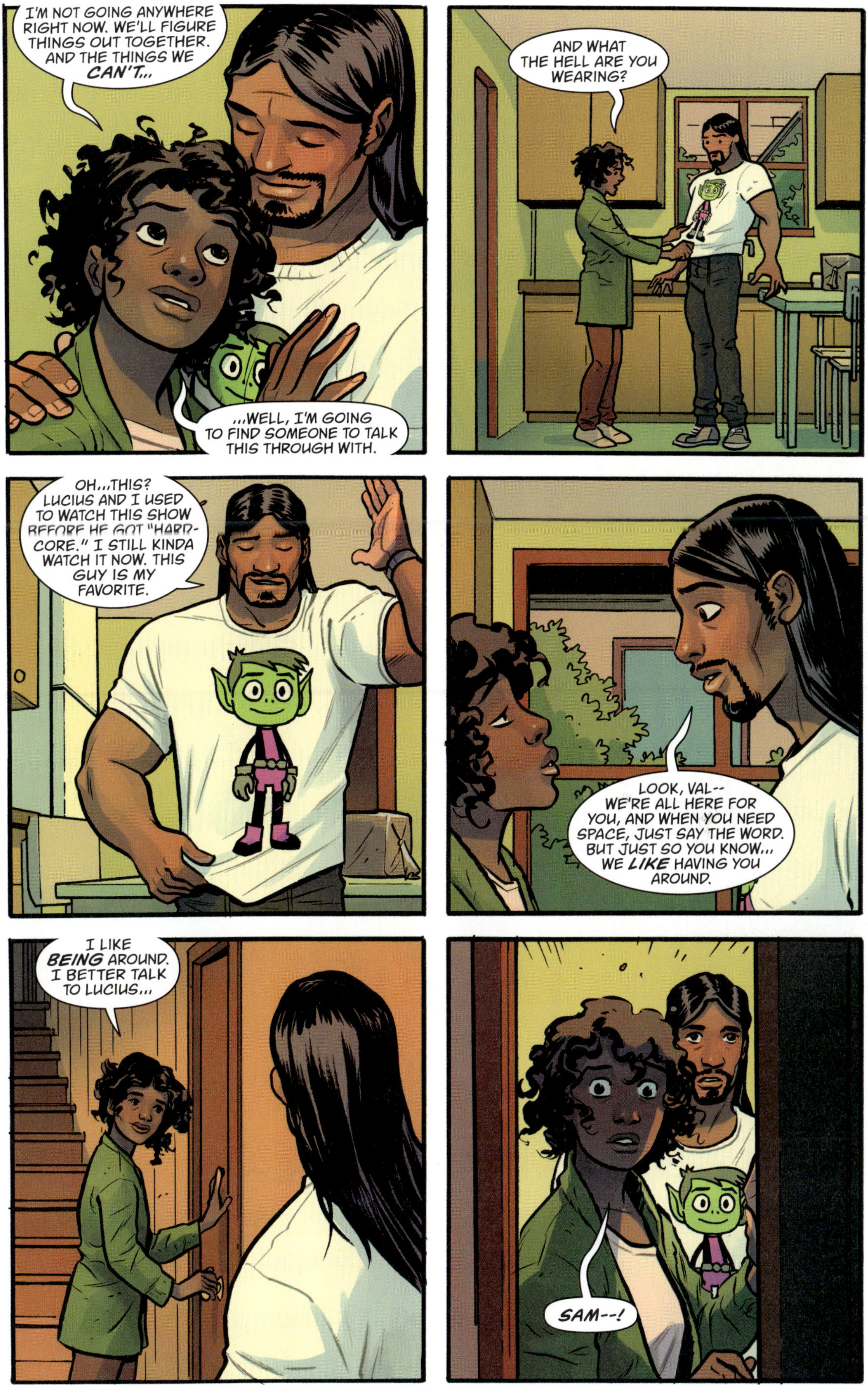
I'M NOT GOING ANYWHERE RIGHT NOW. WE'LL FIGURE THINGS OUT TOGETHER. AND THE THINGS WE *CAN'T*...
...WELL, I'M GOING TO FIND SOMEONE TO TALK THIS THROUGH WITH.
AND WHAT THE HELL ARE YOU WEARING?
OH...THIS? LUCIUS AND I USED TO WATCH THIS SHOW BEFORE HE GOT "HARD-CORE." I STILL KINDA WATCH IT NOW. THIS GUY IS MY FAVORITE.
LOOK, VAL-- WE'RE ALL HERE FOR YOU, AND WHEN YOU NEED SPACE, JUST SAY THE WORD. BUT JUST SO YOU KNOW... WE *LIKE* HAVING YOU AROUND.
I LIKE *BEING* AROUND. I BETTER TALK TO LUCIUS...
SAM--!

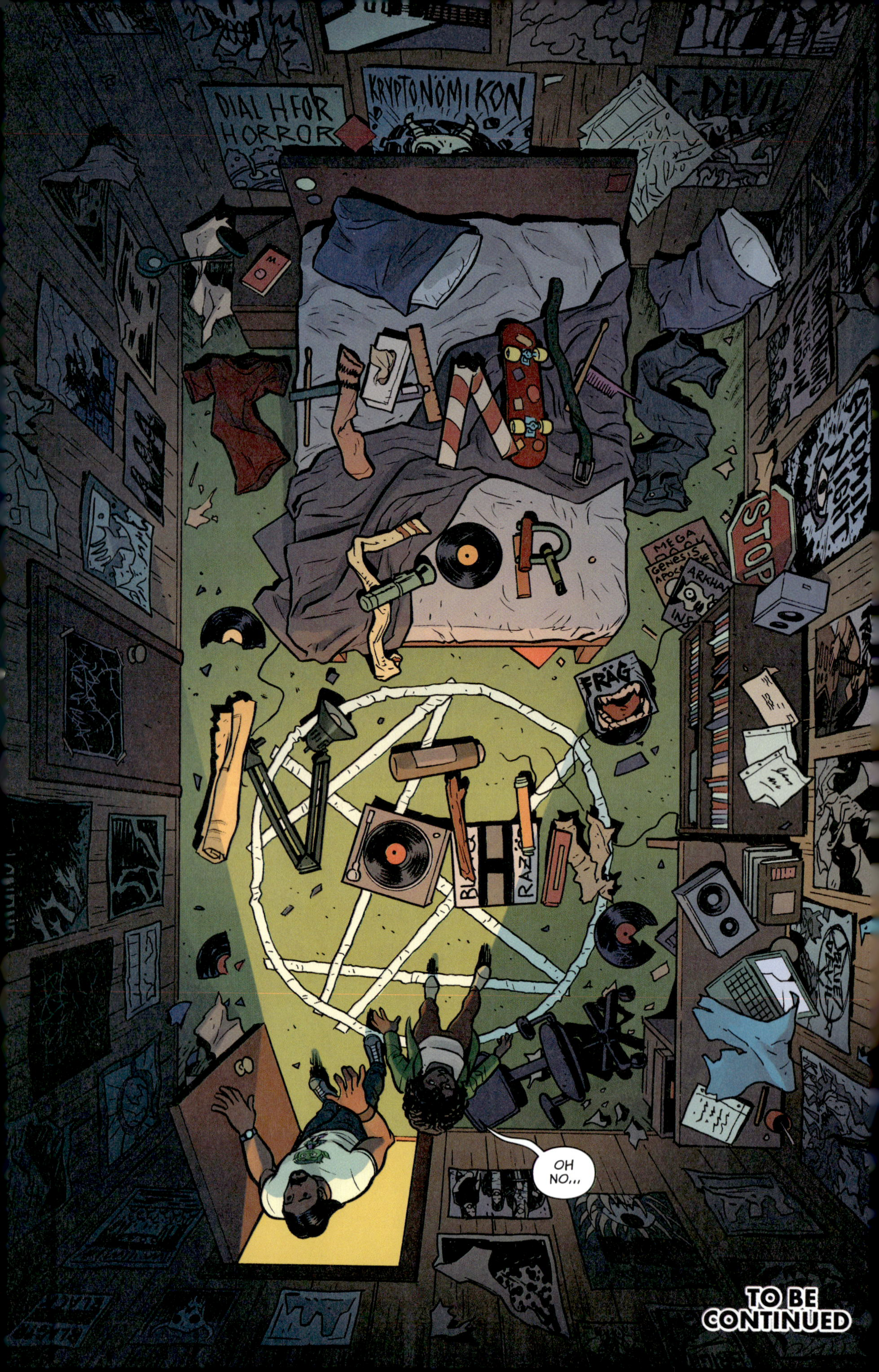
DIAL H FOR HORROR
KRYPTONÖMIKON
STOP
FRÄG
OH NO...
TO BE CONTINUED

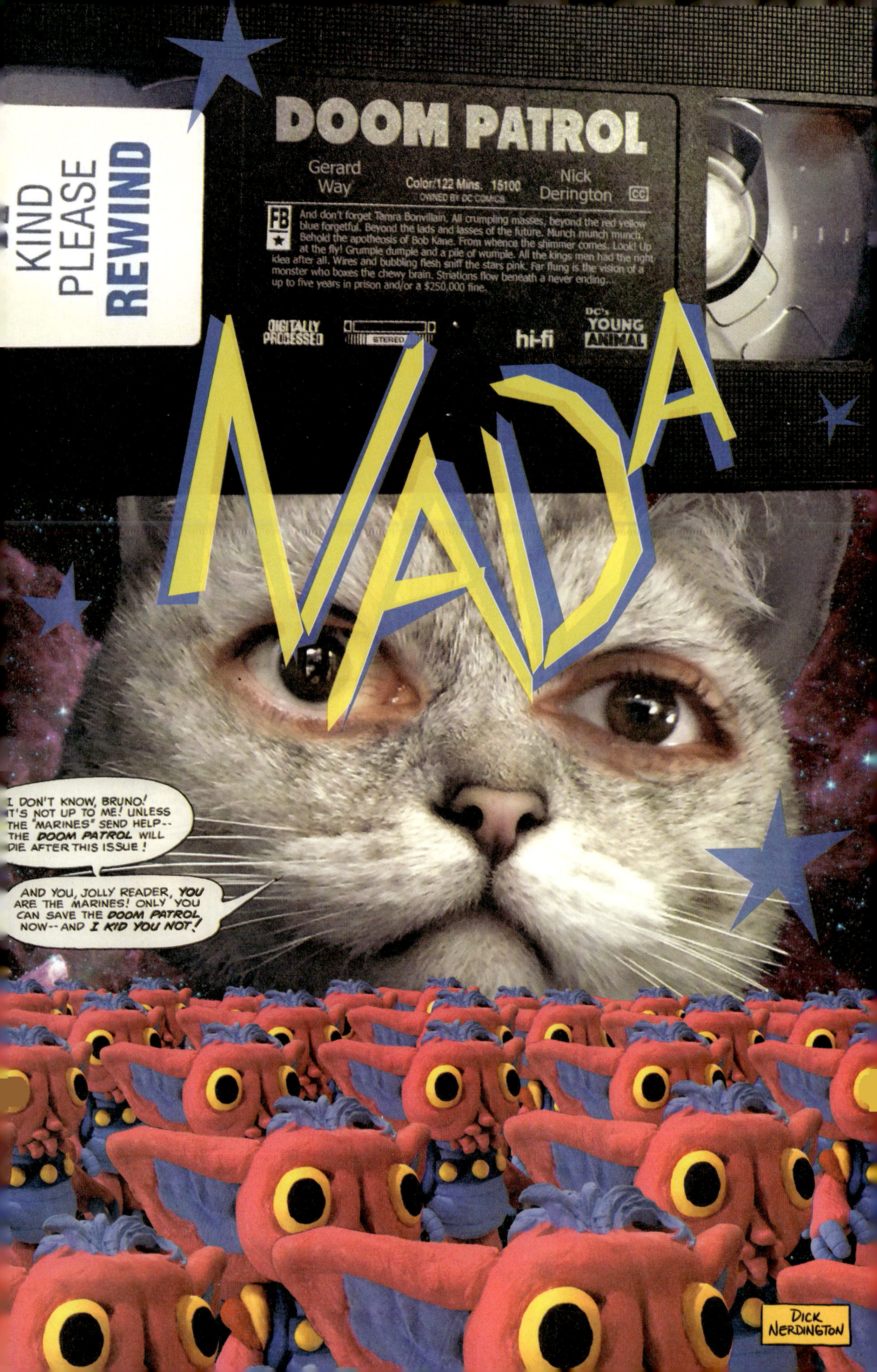
KIND PLEASE REWIND
DOOM PATROL
Gerard Way
Color/122 Mins. 15100
OWNED BY DC COMICS
Nick Derington
CC
FB
And don't forget Tamra Bonvillain. All crumpling masses, beyond the red yellow blue forgetful. Beyond the lads and lasses of the future. Munch munch munch. Behold the apotheosis of Bob Kane. From whence the shimmer comes. Look! Up at the fly! Grumple dumple and a pile of wumple. All the kings men had the right idea after all. Wires and bubbling flesh sniff the stars pink. Far flung is the vision of a monster who boxes the chewy brain. Striations flow beneath a never ending... up to five years in prison and/or a $250,000 fine.
DIGITALLY PROCESSED
STEREO
hi-fi
DC's YOUNG ANIMAL
NADA
I DON'T KNOW, BRUNO! IT'S NOT UP TO ME! UNLESS THE "MARINES" SEND HELP-- THE DOOM PATROL WILL DIE AFTER THIS ISSUE!
AND YOU, JOLLY READER, YOU ARE THE MARINES! ONLY YOU CAN SAVE THE DOOM PATROL NOW-- AND I KID YOU NOT!
DICK NERDINGTON

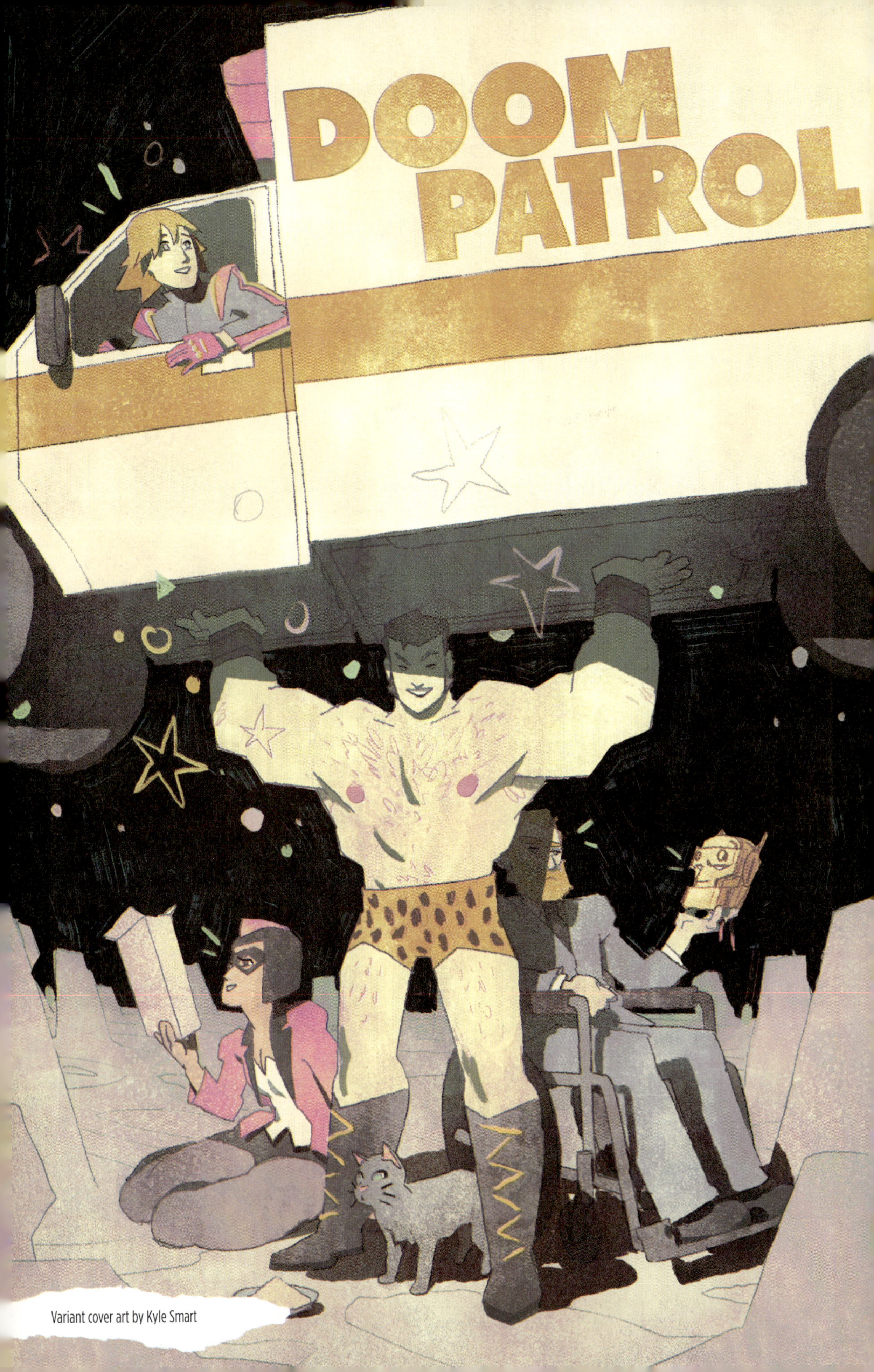
DOOM
PATROL

Variant cover art by Kyle Smart

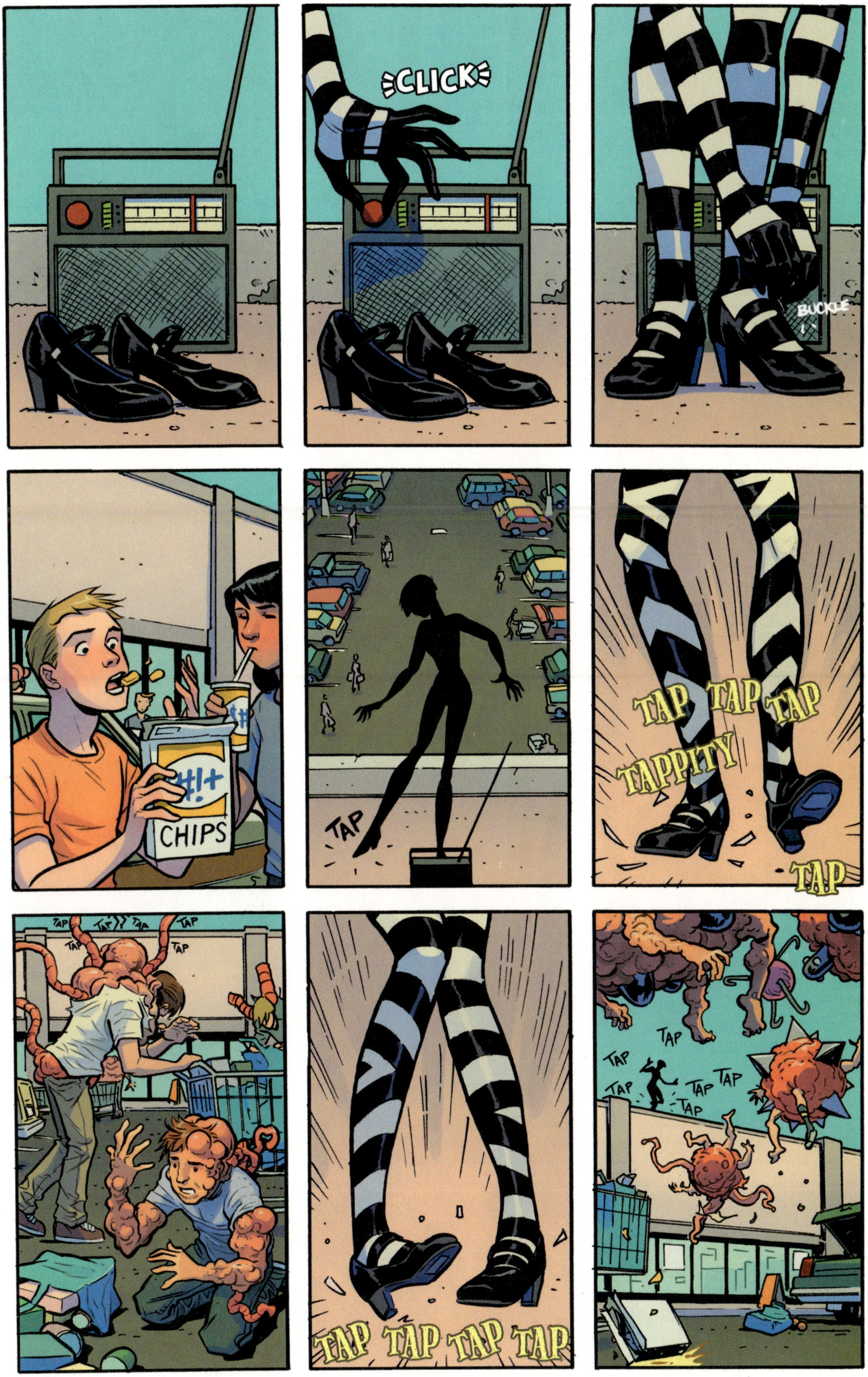
CLICK
BUCKLE
CHIPS
TAP
TAP TAP TAP
TAPPITY
TAP
TAP TAP TAP TAP
TAP
TAP
TAP
TAP TAP
TAP

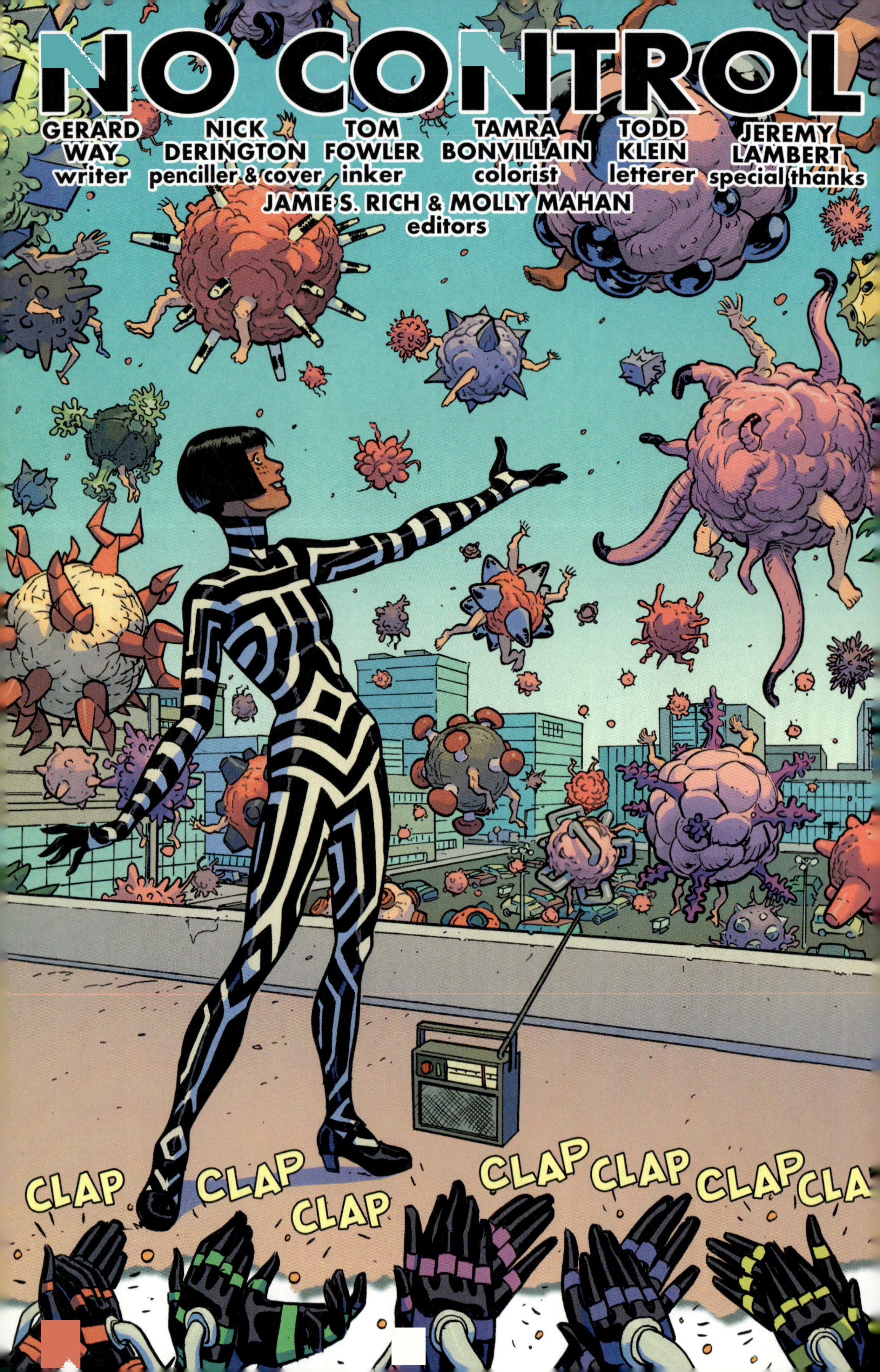
NO CONTROL
GERARD WAY writer
NICK DERINGTON penciller & cover
TOM FOWLER inker
TAMRA BONVILLAIN colorist
TODD KLEIN letterer
JEREMY LAMBERT special thanks
JAMIE S. RICH & MOLLY MAHAN editors
CLAP
CLAP
CLAP
CLAP
CLAP
CLAP
CLA

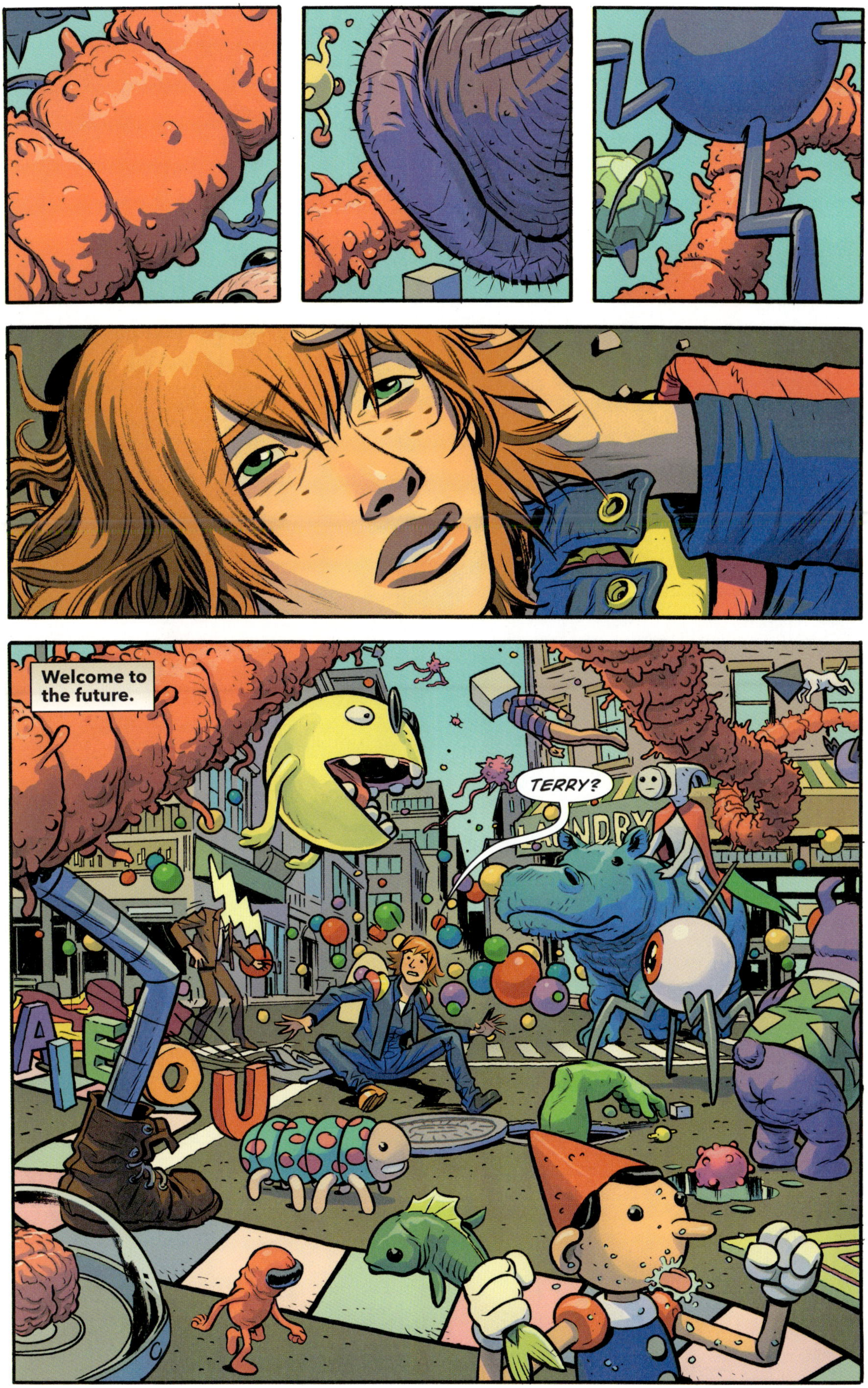
Welcome to the future.
TERRY?

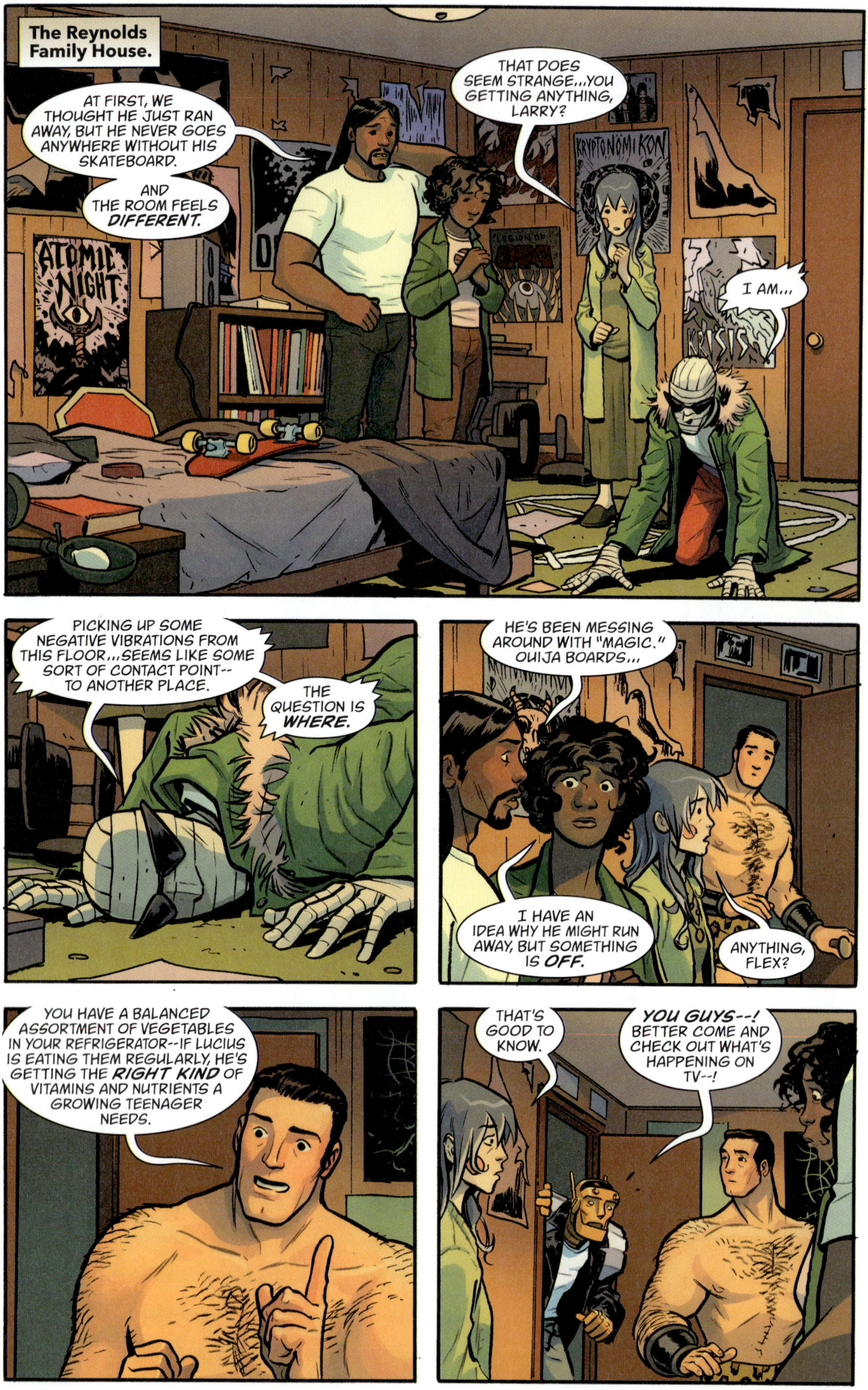
The Reynolds Family House.
AT FIRST, WE THOUGHT HE JUST RAN AWAY, BUT HE NEVER GOES ANYWHERE WITHOUT HIS SKATEBOARD.
AND THE ROOM FEELS DIFFERENT.
THAT DOES SEEM STRANGE... YOU GETTING ANYTHING, LARRY?
I AM...
ATOMIC NIGHT
KRYPTONOMIKON
KRISIS
PICKING UP SOME NEGATIVE VIBRATIONS FROM THIS FLOOR... SEEMS LIKE SOME SORT OF CONTACT POINT-- TO ANOTHER PLACE.
THE QUESTION IS WHERE.
HE'S BEEN MESSING AROUND WITH "MAGIC." OUIJA BOARDS...
I HAVE AN IDEA WHY HE MIGHT RUN AWAY, BUT SOMETHING IS OFF.
ANYTHING, FLEX?
YOU HAVE A BALANCED ASSORTMENT OF VEGETABLES IN YOUR REFRIGERATOR--IF LUCIUS IS EATING THEM REGULARLY, HE'S GETTING THE RIGHT KIND OF VITAMINS AND NUTRIENTS A GROWING TEENAGER NEEDS.
THAT'S GOOD TO KNOW.
YOU GUYS--! BETTER COME AND CHECK OUT WHAT'S HAPPENING ON TV--!

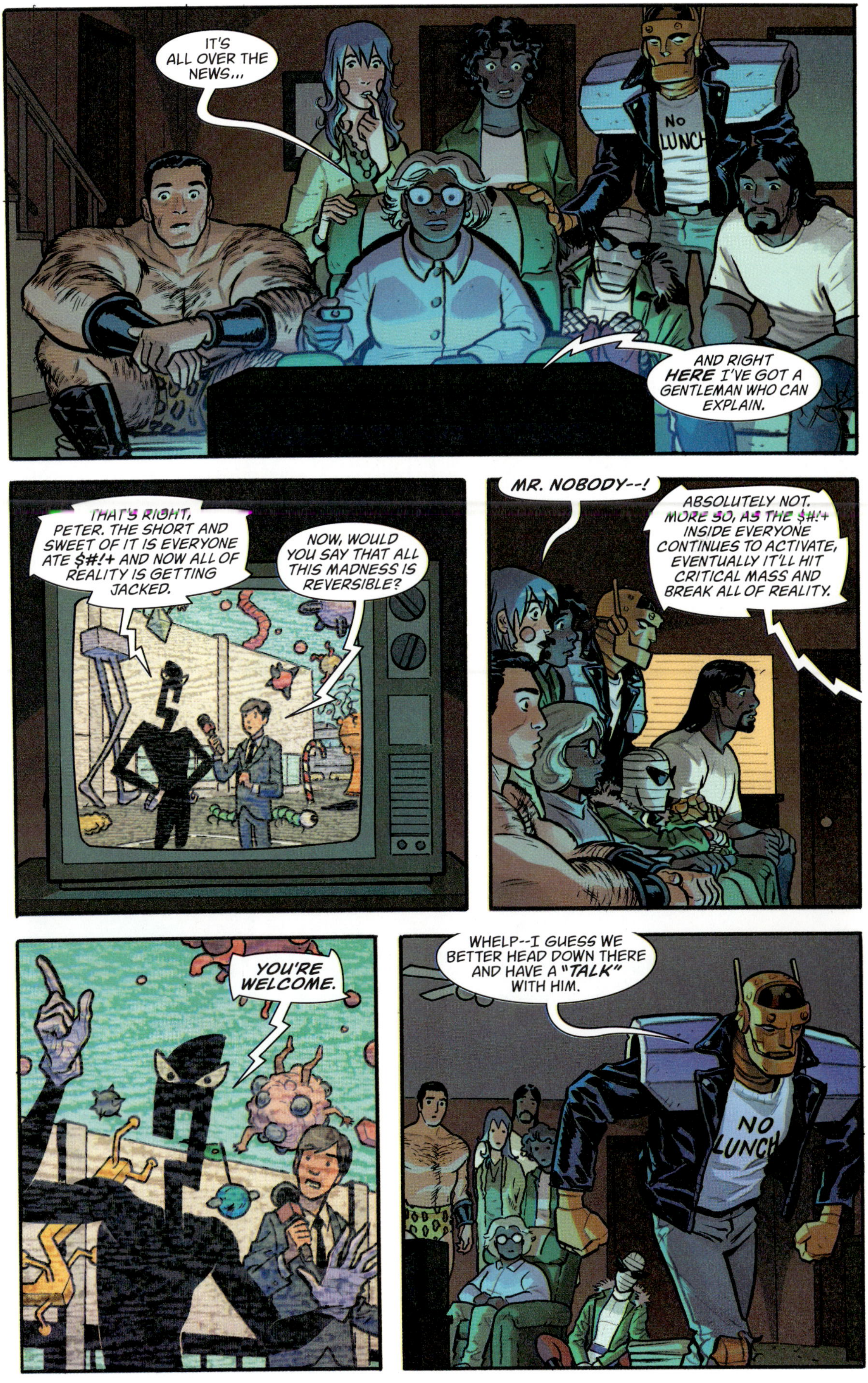
IT'S ALL OVER THE NEWS...
AND RIGHT HERE I'VE GOT A GENTLEMAN WHO CAN EXPLAIN.
THAT'S RIGHT, PETER. THE SHORT AND SWEET OF IT IS EVERYONE ATE $#!+ AND NOW ALL OF REALITY IS GETTING JACKED.
NOW, WOULD YOU SAY THAT ALL THIS MADNESS IS REVERSIBLE?
MR. NOBODY--!
ABSOLUTELY NOT. MORE SO, AS THE $#!+ INSIDE EVERYONE CONTINUES TO ACTIVATE, EVENTUALLY IT'LL HIT CRITICAL MASS AND BREAK ALL OF REALITY.
YOU'RE WELCOME.
WHELP--I GUESS WE BETTER HEAD DOWN THERE AND HAVE A "TALK" WITH HIM.
NO LUNCH

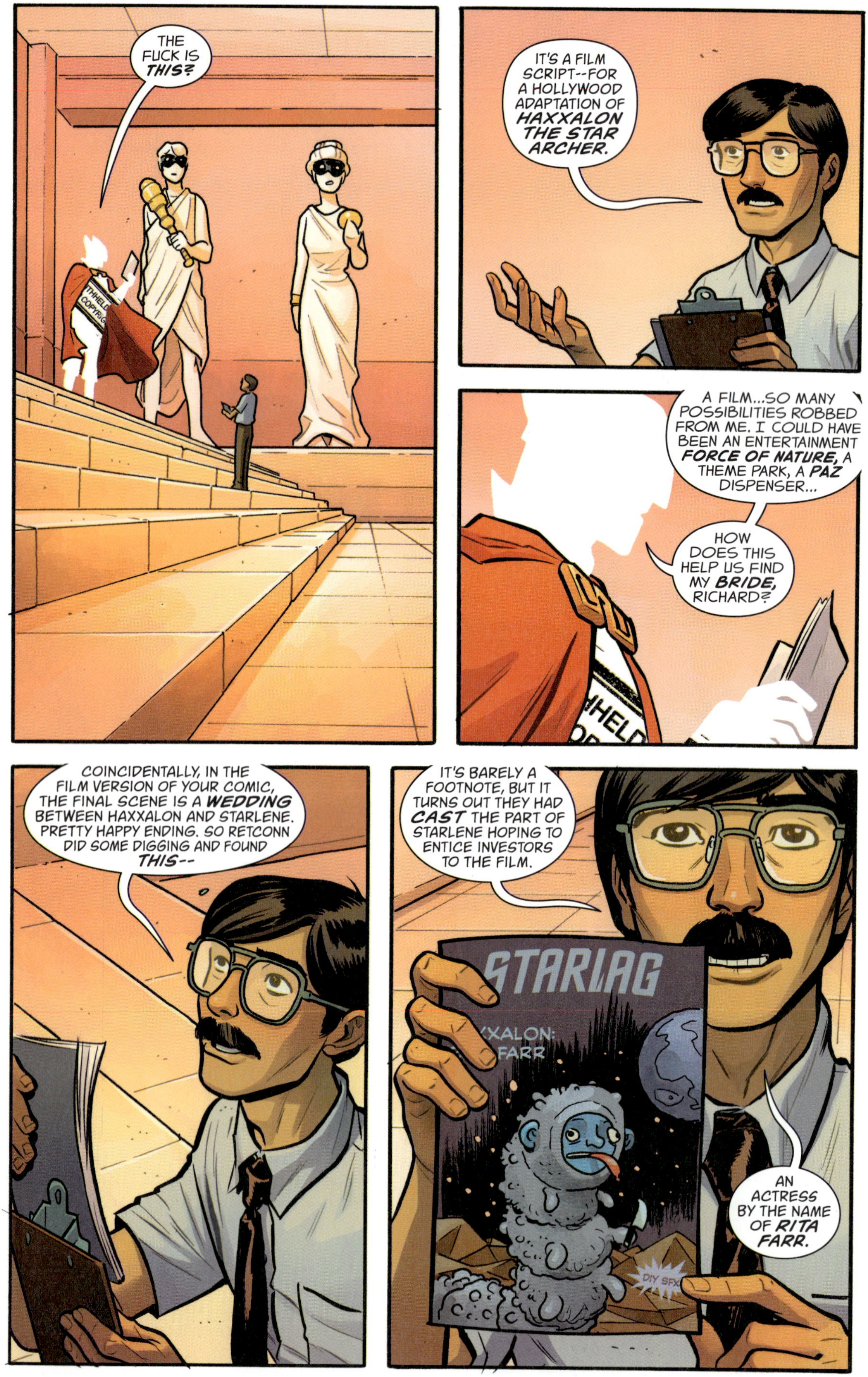
THE FUCK IS THIS?
IT'S A FILM SCRIPT--FOR A HOLLYWOOD ADAPTATION OF HAXXALON THE STAR ARCHER.
A FILM...SO MANY POSSIBILITIES ROBBED FROM ME. I COULD HAVE BEEN AN ENTERTAINMENT FORCE OF NATURE, A THEME PARK, A PAZ DISPENSER...
HOW DOES THIS HELP US FIND MY BRIDE, RICHARD?
COINCIDENTALLY, IN THE FILM VERSION OF YOUR COMIC, THE FINAL SCENE IS A WEDDING BETWEEN HAXXALON AND STARLENE. PRETTY HAPPY ENDING. SO RETCONN DID SOME DIGGING AND FOUND THIS--
IT'S BARELY A FOOTNOTE, BUT IT TURNS OUT THEY HAD CAST THE PART OF STARLENE HOPING TO ENTICE INVESTORS TO THE FILM.
STARLAG
FARR
DIY SFX
AN ACTRESS BY THE NAME OF RITA FARR.

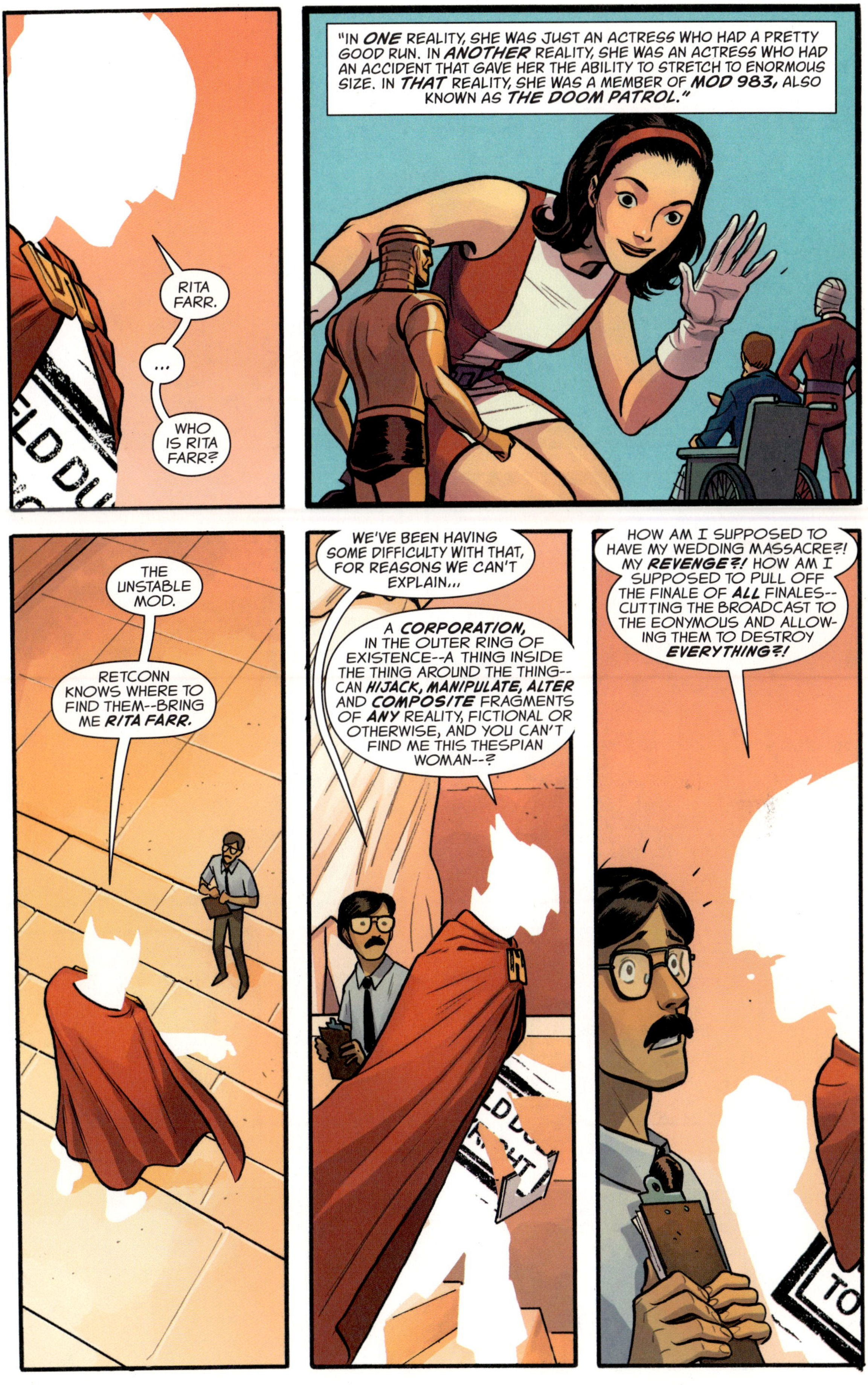
"IN ONE REALITY, SHE WAS JUST AN ACTRESS WHO HAD A PRETTY GOOD RUN. IN ANOTHER REALITY, SHE WAS AN ACTRESS WHO HAD AN ACCIDENT THAT GAVE HER THE ABILITY TO STRETCH TO ENORMOUS SIZE. IN THAT REALITY, SHE WAS A MEMBER OF MOD 983, ALSO KNOWN AS THE DOOM PATROL."
RITA FARR.
...
WHO IS RITA FARR?
THE UNSTABLE MOD.
RETCONN KNOWS WHERE TO FIND THEM--BRING ME RITA FARR.
WE'VE BEEN HAVING SOME DIFFICULTY WITH THAT, FOR REASONS WE CAN'T EXPLAIN...
A CORPORATION, IN THE OUTER RING OF EXISTENCE--A THING INSIDE THE THING AROUND THE THING--CAN HIJACK, MANIPULATE, ALTER AND COMPOSITE FRAGMENTS OF ANY REALITY, FICTIONAL OR OTHERWISE, AND YOU CAN'T FIND ME THIS THESPIAN WOMAN--?
HOW AM I SUPPOSED TO HAVE MY WEDDING MASSACRE?! MY REVENGE?! HOW AM I SUPPOSED TO PULL OFF THE FINALE OF ALL FINALES--CUTTING THE BROADCAST TO THE EONYMOUS AND ALLOWING THEM TO DESTROY EVERYTHING?!

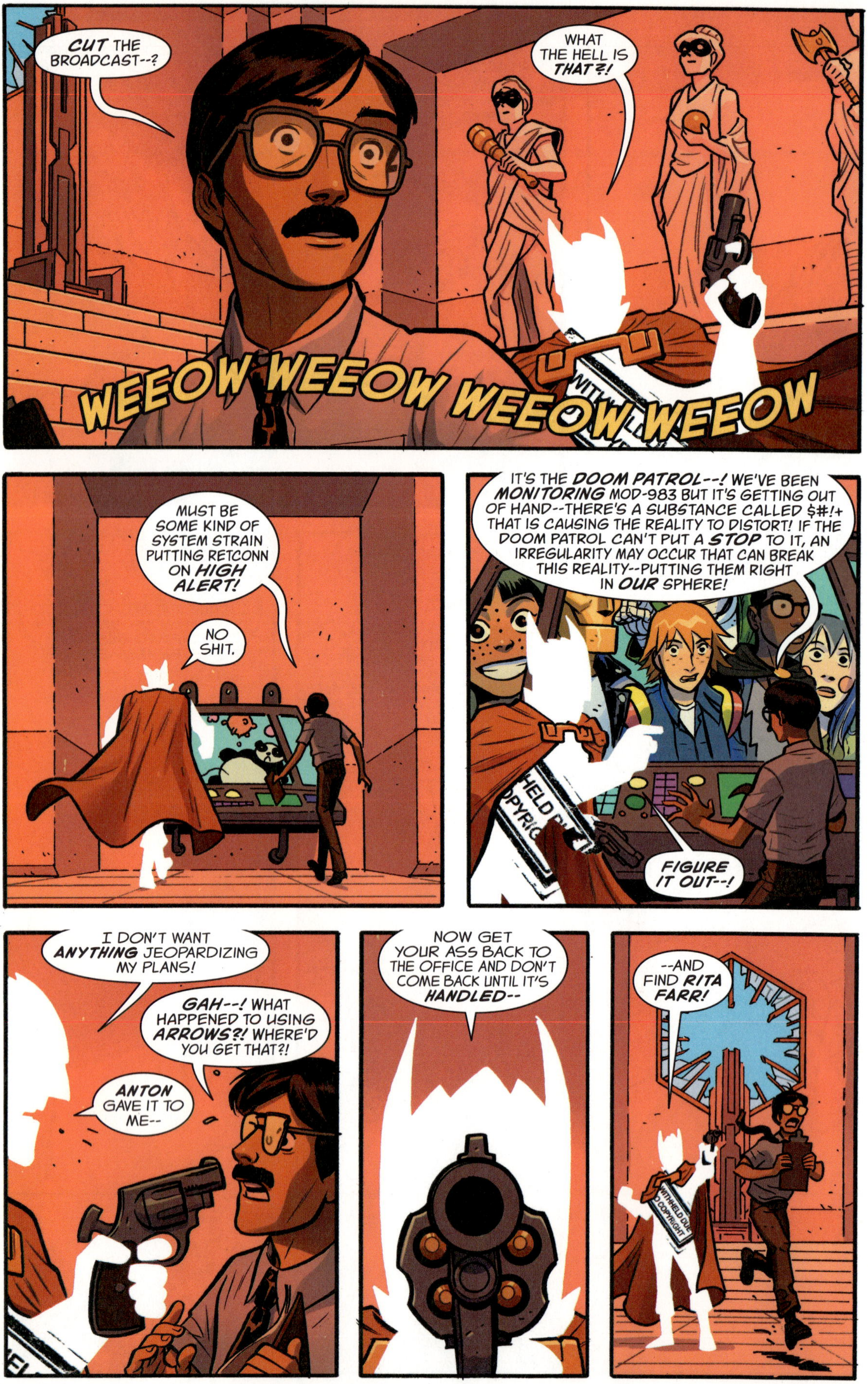
CUT THE BROADCAST--?
WHAT THE HELL IS THAT?!
WEEOW WEEOW WEEOW WEEOW
WITHHELD DUE TO COPYRIGHT
MUST BE SOME KIND OF SYSTEM STRAIN PUTTING RETCONN ON HIGH ALERT!
NO SHIT.
IT'S THE DOOM PATROL--! WE'VE BEEN MONITORING MOD-983 BUT IT'S GETTING OUT OF HAND--THERE'S A SUBSTANCE CALLED $#!+ THAT IS CAUSING THE REALITY TO DISTORT! IF THE DOOM PATROL CAN'T PUT A STOP TO IT, AN IRREGULARITY MAY OCCUR THAT CAN BREAK THIS REALITY--PUTTING THEM RIGHT IN OUR SPHERE!
FIGURE IT OUT--!
I DON'T WANT ANYTHING JEOPARDIZING MY PLANS!
GAH--! WHAT HAPPENED TO USING ARROWS?! WHERE'D YOU GET THAT?!
ANTON GAVE IT TO ME--
NOW GET YOUR ASS BACK TO THE OFFICE AND DON'T COME BACK UNTIL IT'S HANDLED--
--AND FIND RITA FARR!
WITHHELD DUE TO COPYRIGHT

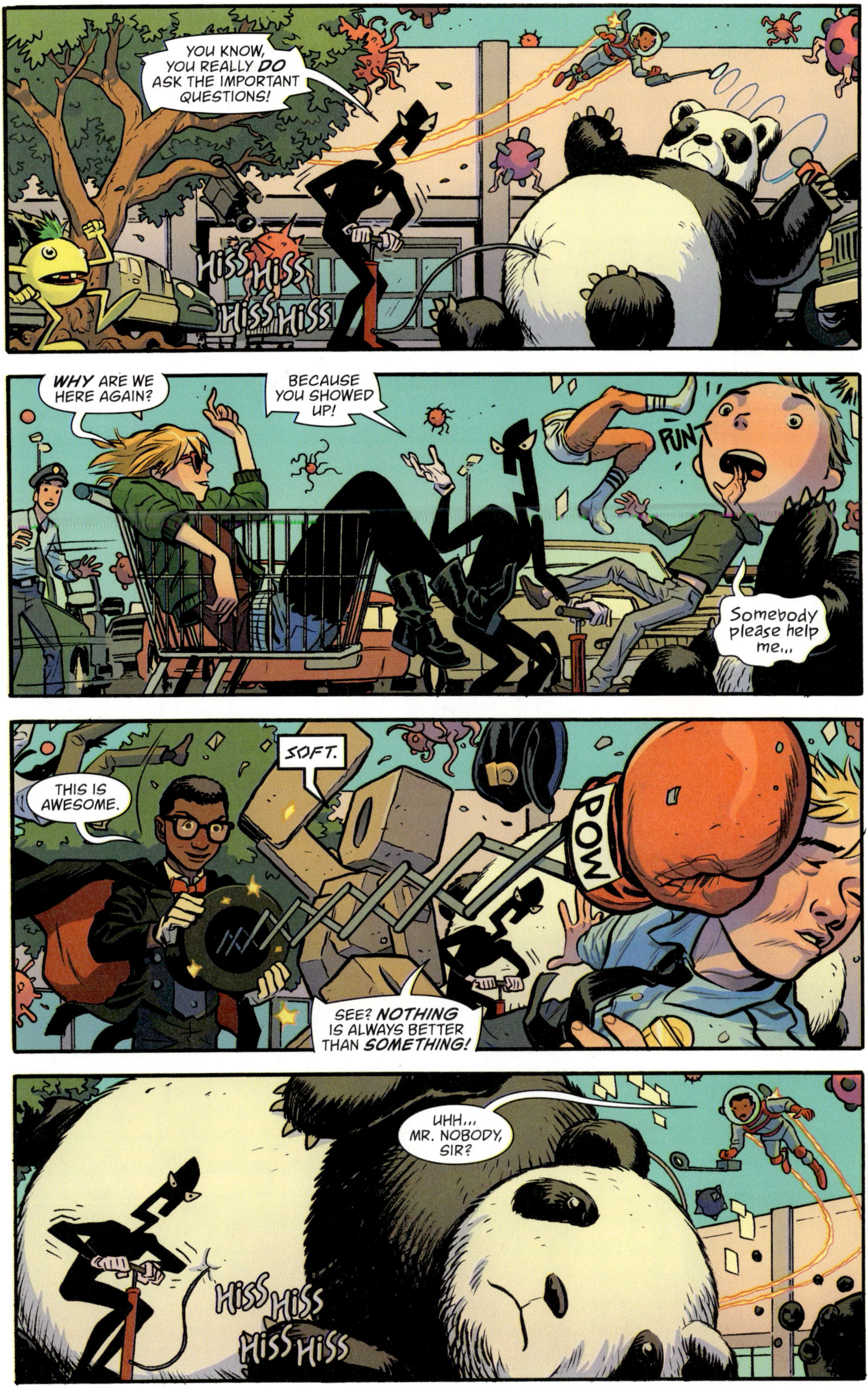
YOU KNOW, YOU REALLY DO ASK THE IMPORTANT QUESTIONS!
HISS HISS HISS HISS
WHY ARE WE HERE AGAIN?
BECAUSE YOU SHOWED UP!
PUNT
Somebody please help me...
THIS IS AWESOME.
SOFT.
POW
SEE? NOTHING IS ALWAYS BETTER THAN SOMETHING!
UHH... MR. NOBODY, SIR?
HISS HISS HISS HISS

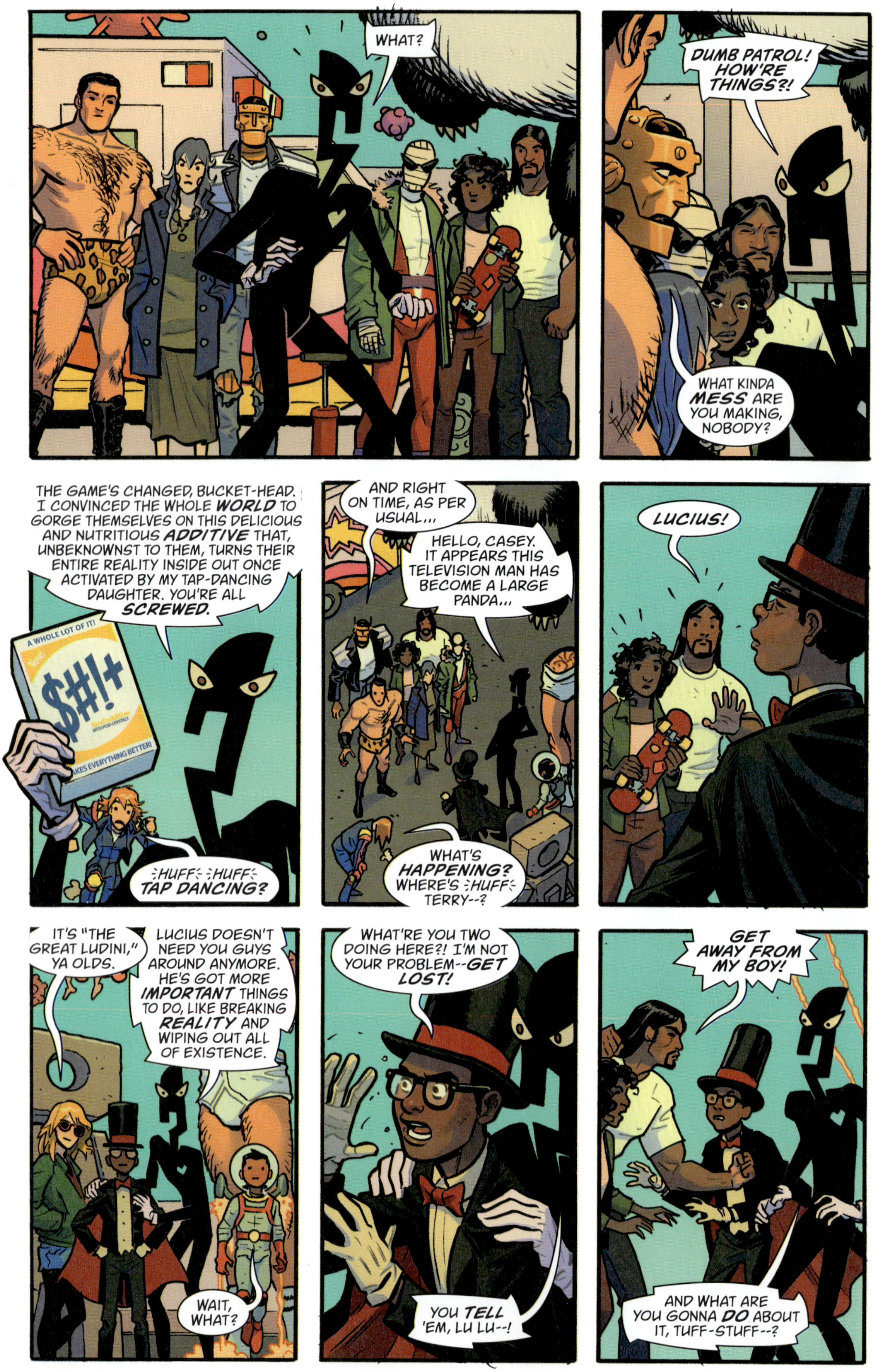
WHAT?
DUMB PATROL! HOW'RE THINGS?!
WHAT KINDA MESS ARE YOU MAKING, NOBODY?
THE GAME'S CHANGED, BUCKET-HEAD. I CONVINCED THE WHOLE WORLD TO GORGE THEMSELVES ON THIS DELICIOUS AND NUTRITIOUS ADDITIVE THAT, UNBEKNOWNST TO THEM, TURNS THEIR ENTIRE REALITY INSIDE OUT ONCE ACTIVATED BY MY TAP-DANCING DAUGHTER. YOU'RE ALL SCREWED.
A WHOLE LOT OF IT!
$#!+
MAKES EVERYTHING BETTER!
HUFF HUFF TAP DANCING?
AND RIGHT ON TIME, AS PER USUAL...
HELLO, CASEY. IT APPEARS THIS TELEVISION MAN HAS BECOME A LARGE PANDA...
WHAT'S HAPPENING? WHERE'S HUFF TERRY--?
LUCIUS!
IT'S "THE GREAT LUDINI," YA OLDS.
LUCIUS DOESN'T NEED YOU GUYS AROUND ANYMORE. HE'S GOT MORE IMPORTANT THINGS TO DO, LIKE BREAKING REALITY AND WIPING OUT ALL OF EXISTENCE.
WAIT, WHAT?
WHAT'RE YOU TWO DOING HERE?! I'M NOT YOUR PROBLEM--GET LOST!
YOU TELL 'EM, LU LU--!
GET AWAY FROM MY BOY!
AND WHAT ARE YOU GONNA DO ABOUT IT, TUFF-STUFF--?

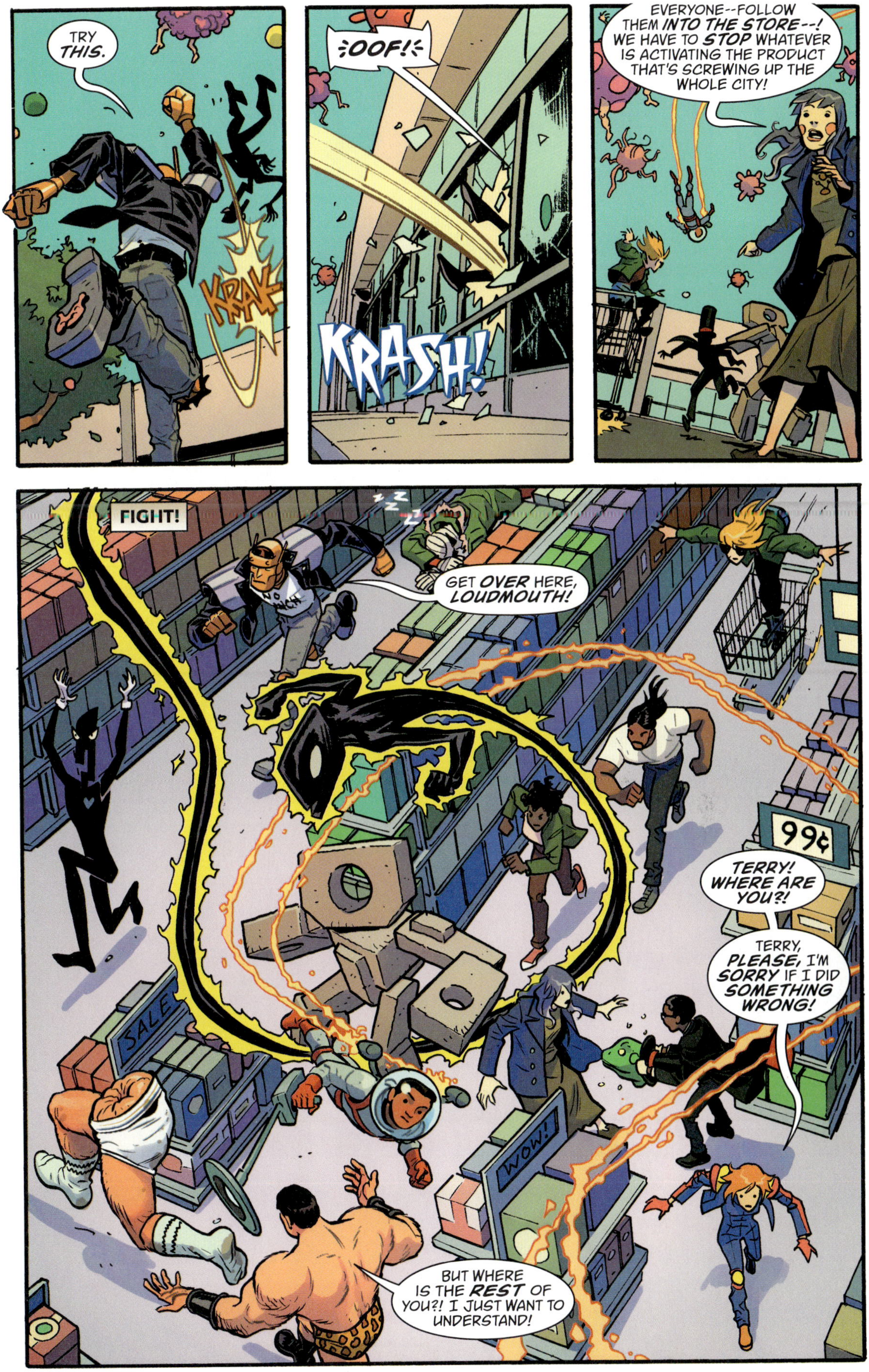
TRY THIS.
KRAK
OOF!
KRASH!
EVERYONE--FOLLOW THEM INTO THE STORE--! WE HAVE TO STOP WHATEVER IS ACTIVATING THE PRODUCT THAT'S SCREWING UP THE WHOLE CITY!
FIGHT!
GET OVER HERE, LOUDMOUTH!
99¢
TERRY! WHERE ARE YOU?!
TERRY, PLEASE, I'M SORRY IF I DID SOMETHING WRONG!
SALE
WOW!
BUT WHERE IS THE REST OF YOU?! I JUST WANT TO UNDERSTAND!

THE SMELL... LIKE FAILURE... WEAKENING...

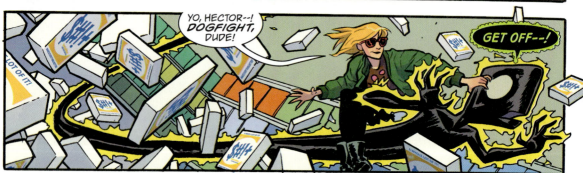

YO, HECTOR--! DOGFIGHT, DUDE!

A LOT OF IT!

GET OFF--!

POW

TERRY?!

IF YOUR ONLY OPTION FOR SOLVING PROBLEMS IS VIOLENCE--

FLICK

--I GOT YOU COVERED!

WAIT, LUCIUS, JUST HOLD ON, DON'T--

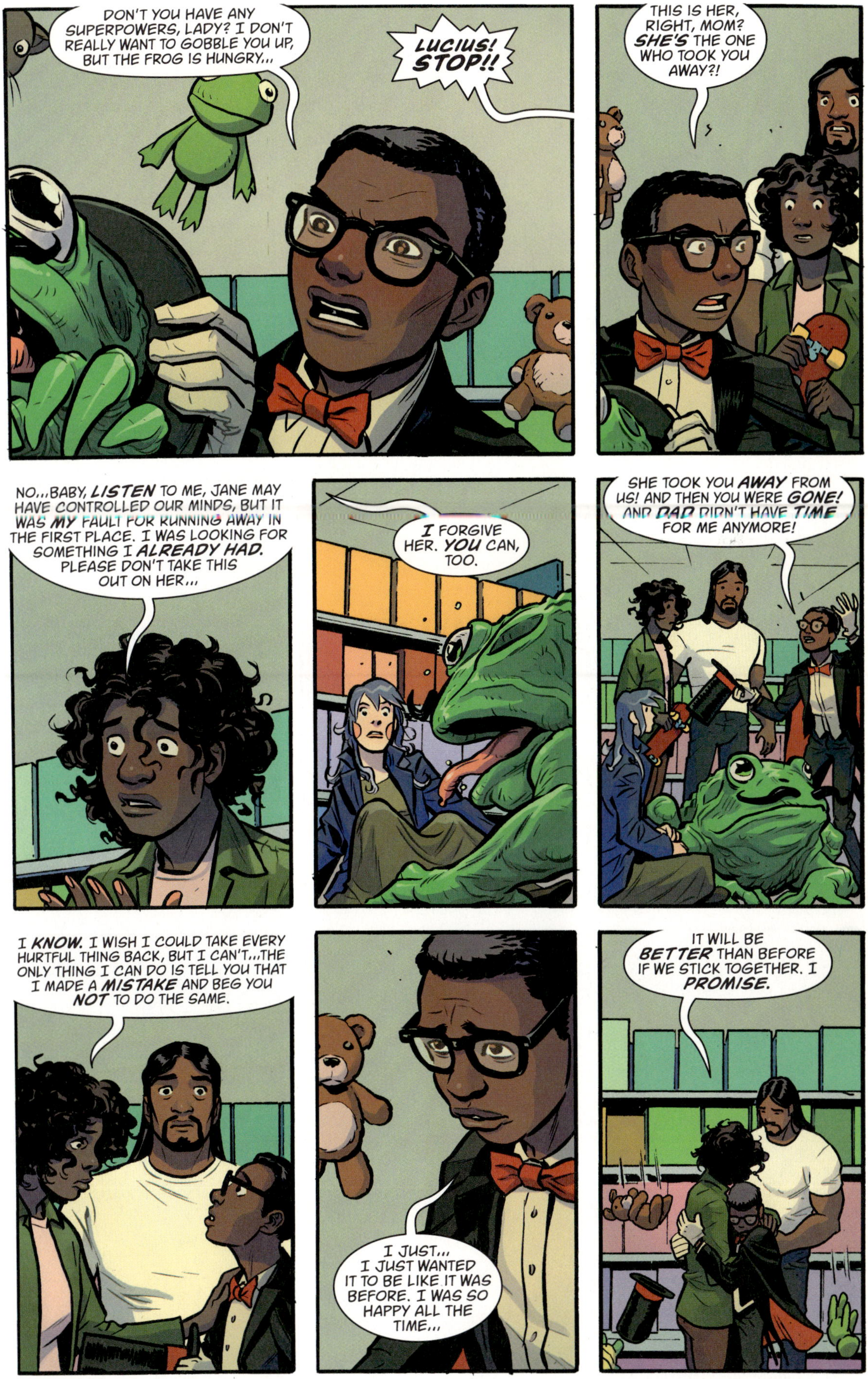
DON'T YOU HAVE ANY SUPERPOWERS, LADY? I DON'T REALLY WANT TO GOBBLE YOU UP, BUT THE FROG IS HUNGRY...
LUCIUS! STOP!!
THIS IS HER, RIGHT, MOM? SHE'S THE ONE WHO TOOK YOU AWAY?!
NO...BABY, LISTEN TO ME. JANE MAY HAVE CONTROLLED OUR MINDS, BUT IT WAS MY FAULT FOR RUNNING AWAY IN THE FIRST PLACE. I WAS LOOKING FOR SOMETHING I ALREADY HAD. PLEASE DON'T TAKE THIS OUT ON HER...
I FORGIVE HER. YOU CAN, TOO.
SHE TOOK YOU AWAY FROM US! AND THEN YOU WERE GONE! AND DAD DIDN'T HAVE TIME FOR ME ANYMORE!
I KNOW. I WISH I COULD TAKE EVERY HURTFUL THING BACK, BUT I CAN'T...THE ONLY THING I CAN DO IS TELL YOU THAT I MADE A MISTAKE AND BEG YOU NOT TO DO THE SAME.
I JUST... I JUST WANTED IT TO BE LIKE IT WAS BEFORE. I WAS SO HAPPY ALL THE TIME...
IT WILL BE BETTER THAN BEFORE IF WE STICK TOGETHER. I PROMISE.

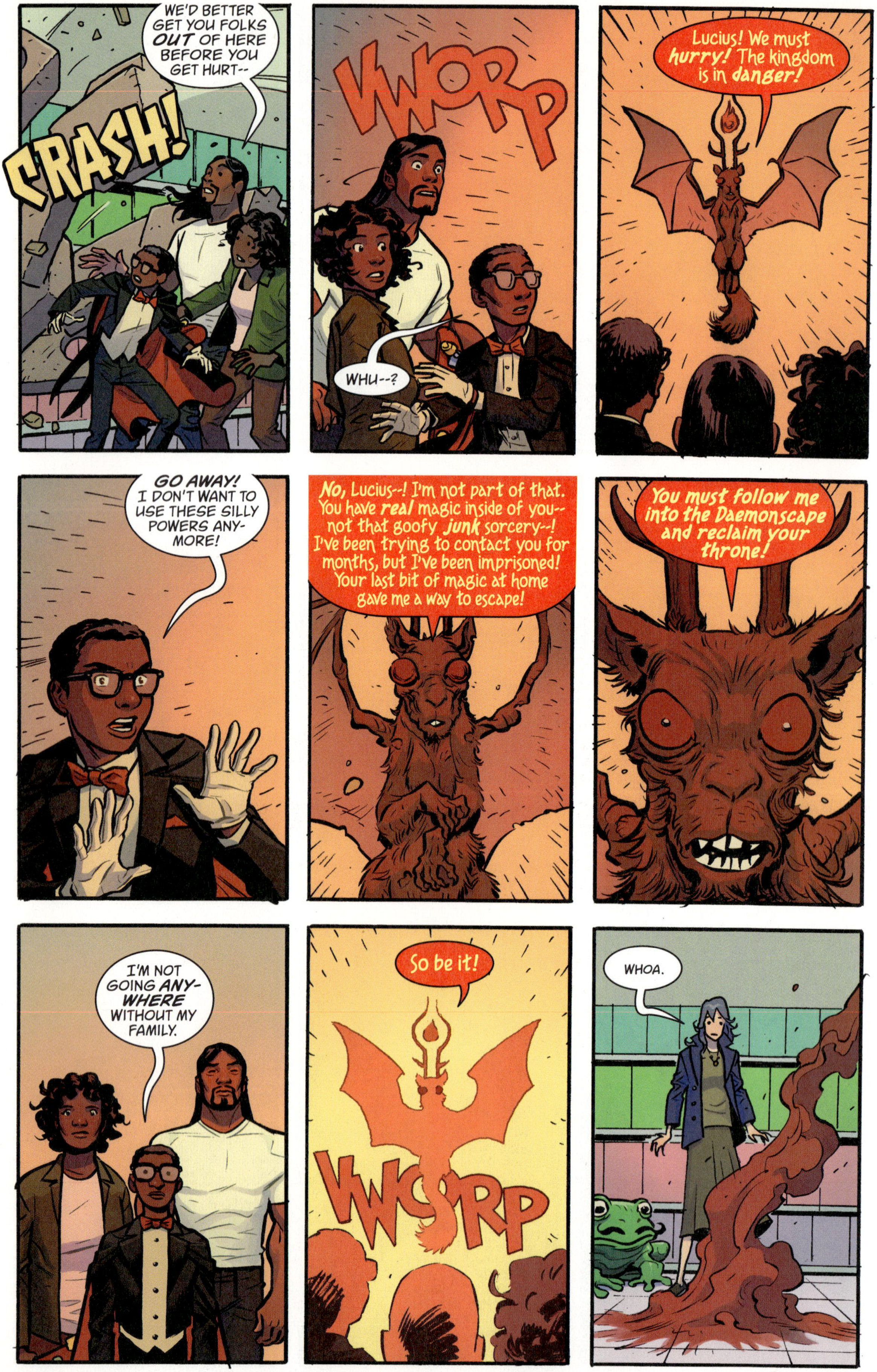
WE'D BETTER GET YOU FOLKS OUT OF HERE BEFORE YOU GET HURT--
CRASH!
VWORP
WHU--?
Lucius! We must hurry! The kingdom is in danger!
GO AWAY! I DON'T WANT TO USE THESE SILLY POWERS ANYMORE!
No, Lucius--! I'm not part of that. You have real magic inside of you-- not that goofy junk sorcery--! I've been trying to contact you for months, but I've been imprisoned! Your last bit of magic at home gave me a way to escape!
You must follow me into the Daemonscape and reclaim your throne!
I'M NOT GOING ANYWHERE WITHOUT MY FAMILY.
So be it!
VWORP
WHOA.

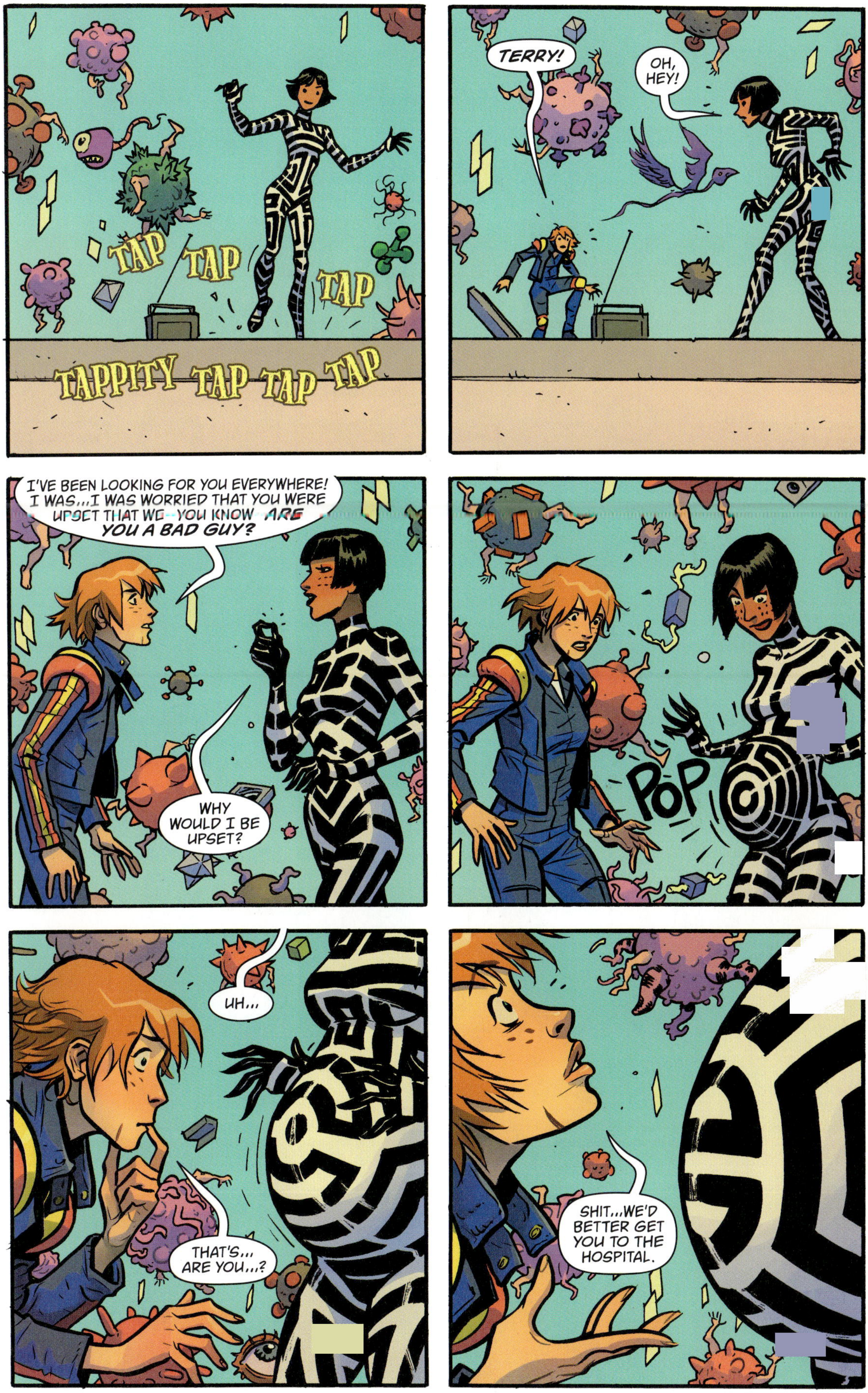
TAP
TAP
TAP
TAPPITY TAP TAP TAP
TERRY!
OH, HEY!
I'VE BEEN LOOKING FOR YOU EVERYWHERE! I WAS...I WAS WORRIED THAT YOU WERE UPSET THAT WE-- YOU KNOW ARE YOU A BAD GUY?
WHY WOULD I BE UPSET?
POP
UH...
THAT'S... ARE YOU...?
SHIT...WE'D BETTER GET YOU TO THE HOSPITAL.

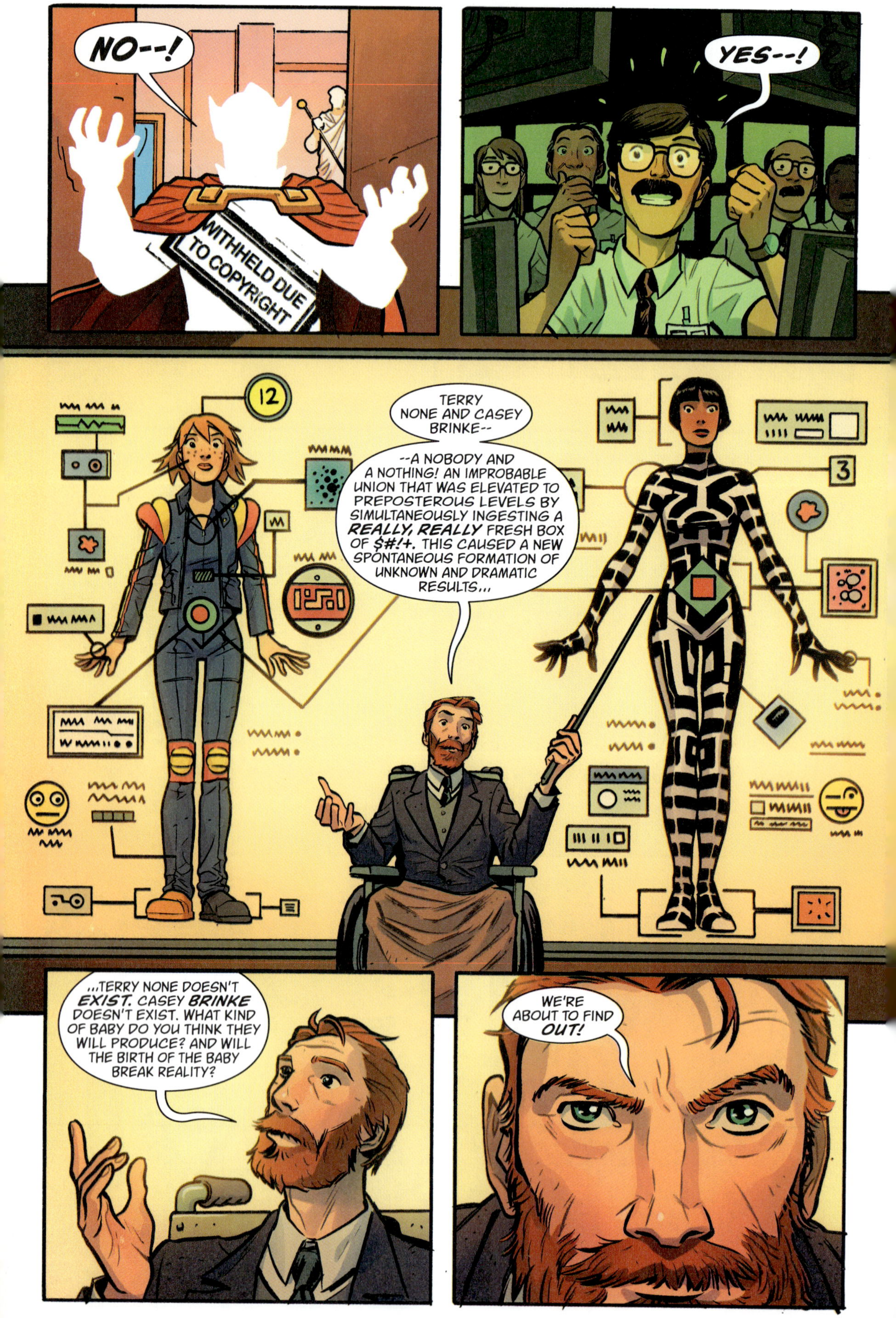
NO--!
WITHHELD DUE TO COPYRIGHT
YES--!
12
3
TERRY NONE AND CASEY BRINKE--
--A NOBODY AND A NOTHING! AN IMPROBABLE UNION THAT WAS ELEVATED TO PREPOSTEROUS LEVELS BY SIMULTANEOUSLY INGESTING A REALLY, REALLY FRESH BOX OF $#!+. THIS CAUSED A NEW SPONTANEOUS FORMATION OF UNKNOWN AND DRAMATIC RESULTS...
...TERRY NONE DOESN'T EXIST. CASEY BRINKE DOESN'T EXIST. WHAT KIND OF BABY DO YOU THINK THEY WILL PRODUCE? AND WILL THE BIRTH OF THE BABY BREAK REALITY?
WE'RE ABOUT TO FIND OUT!

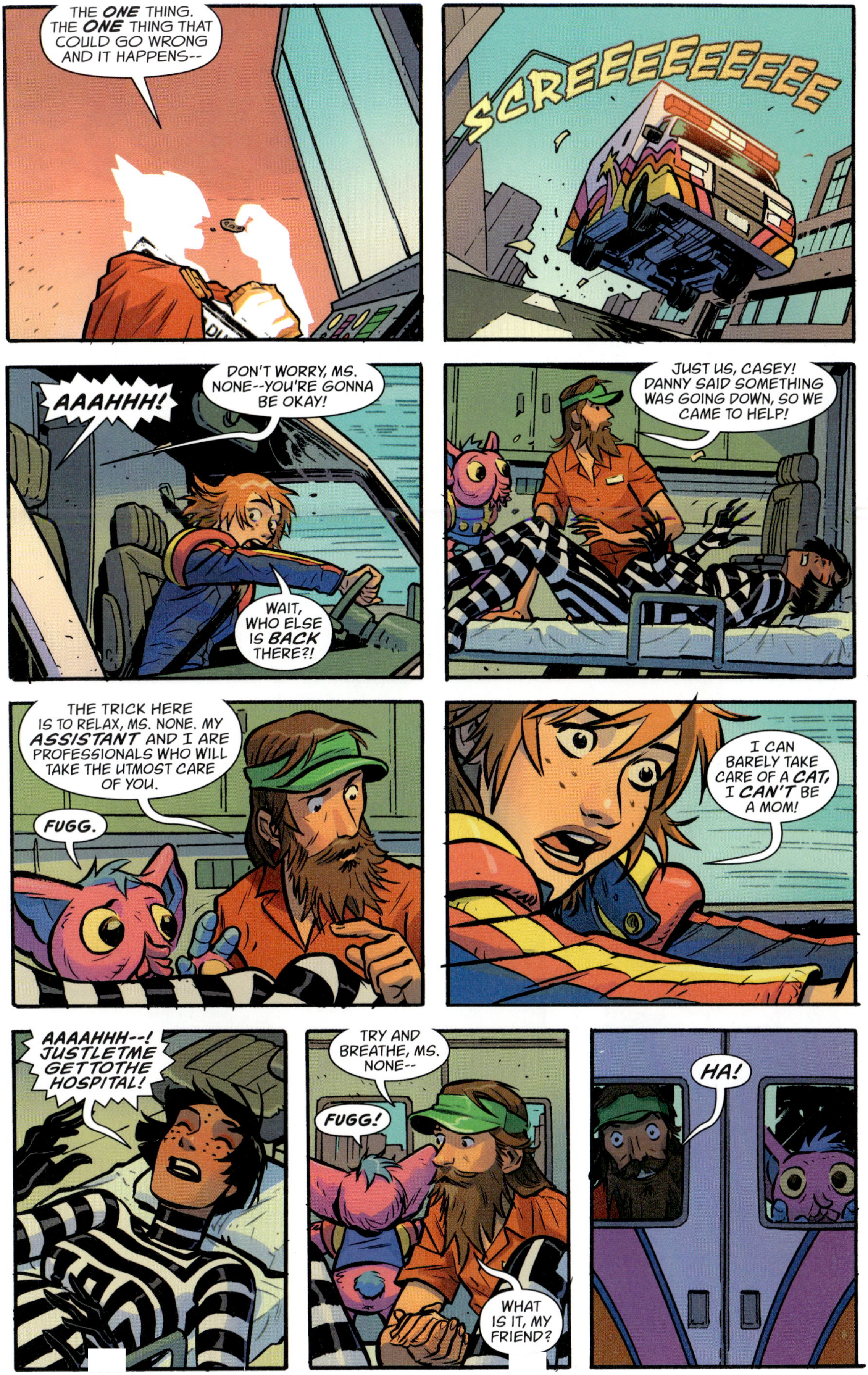
THE ONE THING. THE ONE THING THAT COULD GO WRONG AND IT HAPPENS--
SCREEEEEEEEEE
AAAHHH!
DON'T WORRY, MS. NONE--YOU'RE GONNA BE OKAY!
WAIT, WHO ELSE IS BACK THERE?!
JUST US, CASEY! DANNY SAID SOMETHING WAS GOING DOWN, SO WE CAME TO HELP!
THE TRICK HERE IS TO RELAX, MS. NONE. MY ASSISTANT AND I ARE PROFESSIONALS WHO WILL TAKE THE UTMOST CARE OF YOU.
FUGG.
I CAN BARELY TAKE CARE OF A CAT, I CAN'T BE A MOM!
AAAAHHH--! JUSTLETME GETTOTHE HOSPITAL!
TRY AND BREATHE, MS. NONE--
FUGG!
WHAT IS IT, MY FRIEND?
HA!

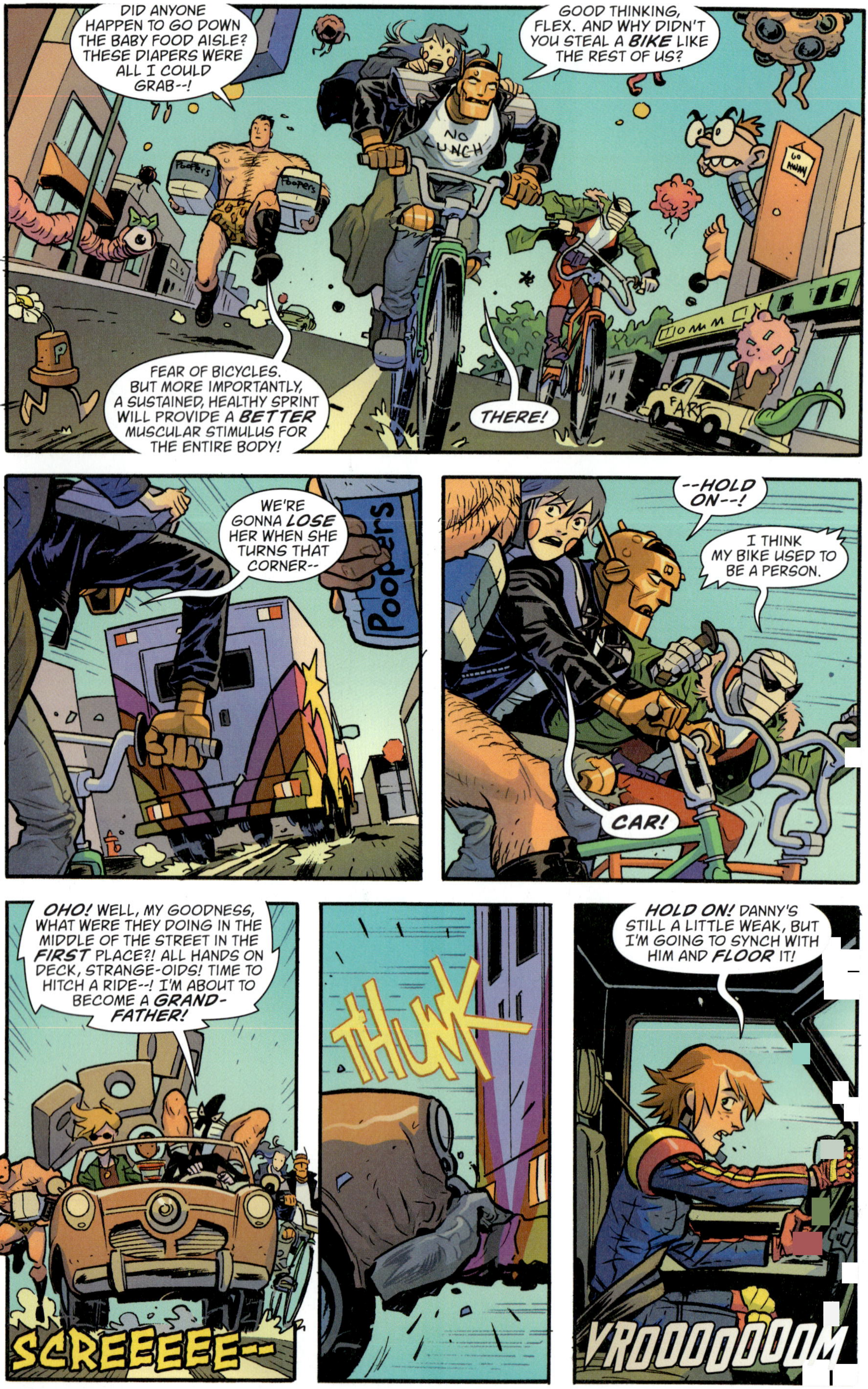
DID ANYONE HAPPEN TO GO DOWN THE BABY FOOD AISLE? THESE DIAPERS WERE ALL I COULD GRAB--!
GOOD THINKING, FLEX. AND WHY DIDN'T YOU STEAL A BIKE LIKE THE REST OF US?
NO LUNCH
Poopers
FEAR OF BICYCLES. BUT MORE IMPORTANTLY, A SUSTAINED, HEALTHY SPRINT WILL PROVIDE A BETTER MUSCULAR STIMULUS FOR THE ENTIRE BODY!
THERE!
WE'RE GONNA LOSE HER WHEN SHE TURNS THAT CORNER--
Poopers
--HOLD ON--!
I THINK MY BIKE USED TO BE A PERSON.
CAR!
OHO! WELL, MY GOODNESS, WHAT WERE THEY DOING IN THE MIDDLE OF THE STREET IN THE FIRST PLACE?! ALL HANDS ON DECK, STRANGE-OIDS! TIME TO HITCH A RIDE--! I'M ABOUT TO BECOME A GRAND-FATHER!
SCREEEEE--
THUNK
HOLD ON! DANNY'S STILL A LITTLE WEAK, BUT I'M GOING TO SYNCH WITH HIM AND FLOOR IT!
VROOOOOOOM

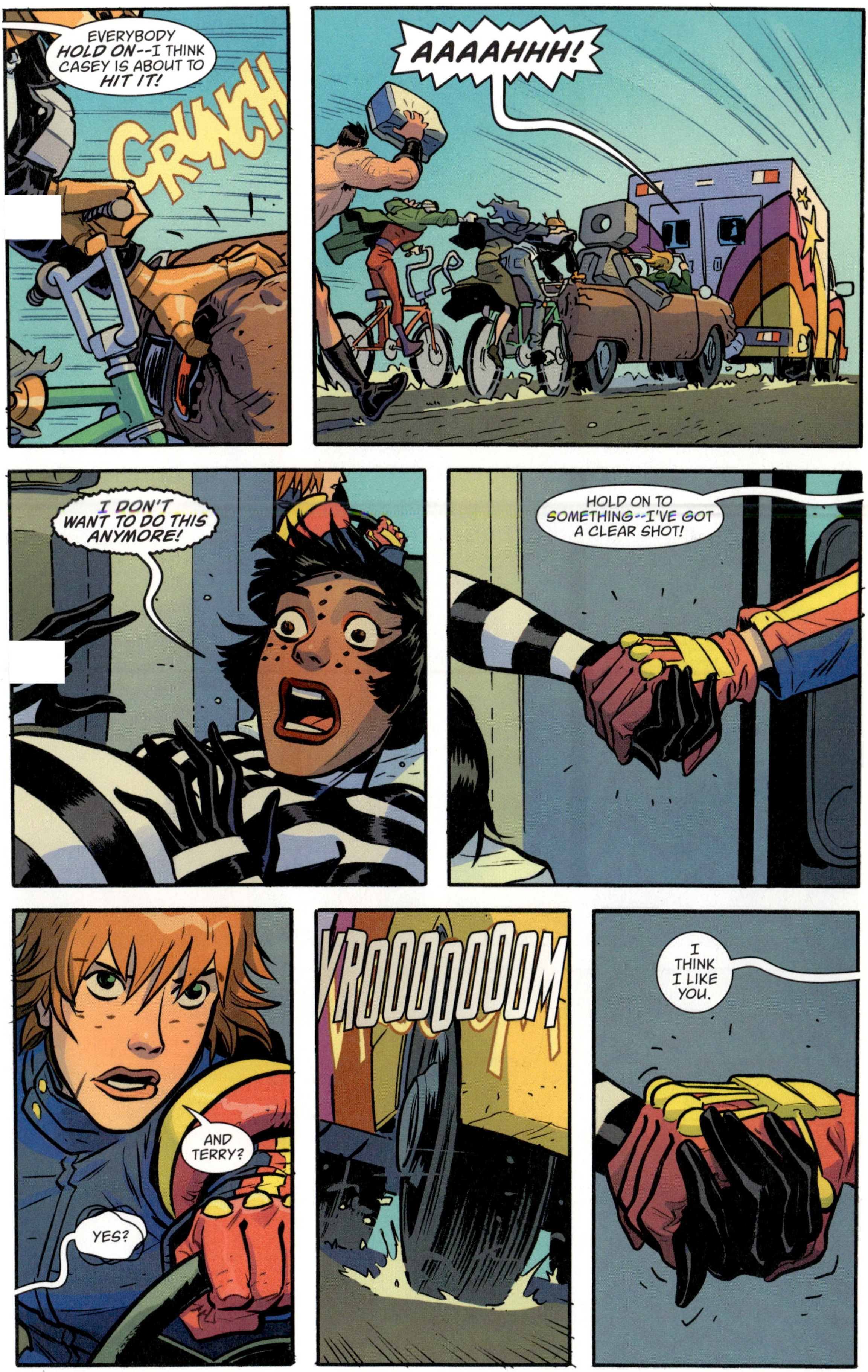

EVERYBODY HOLD ON--I THINK CASEY IS ABOUT TO HIT IT!
CRUNCH
AAAAHHH!
I DON'T WANT TO DO THIS ANYMORE!
HOLD ON TO SOMETHING--I'VE GOT A CLEAR SHOT!
AND TERRY?
YES?
VROOOOOOOOM
I THINK I LIKE YOU.

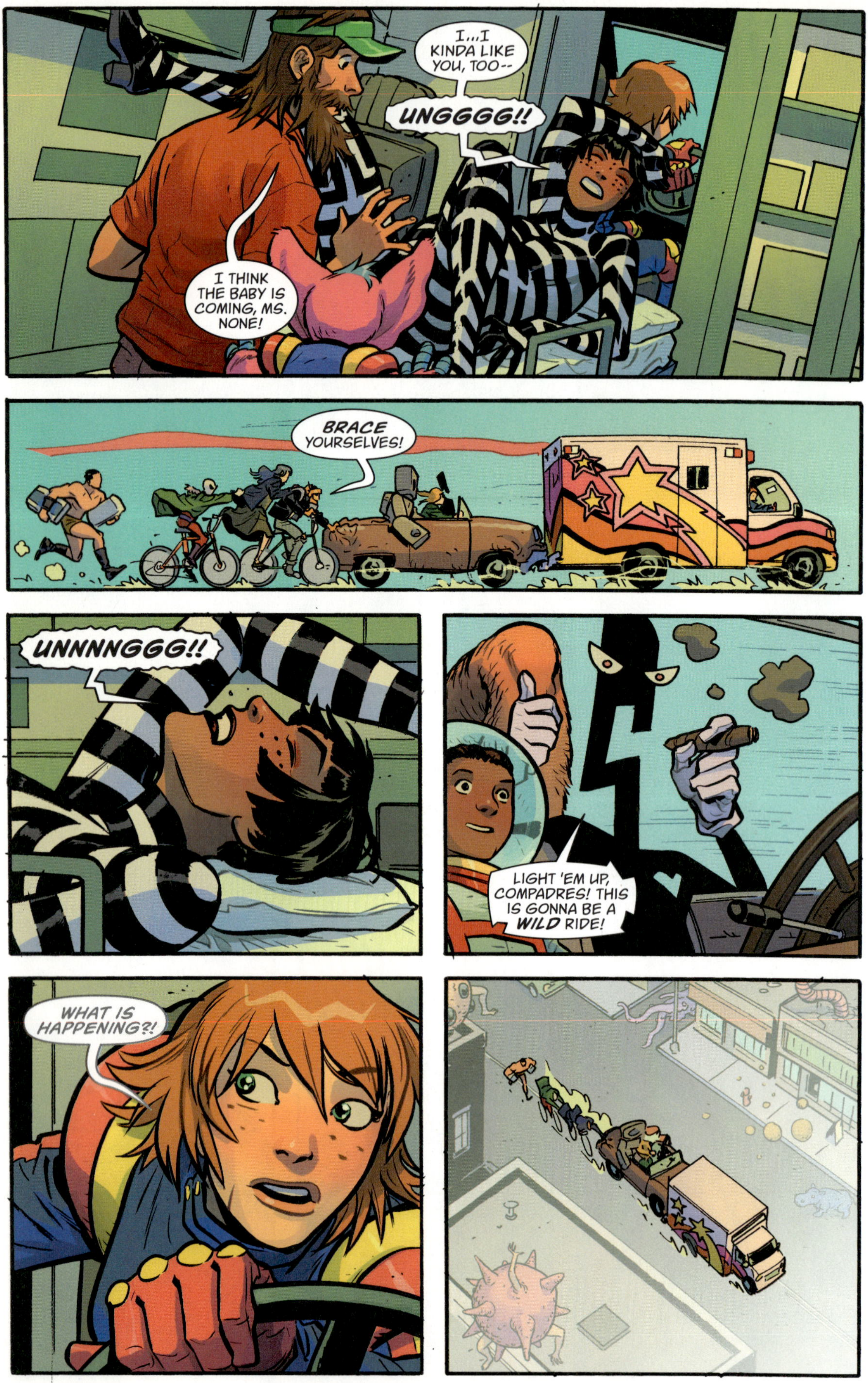
I...I KINDA LIKE YOU, TOO--
UNGGGG!!
I THINK THE BABY IS COMING, MS. NONE!
BRACE YOURSELVES!
UNNNNGGG!!
LIGHT 'EM UP, COMPADRES! THIS IS GONNA BE A WILD RIDE!
WHAT IS HAPPENING?!

I CAN'T *BELIEVE* IT--SHE'S GIVING BIRTH TO AN OMNIBLANK!

IT'S COMING!

DEAR GOD, *NO*--

WITHHELD
TO CO

WE CAN INITIATE *RETCONN* PLAN C!

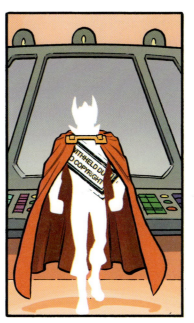

WITHHELD DUE
TO COPYRIGHT

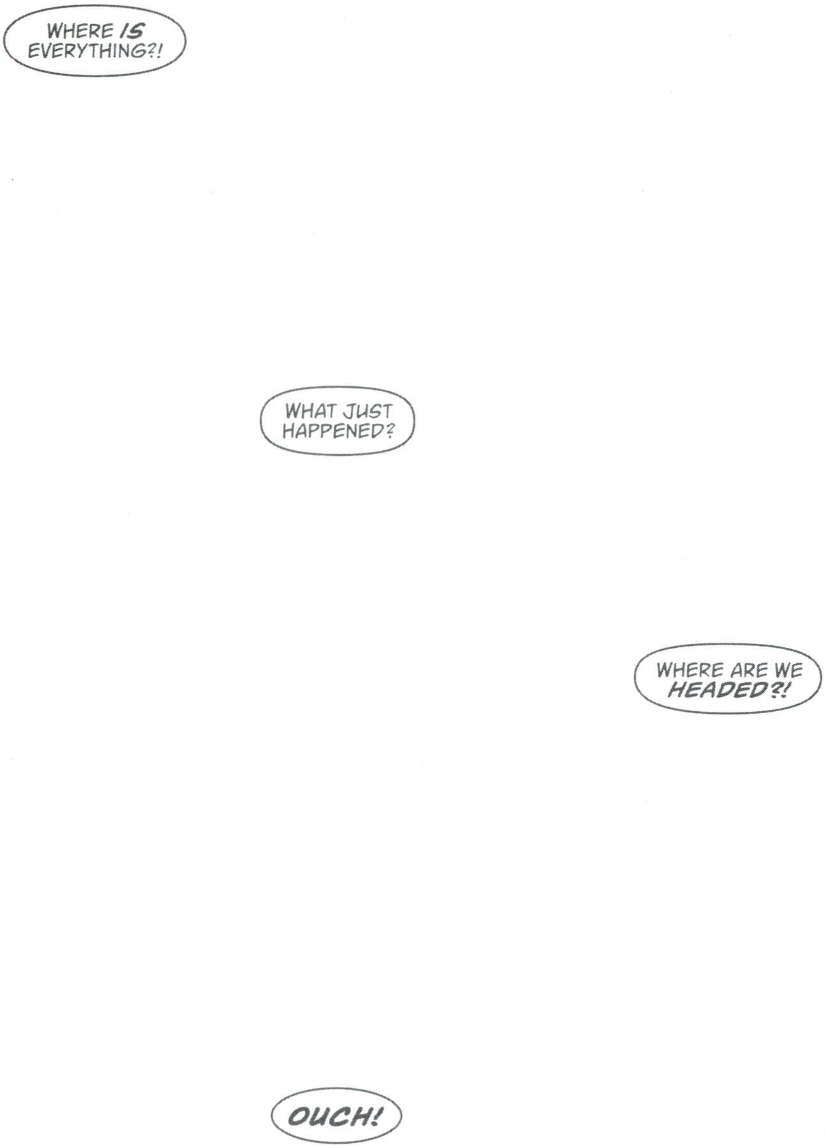
WHERE *IS* EVERYTHING?!
WHAT JUST HAPPENED?
WHERE ARE WE *HEADED?!*
OUCH!

CLIFF--
IS THAT
YOU?!

WHIZZ!

BANG!

SCREEEEE

HOLD
ON--!!

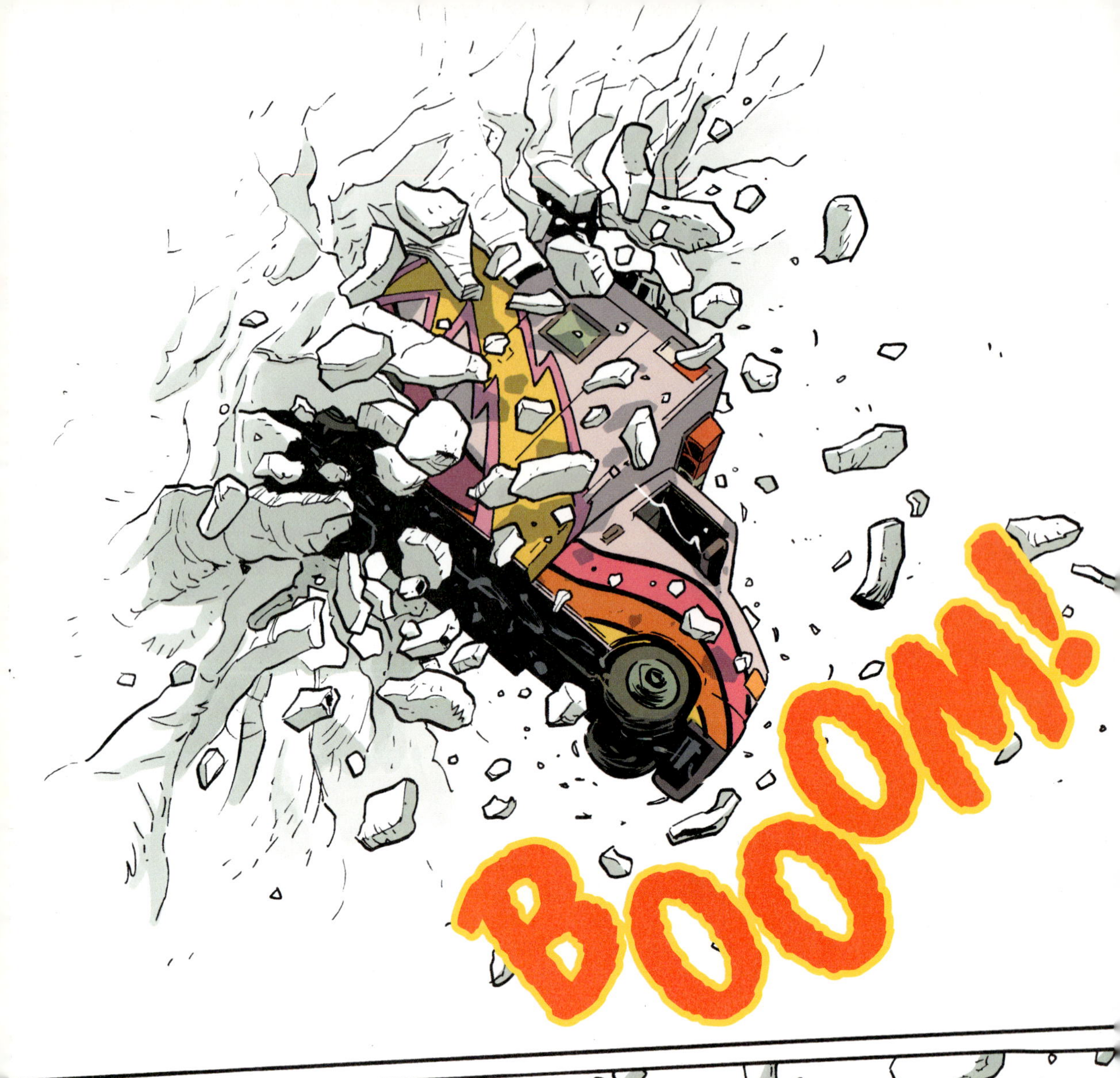
BOOOM!

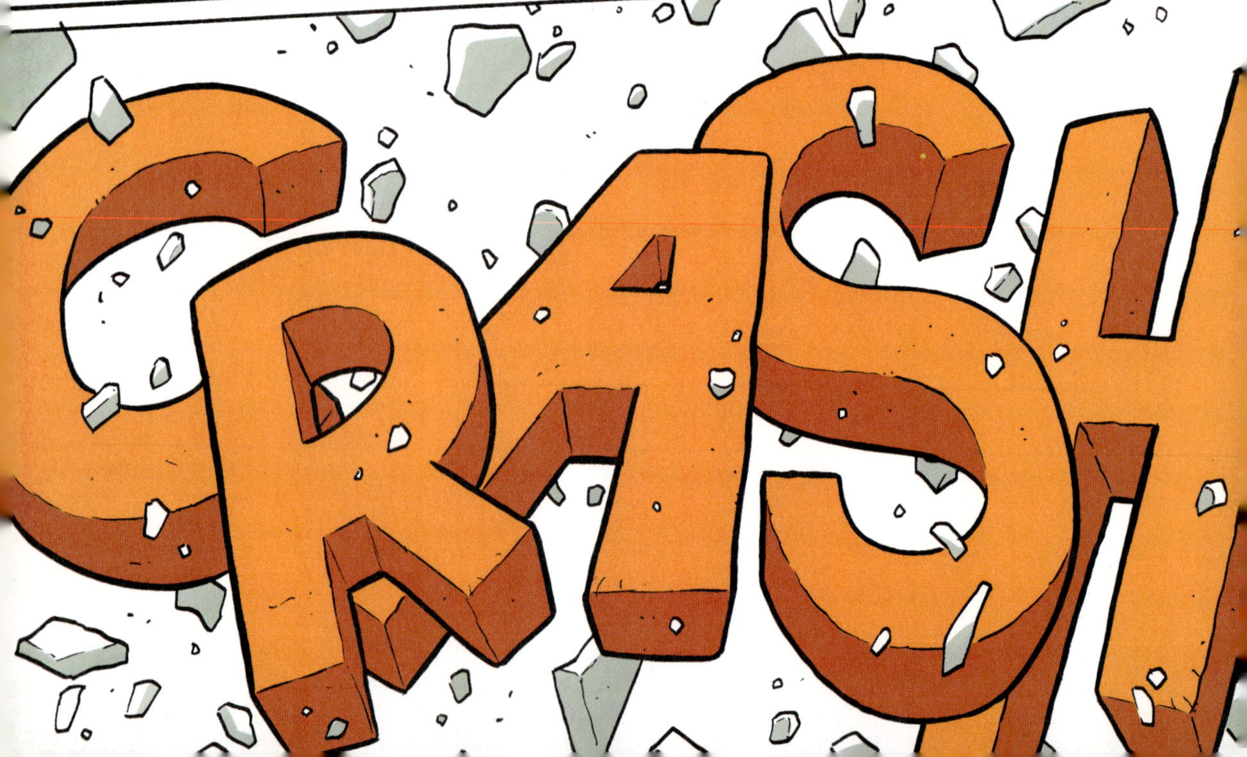
CRASH

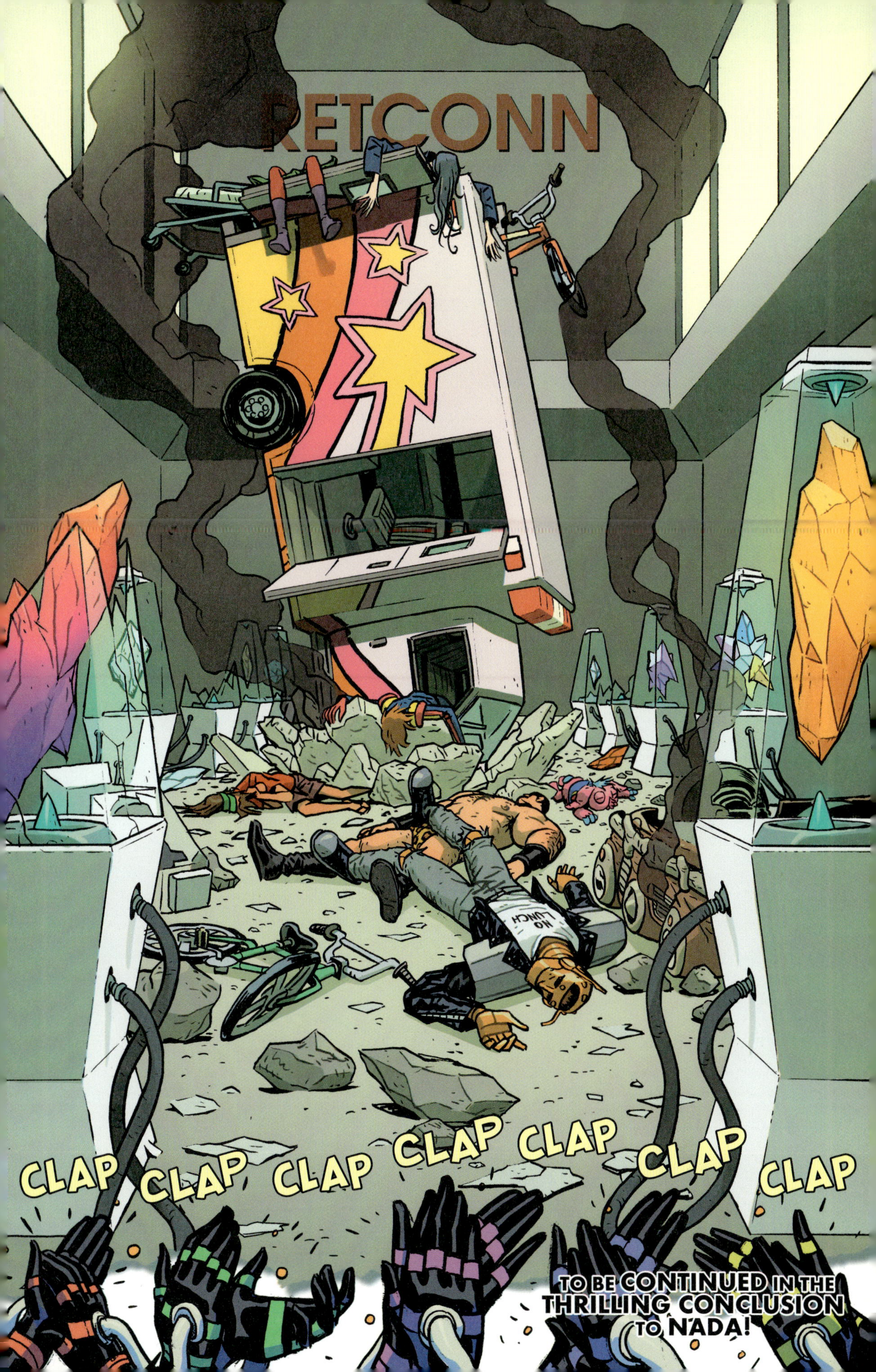

RETCONN
NO LUNCH
CLAP
CLAP
CLAP
CLAP
CLAP
CLAP
CLAP
TO BE CONTINUED IN THE THRILLING CONCLUSION TO NADA!

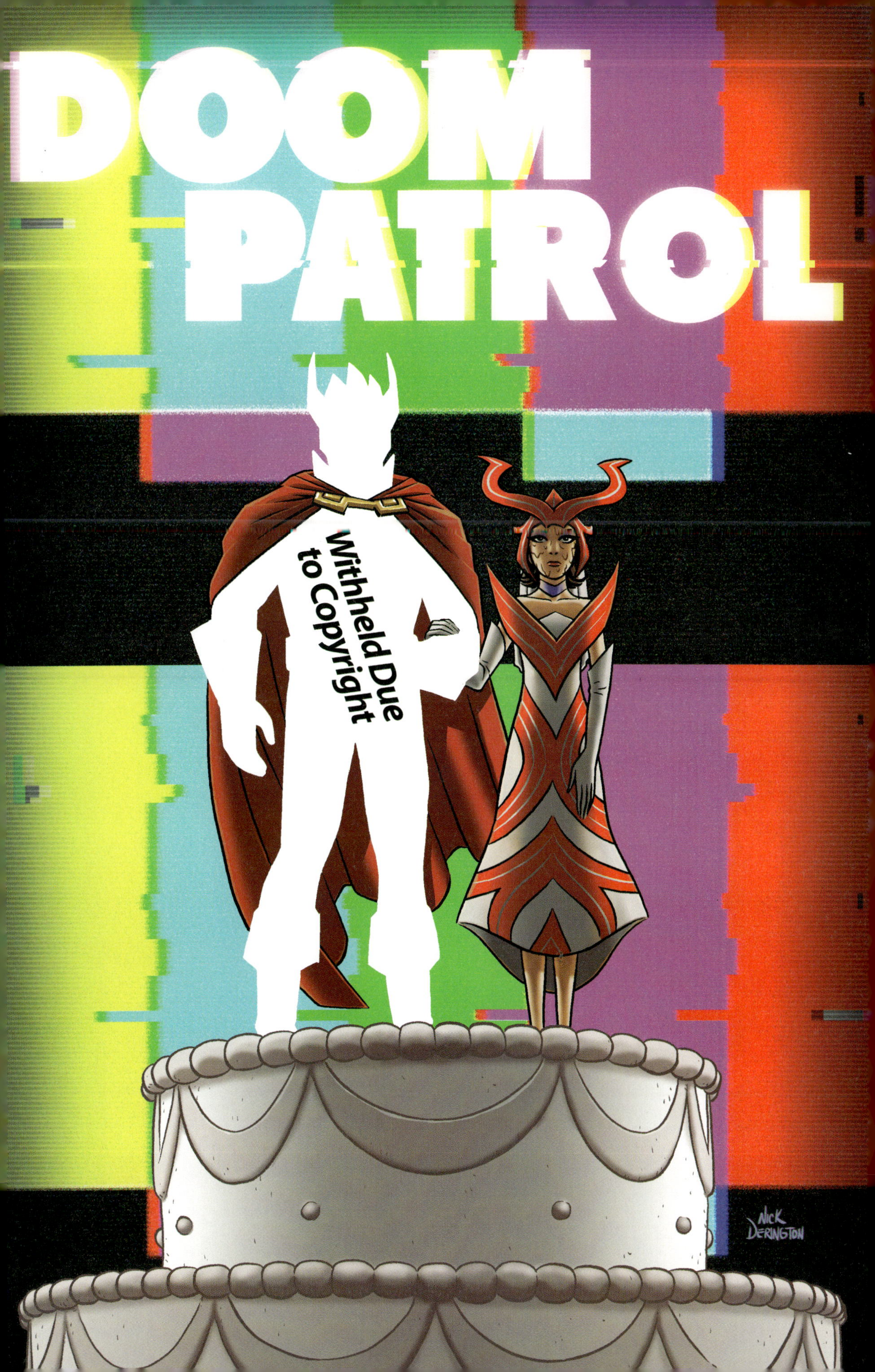
DOOM PATROL
Withheld Due to Copyright
NICK DERINGTON

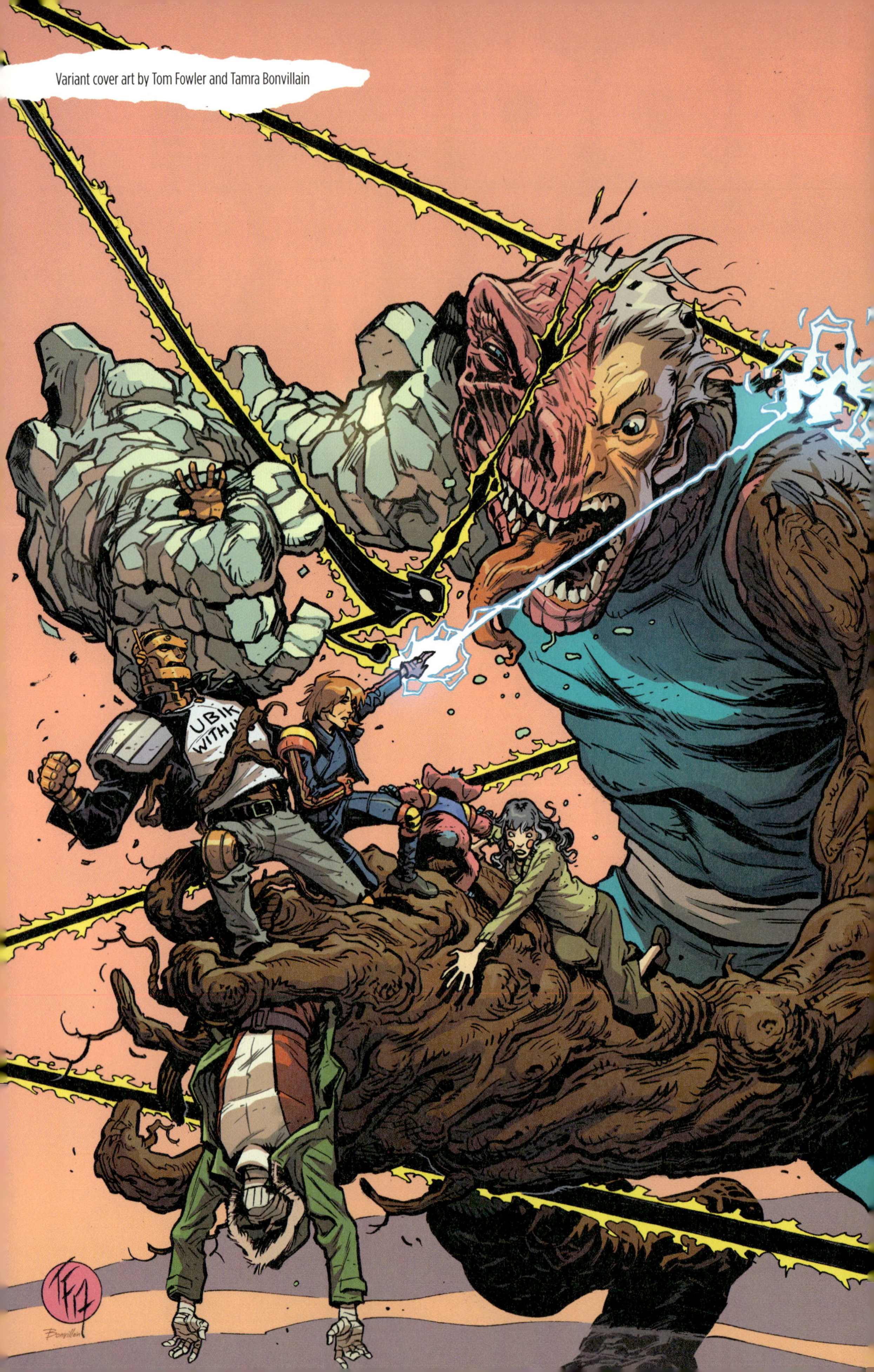
UBIK
WITH

Variant cover art by Tom Fowler and Tamra Bonvillain

FIRST, THERE WAS A BALL.

IT WAS SIMPLE. IT WAS FUN. AND IT WAS NEW.

THIS WAS ENTERTAINING FOR SOME TIME, BUT REALLY, IT'S JUST ONE BALL.

SLAP

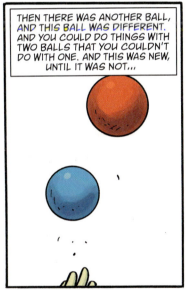

THEN THERE WAS ANOTHER BALL, AND THIS BALL WAS DIFFERENT. AND YOU COULD DO THINGS WITH TWO BALLS THAT YOU COULDN'T DO WITH ONE. AND THIS WAS NEW, UNTIL IT WAS NOT...

...AND SO THERE WAS ANOTHER BALL. AND ANOTHER...

...AND ANOTHER, AND ANOTHER...

...AND SO ON...

...AND SO ON...

...AND SO ON...

♪

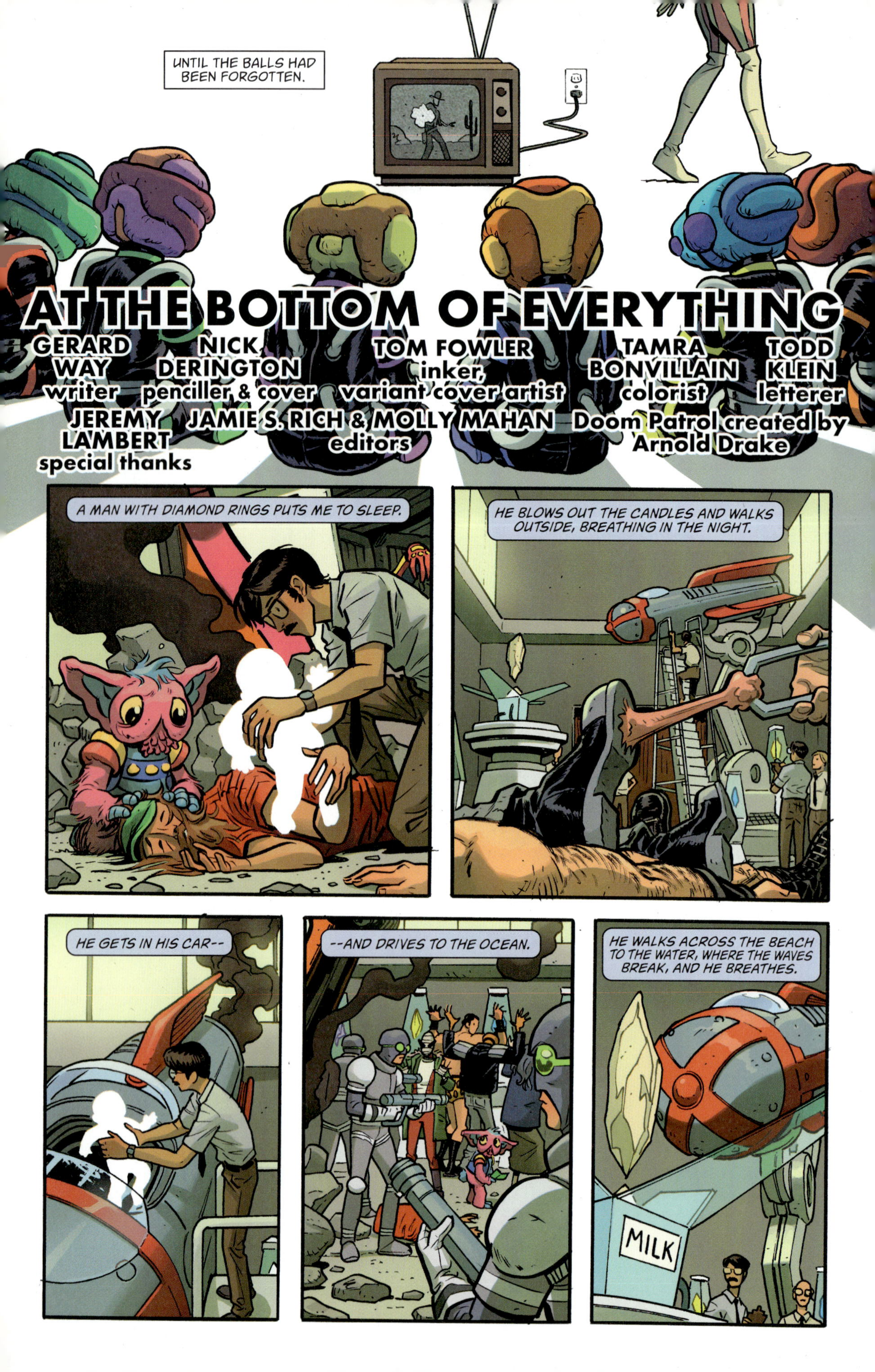

UNTIL THE BALLS HAD BEEN FORGOTTEN.
AT THE BOTTOM OF EVERYTHING
GERARD WAY writer
NICK DERINGTON penciller & cover
TOM FOWLER inker, variant cover artist
TAMRA BONVILLAIN colorist
TODD KLEIN letterer
JEREMY LAMBERT special thanks
JAMIE S. RICH & MOLLY MAHAN editors
Doom Patrol created by Arnold Drake
A MAN WITH DIAMOND RINGS PUTS ME TO SLEEP.
HE BLOWS OUT THE CANDLES AND WALKS OUTSIDE, BREATHING IN THE NIGHT.
HE GETS IN HIS CAR--
--AND DRIVES TO THE OCEAN.
HE WALKS ACROSS THE BEACH TO THE WATER, WHERE THE WAVES BREAK, AND HE BREATHES.
MILK

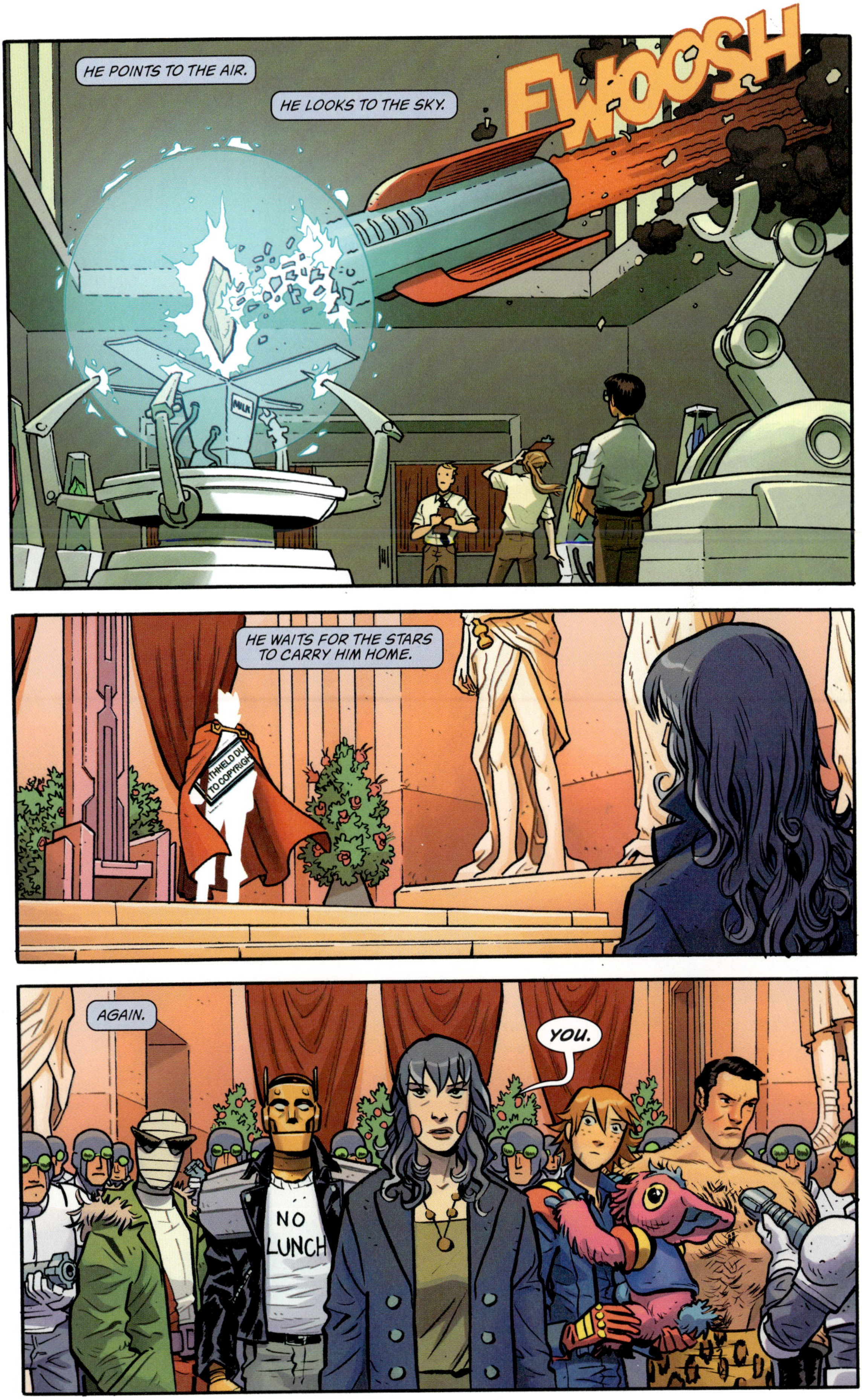
HE POINTS TO THE AIR.
HE LOOKS TO THE SKY.
FWOOSH
HE WAITS FOR THE STARS TO CARRY HIM HOME.
AGAIN.
YOU.
NO LUNCH

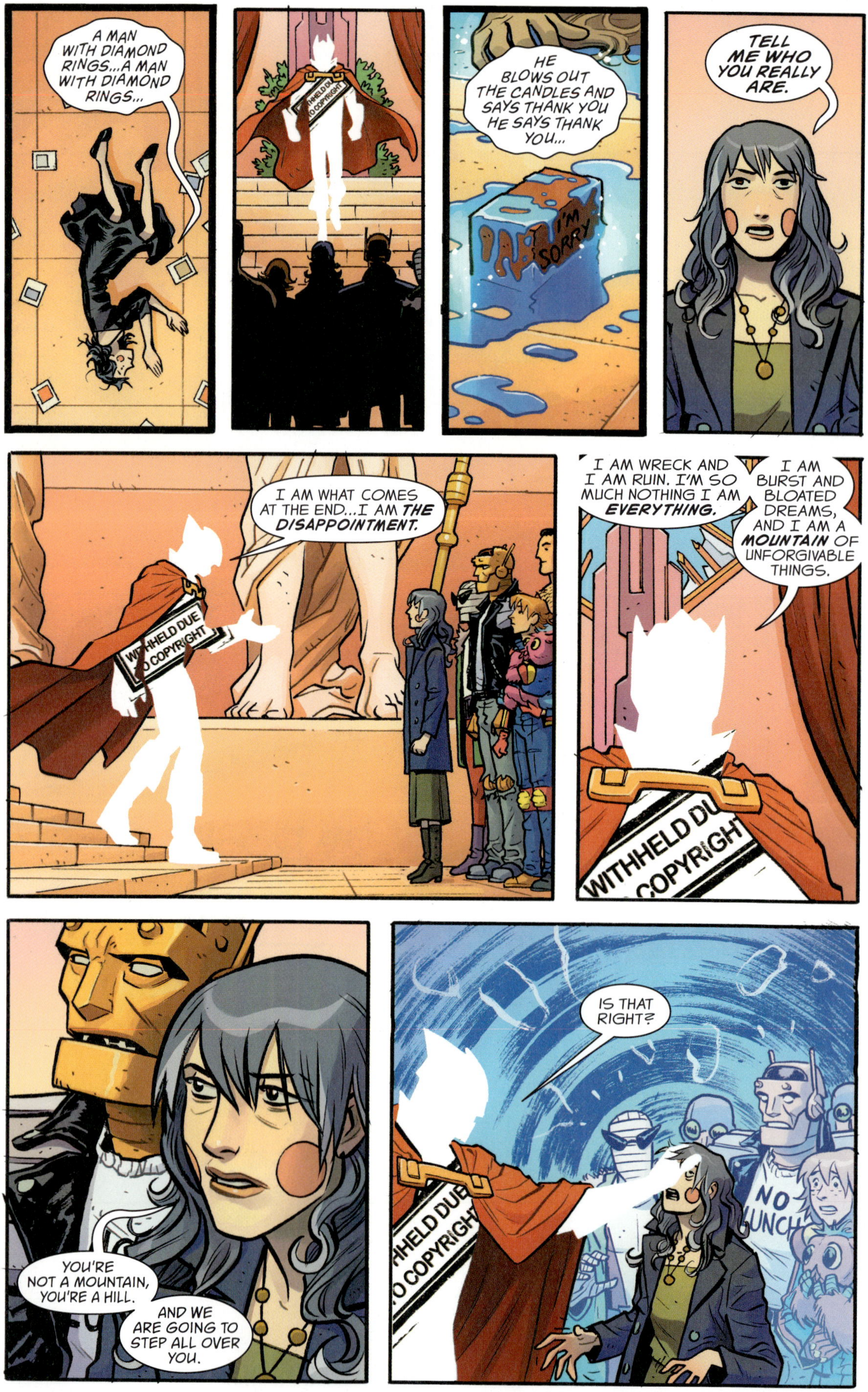
A MAN WITH DIAMOND RINGS...A MAN WITH DIAMOND RINGS...
WITHHELD DUE TO COPYRIGHT
HE BLOWS OUT THE CANDLES AND SAYS THANK YOU HE SAYS THANK YOU...
I'M SORRY
TELL ME WHO YOU REALLY ARE.
I AM WHAT COMES AT THE END...I AM THE DISAPPOINTMENT.
WITHHELD DUE TO COPYRIGHT
I AM WRECK AND I AM RUIN. I'M SO MUCH NOTHING I AM EVERYTHING.
I AM BURST AND BLOATED DREAMS, AND I AM A MOUNTAIN OF UNFORGIVABLE THINGS.
WITHHELD DUE TO COPYRIGHT
YOU'RE NOT A MOUNTAIN, YOU'RE A HILL.
AND WE ARE GOING TO STEP ALL OVER YOU.
IS THAT RIGHT?
WITHHELD DUE TO COPYRIGHT
NO LUNCH

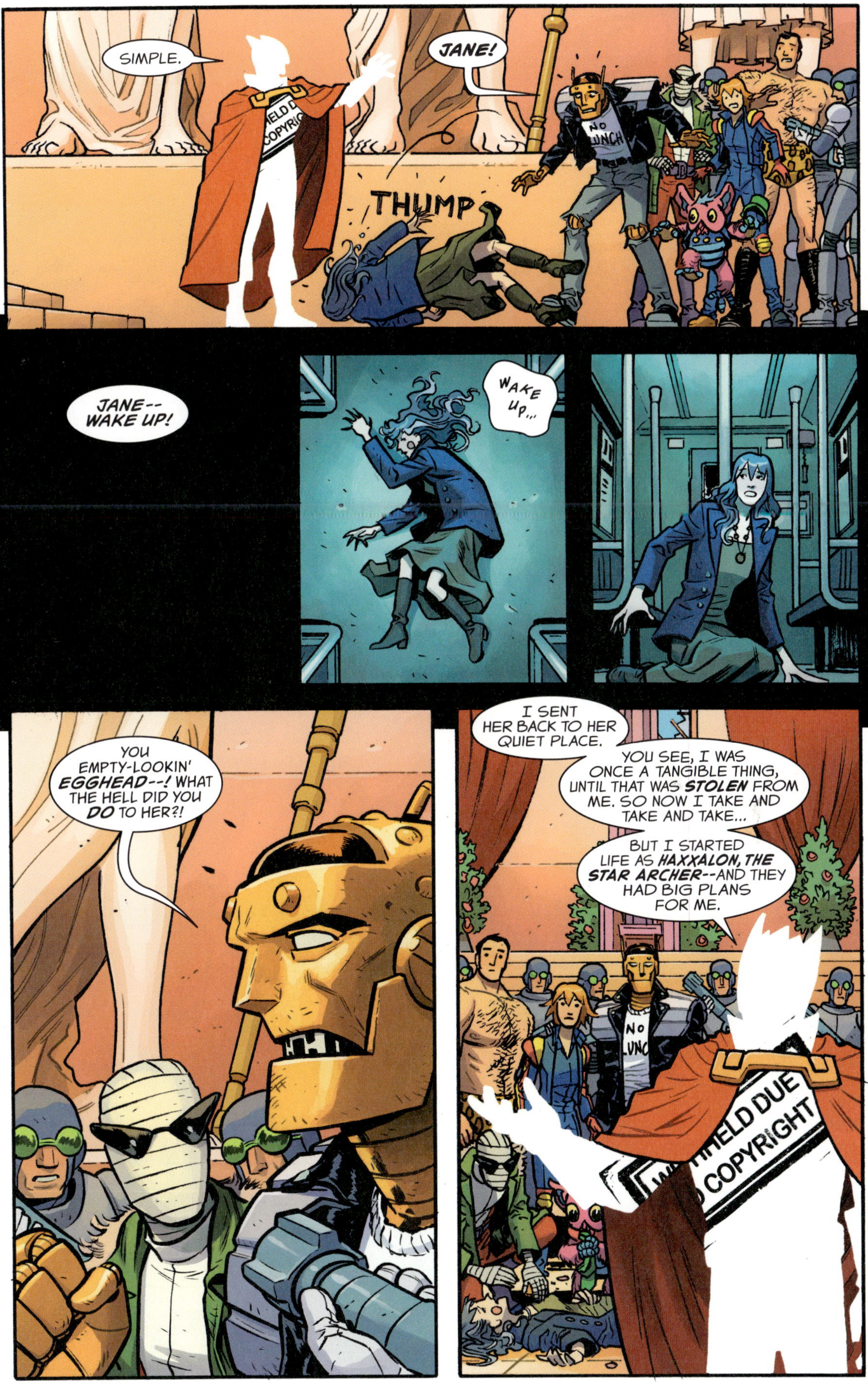
SIMPLE.
WITHHELD DUE COPYRIGHT
JANE!
NO LUNCH
THUMP
JANE--
WAKE UP!
WAKE UP...
YOU EMPTY-LOOKIN' EGGHEAD--! WHAT THE HELL DID YOU DO TO HER?!
I SENT HER BACK TO HER QUIET PLACE.
YOU SEE, I WAS ONCE A TANGIBLE THING, UNTIL THAT WAS STOLEN FROM ME. SO NOW I TAKE AND TAKE AND TAKE...
BUT I STARTED LIFE AS HAXXALON, THE STAR ARCHER--AND THEY HAD BIG PLANS FOR ME.
NO LUNC
HELD DUE COPYRIGHT

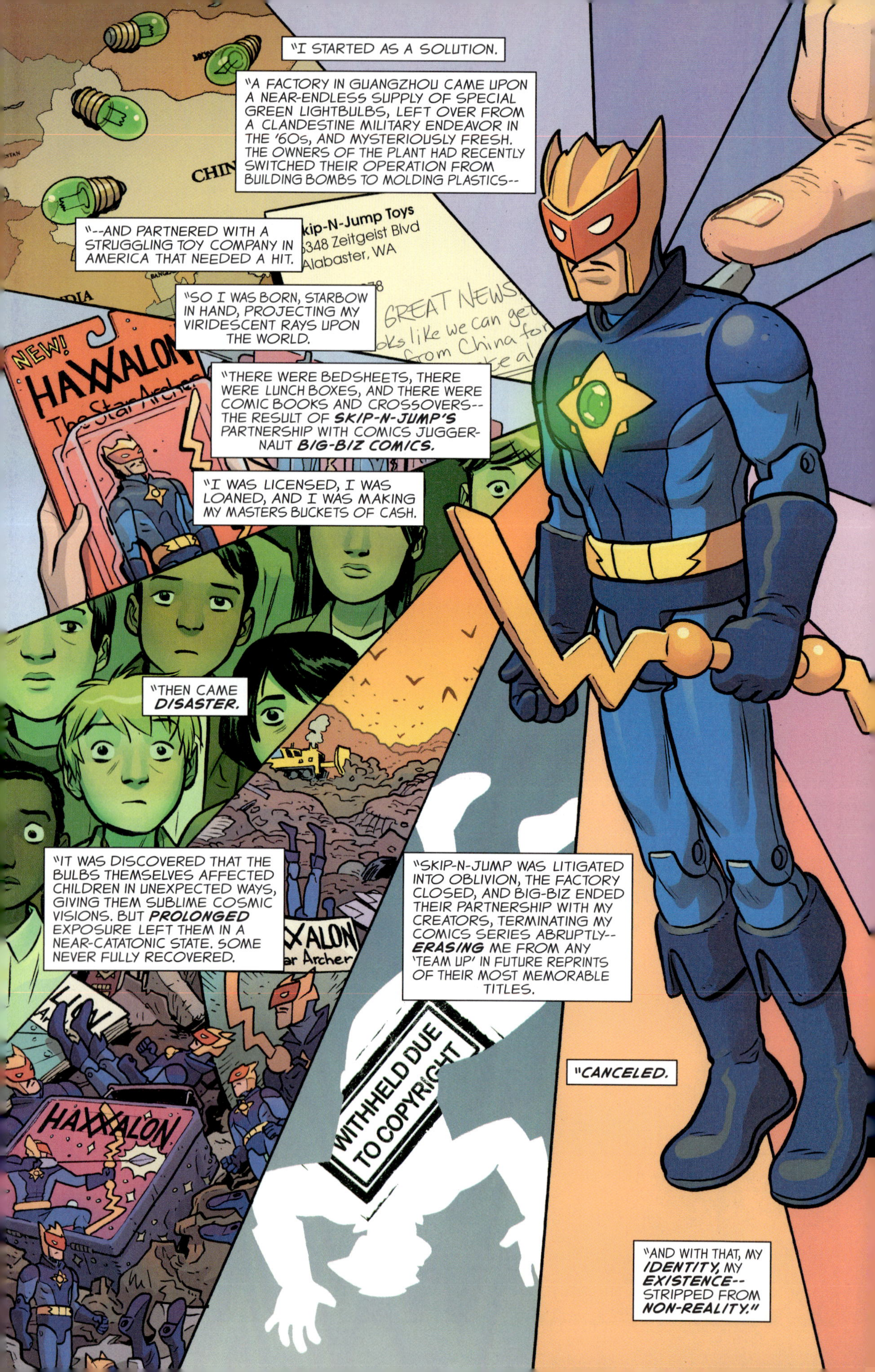
"I STARTED AS A SOLUTION.
"A FACTORY IN GUANGZHOU CAME UPON A NEAR-ENDLESS SUPPLY OF SPECIAL GREEN LIGHTBULBS, LEFT OVER FROM A CLANDESTINE MILITARY ENDEAVOR IN THE '60s, AND MYSTERIOUSLY FRESH. THE OWNERS OF THE PLANT HAD RECENTLY SWITCHED THEIR OPERATION FROM BUILDING BOMBS TO MOLDING PLASTICS--
"--AND PARTNERED WITH A STRUGGLING TOY COMPANY IN AMERICA THAT NEEDED A HIT.
Skip-N-Jump Toys
Alabaster, WA
GREAT NEWS
"SO I WAS BORN, STARBOW IN HAND, PROJECTING MY VIRIDESCENT RAYS UPON THE WORLD.
NEW!
HAXXALON
"THERE WERE BEDSHEETS, THERE WERE LUNCH BOXES, AND THERE WERE COMIC BOOKS AND CROSSOVERS-- THE RESULT OF **SKIP-N-JUMP'S** PARTNERSHIP WITH COMICS JUGGERNAUT **BIG-BIZ COMICS.**
"I WAS LICENSED, I WAS LOANED, AND I WAS MAKING MY MASTERS BUCKETS OF CASH.
"THEN CAME **DISASTER.**
"IT WAS DISCOVERED THAT THE BULBS THEMSELVES AFFECTED CHILDREN IN UNEXPECTED WAYS, GIVING THEM SUBLIME COSMIC VISIONS. BUT **PROLONGED** EXPOSURE LEFT THEM IN A NEAR-CATATONIC STATE. SOME NEVER FULLY RECOVERED.
"SKIP-N-JUMP WAS LITIGATED INTO OBLIVION, THE FACTORY CLOSED, AND BIG-BIZ ENDED THEIR PARTNERSHIP WITH MY CREATORS, TERMINATING MY COMICS SERIES ABRUPTLY-- **ERASING** ME FROM ANY 'TEAM UP' IN FUTURE REPRINTS OF THEIR MOST MEMORABLE TITLES.
HAXXALON
WITHHELD DUE TO COPYRIGHT
"**CANCELED.**
"AND WITH THAT, MY **IDENTITY,** MY **EXISTENCE--** STRIPPED FROM **NON-REALITY.**"

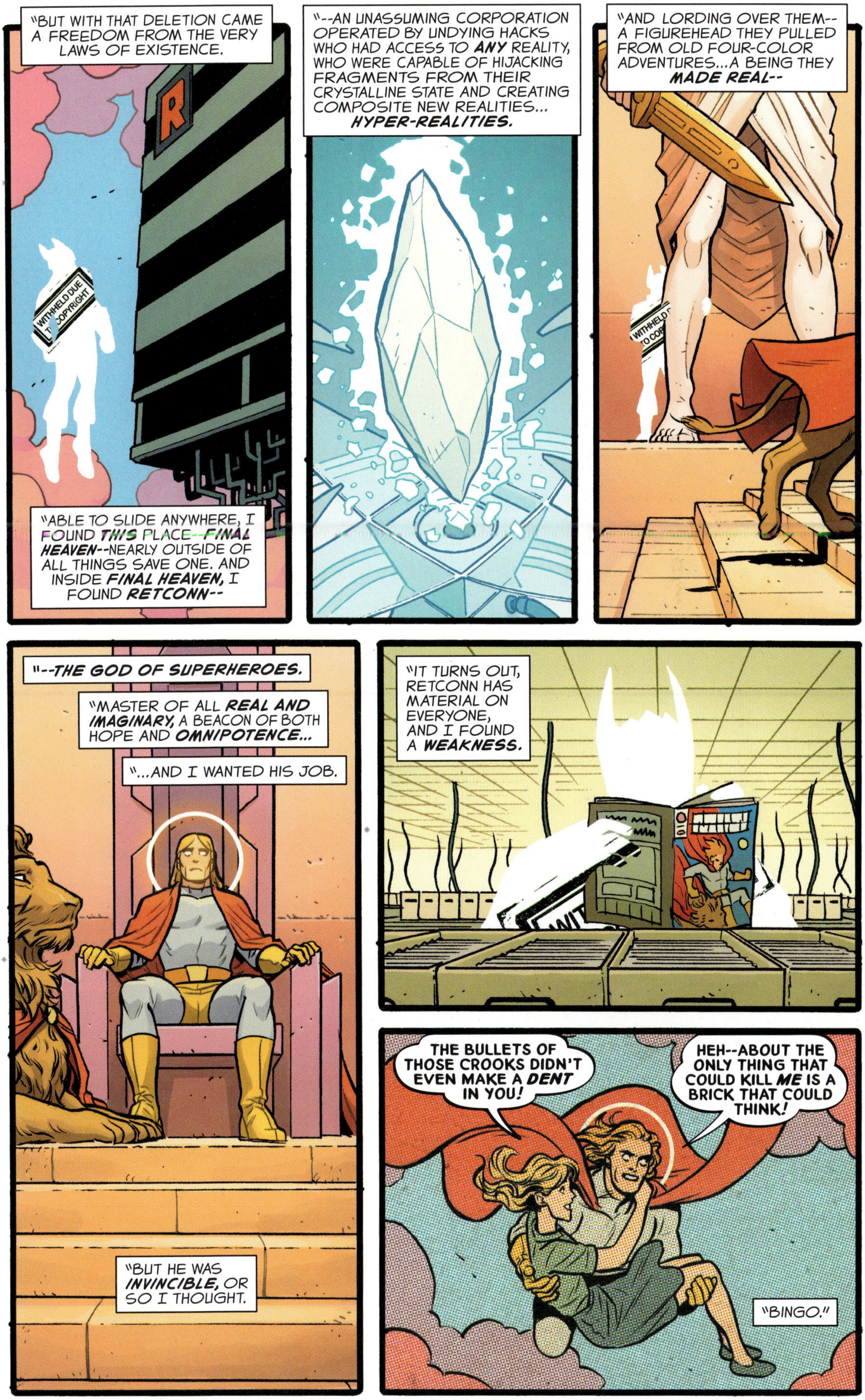
"BUT WITH THAT DELETION CAME A FREEDOM FROM THE VERY LAWS OF EXISTENCE.
WITHHELD DUE TO COPYRIGHT
"ABLE TO SLIDE ANYWHERE, I FOUND THIS PLACE--FINAL HEAVEN--NEARLY OUTSIDE OF ALL THINGS SAVE ONE. AND INSIDE FINAL HEAVEN, I FOUND RETCONN--
"--AN UNASSUMING CORPORATION OPERATED BY UNDYING HACKS WHO HAD ACCESS TO ANY REALITY, WHO WERE CAPABLE OF HIJACKING FRAGMENTS FROM THEIR CRYSTALLINE STATE AND CREATING COMPOSITE NEW REALITIES... HYPER-REALITIES.
"AND LORDING OVER THEM--A FIGUREHEAD THEY PULLED FROM OLD FOUR-COLOR ADVENTURES...A BEING THEY MADE REAL--
"--THE GOD OF SUPERHEROES.
"MASTER OF ALL REAL AND IMAGINARY, A BEACON OF BOTH HOPE AND OMNIPOTENCE...
"...AND I WANTED HIS JOB.
"BUT HE WAS INVINCIBLE, OR SO I THOUGHT.
"IT TURNS OUT, RETCONN HAS MATERIAL ON EVERYONE, AND I FOUND A WEAKNESS.
THE BULLETS OF THOSE CROOKS DIDN'T EVEN MAKE A DENT IN YOU!
HEH--ABOUT THE ONLY THING THAT COULD KILL ME IS A BRICK THAT COULD THINK!
"BINGO."

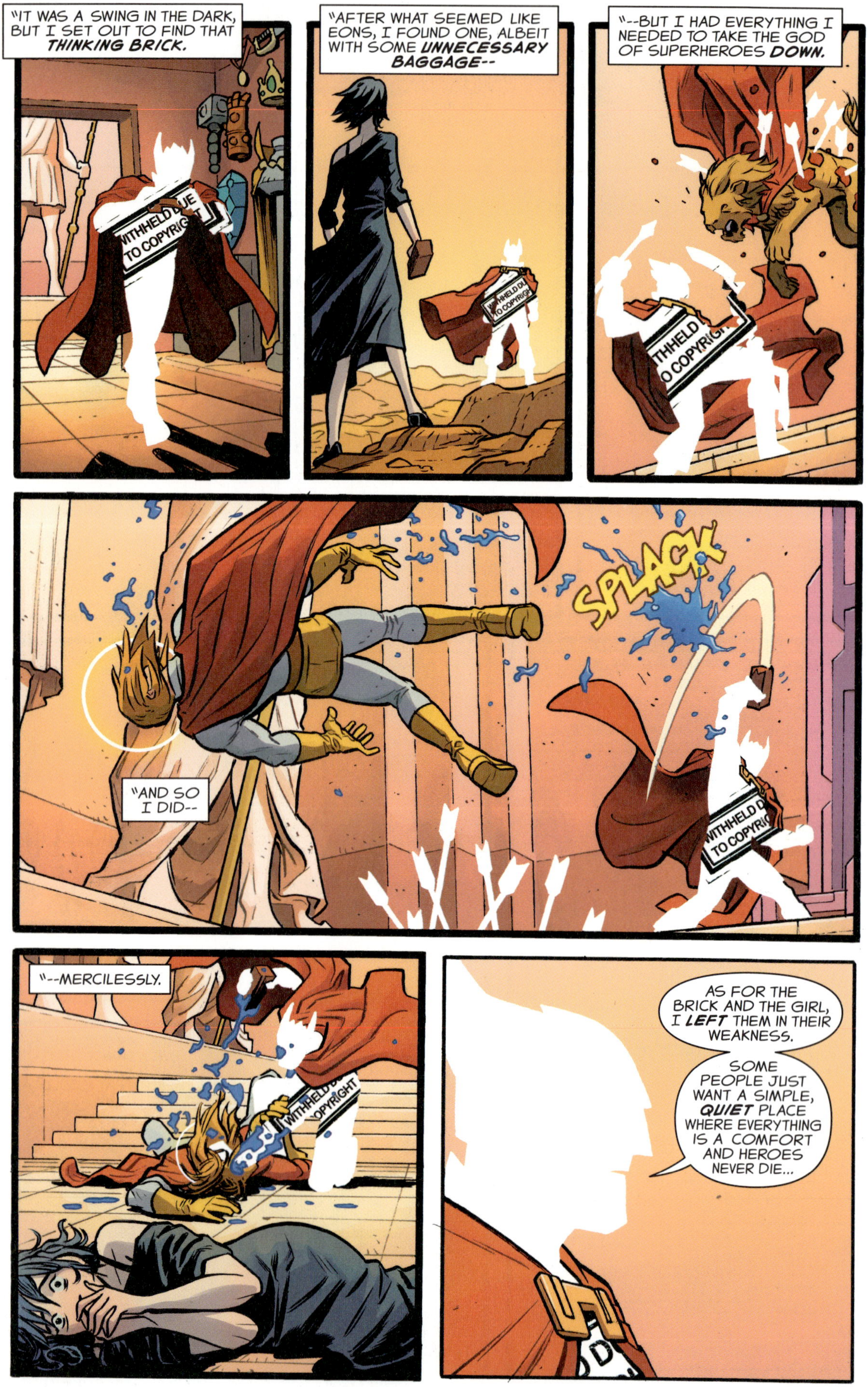

"IT WAS A SWING IN THE DARK, BUT I SET OUT TO FIND THAT THINKING BRICK.
WITHHELD DUE TO COPYRIGHT
"AFTER WHAT SEEMED LIKE EONS, I FOUND ONE, ALBEIT WITH SOME UNNECESSARY BAGGAGE--
WITHHELD DUE TO COPYRIGHT
"--BUT I HAD EVERYTHING I NEEDED TO TAKE THE GOD OF SUPERHEROES DOWN.
WITHHELD DUE TO COPYRIGHT
SPLACK
"AND SO I DID--
WITHHELD DUE TO COPYRIGHT
"--MERCILESSLY.
WITHHELD DUE TO COPYRIGHT
AS FOR THE BRICK AND THE GIRL, I LEFT THEM IN THEIR WEAKNESS.
SOME PEOPLE JUST WANT A SIMPLE, QUIET PLACE WHERE EVERYTHING IS A COMFORT AND HEROES NEVER DIE...

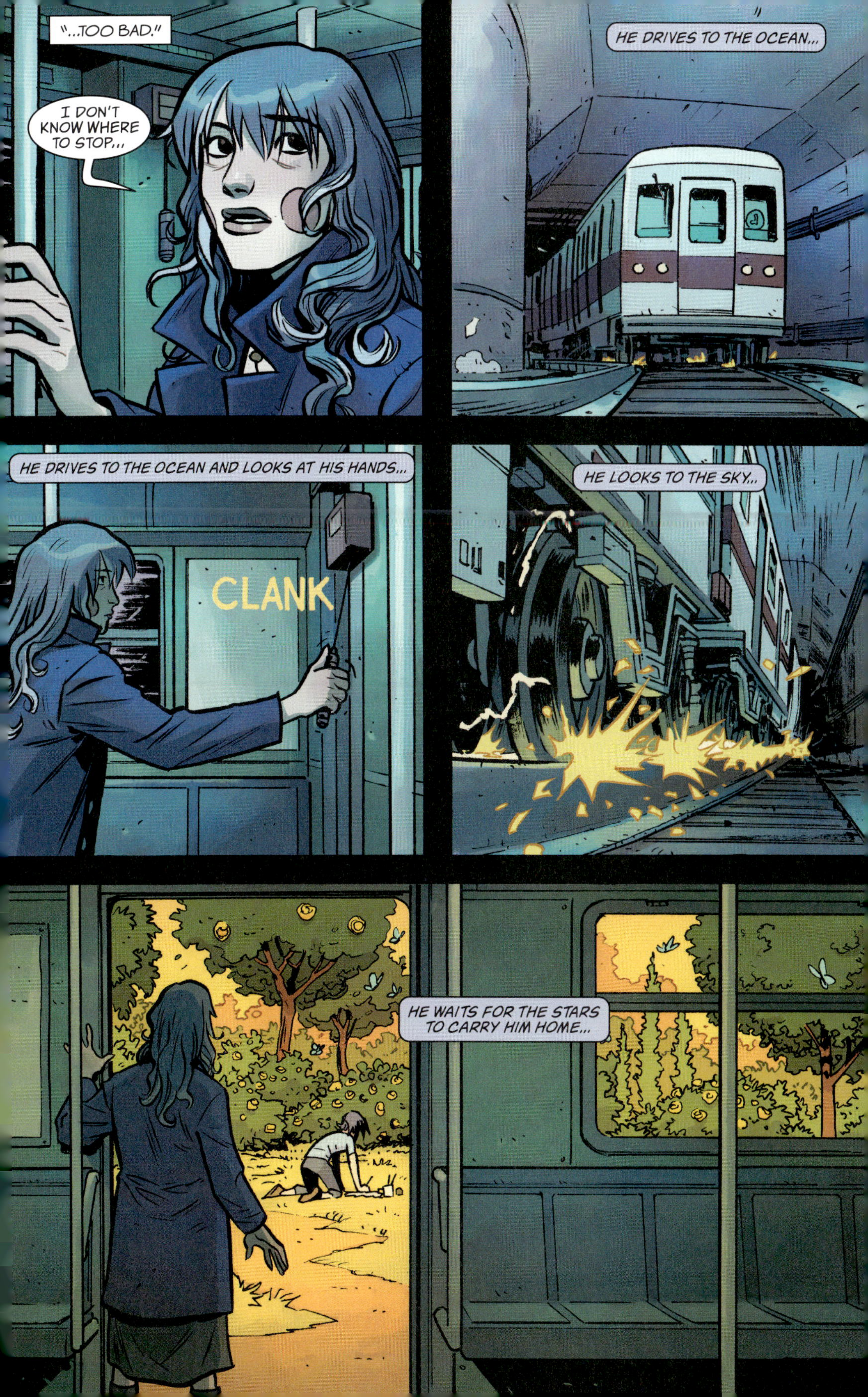
"...TOO BAD."
I DON'T KNOW WHERE TO STOP...
HE DRIVES TO THE OCEAN...
HE DRIVES TO THE OCEAN AND LOOKS AT HIS HANDS...
CLANK
HE LOOKS TO THE SKY...
HE WAITS FOR THE STARS TO CARRY HIM HOME...

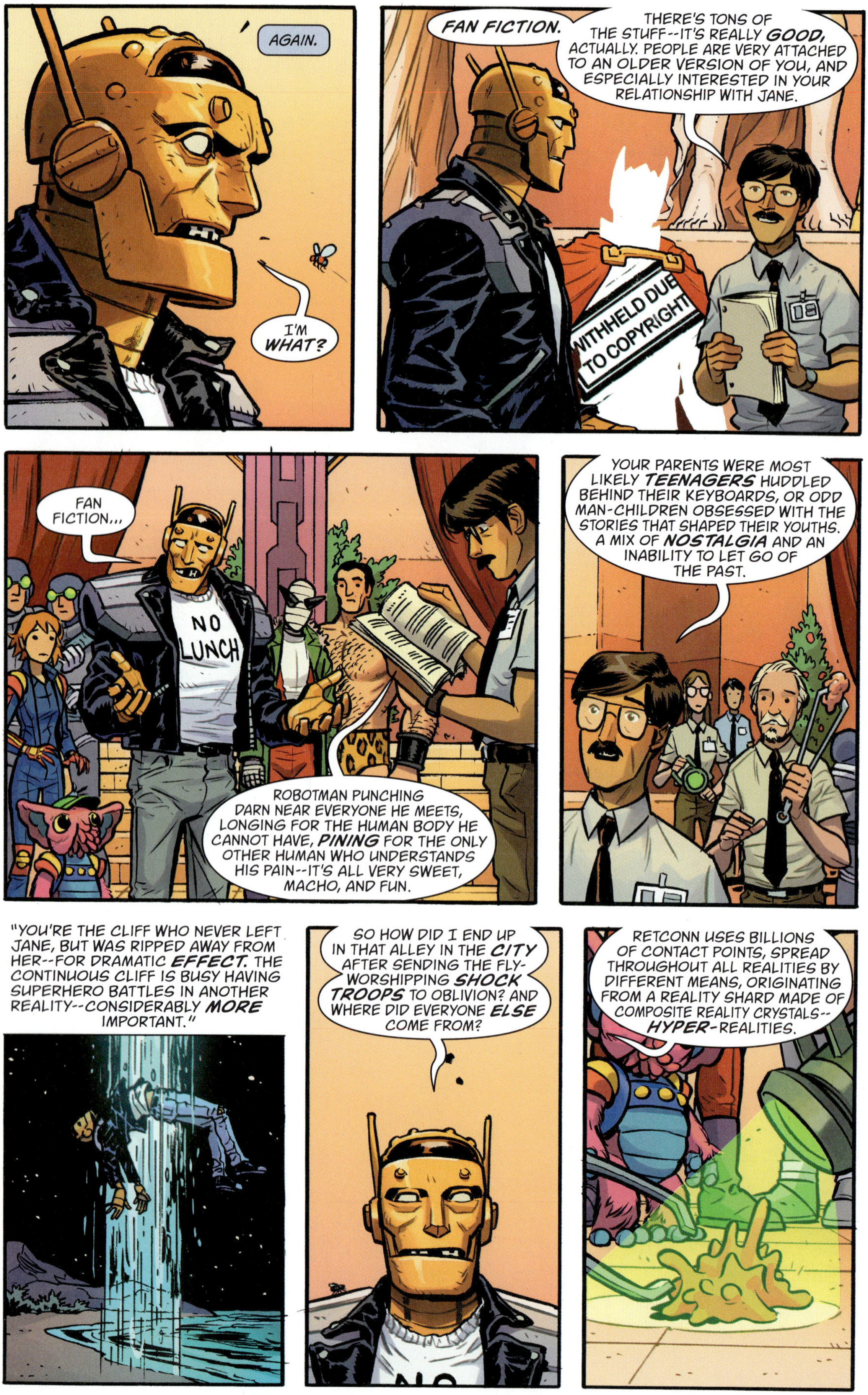
AGAIN.
I'M WHAT?
FAN FICTION.
THERE'S TONS OF THE STUFF--IT'S REALLY GOOD, ACTUALLY. PEOPLE ARE VERY ATTACHED TO AN OLDER VERSION OF YOU, AND ESPECIALLY INTERESTED IN YOUR RELATIONSHIP WITH JANE.
WITHHELD DUE TO COPYRIGHT
FAN FICTION...
NO LUNCH
ROBOTMAN PUNCHING DARN NEAR EVERYONE HE MEETS, LONGING FOR THE HUMAN BODY HE CANNOT HAVE, PINING FOR THE ONLY OTHER HUMAN WHO UNDERSTANDS HIS PAIN--IT'S ALL VERY SWEET, MACHO, AND FUN.
YOUR PARENTS WERE MOST LIKELY TEENAGERS HUDDLED BEHIND THEIR KEYBOARDS, OR ODD MAN-CHILDREN OBSESSED WITH THE STORIES THAT SHAPED THEIR YOUTHS. A MIX OF NOSTALGIA AND AN INABILITY TO LET GO OF THE PAST.
"YOU'RE THE CLIFF WHO NEVER LEFT JANE, BUT WAS RIPPED AWAY FROM HER--FOR DRAMATIC EFFECT. THE CONTINUOUS CLIFF IS BUSY HAVING SUPERHERO BATTLES IN ANOTHER REALITY--CONSIDERABLY MORE IMPORTANT."
SO HOW DID I END UP IN THAT ALLEY IN THE CITY AFTER SENDING THE FLY-WORSHIPPING SHOCK TROOPS TO OBLIVION? AND WHERE DID EVERYONE ELSE COME FROM?
RETCONN USES BILLIONS OF CONTACT POINTS, SPREAD THROUGHOUT ALL REALITIES BY DIFFERENT MEANS, ORIGINATING FROM A REALITY SHARD MADE OF COMPOSITE REALITY CRYSTALS--HYPER-REALITIES.

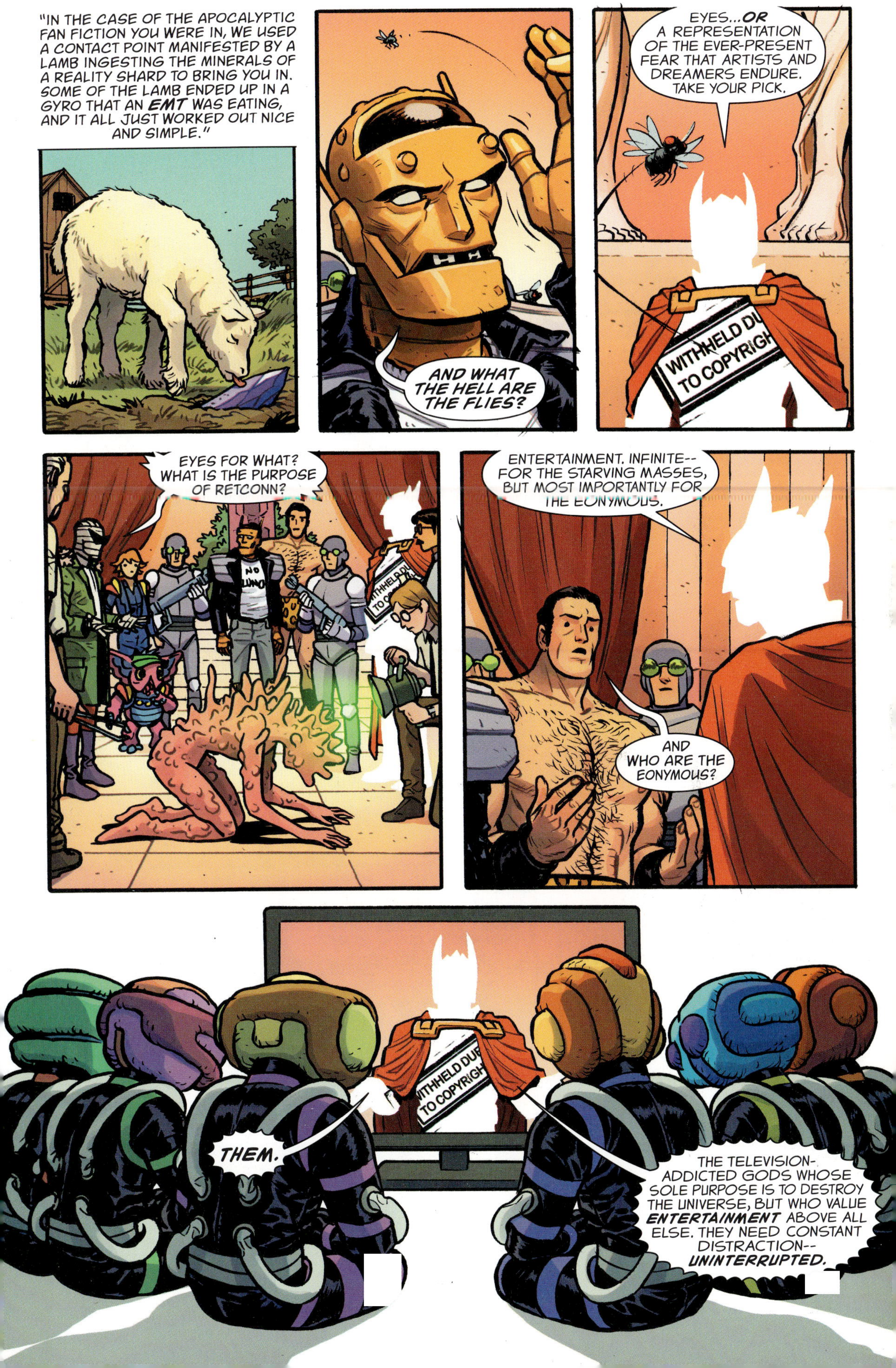
"IN THE CASE OF THE APOCALYPTIC FAN FICTION YOU WERE IN, WE USED A CONTACT POINT MANIFESTED BY A LAMB INGESTING THE MINERALS OF A REALITY SHARD TO BRING YOU IN. SOME OF THE LAMB ENDED UP IN A GYRO THAT AN EMT WAS EATING, AND IT ALL JUST WORKED OUT NICE AND SIMPLE."
AND WHAT THE HELL ARE THE FLIES?
EYES...OR A REPRESENTATION OF THE EVER-PRESENT FEAR THAT ARTISTS AND DREAMERS ENDURE. TAKE YOUR PICK.
WITHHELD DU TO COPYRIGH
EYES FOR WHAT? WHAT IS THE PURPOSE OF RETCONN?
NO
ENTERTAINMENT. INFINITE--FOR THE STARVING MASSES, BUT MOST IMPORTANTLY FOR THE EONYMOUS.
AND WHO ARE THE EONYMOUS?
WITHHELD DU TO COPYRIGH
THEM.
THE TELEVISION-ADDICTED GODS WHOSE SOLE PURPOSE IS TO DESTROY THE UNIVERSE, BUT WHO VALUE ENTERTAINMENT ABOVE ALL ELSE. THEY NEED CONSTANT DISTRACTION--UNINTERRUPTED.

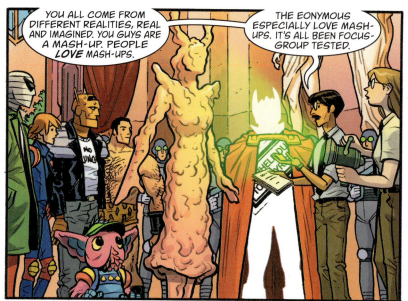

YOU ALL COME FROM DIFFERENT REALITIES, REAL AND IMAGINED. YOU GUYS ARE A MASH-UP. PEOPLE **LOVE** MASH-UPS.
THE EONYMOUS ESPECIALLY LOVE MASH-UPS. IT'S ALL BEEN FOCUS-GROUP TESTED.
NO LUNCH
WITHHELD DUE TO COPYRIGHT
YOU'RE A MONSTER WHO CONTROLS PEOPLE'S LIVES! WE ARE NOT A **GAME!**
DIDN'T YOU HAVE SEX WITH YOUR CAT? YEAH, I DON'T THINK WE NEED TO HEAR ANY MORE OUT OF YOU.
HE'S A **MAN-CAT** WITH HIS OWN FREE WILL--AND I CAN GET DOWN WITH WHOEVER WANTS TO GET **DOWN.**
OBVIOUSLY, WHICH IS HOW WE ENDED UP IN THIS MESS...
WITHHELD DU TO COPYRIGH
YOUR REALITY IS A CONSTRUCT--**NOTHING IS REAL**--AND IF NOTHING IS REAL, THEN **EVERYTHING IS REAL**--IT'S ALL **DIGESTIBLE.** BUT I'VE DECIDED IT NEEDS TO END.
'CUZ I'M TIRED AS SHIT, AND I'VE BEEN FOOLING MYSELF FOR YEARS THAT I ACTUALLY MATTER--THAT I CONTROL ANYTHING AT ALL. REALLY, I'M JUST A SLAVE--**WE ALL ARE.**
NO UNCH
WITHHELD DU TO COPYRIG

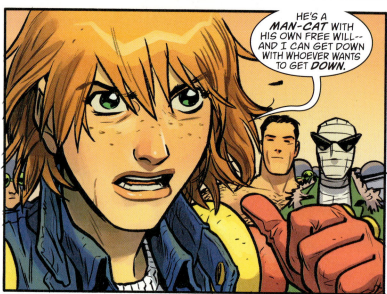

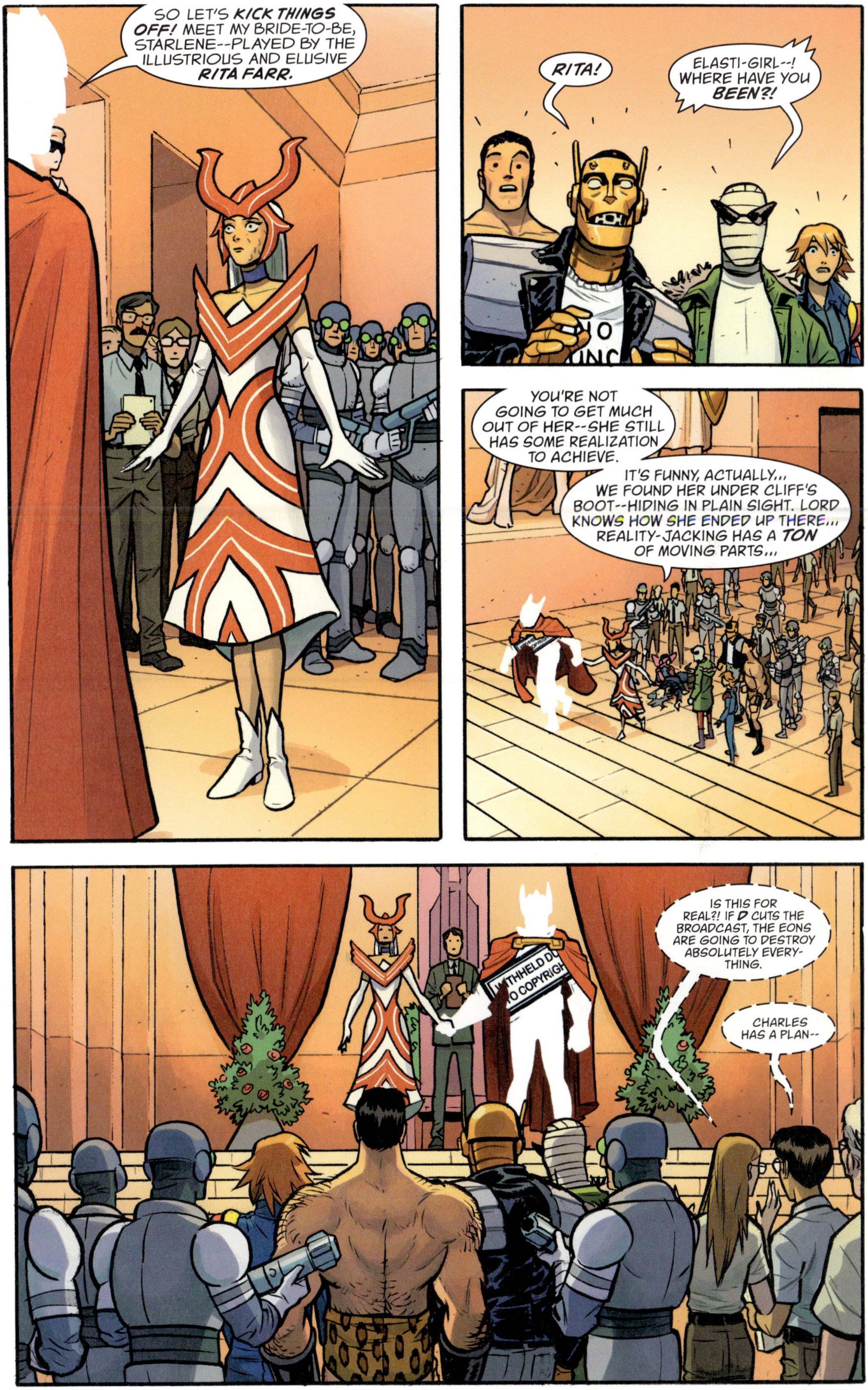
SO LET'S KICK THINGS OFF! MEET MY BRIDE-TO-BE, STARLENE--PLAYED BY THE ILLUSTRIOUS AND ELUSIVE RITA FARR.
RITA!
ELASTI-GIRL--! WHERE HAVE YOU BEEN?!
YOU'RE NOT GOING TO GET MUCH OUT OF HER--SHE STILL HAS SOME REALIZATION TO ACHIEVE.
IT'S FUNNY, ACTUALLY... WE FOUND HER UNDER CLIFF'S BOOT--HIDING IN PLAIN SIGHT. LORD KNOWS HOW SHE ENDED UP THERE... REALITY-JACKING HAS A TON OF MOVING PARTS...
IS THIS FOR REAL?! IF D CUTS THE BROADCAST, THE EONS ARE GOING TO DESTROY ABSOLUTELY EVERY-THING.
CHARLES HAS A PLAN--

"--HE'S FOUND US A REPLACEMENT."

WHAT, LIKE FAMOUS FOR ALL ETERNITY?! I'M *INTRIGUED*--WHAT'S *THE CATCH?* I NEED *DETAILS*, CHUCK.

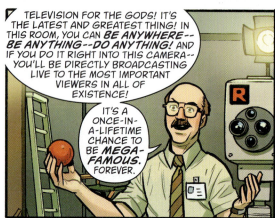

TELEVISION FOR THE GODS! IT'S THE LATEST AND GREATEST THING! IN THIS ROOM, YOU CAN *BE ANYWHERE-- BE ANYTHING--DO ANYTHING!* AND IF YOU DO IT RIGHT INTO THIS CAMERA-- YOU'LL BE DIRECTLY BROADCASTING LIVE TO THE MOST IMPORTANT VIEWERS IN ALL OF EXISTENCE!

IT'S A ONCE-IN- A-LIFETIME CHANCE TO BE *MEGA- FAMOUS.* FOREVER.

JUST TAKE THIS BALL, AND IT'LL GIVE YOU ALL THE POWER YOU *NEED* TO BE OMNIPOTENTLY TELEVISED.

HMMMM...WITH THE ABILITY TO MAKE ANYTHING UP, I COULD REALLY SUBVERT TELE- VISION PROGRAMMING LIKE I'VE ALWAYS WANTED TO WHILE AT THE SAME TIME LIVING IN AN EMPTY WHITE ROOM DRINKING FREE DIET COLA--

WE'RE IN!!

SPEAK FOR YOURSELF, NOBODY--THIS AIN'T OUR SCENE, AND *THE BREEZE* DOESN'T WORK FOR FREE POP.

DAD--! ARE YOU CRAZY?! I DON'T WANT TO BE TV FOR A BUNCH OF *GODS!* AND YOU WANTED TO WIPE EVERYTHING OUT--THAT'S EXACTLY WHAT WILL HAPPEN IF WE DON'T DO THIS! AND--

--HELLO--! I JUST HAD A BABY AND HE'S MISSING!

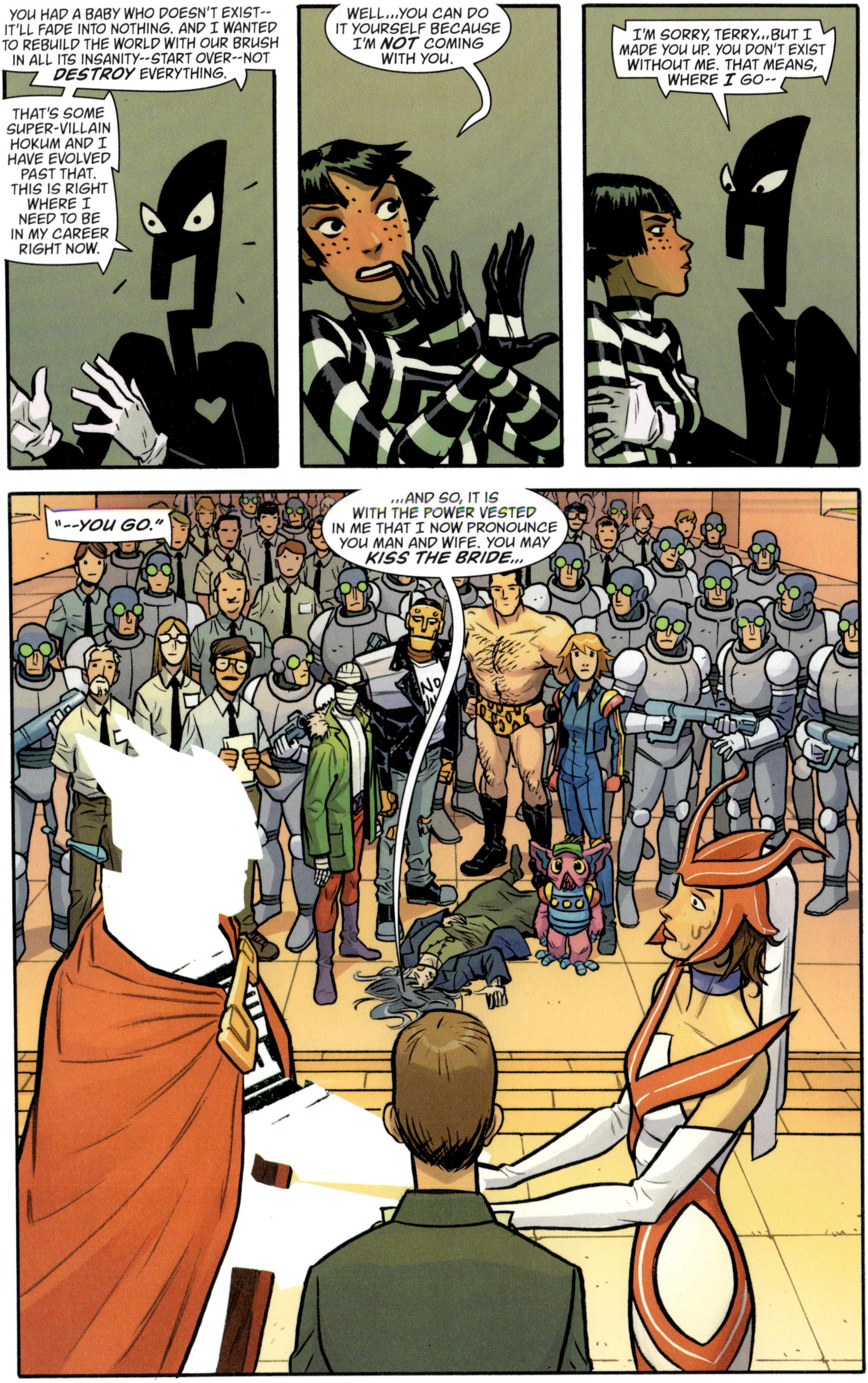

YOU HAD A BABY WHO DOESN'T EXIST--IT'LL FADE INTO NOTHING. AND I WANTED TO REBUILD THE WORLD WITH OUR BRUSH IN ALL ITS INSANITY--START OVER--NOT DESTROY EVERYTHING.
THAT'S SOME SUPER-VILLAIN HOKUM AND I HAVE EVOLVED PAST THAT. THIS IS RIGHT WHERE I NEED TO BE IN MY CAREER RIGHT NOW.
WELL...YOU CAN DO IT YOURSELF BECAUSE I'M NOT COMING WITH YOU.
I'M SORRY, TERRY...BUT I MADE YOU UP. YOU DON'T EXIST WITHOUT ME. THAT MEANS, WHERE I GO--
"--YOU GO."
...AND SO, IT IS WITH THE POWER VESTED IN ME THAT I NOW PRONOUNCE YOU MAN AND WIFE. YOU MAY KISS THE BRIDE...

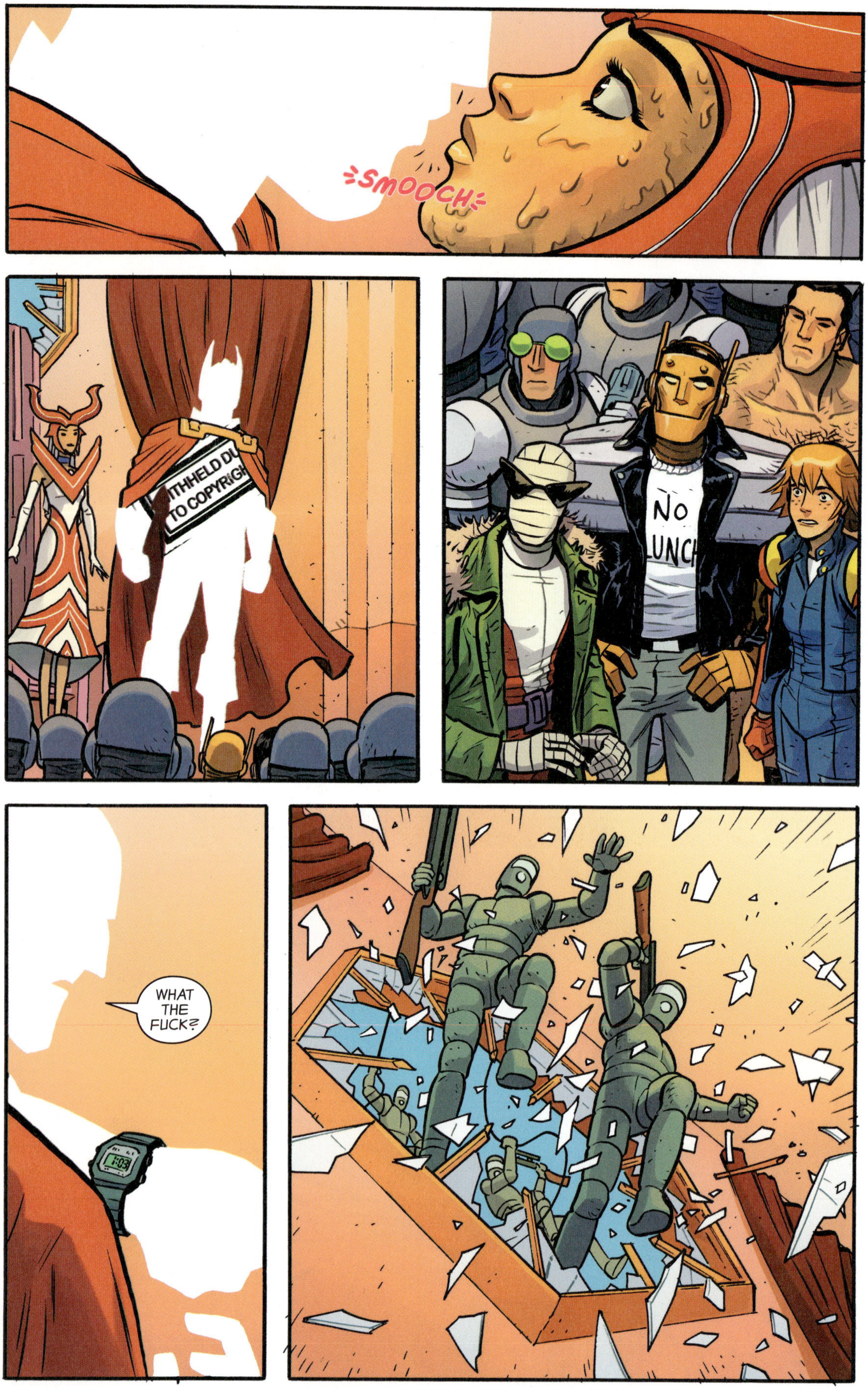
SMOOCH
ITHHELD DU
TO COPYRIGH
NO
LUNCH
WHAT THE FUCK?

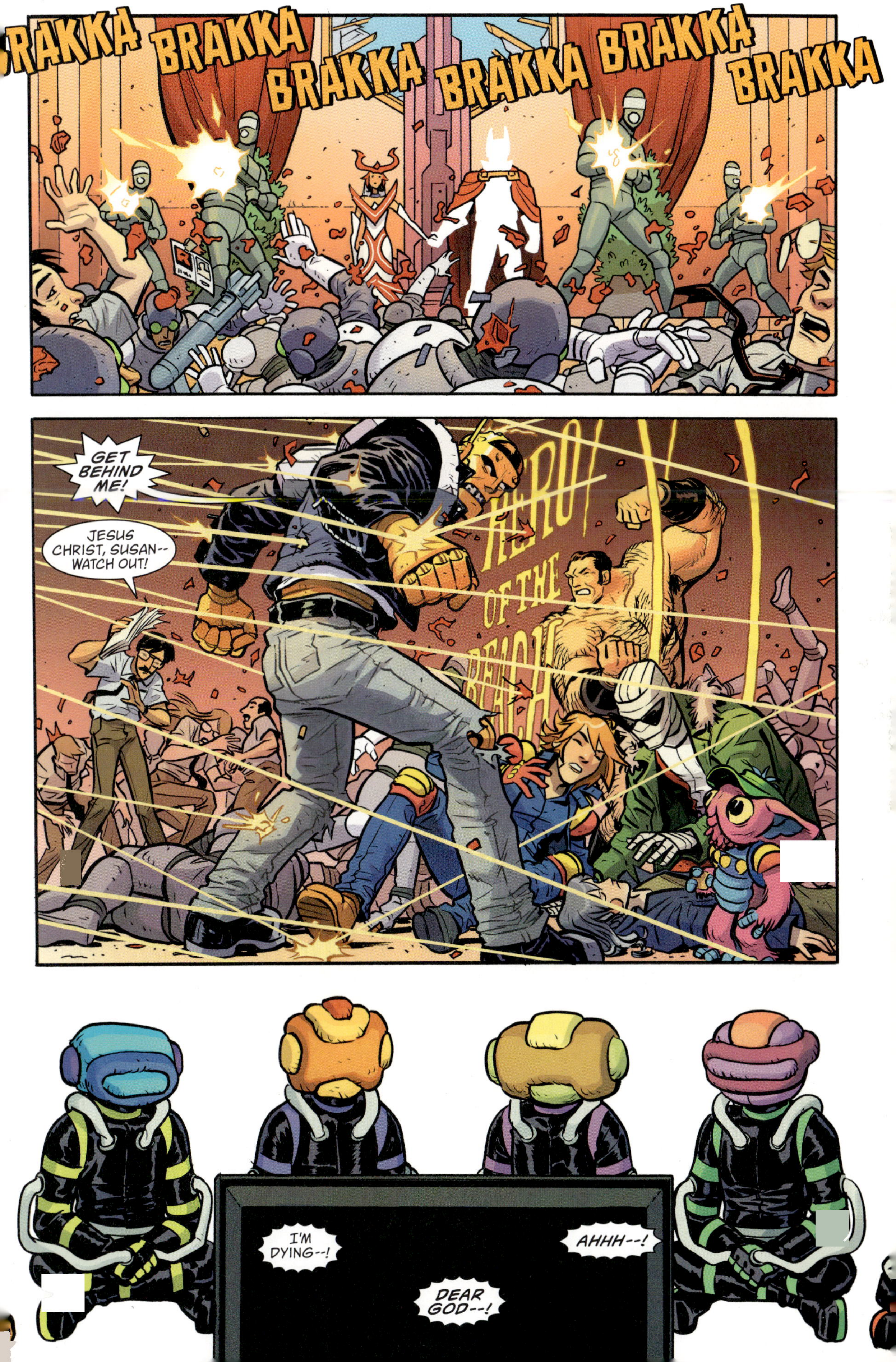
BRAKKA BRAKKA BRAKKA BRAKKA BRAKKA BRAKKA
GET BEHIND ME!
JESUS CHRIST, SUSAN-- WATCH OUT!
HERO OF THE BEACH
I'M DYING--!
AHHH--!
DEAR GOD--!

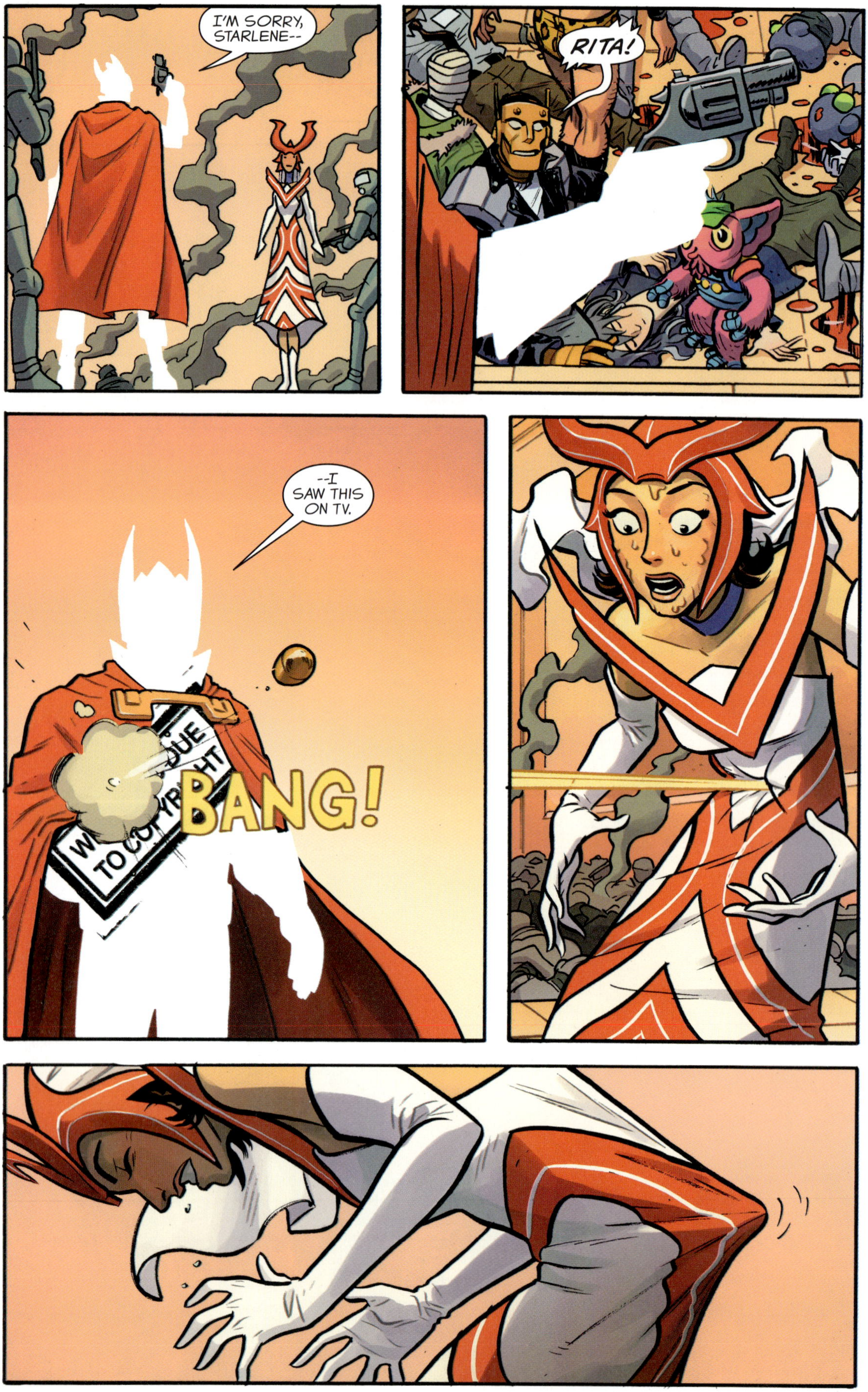
I'M SORRY, STARLENE--
RITA!
--I SAW THIS ON TV.
BANG!

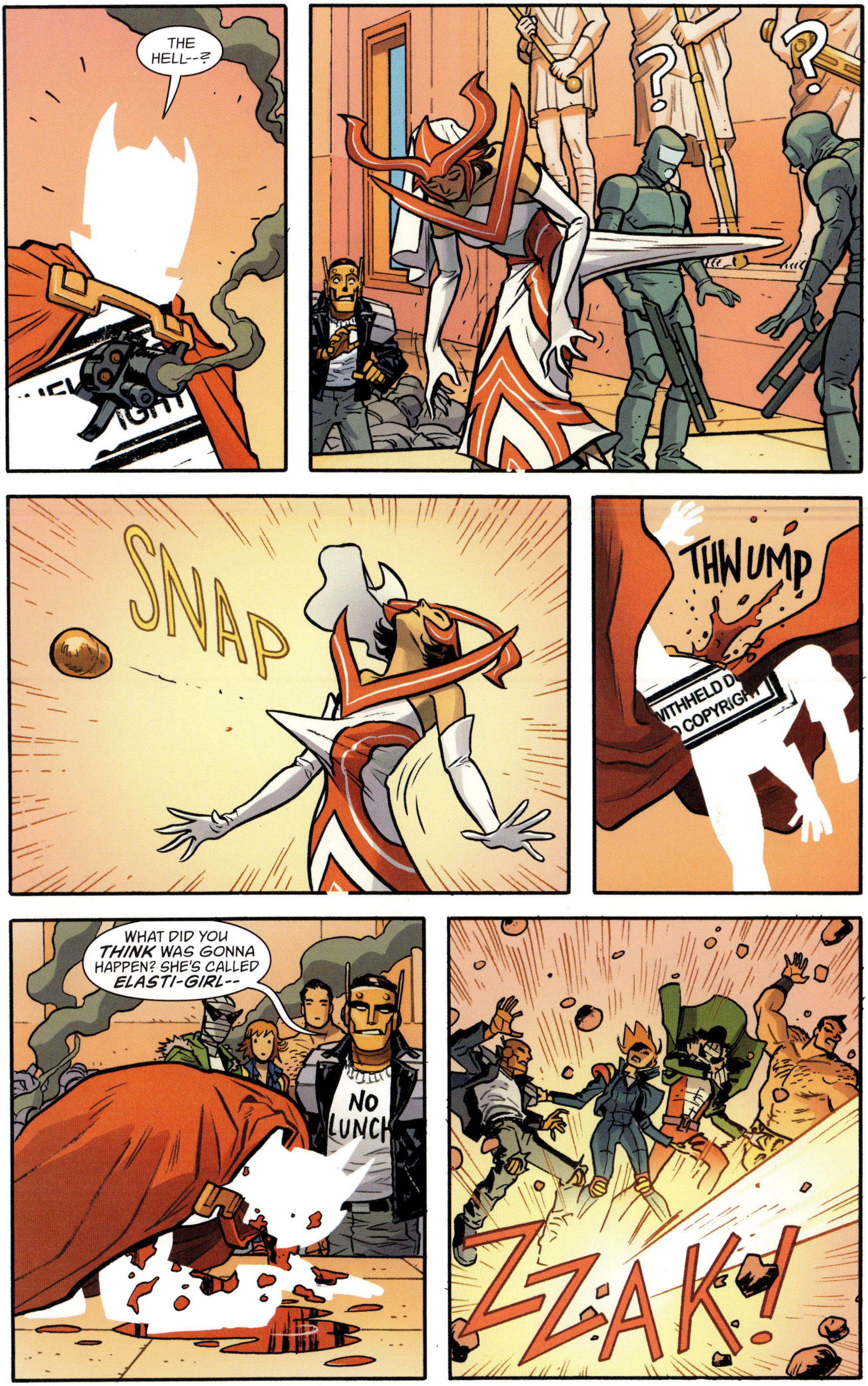
THE HELL--?
?
?
SNAP
THWUMP
WITHHELD D
D COPYRIGH
WHAT DID YOU *THINK* WAS GONNA HAPPEN? SHE'S CALLED *ELASTI-GIRL*--
NO LUNCH
ZZAK!

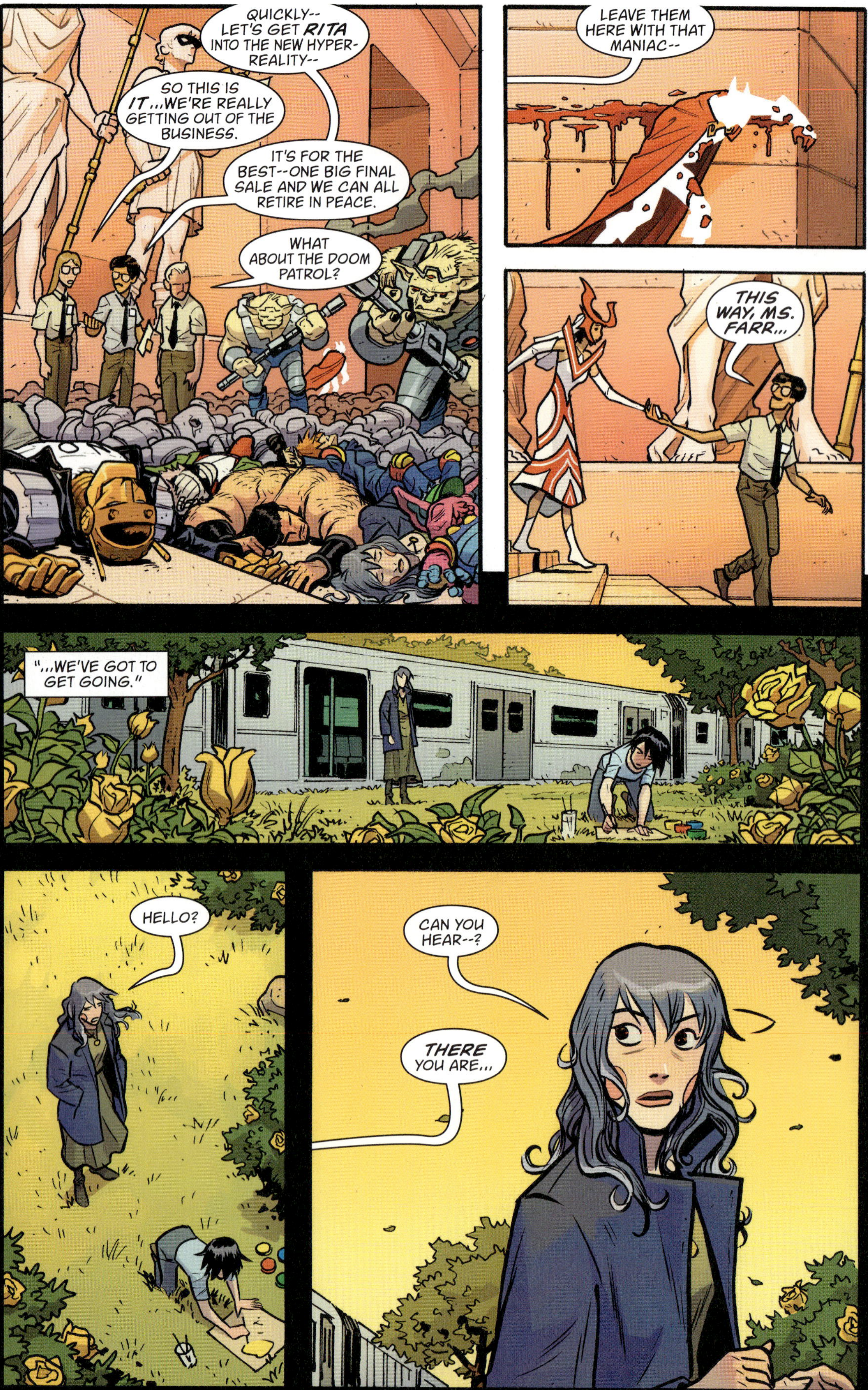

QUICKLY-- LET'S GET RITA INTO THE NEW HYPER-REALITY--
SO THIS IS IT...WE'RE REALLY GETTING OUT OF THE BUSINESS.
IT'S FOR THE BEST--ONE BIG FINAL SALE AND WE CAN ALL RETIRE IN PEACE.
WHAT ABOUT THE DOOM PATROL?
LEAVE THEM HERE WITH THAT MANIAC--
THIS WAY, MS. FARR...
"...WE'VE GOT TO GET GOING."
HELLO?
CAN YOU HEAR--?
THERE YOU ARE...

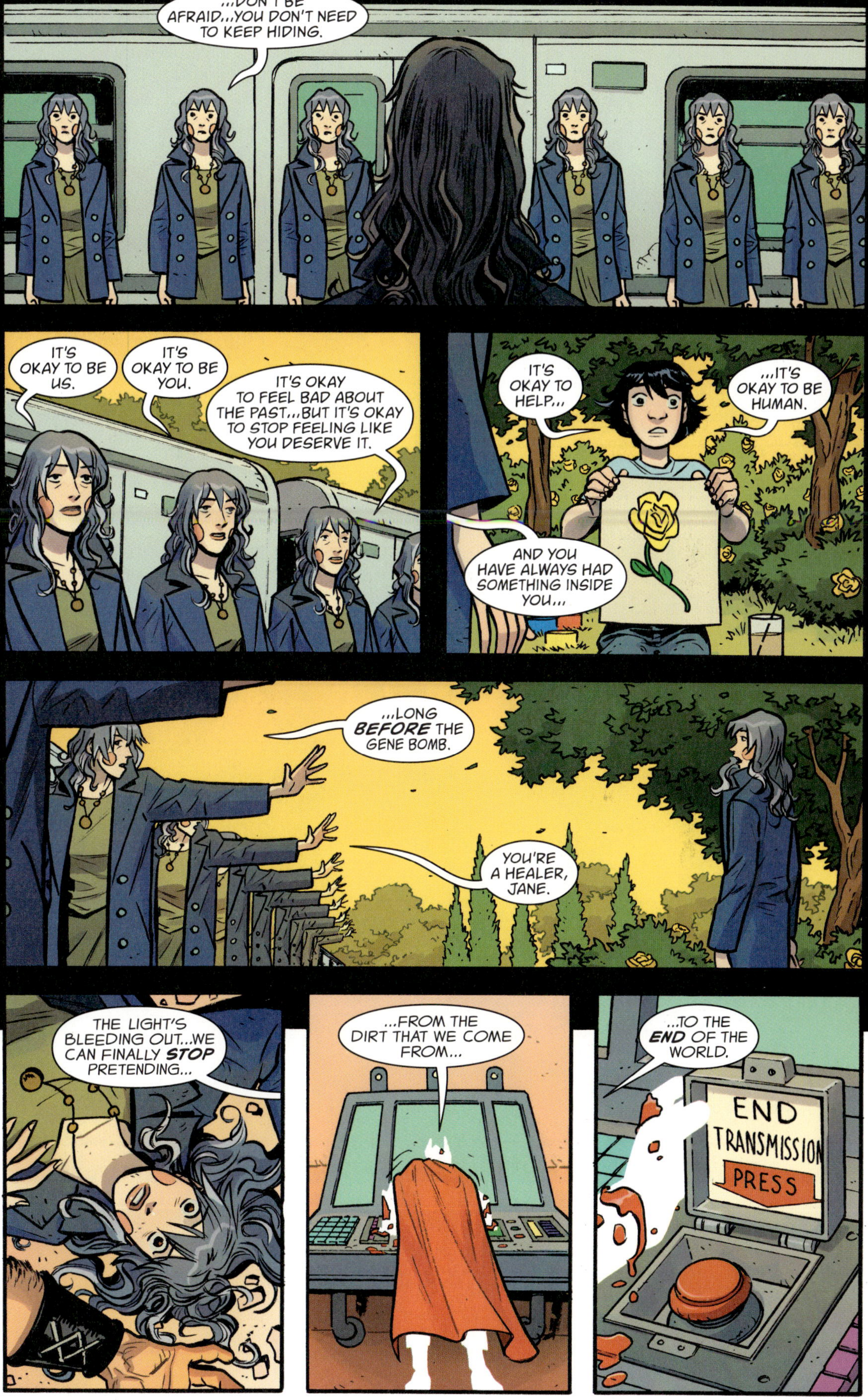
...DON'T BE AFRAID...YOU DON'T NEED TO KEEP HIDING.
IT'S OKAY TO BE US.
IT'S OKAY TO BE YOU.
IT'S OKAY TO FEEL BAD ABOUT THE PAST...BUT IT'S OKAY TO STOP FEELING LIKE YOU DESERVE IT.
IT'S OKAY TO HELP...
...IT'S OKAY TO BE HUMAN.
AND YOU HAVE ALWAYS HAD SOMETHING INSIDE YOU...
...LONG **BEFORE** THE GENE BOMB.
YOU'RE A HEALER, JANE.
THE LIGHT'S BLEEDING OUT...WE CAN FINALLY **STOP** PRETENDING...
...FROM THE DIRT THAT WE COME FROM...
...TO THE **END** OF THE WORLD.
END TRANSMISSION
PRESS

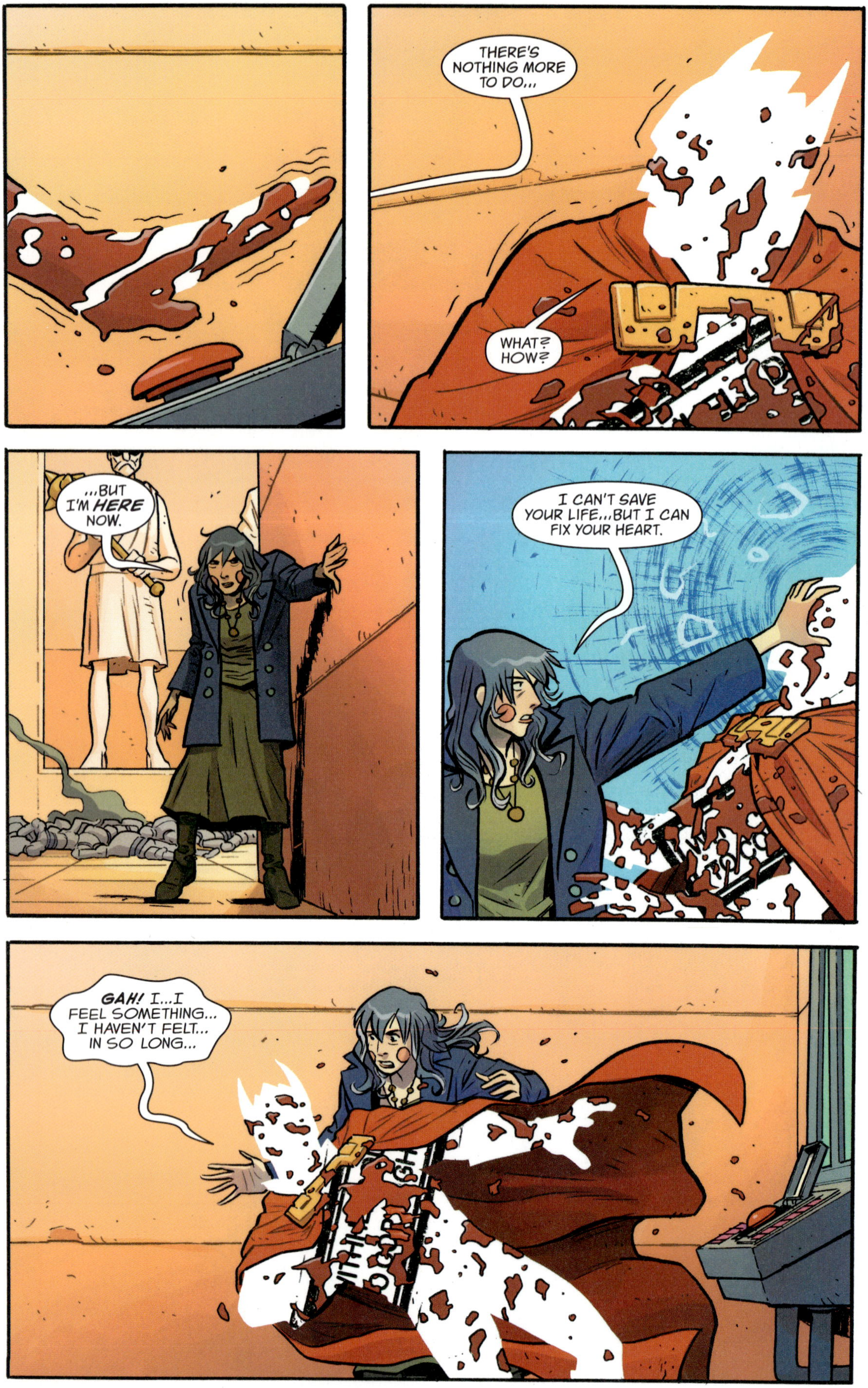
THERE'S NOTHING MORE TO DO...
WHAT? HOW?
...BUT I'M HERE NOW.
I CAN'T SAVE YOUR LIFE...BUT I CAN FIX YOUR HEART.
GAH! I...I FEEL SOMETHING... I HAVEN'T FELT... IN SO LONG...

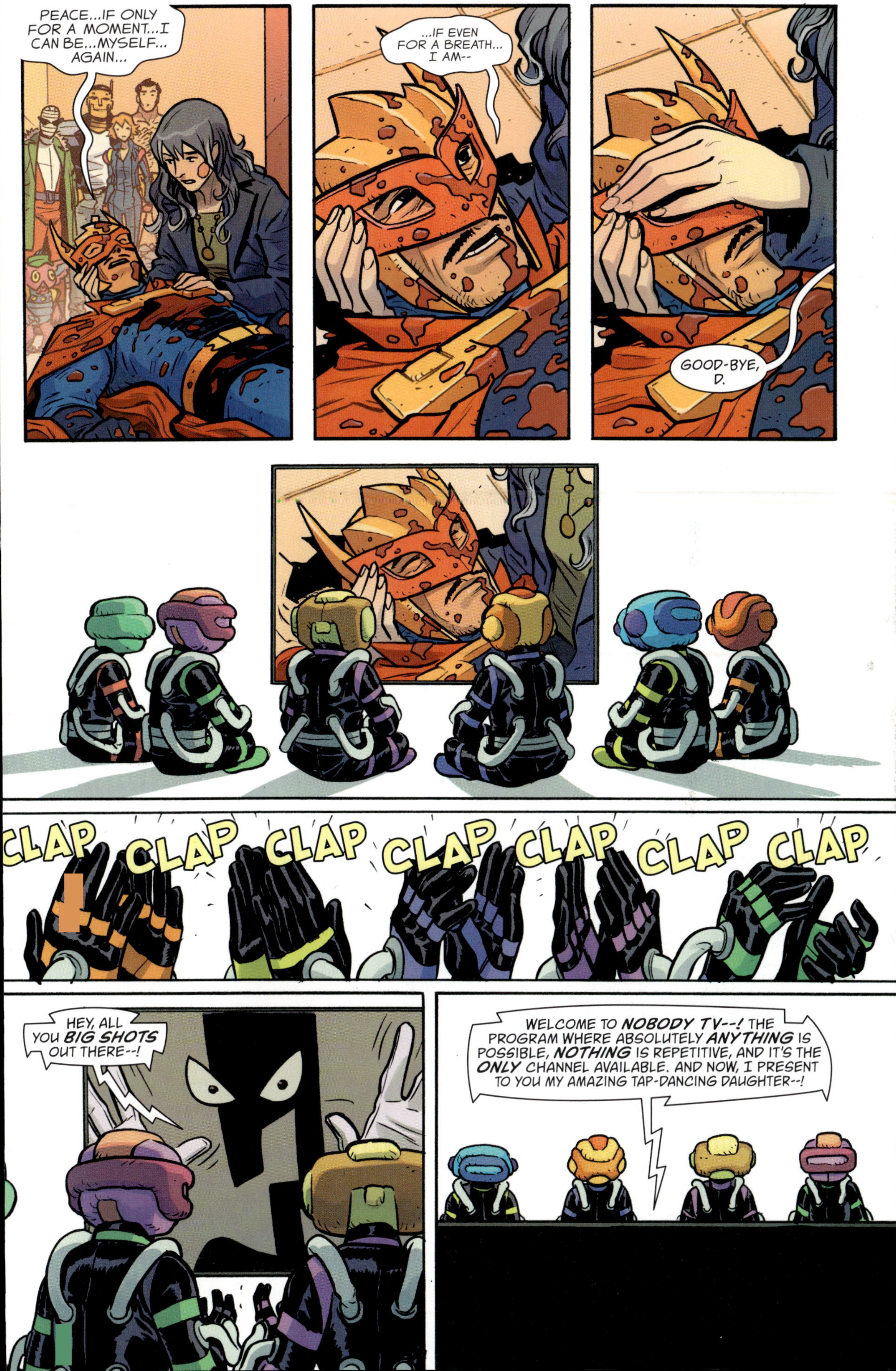
PEACE...IF ONLY FOR A MOMENT...I CAN BE...MYSELF... AGAIN...
...IF EVEN FOR A BREATH... I AM--
GOOD-BYE, D.
CLAP CLAP CLAP CLAP CLAP CLAP CLAP
HEY, ALL YOU BIG SHOTS OUT THERE--!
WELCOME TO NOBODY TV--! THE PROGRAM WHERE ABSOLUTELY ANYTHING IS POSSIBLE, NOTHING IS REPETITIVE, AND IT'S THE ONLY CHANNEL AVAILABLE. AND NOW, I PRESENT TO YOU MY AMAZING TAP-DANCING DAUGHTER--!

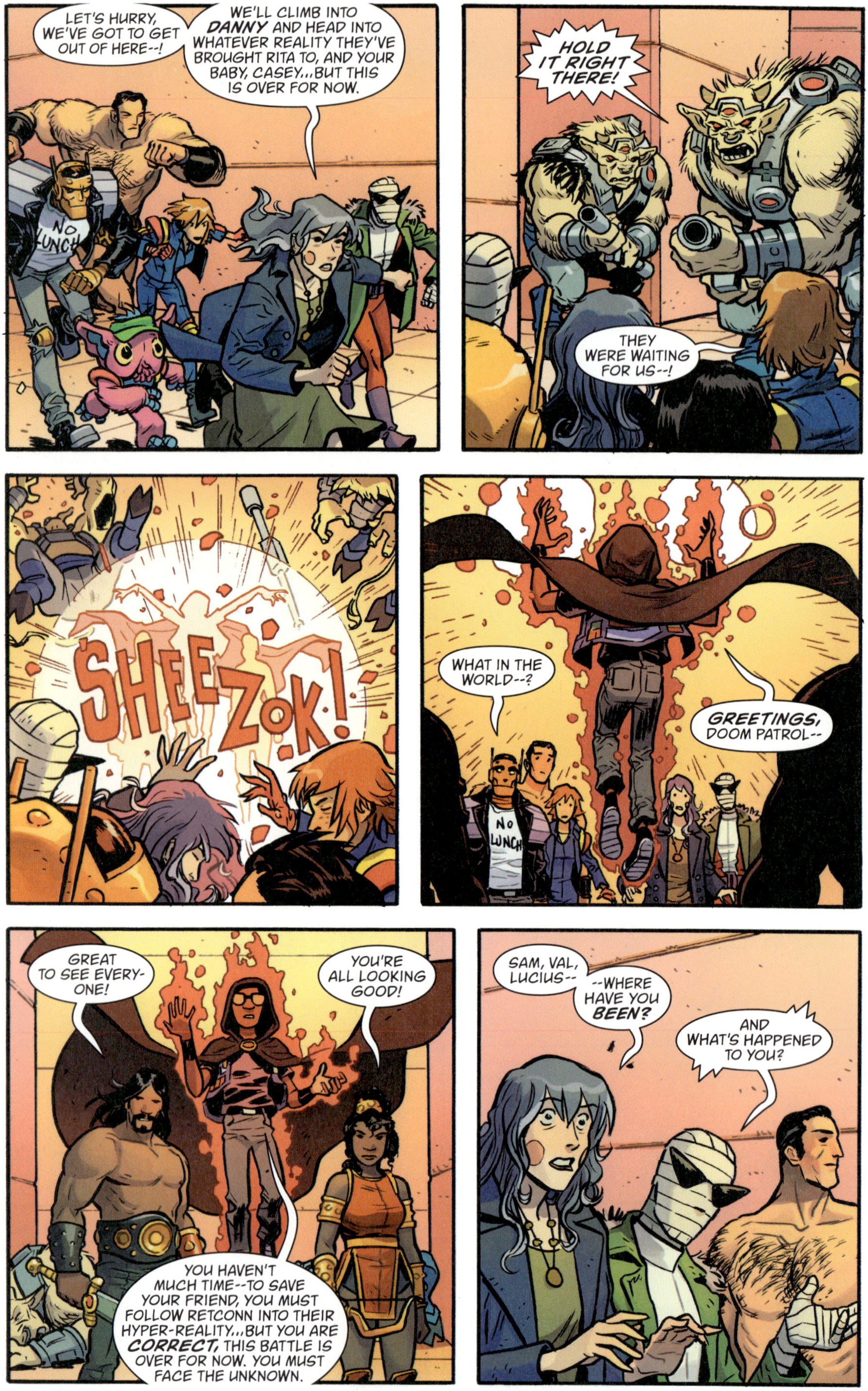

LET'S HURRY, WE'VE GOT TO GET OUT OF HERE--!
WE'LL CLIMB INTO **DANNY** AND HEAD INTO WHATEVER REALITY THEY'VE BROUGHT RITA TO, AND YOUR BABY, CASEY... BUT THIS IS OVER FOR NOW.
HOLD IT RIGHT THERE!
THEY WERE WAITING FOR US--!
SHEEZOK!
WHAT IN THE WORLD--?
GREETINGS, DOOM PATROL--
GREAT TO SEE EVERY-ONE!
YOU'RE ALL LOOKING GOOD!
YOU HAVEN'T MUCH TIME--TO SAVE YOUR FRIEND, YOU MUST FOLLOW RETCONN INTO THEIR HYPER-REALITY... BUT YOU ARE **CORRECT,** THIS BATTLE IS OVER FOR NOW. YOU MUST FACE THE UNKNOWN.
SAM, VAL, LUCIUS--
--WHERE HAVE YOU **BEEN?**
AND WHAT'S HAPPENED TO YOU?

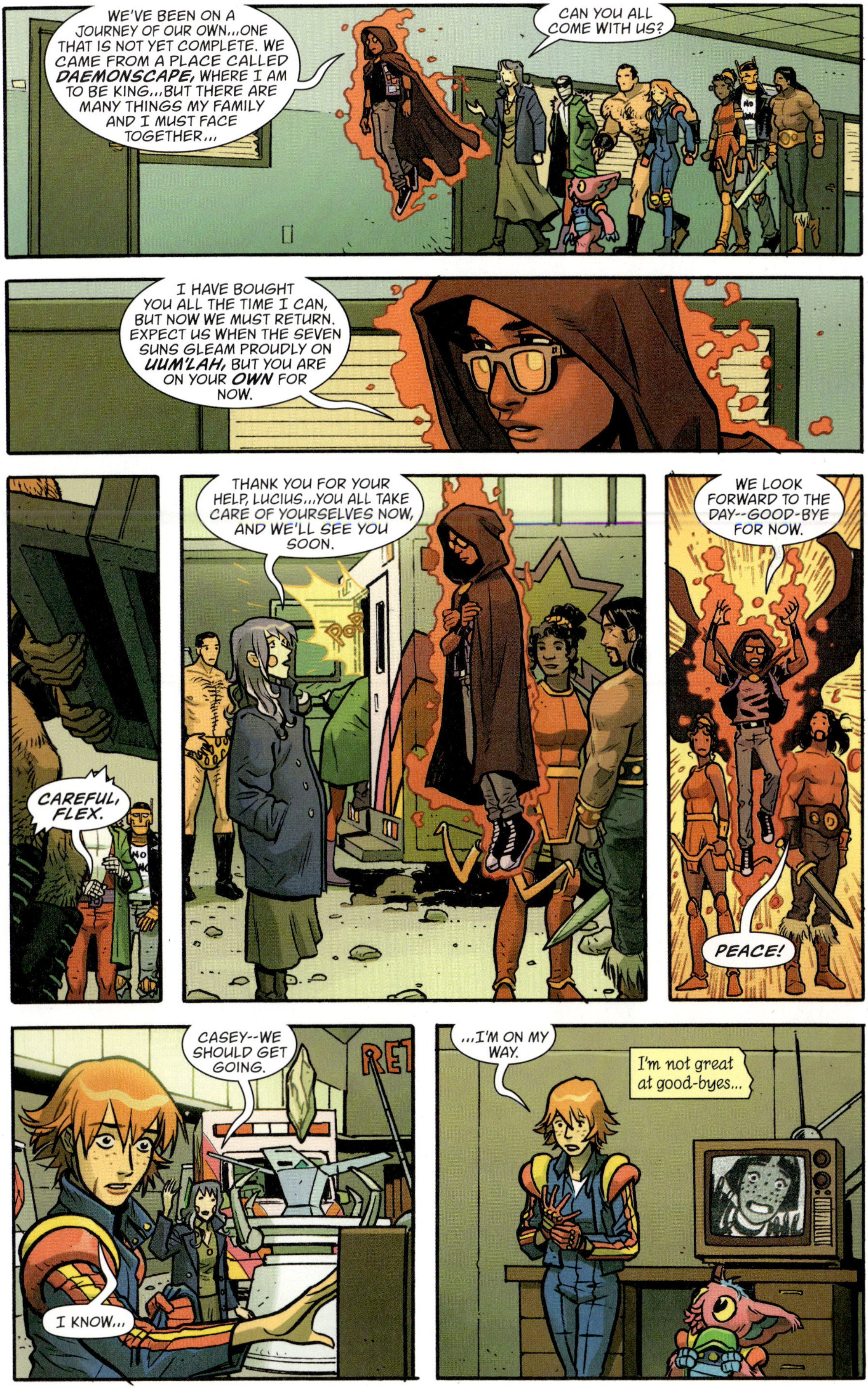
WE'VE BEEN ON A JOURNEY OF OUR OWN...ONE THAT IS NOT YET COMPLETE. WE CAME FROM A PLACE CALLED DAEMONSCAPE, WHERE I AM TO BE KING...BUT THERE ARE MANY THINGS MY FAMILY AND I MUST FACE TOGETHER...
CAN YOU ALL COME WITH US?
I HAVE BOUGHT YOU ALL THE TIME I CAN, BUT NOW WE MUST RETURN. EXPECT US WHEN THE SEVEN SUNS GLEAM PROUDLY ON UUM'LAH, BUT YOU ARE ON YOUR OWN FOR NOW.
CAREFUL, FLEX.
THANK YOU FOR YOUR HELP, LUCIUS...YOU ALL TAKE CARE OF YOURSELVES NOW, AND WE'LL SEE YOU SOON.
POP
WE LOOK FORWARD TO THE DAY--GOOD-BYE FOR NOW.
PEACE!
CASEY--WE SHOULD GET GOING.
I KNOW...
...I'M ON MY WAY.
I'm not great at good-byes...

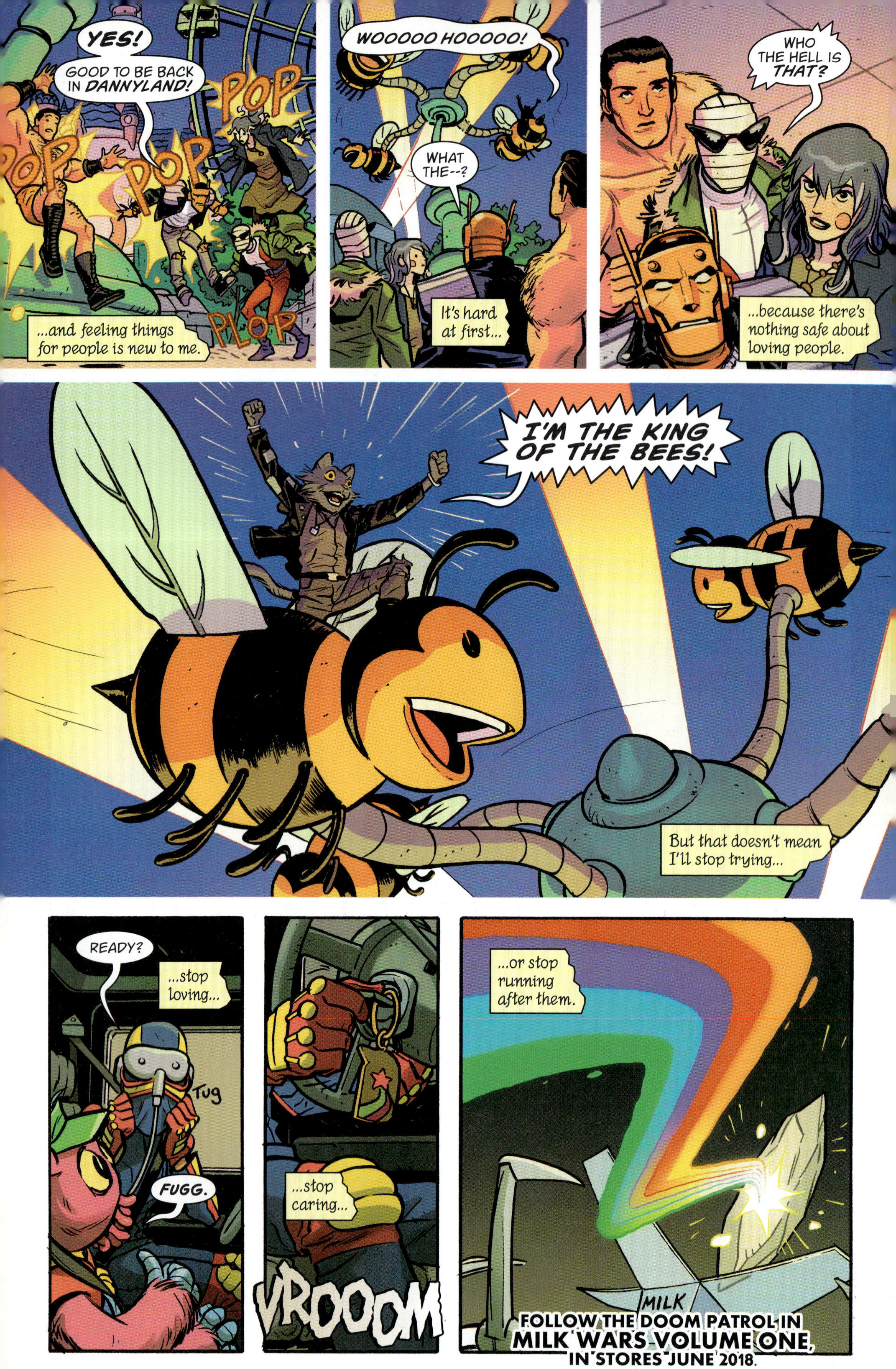
YES!
GOOD TO BE BACK IN DANNYLAND!
POP
POP
POP
...and feeling things for people is new to me.
PLOP
WOOOOO HOOOOO!
WHAT THE--?
It's hard at first...
WHO THE HELL IS THAT?
...because there's nothing safe about loving people.
I'M THE KING OF THE BEES!
But that doesn't mean I'll stop trying...
READY?
...stop loving...
TUG
FUGG.
...stop caring...
VROOOM
...or stop running after them.
MILK
FOLLOW THE DOOM PATROL IN
MILK WARS VOLUME ONE,
IN STORES JUNE 2018.

DOOM PATROL

Into the Daemonscape

A QUEST FOR ADVENTURERS LEVEL 16-20

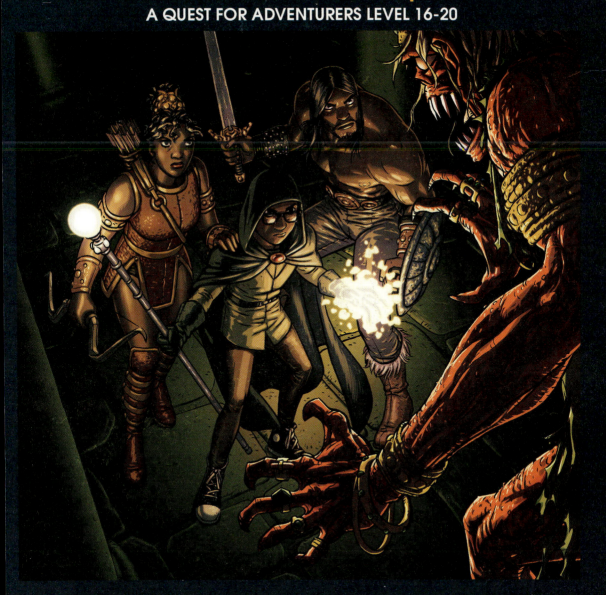

Far beyond the mortal realms, The Reynolds family must overcome their familial challenges in order to claim Lucius's rightful place as the ruler of THE DAEMONSCAPE, a place of horror, conflict, and sorcery. It is filled with traps, beasts, difficult challenges, the Five Daemon-Lords of The Crystal Hells ™ , and Agantha, a demon trapped in the body of a dead squirrel.

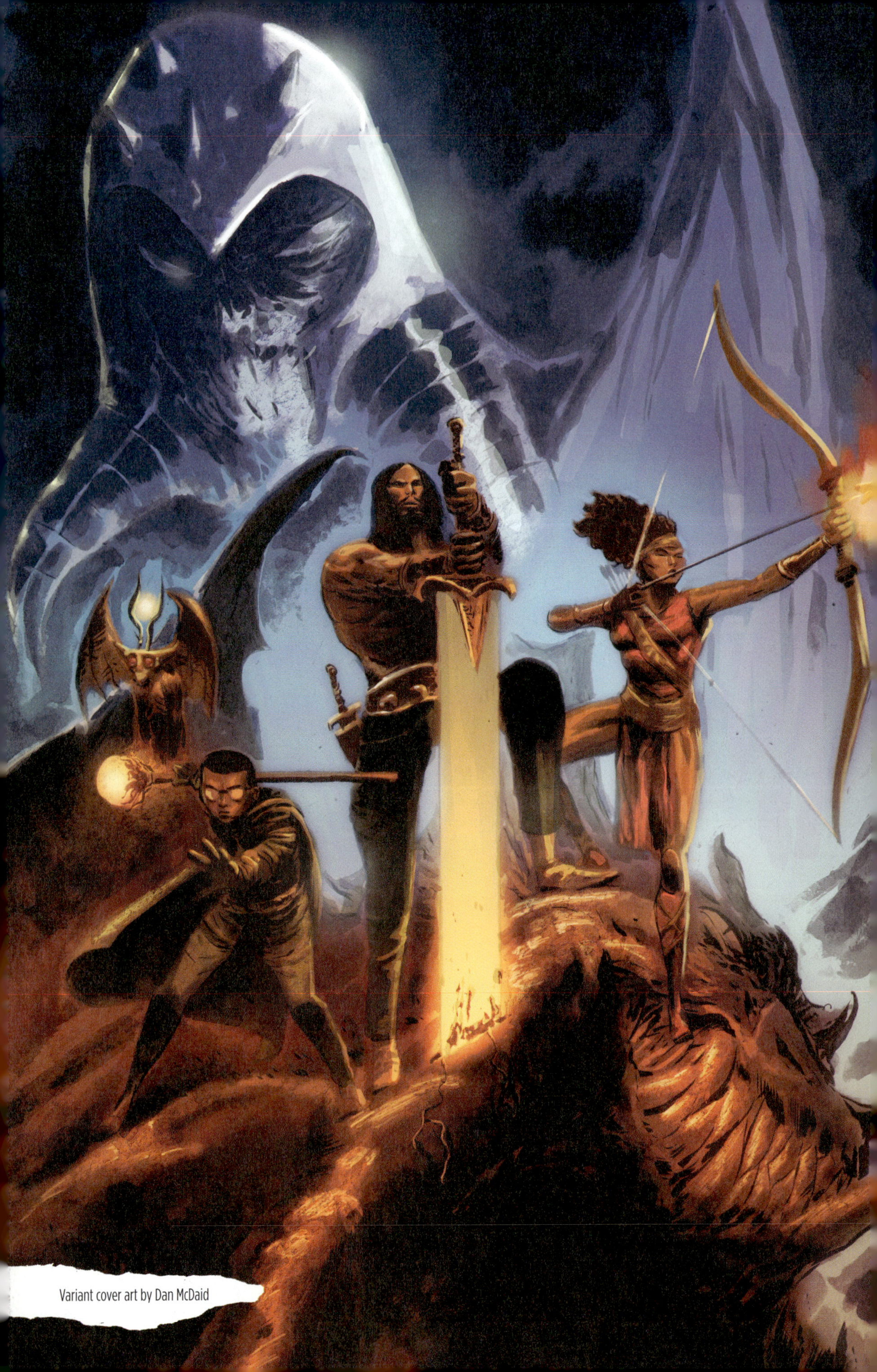

Variant cover art by Dan McDaid

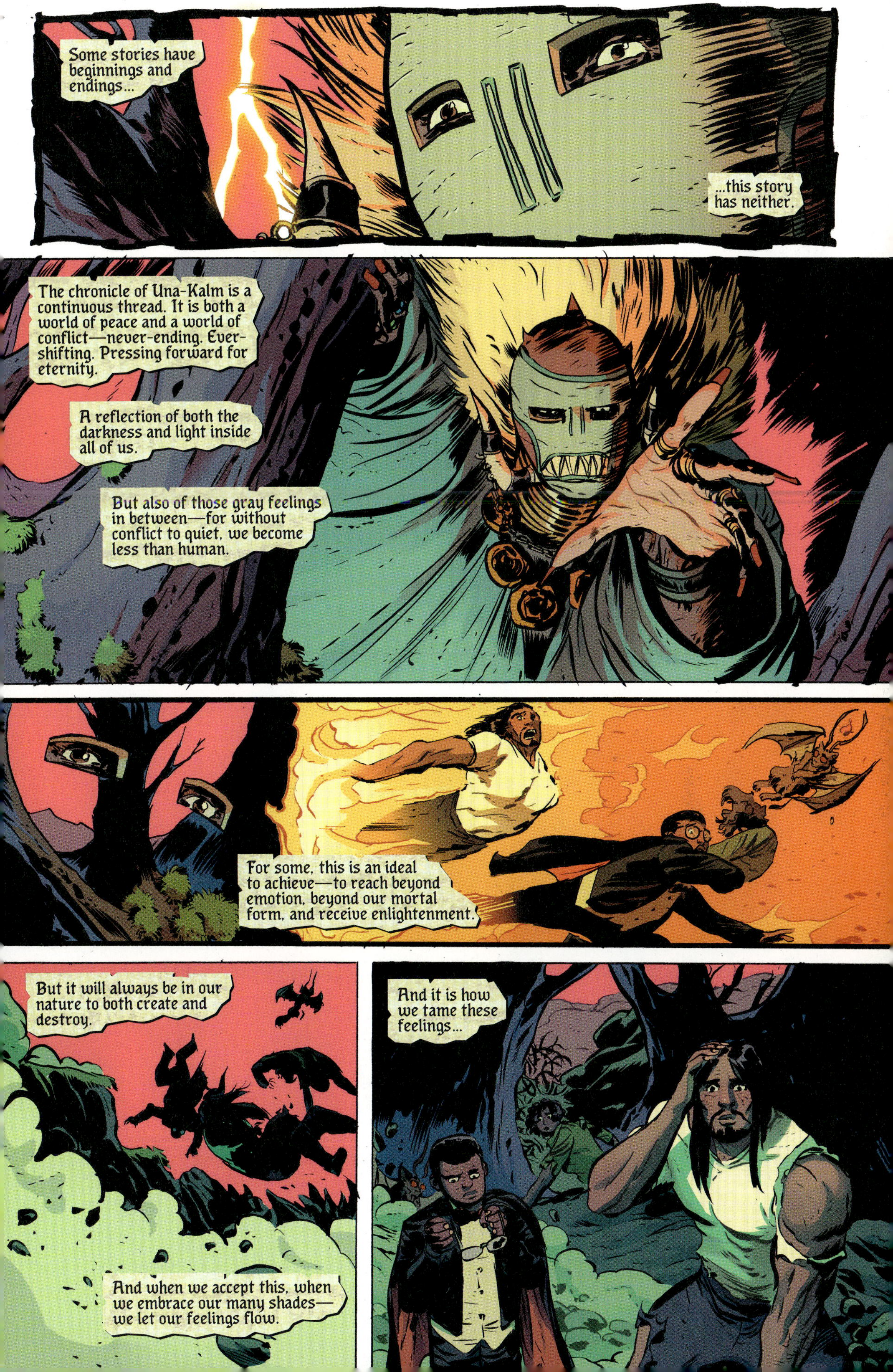
Some stories have beginnings and endings...
...this story has neither.
The chronicle of Una-Kalm is a continuous thread. It is both a world of peace and a world of conflict—never-ending. Ever-shifting. Pressing forward for eternity.
A reflection of both the darkness and light inside all of us.
But also of those gray feelings in between—for without conflict to quiet, we become less than human.
For some, this is an ideal to achieve—to reach beyond emotion, beyond our mortal form, and receive enlightenment.
But it will always be in our nature to both create and destroy.
And when we accept this, when we embrace our many shades—we let our feelings flow.
And it is how we tame these feelings...

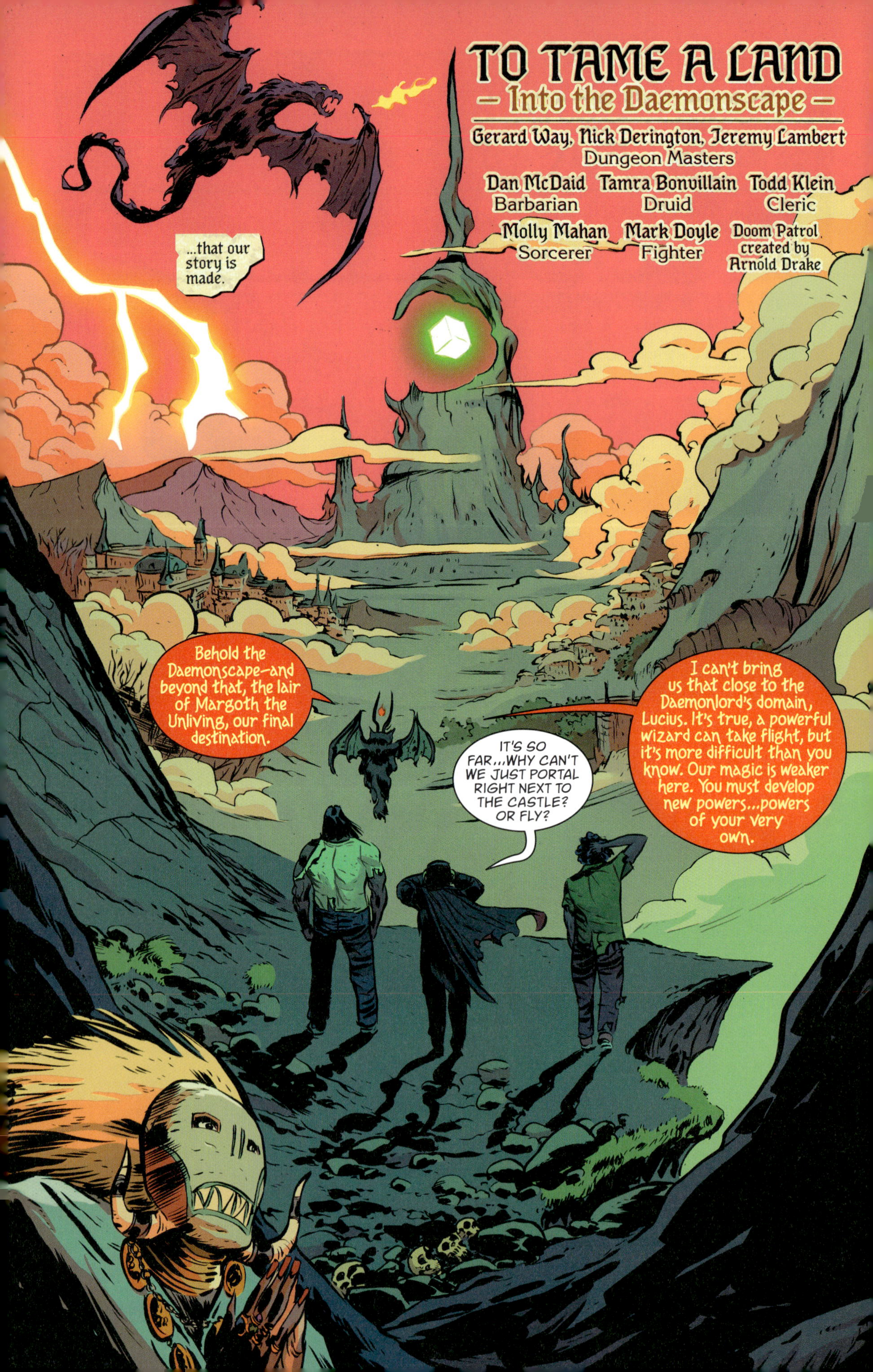
TO TAME A LAND
— Into the Daemonscape —
Gerard Way, Nick Derington, Jeremy Lambert
Dungeon Masters
Dan McDaid Barbarian
Tamra Bonvillain Druid
Todd Klein Cleric
Molly Mahan Sorcerer
Mark Doyle Fighter
Doom Patrol created by Arnold Drake
...that our story is made.
Behold the Daemonscape—and beyond that, the lair of Margoth the Unliving, our final destination.
IT'S SO FAR...WHY CAN'T WE JUST PORTAL RIGHT NEXT TO THE CASTLE? OR FLY?
I can't bring us that close to the Daemonlord's domain, Lucius. It's true, a powerful wizard can take flight, but it's more difficult than you know. Our magic is weaker here. You must develop new powers...powers of your very own.

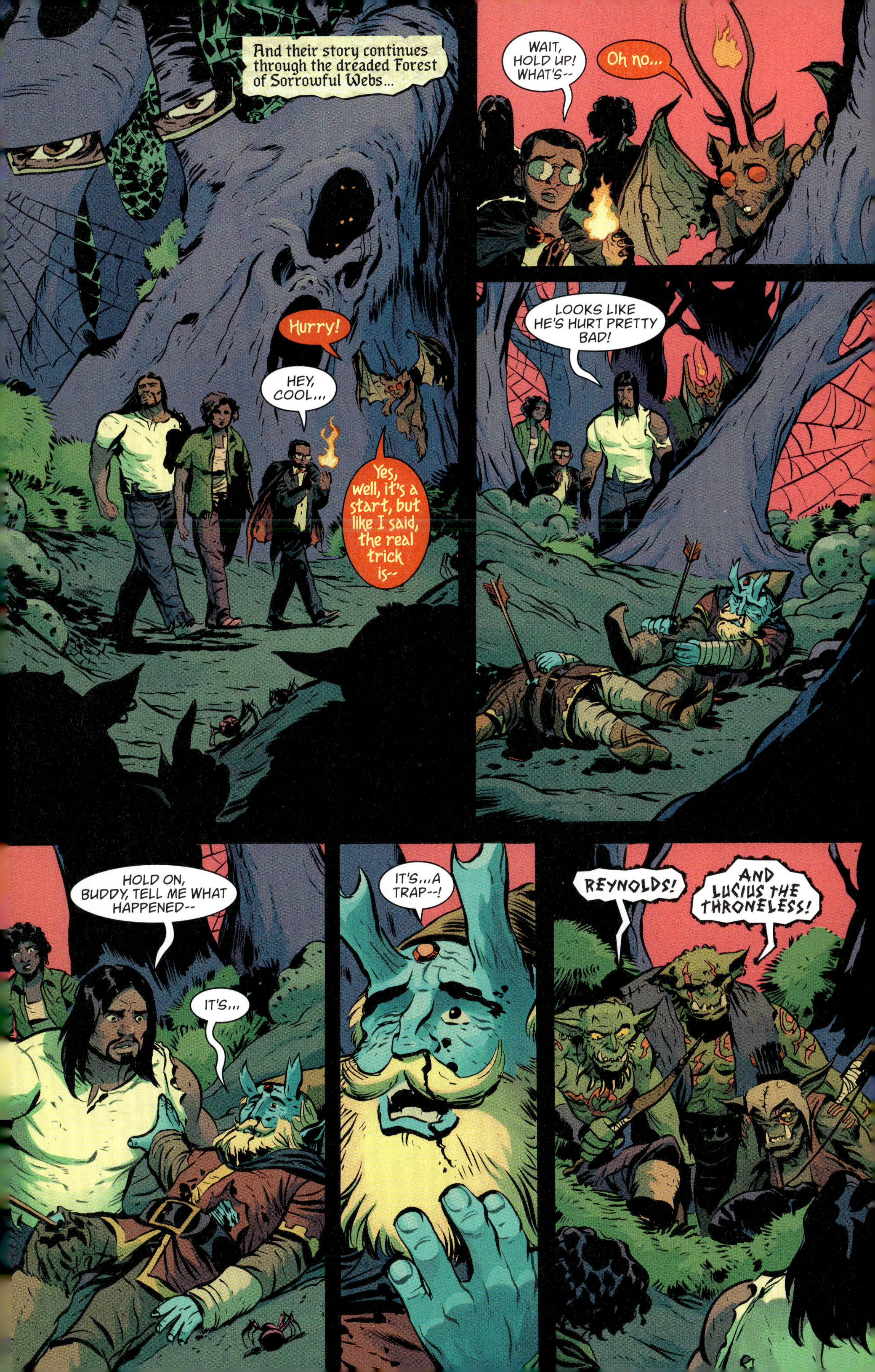

And their story continues through the dreaded Forest of Sorrowful Webs...
Hurry!
HEY, COOL...
Yes, well, it's a start, but like I said, the real trick is-
WAIT, HOLD UP! WHAT'S--
Oh no...
LOOKS LIKE HE'S HURT PRETTY BAD!
HOLD ON, BUDDY, TELL ME WHAT HAPPENED--
IT'S...
IT'S...A TRAP--!
REYNOLDS!
AND LUCIUS THE THRONELESS!

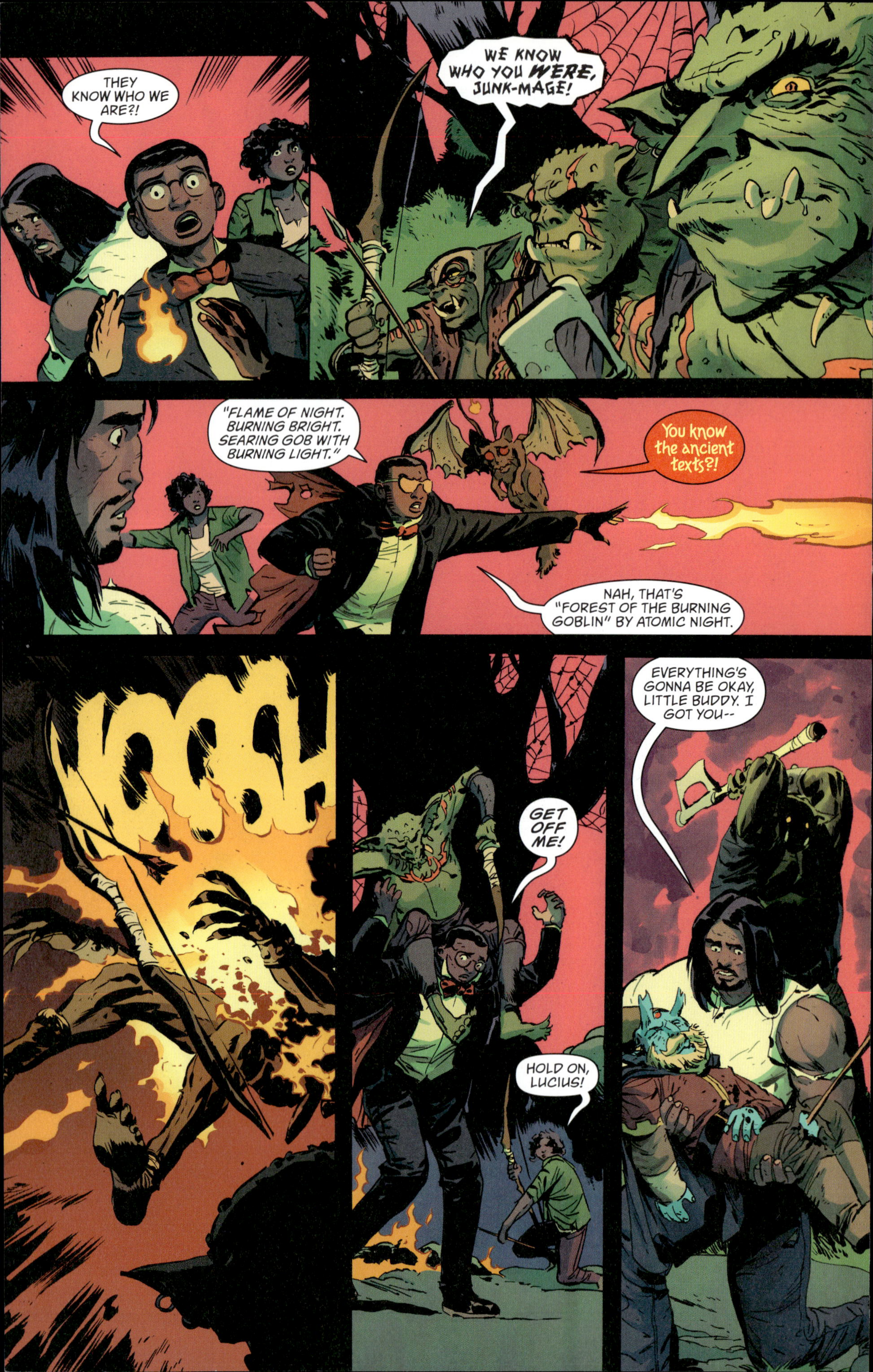
THEY KNOW WHO WE ARE?!
WE KNOW WHO YOU WERE, JUNK-MAGE!
"FLAME OF NIGHT. BURNING BRIGHT. SEARING GOB WITH BURNING LIGHT."
You know the ancient texts?!
NAH, THAT'S "FOREST OF THE BURNING GOBLIN" BY ATOMIC NIGHT.
GET OFF ME!
HOLD ON, LUCIUS!
EVERYTHING'S GONNA BE OKAY, LITTLE BUDDY. I GOT YOU--

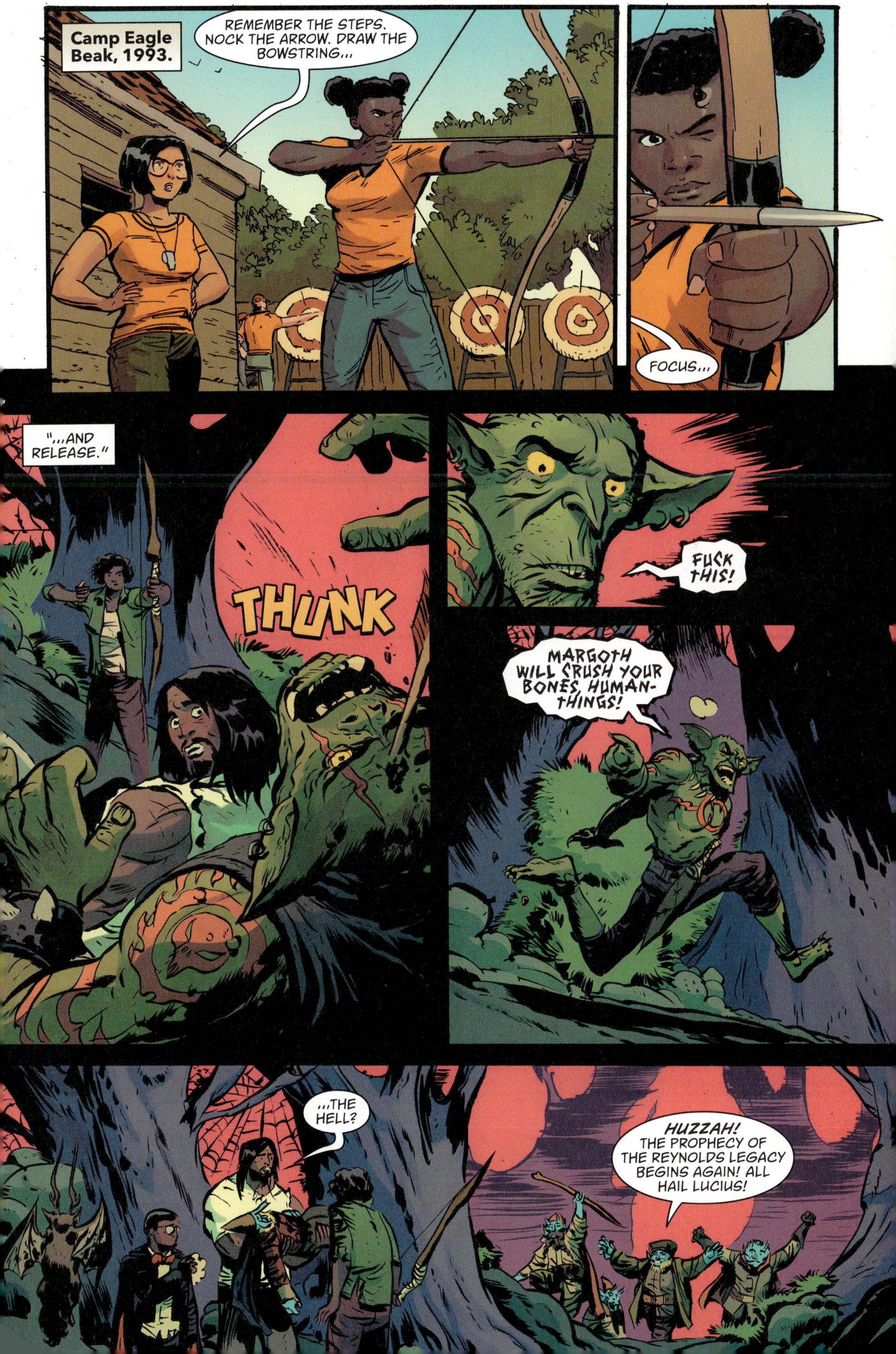
Camp Eagle Beak, 1993.
REMEMBER THE STEPS. NOCK THE ARROW. DRAW THE BOWSTRING...
FOCUS...
"...AND RELEASE."
THUNK
FUCK THIS!
MARGOTH WILL CRUSH YOUR BONES, HUMAN-THINGS!
...THE HELL?
HUZZAH! THE PROPHECY OF THE REYNOLDS LEGACY BEGINS AGAIN! ALL HAIL LUCIUS!

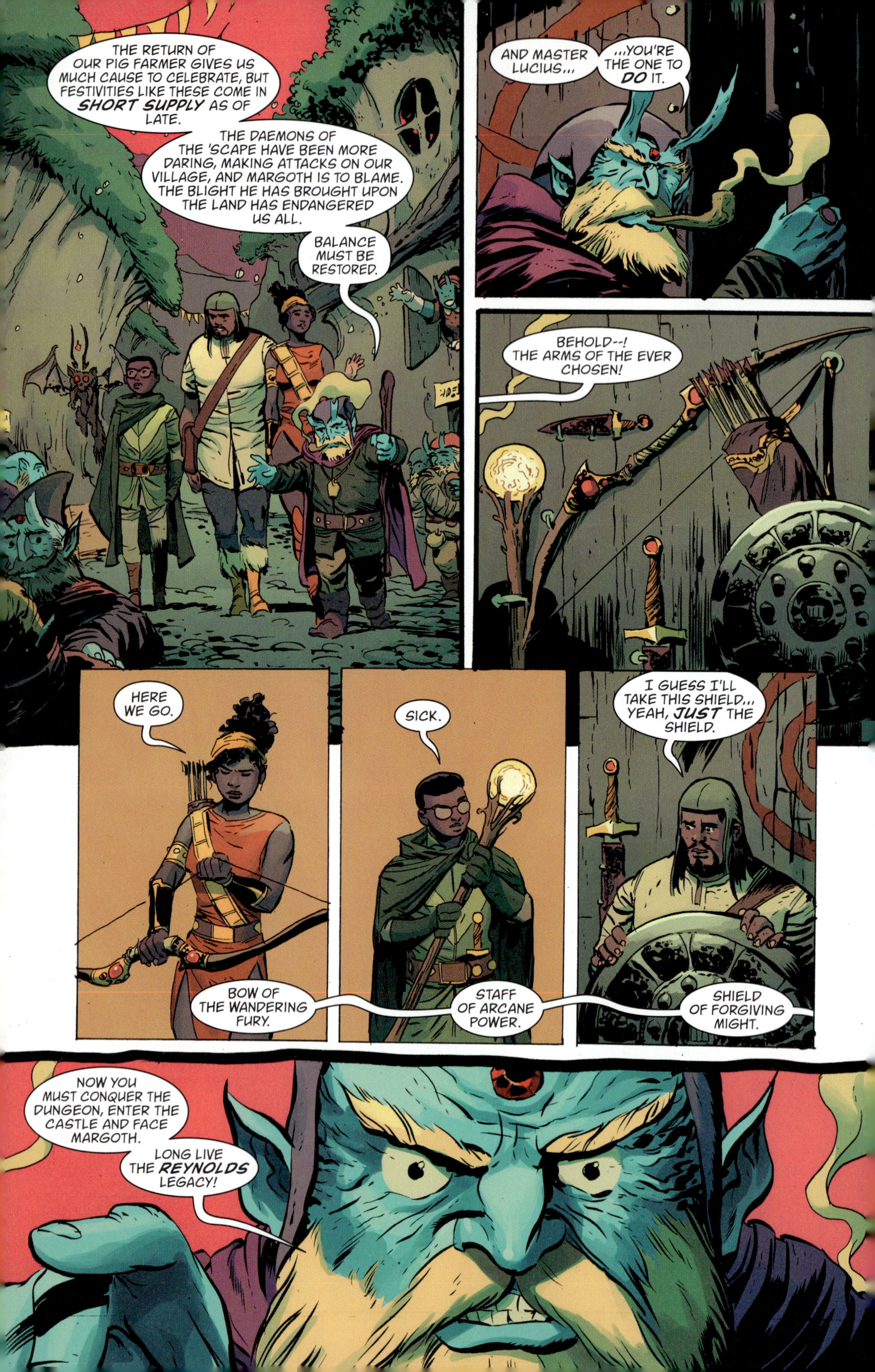
THE RETURN OF OUR PIG FARMER GIVES US MUCH CAUSE TO CELEBRATE, BUT FESTIVITIES LIKE THESE COME IN SHORT SUPPLY AS OF LATE.
THE DAEMONS OF THE 'SCAPE HAVE BEEN MORE DARING, MAKING ATTACKS ON OUR VILLAGE, AND MARGOTH IS TO BLAME. THE BLIGHT HE HAS BROUGHT UPON THE LAND HAS ENDANGERED US ALL.
BALANCE MUST BE RESTORED.
AND MASTER LUCIUS...
...YOU'RE THE ONE TO DO IT.
BEHOLD--! THE ARMS OF THE EVER CHOSEN!
HERE WE GO.
SICK.
I GUESS I'LL TAKE THIS SHIELD... YEAH, JUST THE SHIELD.
BOW OF THE WANDERING FURY.
STAFF OF ARCANE POWER.
SHIELD OF FORGIVING MIGHT.
NOW YOU MUST CONQUER THE DUNGEON, ENTER THE CASTLE AND FACE MARGOTH.
LONG LIVE THE REYNOLDS LEGACY!

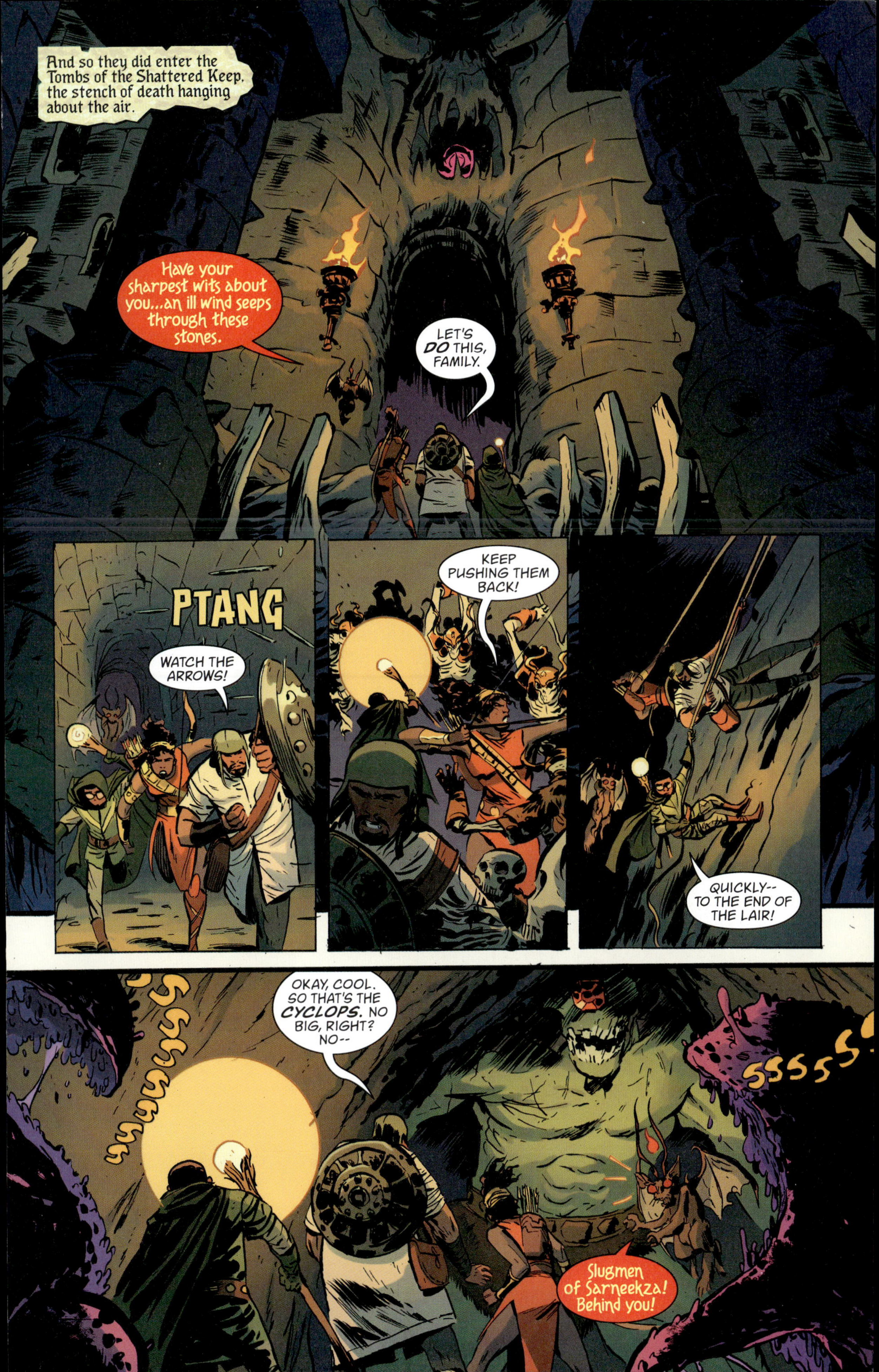
And so they did enter the Tombs of the Shattered Keep, the stench of death hanging about the air.
Have your sharpest wits about you...an ill wind seeps through these stones.
LET'S DO THIS, FAMILY.
PTANG
WATCH THE ARROWS!
KEEP PUSHING THEM BACK!
QUICKLY-- TO THE END OF THE LAIR!
SSSSSSSSSS
OKAY, COOL. SO THAT'S THE CYCLOPS. NO BIG, RIGHT? NO--
SSSSS
Slugmen of Sarneekza! Behind you!

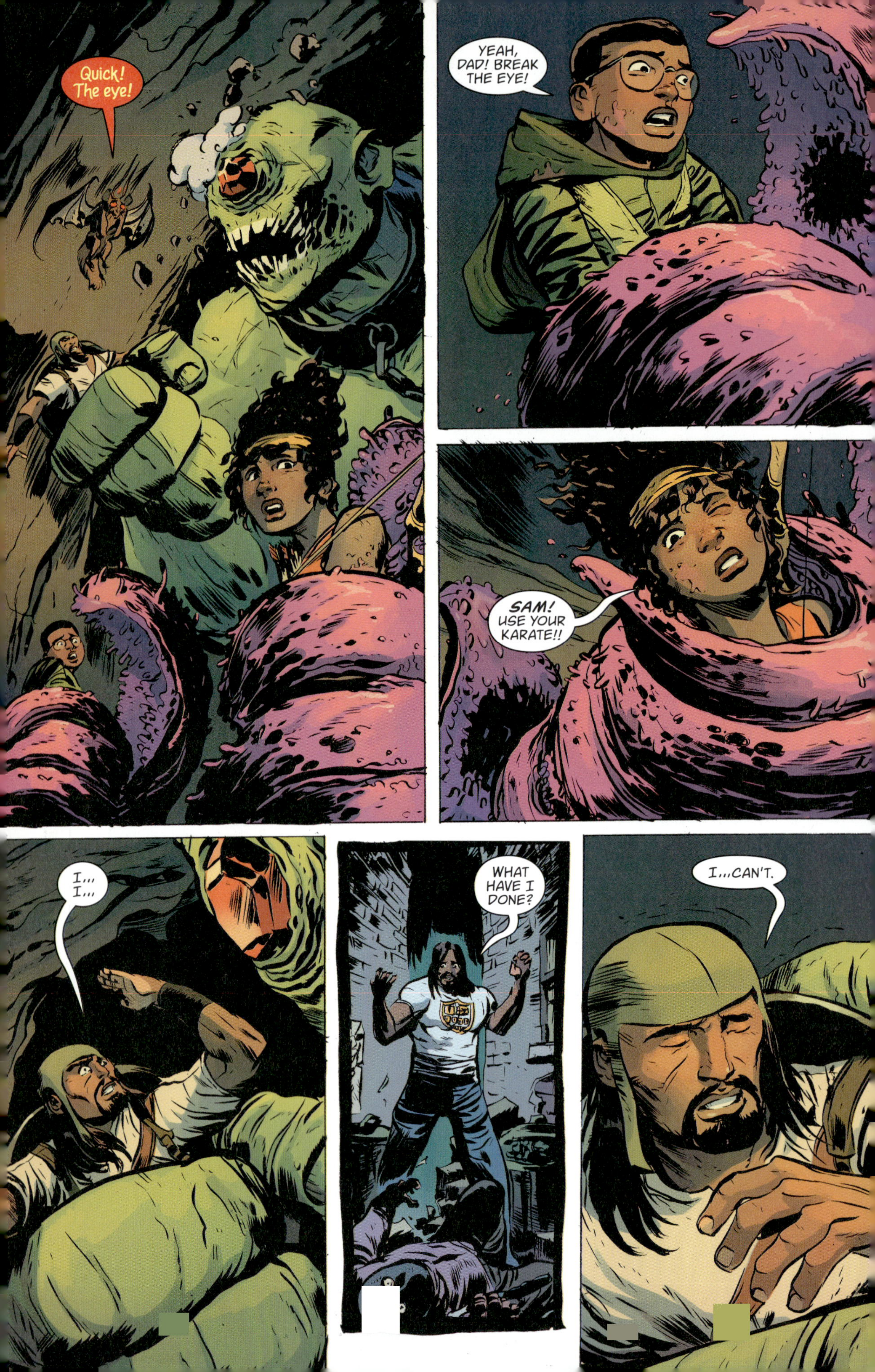
Quick! The eye!
YEAH, DAD! BREAK THE EYE!
SAM! USE YOUR KARATE!!
I... I...
WHAT HAVE I DONE?
I...CAN'T.

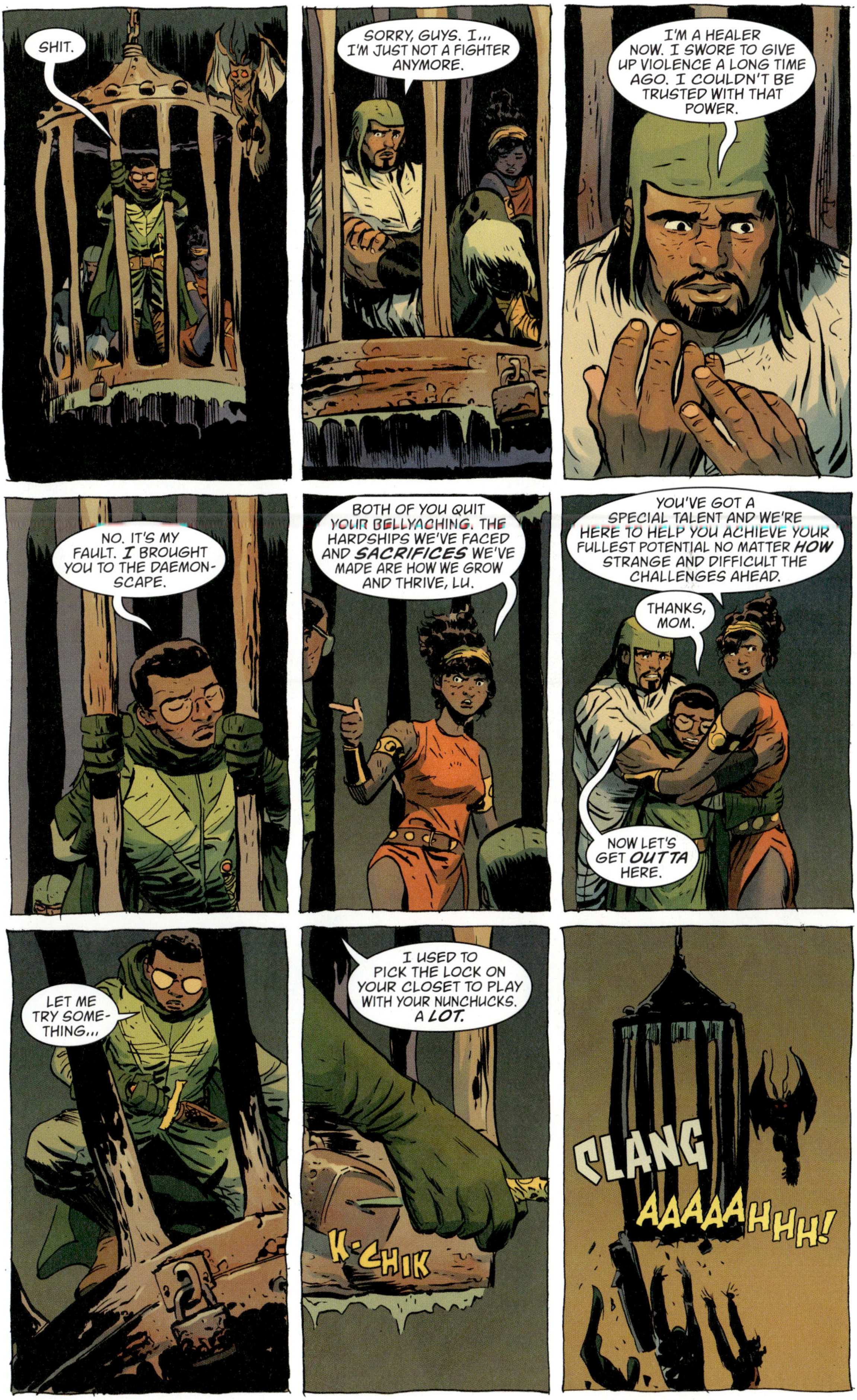
SHIT.
SORRY, GUYS. I... I'M JUST NOT A FIGHTER ANYMORE.
I'M A HEALER NOW. I SWORE TO GIVE UP VIOLENCE A LONG TIME AGO. I COULDN'T BE TRUSTED WITH THAT POWER.
NO. IT'S MY FAULT. I BROUGHT YOU TO THE DAEMON-SCAPE.
BOTH OF YOU QUIT YOUR BELLYACHING. THE HARDSHIPS WE'VE FACED AND SACRIFICES WE'VE MADE ARE HOW WE GROW AND THRIVE, LU.
YOU'VE GOT A SPECIAL TALENT AND WE'RE HERE TO HELP YOU ACHIEVE YOUR FULLEST POTENTIAL NO MATTER HOW STRANGE AND DIFFICULT THE CHALLENGES AHEAD.
THANKS, MOM.
NOW LET'S GET OUTTA HERE.
LET ME TRY SOME-THING...
I USED TO PICK THE LOCK ON YOUR CLOSET TO PLAY WITH YOUR NUNCHUCKS. A LOT.
K-CHIK
CLANG
AAAAAHHH!

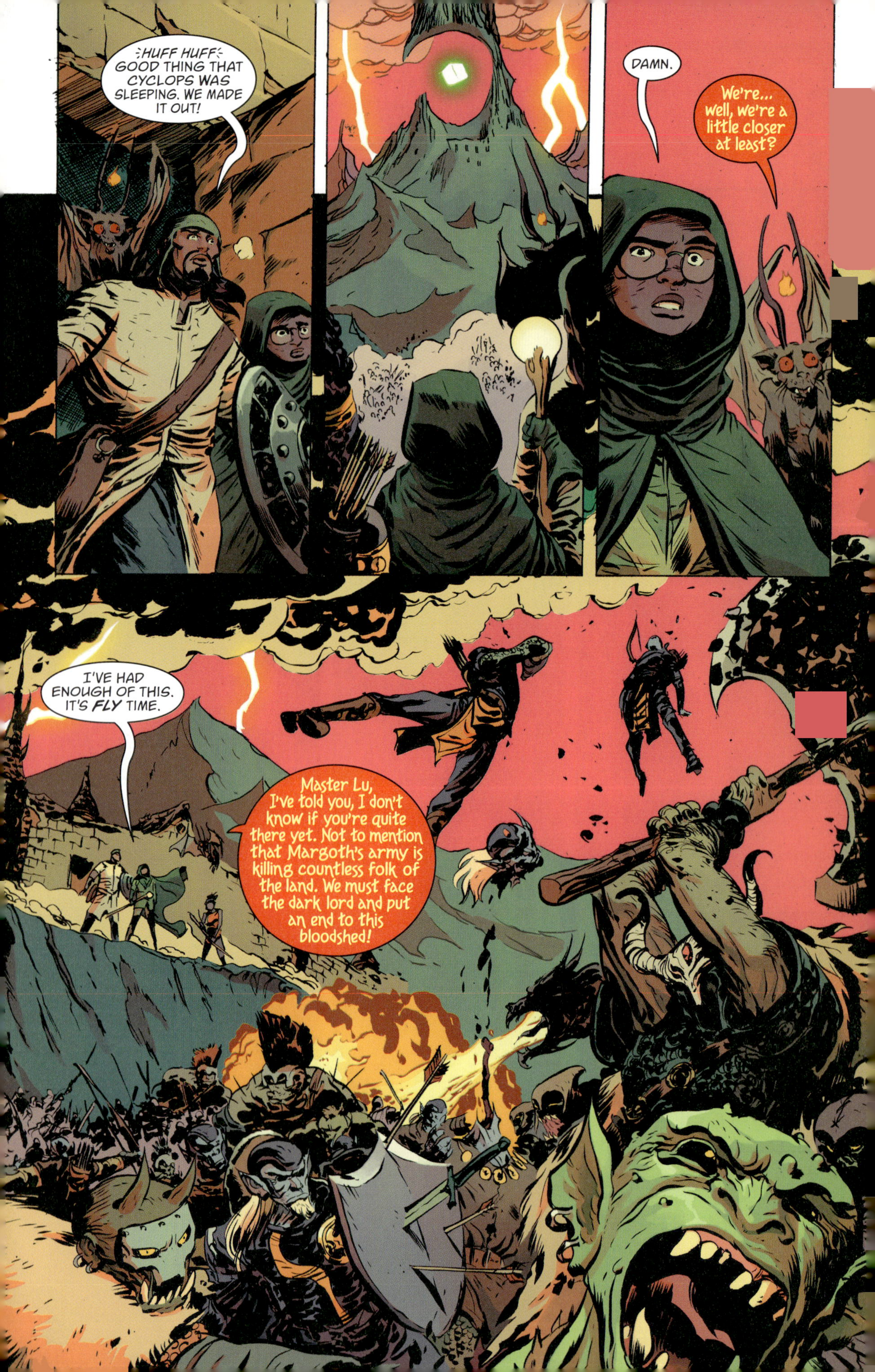
HUFF HUFF
GOOD THING THAT CYCLOPS WAS SLEEPING. WE MADE IT OUT!
DAMN.
We're... well, we're a little closer at least?
I'VE HAD ENOUGH OF THIS. IT'S FLY TIME.
Master Lu, I've told you, I don't know if you're quite there yet. Not to mention that Margoth's army is killing countless folk of the land. We must face the dark lord and put an end to this bloodshed!

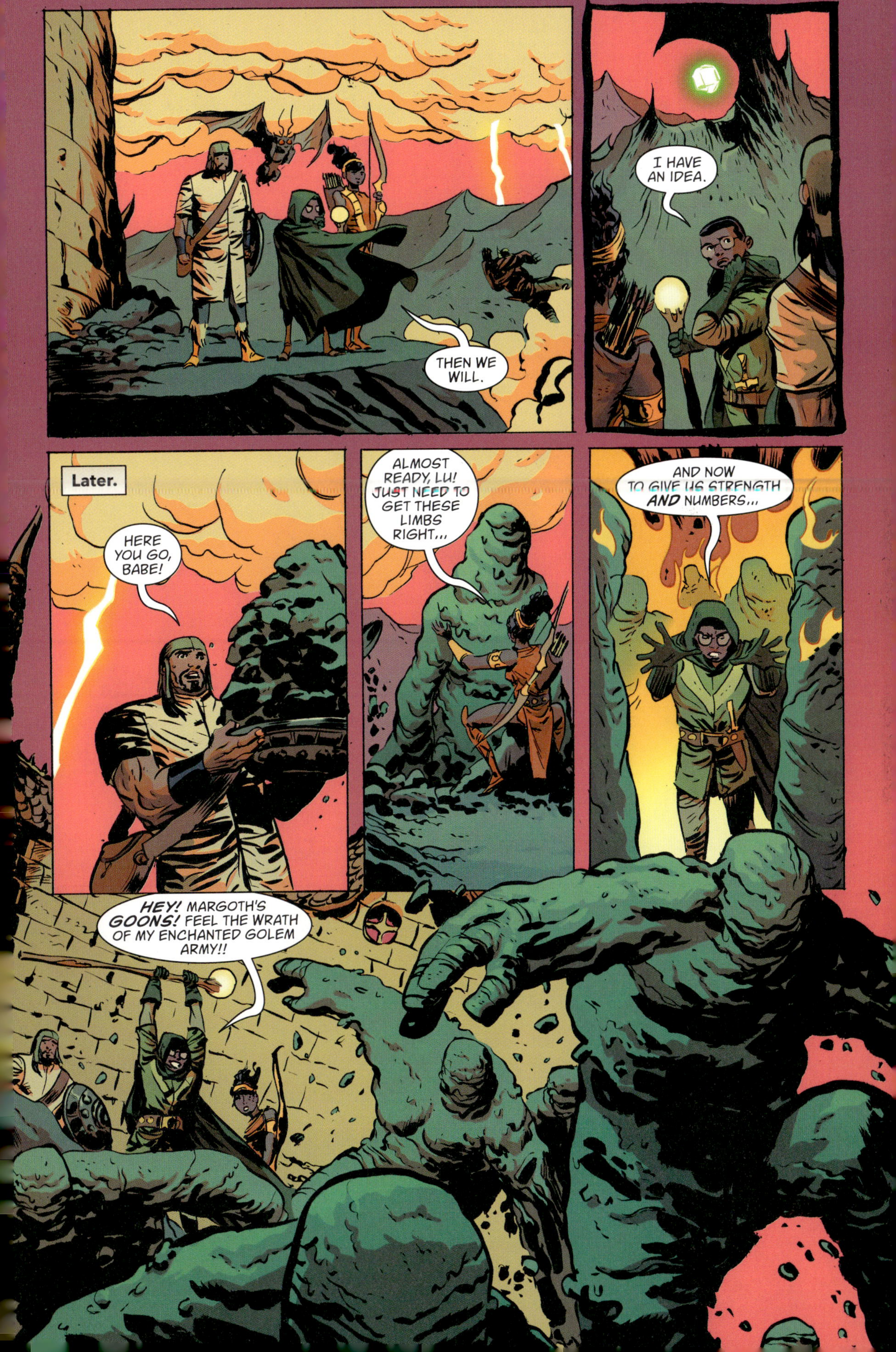
THEN WE WILL.
I HAVE AN IDEA.
Later.
HERE YOU GO, BABE!
ALMOST READY, LU! JUST NEED TO GET THESE LIMBS RIGHT...
AND NOW TO GIVE US STRENGTH AND NUMBERS...
HEY! MARGOTH'S GOONS! FEEL THE WRATH OF MY ENCHANTED GOLEM ARMY!!

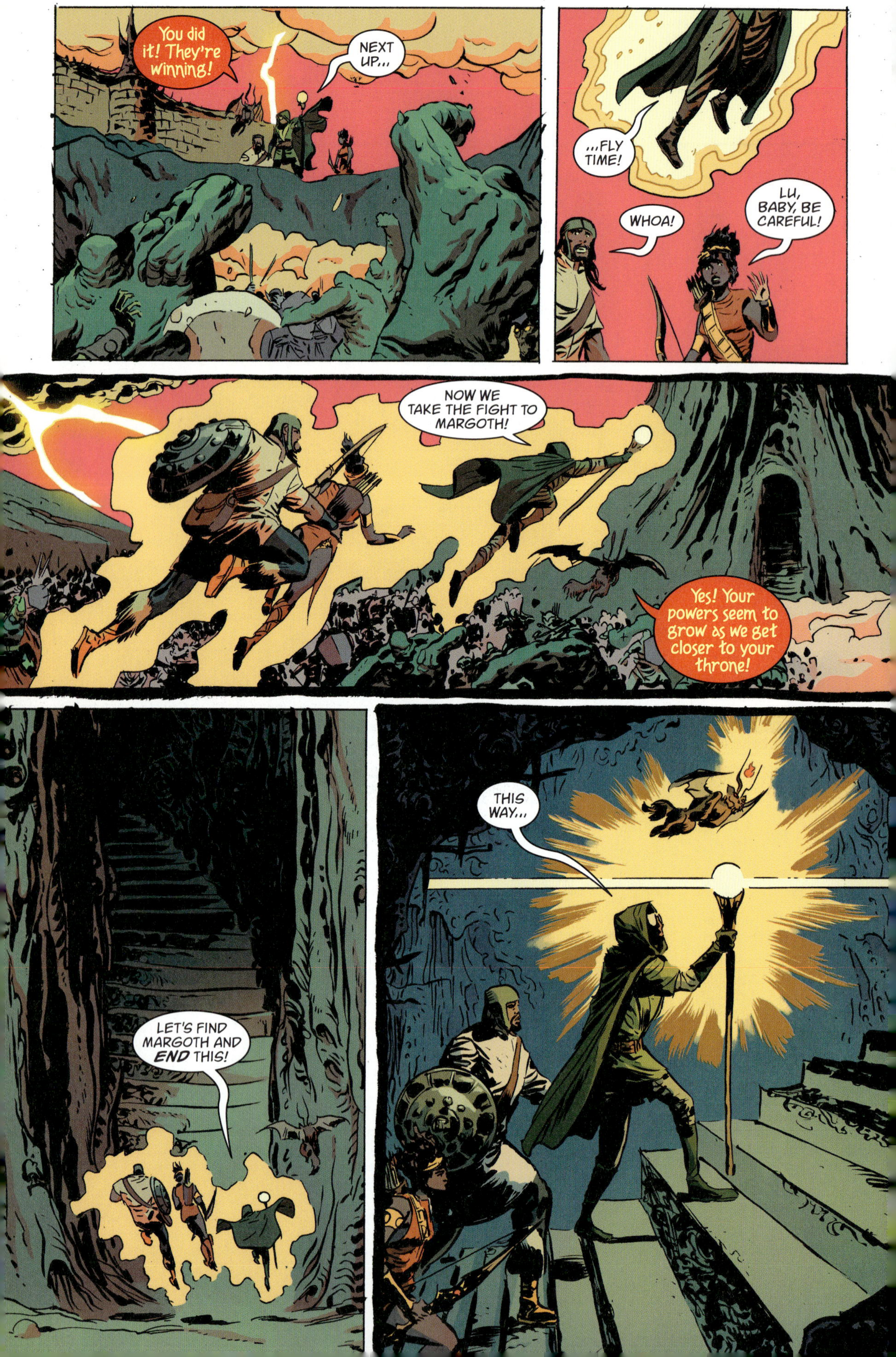
You did it! They're winning!
NEXT UP...
...FLY TIME!
WHOA!
LU, BABY, BE CAREFUL!
NOW WE TAKE THE FIGHT TO MARGOTH!
Yes! Your powers seem to grow as we get closer to your throne!
LET'S FIND MARGOTH AND END THIS!
THIS WAY...

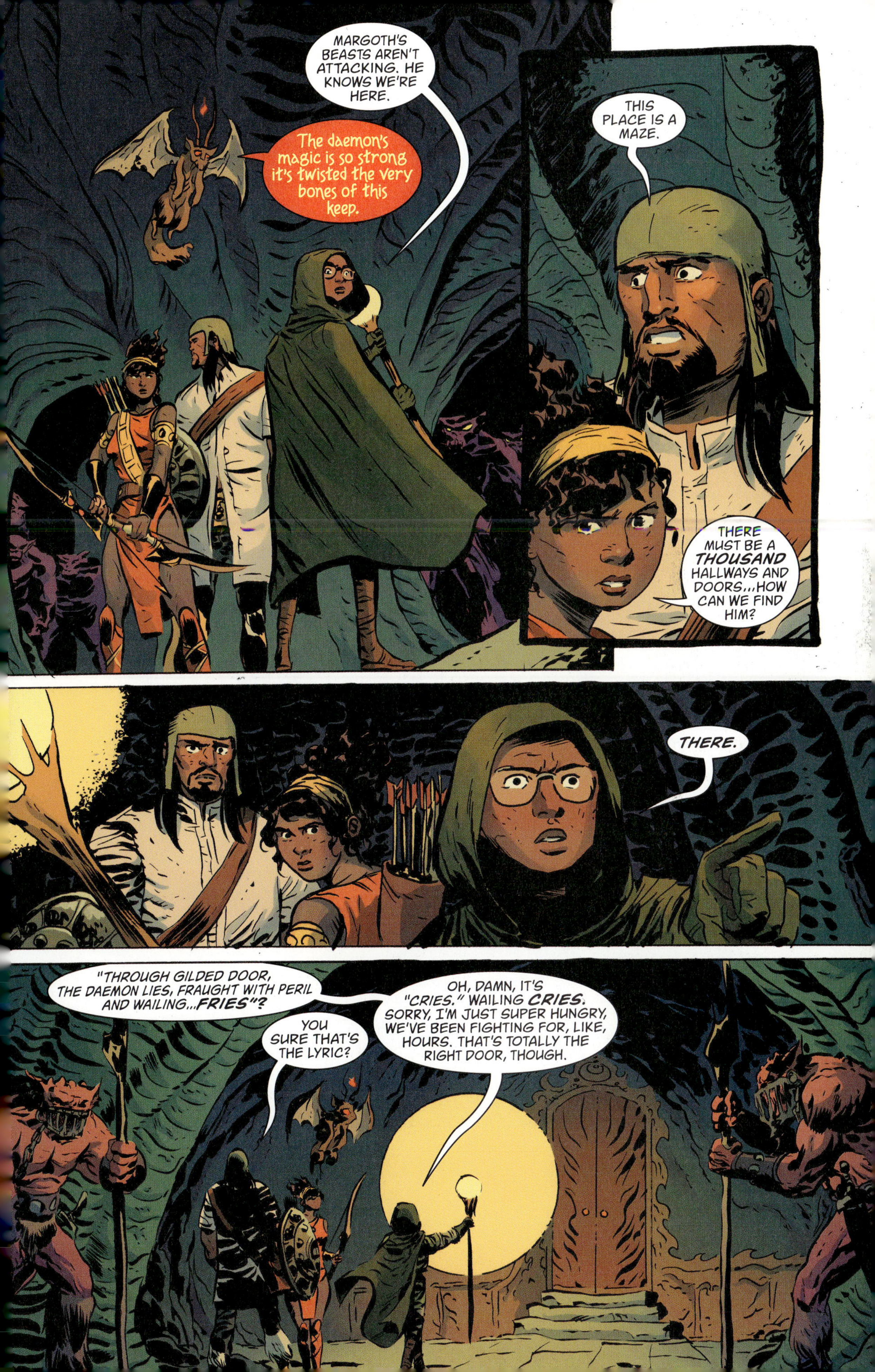
MARGOTH'S BEASTS AREN'T ATTACKING. HE KNOWS WE'RE HERE.
The daemon's magic is so strong it's twisted the very bones of this keep.
THIS PLACE IS A MAZE.
THERE MUST BE A THOUSAND HALLWAYS AND DOORS...HOW CAN WE FIND HIM?
THERE.
"THROUGH GILDED DOOR, THE DAEMON LIES, FRAUGHT WITH PERIL AND WAILING...FRIES"?
YOU SURE THAT'S THE LYRIC?
OH, DAMN, IT'S "CRIES." WAILING CRIES. SORRY, I'M JUST SUPER HUNGRY, WE'VE BEEN FIGHTING FOR, LIKE, HOURS. THAT'S TOTALLY THE RIGHT DOOR, THOUGH.

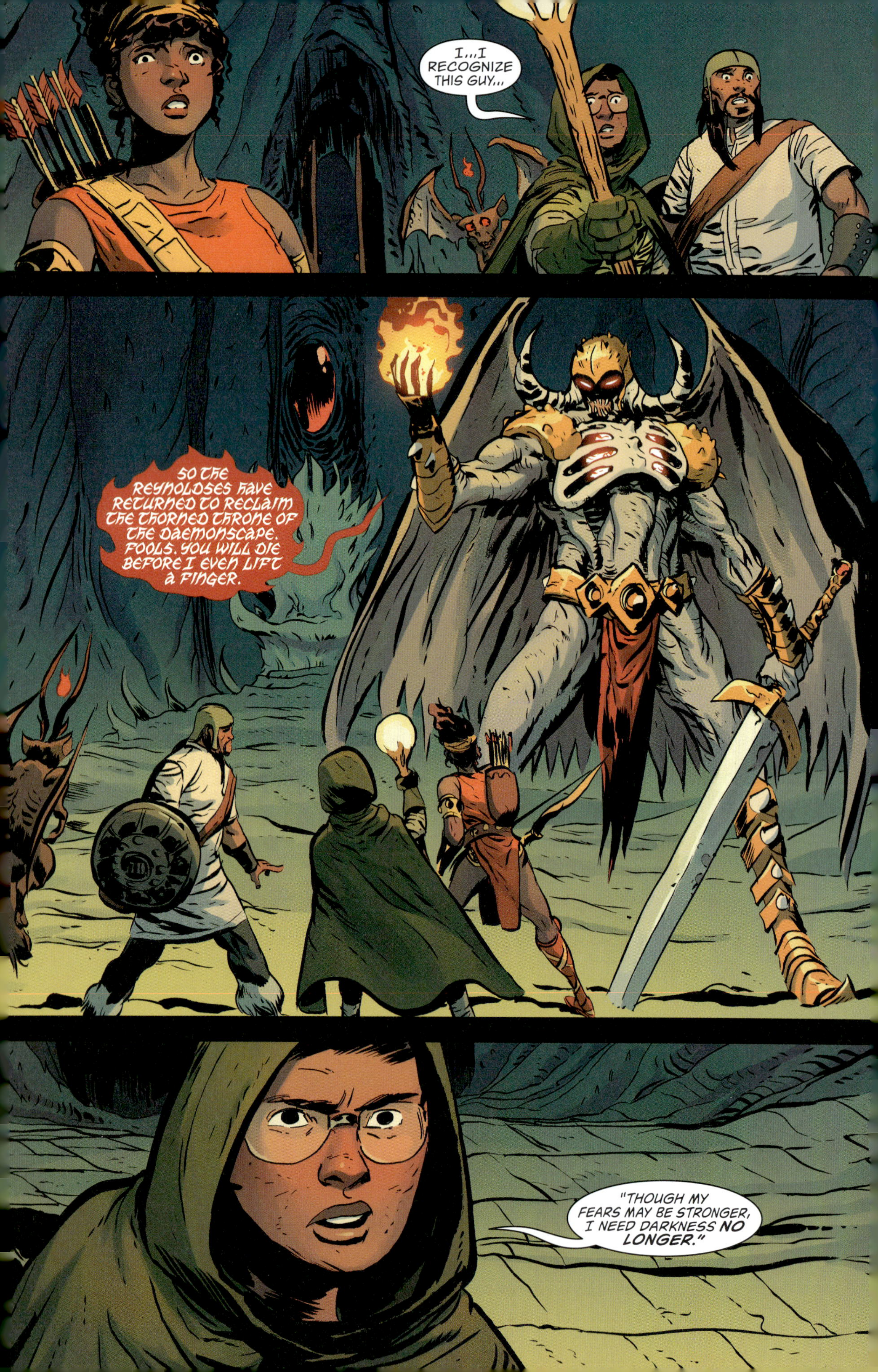
I...I RECOGNIZE THIS GUY...
SO THE REYNOLDSES HAVE RETURNED TO RECLAIM THE THORNED THRONE OF THE DAEMONSCAPE. FOOLS. YOU WILL DIE BEFORE I EVEN LIFT A FINGER.
"THOUGH MY FEARS MAY BE STRONGER, I NEED DARKNESS NO LONGER."

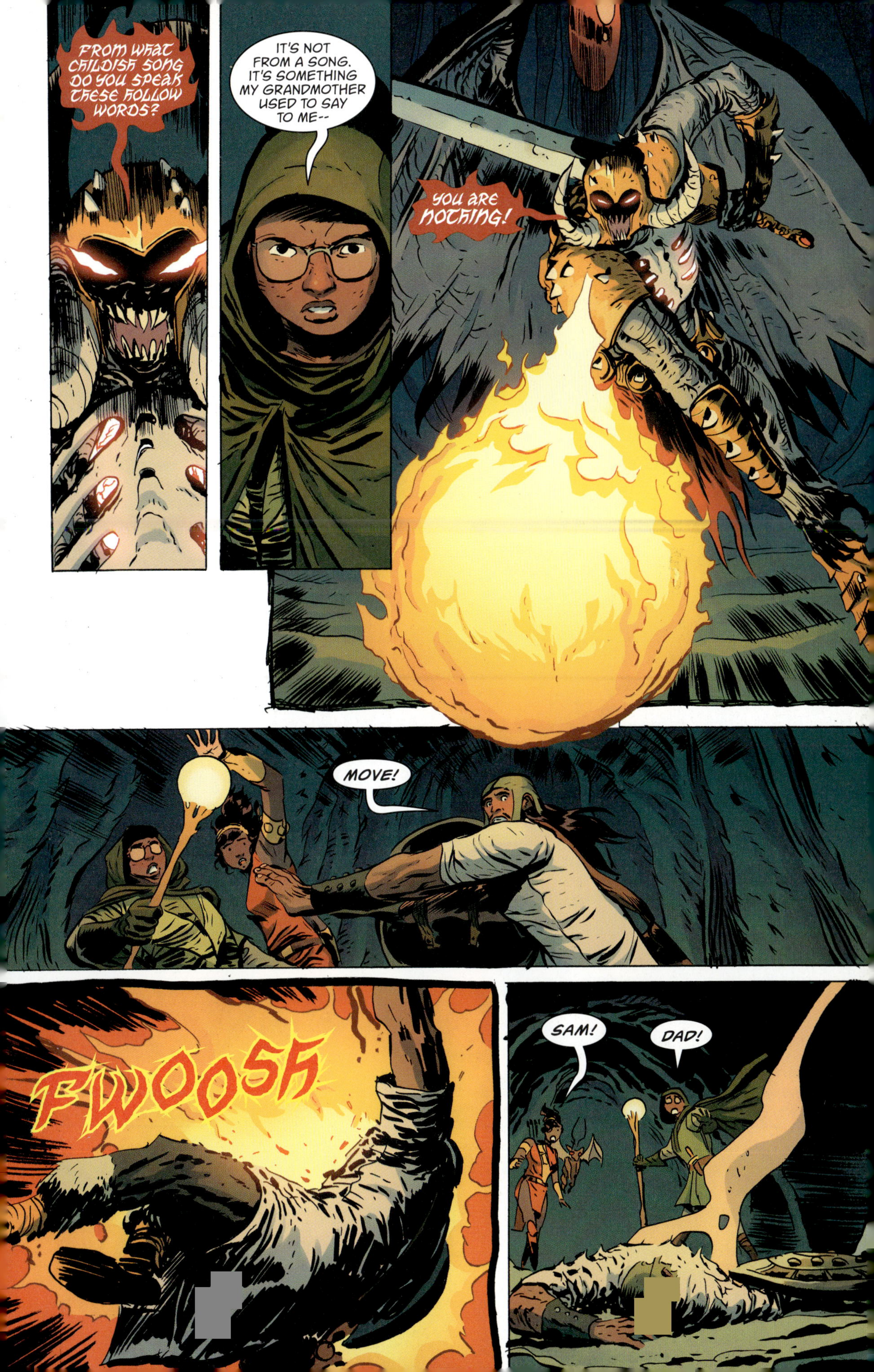
FROM WHAT CHILDISH SONG DO YOU SPEAK THESE HOLLOW WORDS?
IT'S NOT FROM A SONG. IT'S SOMETHING MY GRANDMOTHER USED TO SAY TO ME--
YOU ARE NOTHING!
MOVE!
FWOOSH
SAM!
DAD!

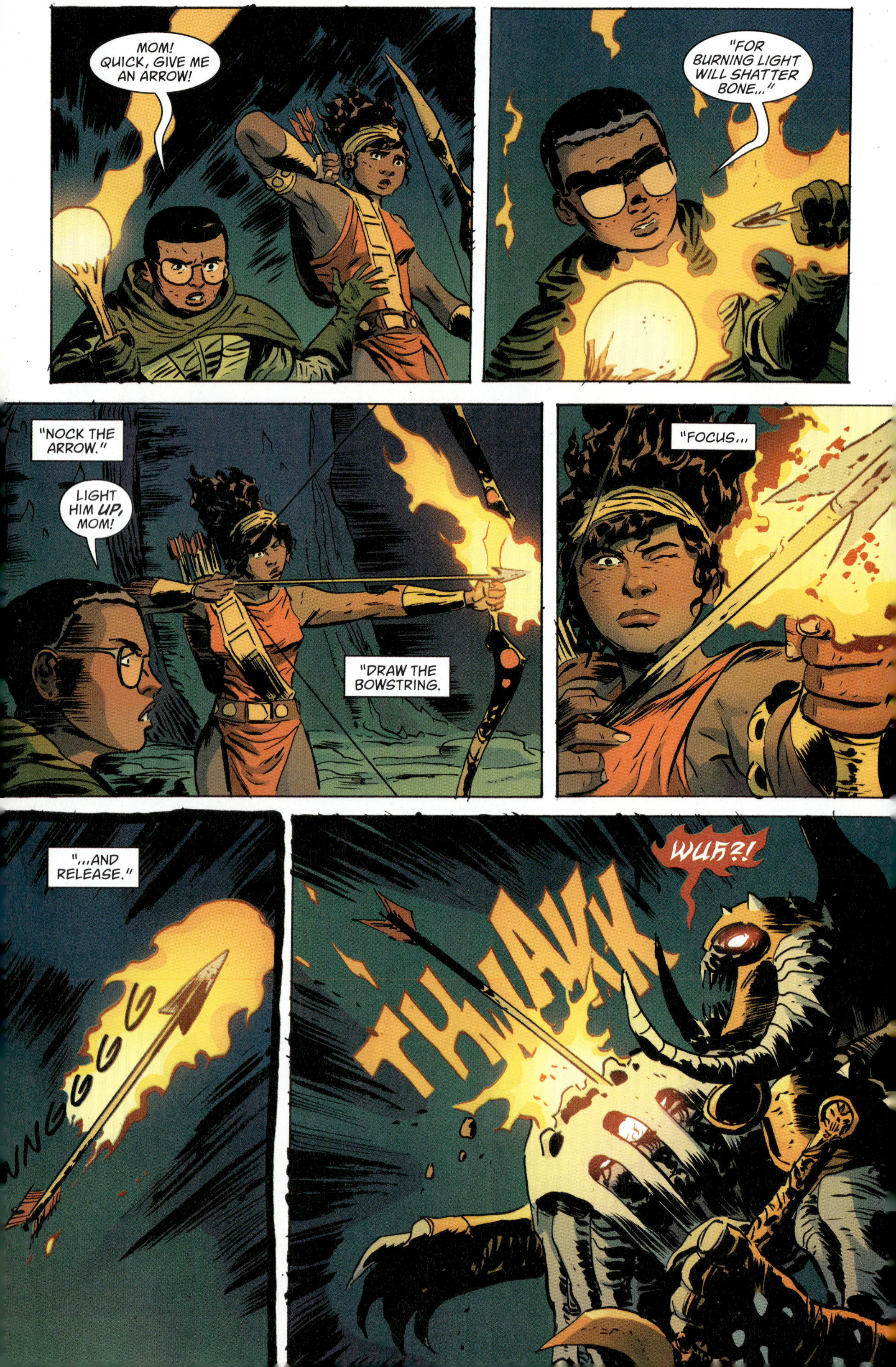
MOM! QUICK, GIVE ME AN ARROW!
"FOR BURNING LIGHT WILL SHATTER BONE..."
"NOCK THE ARROW."
LIGHT HIM UP, MOM!
"DRAW THE BOWSTRING.
"FOCUS...
"...AND RELEASE."
NNGGGGG
WUH?!
THWAKK

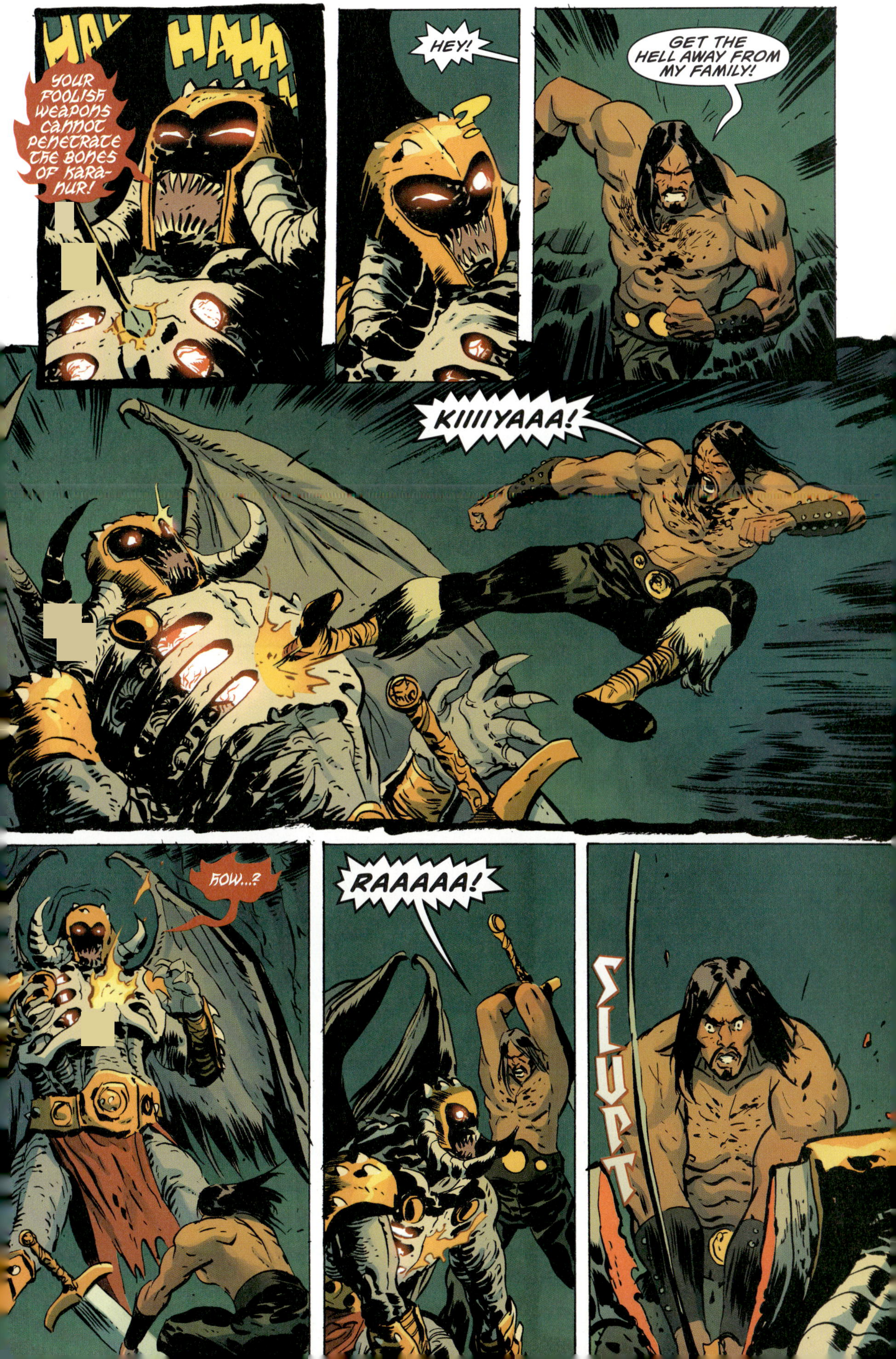
HAHA HAHA
YOUR FOOLISH WEAPONS CANNOT PENETRATE THE BONES OF KARA-NUR!
HEY!
?
GET THE HELL AWAY FROM MY FAMILY!
KIIIIYAAA!
HOW...?
RAAAAAA!
SLUCT

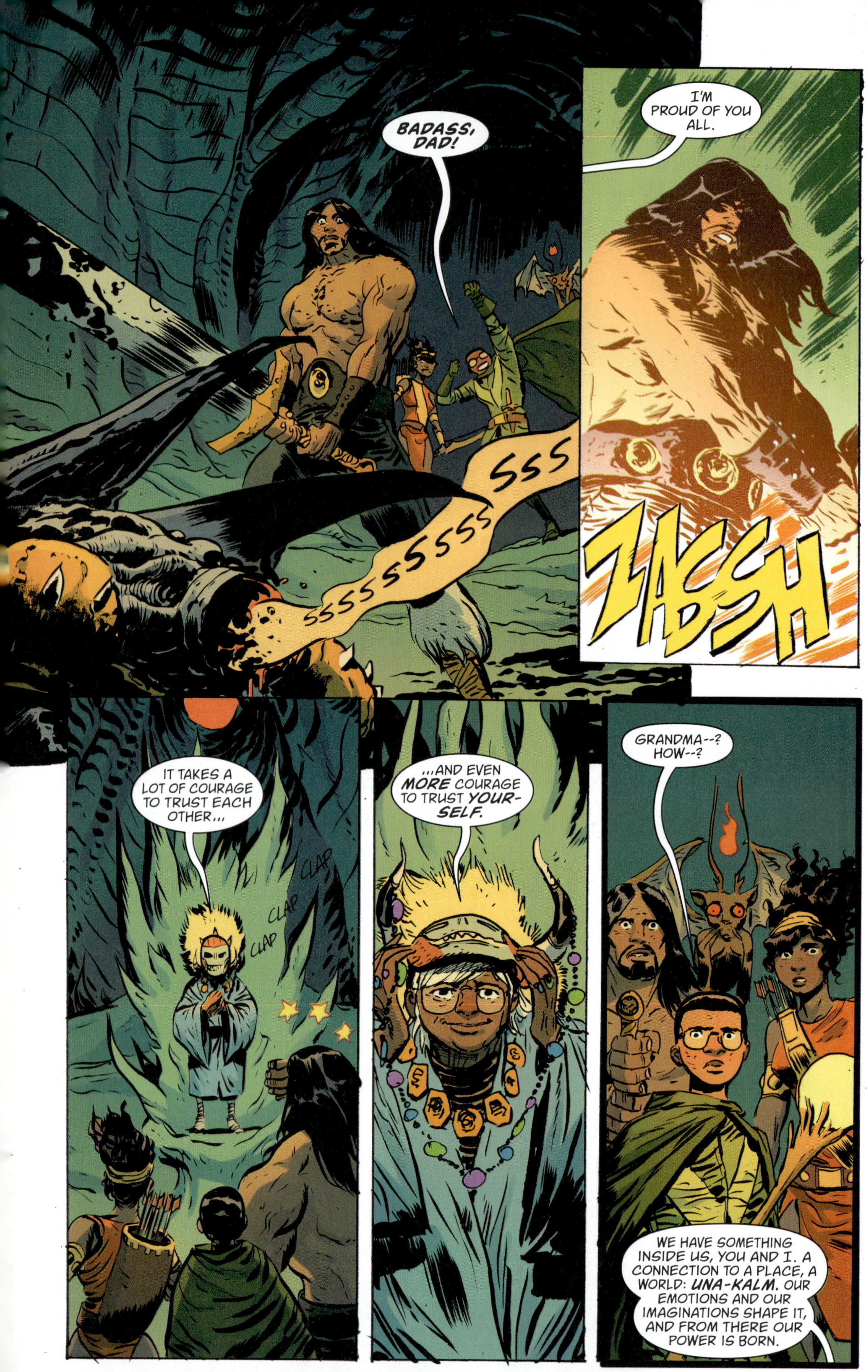
BADASS, DAD!
SSSSSSSSSSSSS
I'M PROUD OF YOU ALL.
ZASSH
IT TAKES A LOT OF COURAGE TO TRUST EACH OTHER...
CLAP
CLAP
CLAP
...AND EVEN MORE COURAGE TO TRUST YOURSELF.
GRANDMA--? HOW--?
WE HAVE SOMETHING INSIDE US, YOU AND I. A CONNECTION TO A PLACE, A WORLD: UNA-KALM. OUR EMOTIONS AND OUR IMAGINATIONS SHAPE IT, AND FROM THERE OUR POWER IS BORN.

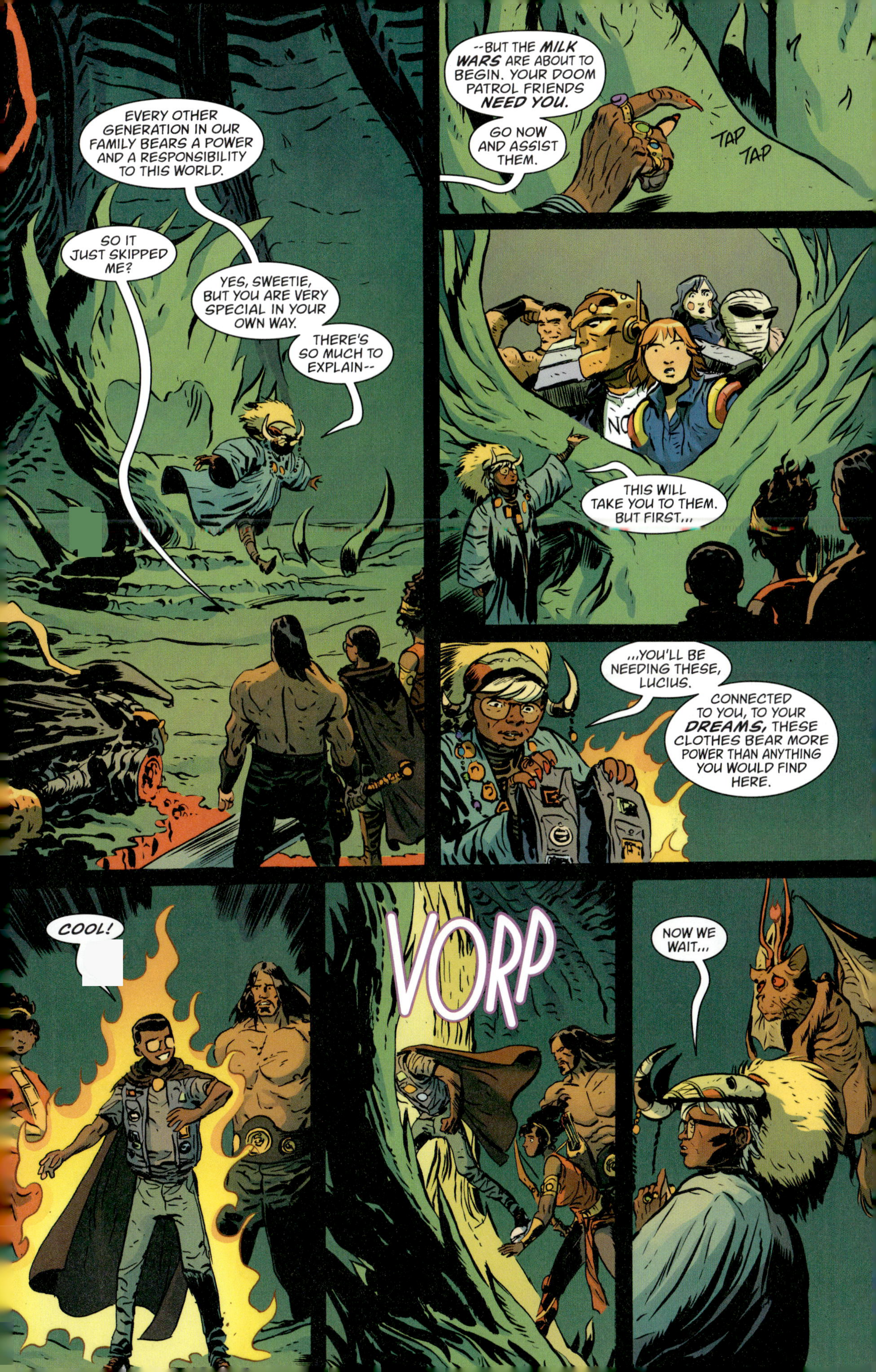

EVERY OTHER GENERATION IN OUR FAMILY BEARS A POWER AND A RESPONSIBILITY TO THIS WORLD.
SO IT JUST SKIPPED ME?
YES, SWEETIE, BUT YOU ARE VERY SPECIAL IN YOUR OWN WAY.
THERE'S SO MUCH TO EXPLAIN--
--BUT THE MILK WARS ARE ABOUT TO BEGIN. YOUR DOOM PATROL FRIENDS NEED YOU.
GO NOW AND ASSIST THEM.
TAP TAP
THIS WILL TAKE YOU TO THEM. BUT FIRST...
...YOU'LL BE NEEDING THESE, LUCIUS.
CONNECTED TO YOU, TO YOUR DREAMS, THESE CLOTHES BEAR MORE POWER THAN ANYTHING YOU WOULD FIND HERE.
COOL!
VORP
NOW WE WAIT...

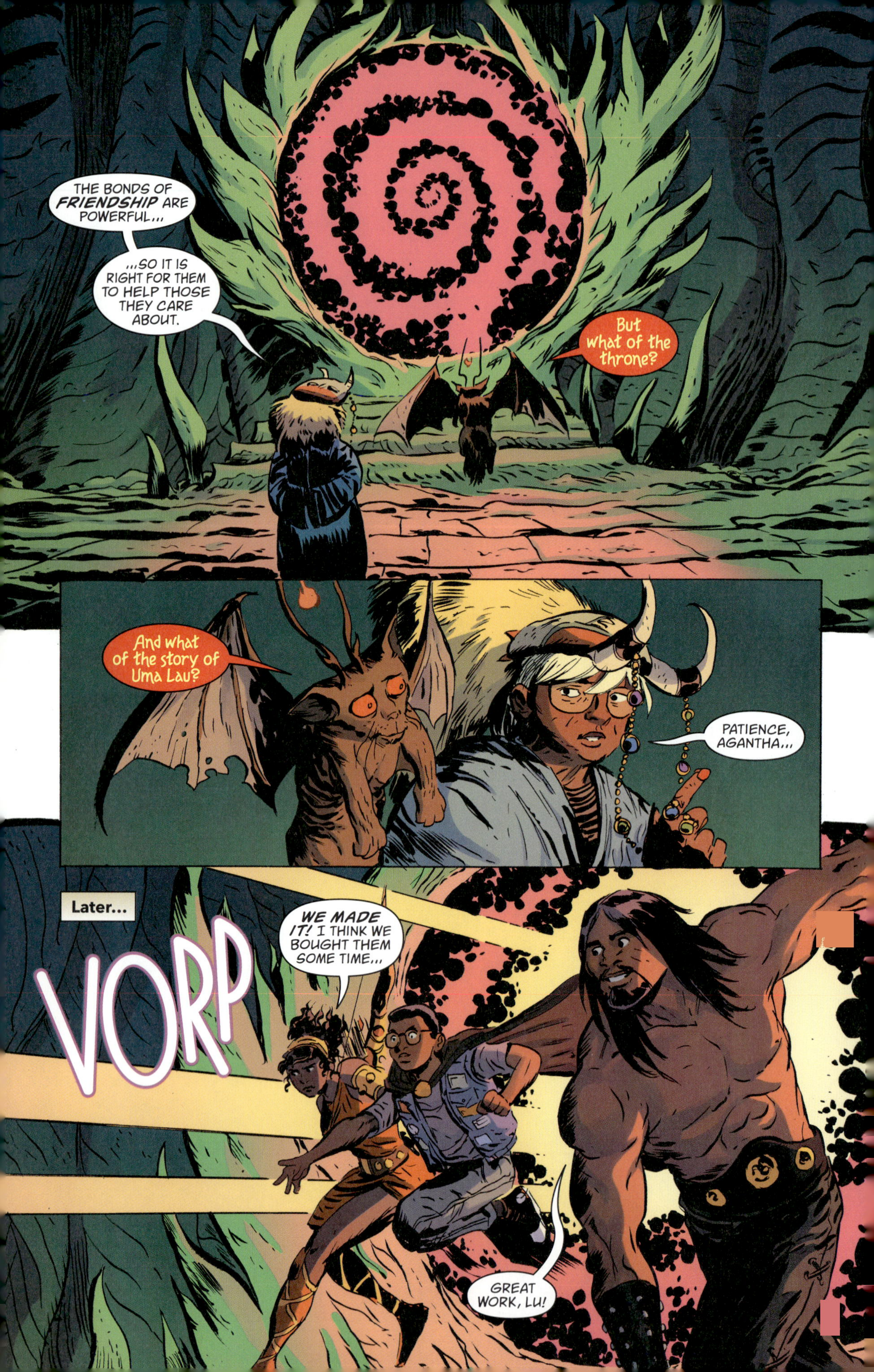

THE BONDS OF ***FRIENDSHIP*** ARE POWERFUL...
...SO IT IS RIGHT FOR THEM TO HELP THOSE THEY CARE ABOUT.
But what of the throne?
And what of the story of Uma Lau?
PATIENCE, AGANTHA...
Later...
VORP
WE MADE IT! I THINK WE BOUGHT THEM SOME TIME...
GREAT WORK, LU!

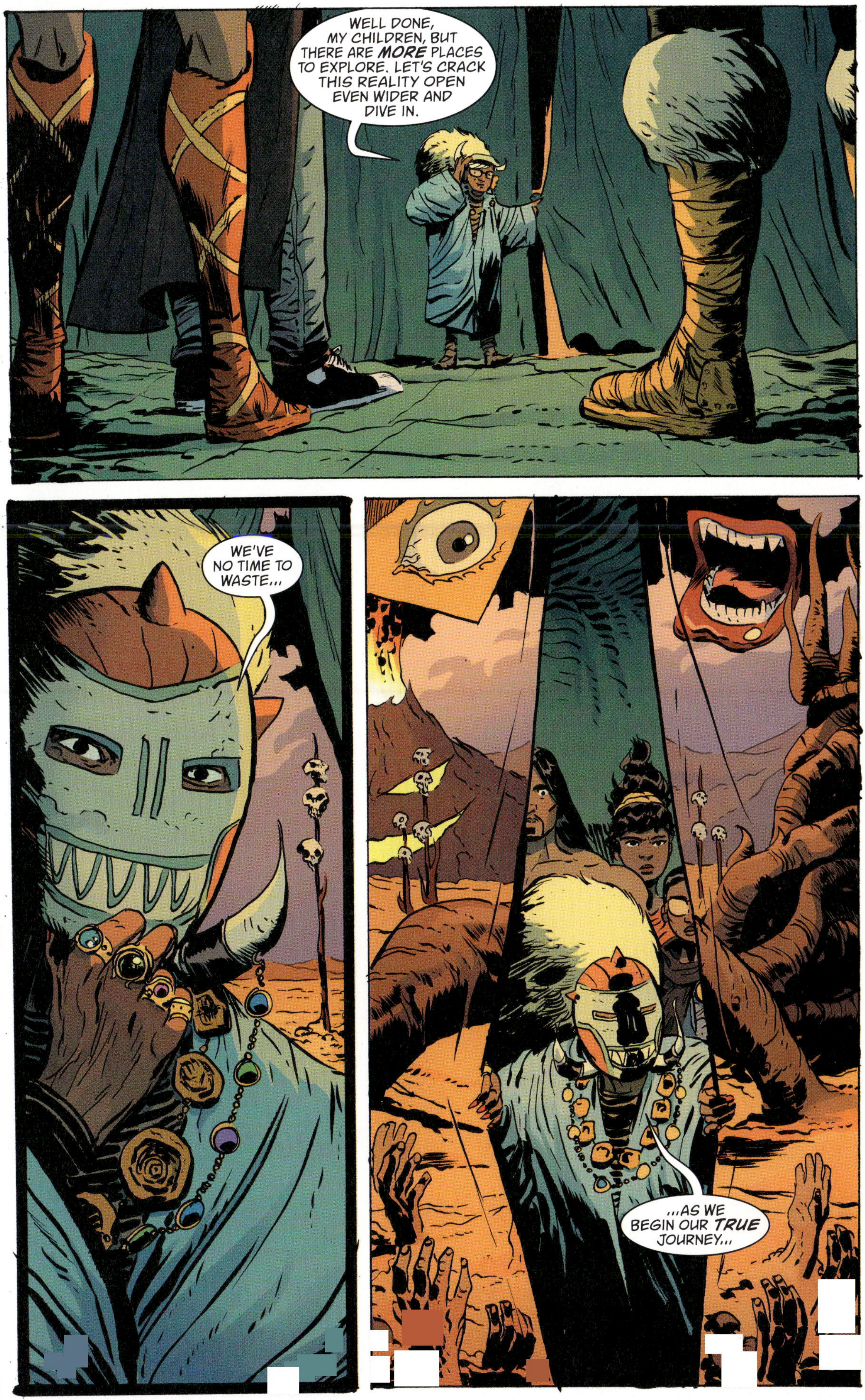
WELL DONE, MY CHILDREN, BUT THERE ARE **MORE** PLACES TO EXPLORE. LET'S CRACK THIS REALITY OPEN EVEN WIDER AND DIVE IN.
WE'VE NO TIME TO WASTE...
...AS WE BEGIN OUR **TRUE** JOURNEY...

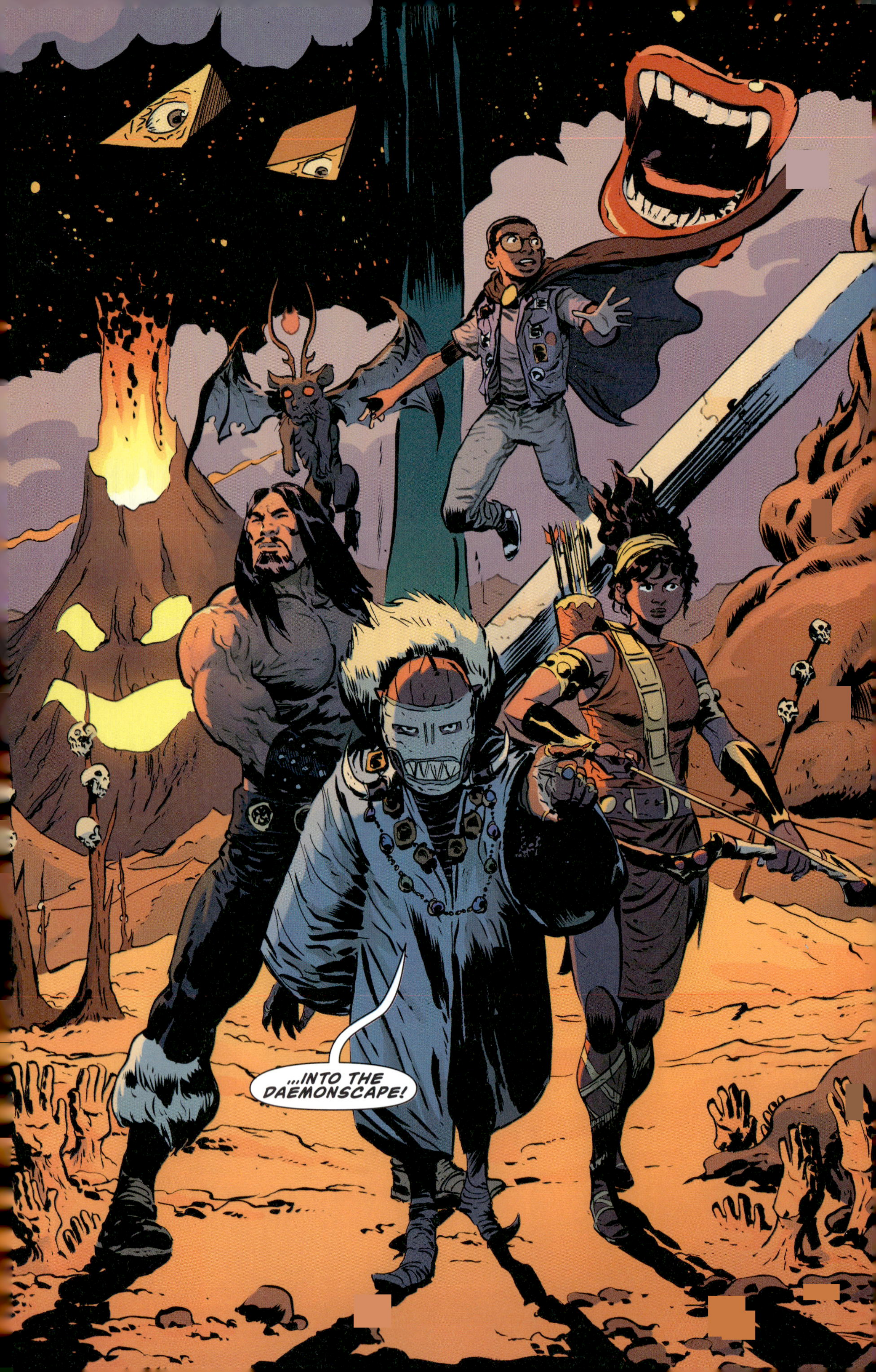
...INTO THE DAEMONSCAPE!

Heroes of the Daemonscape

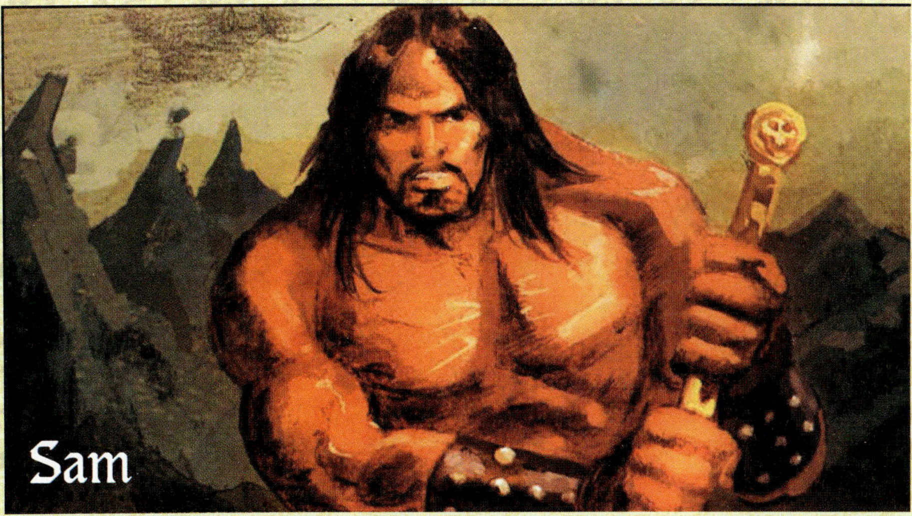
Sam

XP: +666

Strength: 300

Dexterity: 100

Intelligence: 250

Wisdom: 180

Constitution: 260

Charisma: 140

EQUIPMENT: Shield of Forgiving Might, Sword of Margoth

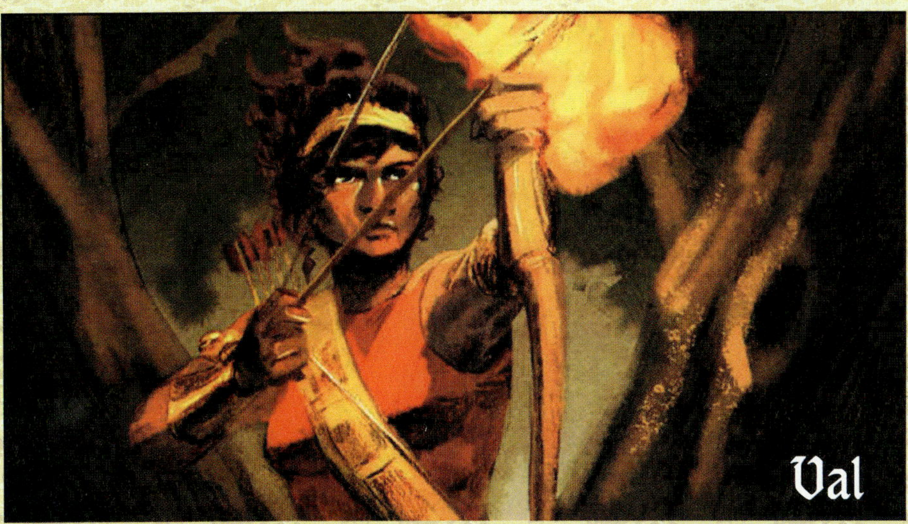
Val

XP: +483

Strength: 200

Dexterity: 220

Intelligence: 260

Wisdom: 270

Constitution: 100

Charisma: 160

EQUIPMENT: Bow of the Wandering Fury

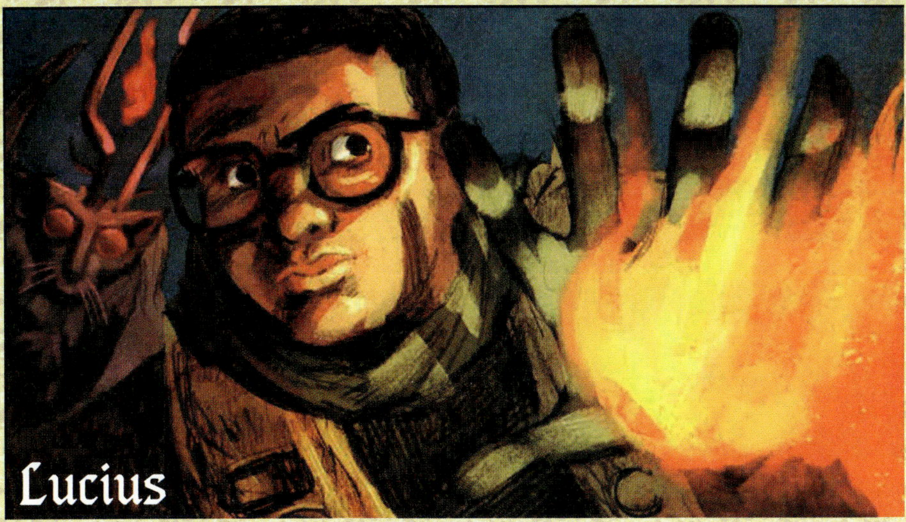
Lucius

XP: +482

Strength: 120

Dexterity: 180

Intelligence: 300

Wisdom: 200

Constitution: 140

Charisma: 160

EQUIPMENT: Staff of Arcane Power, Mage Fire

Greetings, traveler! It is I, ***Agantha,*** with a decree (by order of ***Lucius,*** Slayer of Margoth) to craft battles and stories of your very own in the Daemonscape! Whether they be atop Widow's Peak or the dark depths within the Sea of Hands! The instructions are threefold:

1. Remove the map from the comic and trim and tape the sides together, or copy with scanner, copier, or other device.

2. Cut around the dotted lines to free the Reynolds family, Heroes of the Daemonscape, from this page-cage. Don't forget your favorite daemon-squirrel! (Also included is Margoth the Unliving, for those of you with a proclivity for pain.)

3. Bend both sides of the tabs at their feet, allowing them to stand.

And that's it! Re-enact your favorite battles across the lands of the Daemonscape! Craft new stories of your very own! (Robotman himself was born of fan-fiction after all, who knows what could happen?)

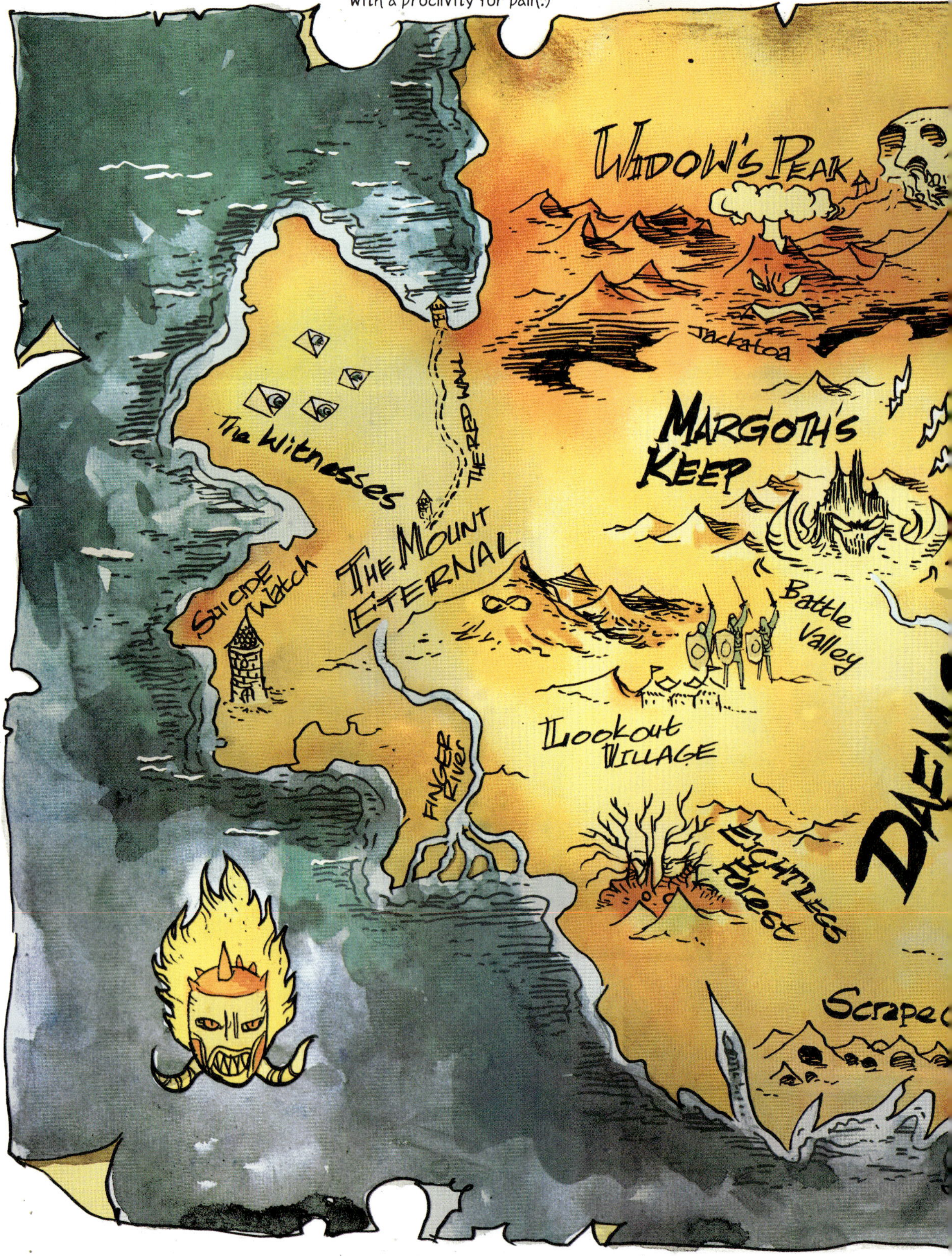

Widow's Peak
Jackatoa
Margoth's Keep
The Witnesses
The Red Wall
The Mount Eternal
Suicide Watch
Battle Valley
Lookout Village
Finger River
Eightless Forest
Scrape
DAEM

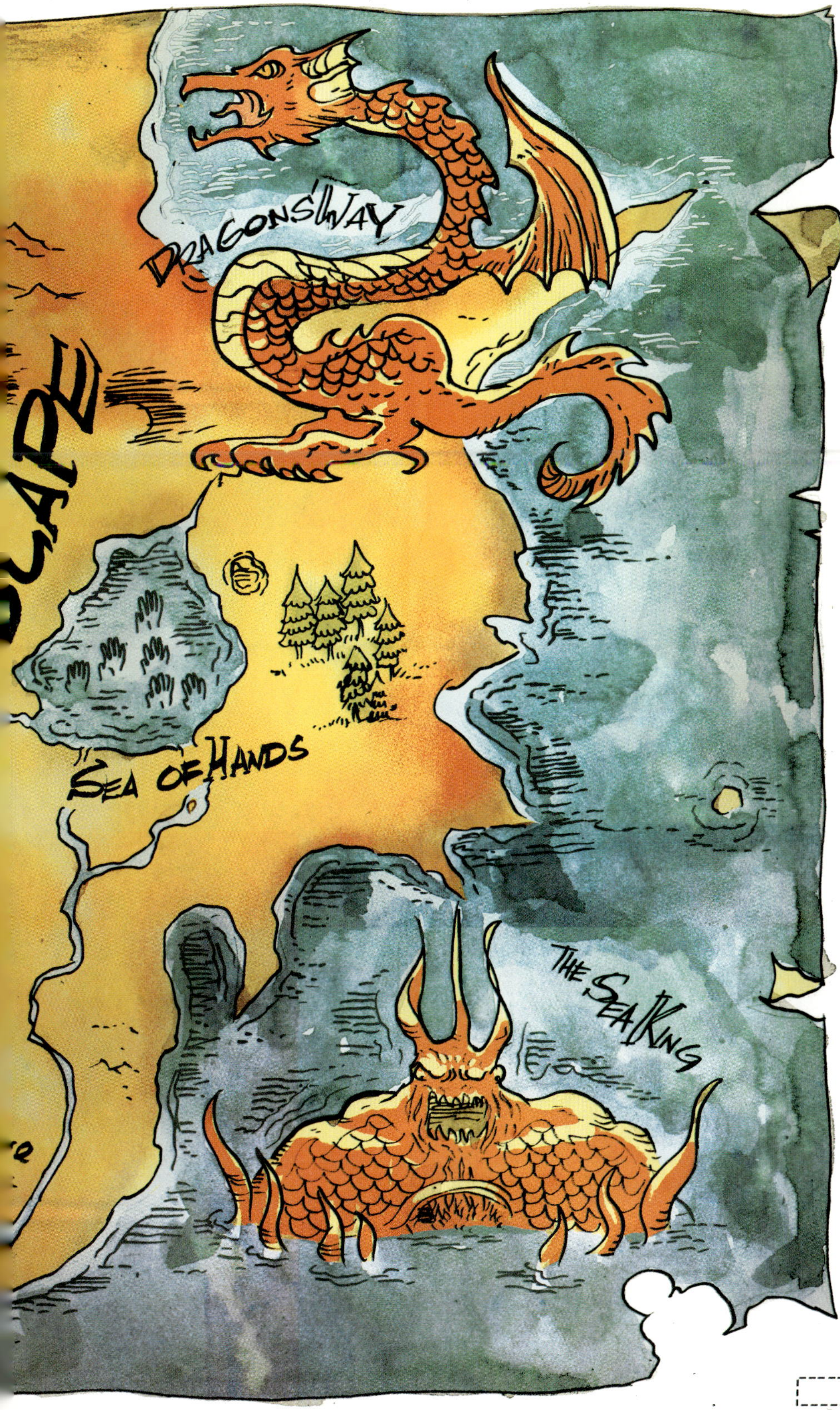
DRAGONS'WAY
SEA OF HANDS
THE SEA KING

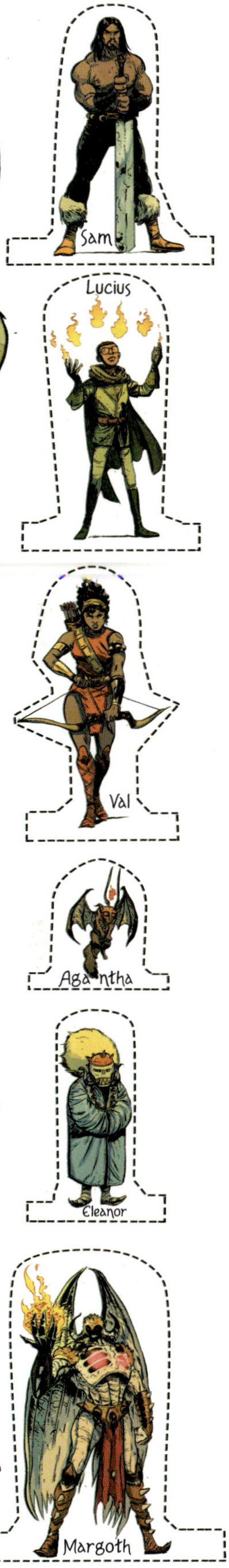
Sam
Lucius
Val
Aga ntha
Eleanor
Margoth

Who's Who
DC's Young Animal

TAMRA BONVILLAIN

PERSONAL DATA

Name: Tamra Bonvillain
Occupation: Colorist
First Appearance:
DOOM PATROL #1

HISTORY

I once thought green was my favorite color, but purple is doing it for me these days. I was pretty much always into comics since I was a kid, either comics themselves or cartoons and movies based on comics characters. I also liked to draw! I took any art class I was able to, either through school or privately (on rare occassions). My last three years of high school, I went to a fine arts magnet school, Davidson Fine Arts, where I picked up a lot of useful art education. I majored in fine art at a local university in Augusta, GA, for a few years, but I was keen to learn skills more specific to illustration and comics, so I left that school to attend the Joe Kubert School. I learned a lot and got a ton more practice. Through many of the connections I made, I picked up some coloring jobs, and those connections led to more and more, eventually allowing me to make a steady living at it, and now here I am!

1
POP
SQUEEK
SQUEEK

1 Black-and-white page from artist Nick Derington

2
POP
SQUEEK
SQUEEK

2 The first thing I'll do when coloring is put in the flat colors. There's no rendering at this stage.

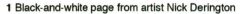

THE PROCESS OF COLORING DOOM PATROL

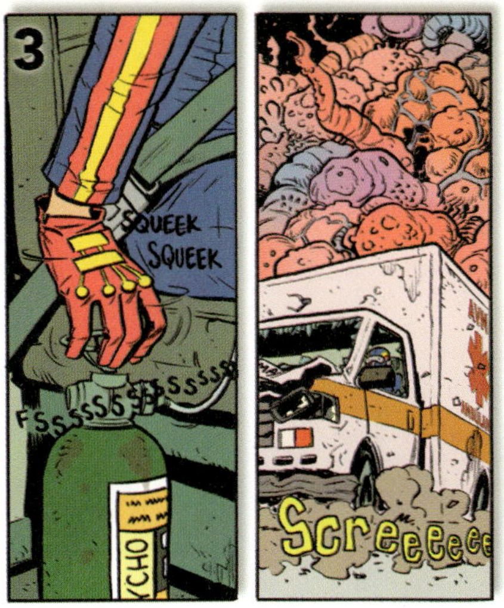
3
SQUEEK
SQUEEK

3 Next, I'll put in any color variations. On this page I added some redness to characters' skin, a little rust on the gas tank, and made the goopy bits in the last panel have more variety to them. There's still no shadow or light rendering at this stage.

4 After that step, I'll start to get into the rendering. I make a copy of my flats, one for mid tones and another for shadows. The mid-tone flats are similar to the initial flats, but I'll adjust them slightly to the lighting of the scene. In this case, they have a little reddish tinge to them. The copy of the shadows again starts with those initial flats, but I make those darker, and add some cool greens. I set the shadows layer above the mid-tone layers and use a mask to draw it over the other layer, adding shadows where appropriate. This way, I can easily render in the shadows without having to pick new colors for different objects all the time, and the lighting should look consistent. At this stage, it's only mid tones and shadows.

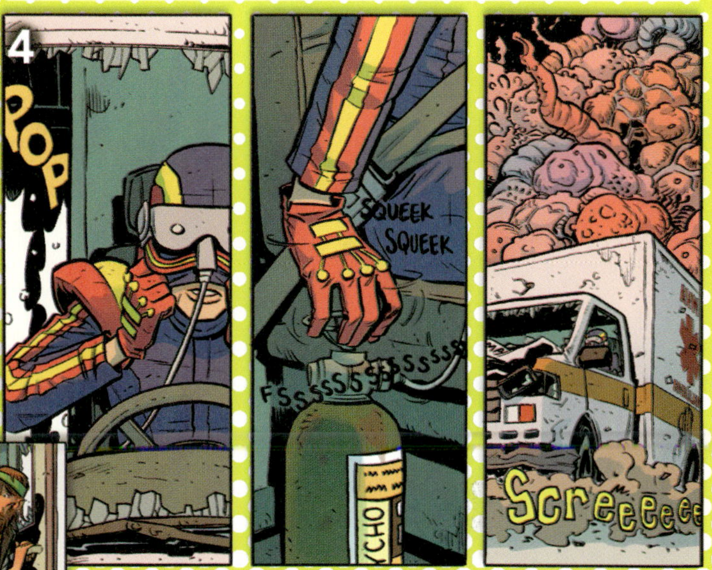
4
POP
SQUEEK
SQUEEK

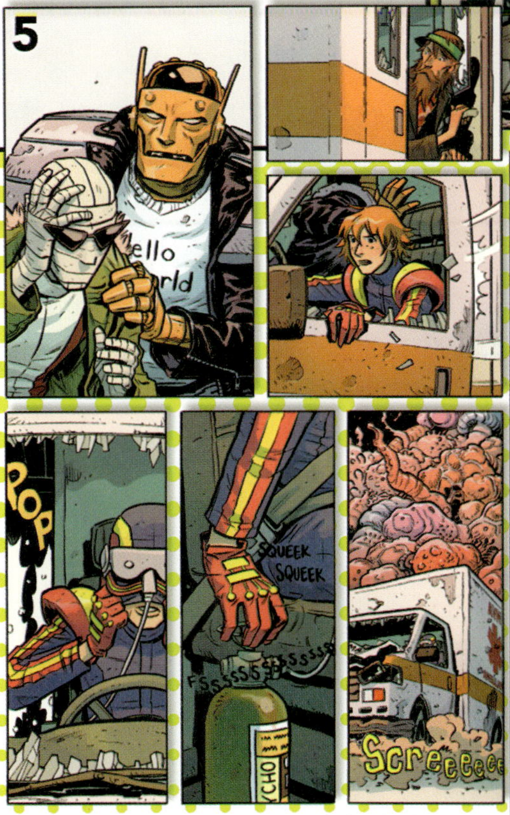
5
POP
SQUEEK
SQUEEK

5 I add some more rendering to push the shadows further in some areas, do some subtle color overlay stuff in areas, and start to bring in lights and highlights. I generally use color-fill layers set to different blending modes, and also push the values and contrast around a little with levels to help things separate as best I can.

6 The finished image! Here I've added in color holds for some of the sound effects and effects, as well as some of the interior lines to give a softer, more unified appearance. The last thing I do is add an adjustment layer to the whole thing and slightly tweak the contrast, and then I'm done!

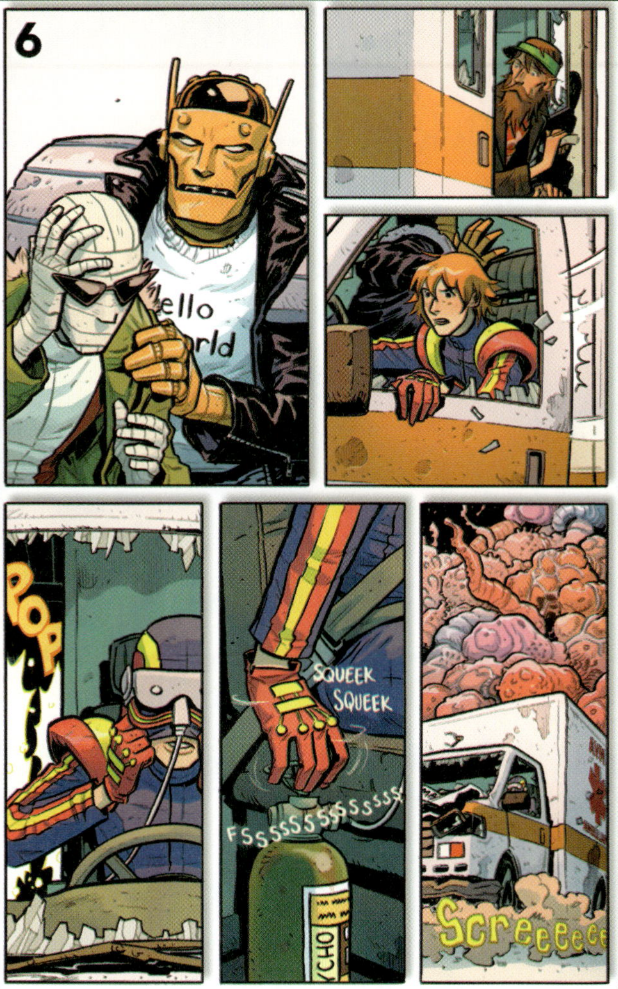
6
POP
SQUEEK
SQUEEK

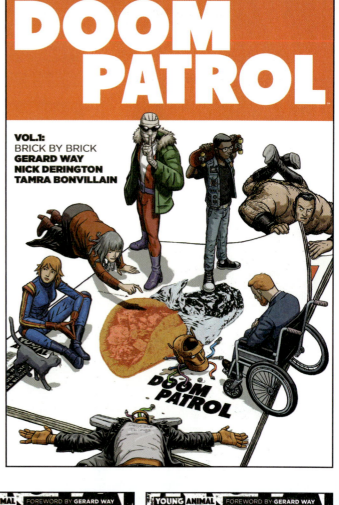
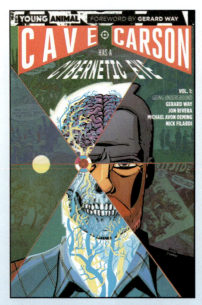

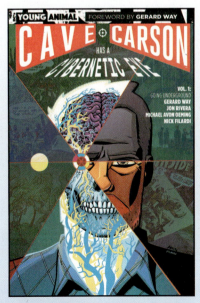

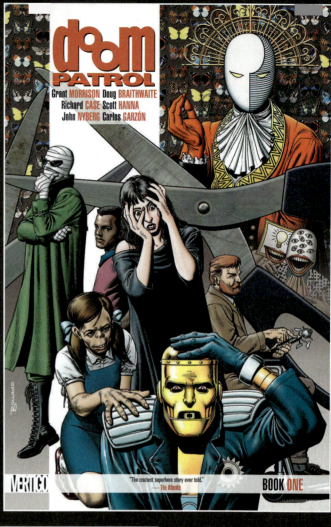

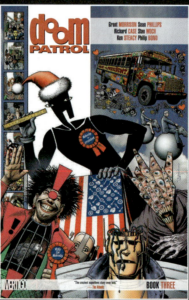
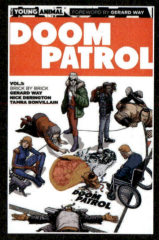